THE
PHILOSOPHY
OF
RELIGION

THE
PHILOSOPHY
OF
RELIGION

YEAGER HUDSON

Colby College

MAYFIELD PUBLISHING COMPANY

Mountain View, California
London • Toronto

Library of Congress Cataloging-in-Publication Data
Hudson, Yeager
    The philosophy of religion / by Yeager Hudson.
        p.   cm.
    Includes bibliographical references and index.
    ISBN 0-87484-902-0
    1. Religion — Philosophy.   I. Title.
BL51.H895   1990
200'.1 — dc20   90-37428
                                                                            CIP

Manufactured in the United States of America

10   9   8   7   6   5   4   3   2   1

Mayfield Publishing Company
1240 Villa Street
Mountain View, California 94041

Sponsoring editor, James Bull; managing editor, Linda Toy; production editor, Carol Zafiropoulos; manuscript editor, Victoria Nelson; text and cover design, Anna George. This text was set in 10½/12 Goudy by TypeLink, Inc., and printed on 50# Glatfelter Spring Forge by Thomson-Shore.

Excerpts from "God's Trombones" in *God's Trombones* by James Weldon Johnson. Copyright 1927 by The Viking Press, Inc.; copyright renewed 1955 by Grace Nail Johnson. Used by permission of Viking Penguin, a division of Penguin USA. Poem Number 3 from *Shyamali* is used by permission of Visva-Bharati, Calcutta. The Bible text is from the Revised Standard Version Bible, copyright 1946, 1952, 1971 by the Division of Christian Education of the National Council of Churches of Christ in the USA, and is used by permission.

Contents

Preface

In the long sweep of human history, religion has been a central force in every society and in every era. Even in our so-called skeptical age, religion remains of primary importance in the lives of vast numbers throughout the world. A large majority believe in and faithfully practice religion; a small minority regard it with indifference; and only a much smaller minority explicitly reject religion and take a hostile attitude toward it. Probably religion outstrips even politics as a topic for heated discussions among persons involved in the intellectual life. The issues that arise when we begin to reason about religious beliefs are not only intriguing but also very important. For a few people, the arguments may be largely academic; but many feel that all that they hold dear is at stake. And sometimes the defense of belief becomes so crucial that it takes precedence over an objective and dispassionate search for the truth.

Some people fear that a philosophical scrutiny of religious beliefs might undermine their faith. But surely, we are inclined to say, a faith with any substantial intellectual substance should stand up to rational scrutiny, and a faith that can be destroyed by an honest search for the truth is not worth defending. An honest examination may indeed lead to a revision of one's beliefs, but if it is carried out with candor and sincerity it can be expected to result in a set of beliefs that is superior to the old set. In the process of growing up, most of us acquire religious beliefs in a fairly haphazard way. We often have only the vaguest understanding about what such beliefs mean, and even less about why people have thought it important to hold them. The philosophical study of religion is designed to make the meanings of our beliefs clear and to discover which can and which cannot be rationally justified.

The philosopher's objective is neither to undermine nor to shore up any one set of beliefs. Rather, the goal is to understand our beliefs so that we can decide whether or not it is reasonable to hold them. The philosopher refuses to accept any teaching merely on the basis of tradition or authority and roundly rejects the claim that matters religious are too sublime or mysterious to be understood by human reason. Every belief is subject to examination. If it is to pass muster, a belief must be intelligible — capable of being understood and reasoned about — and if it is to be accepted, it must have rational support. The philosopher is convinced that beliefs which are truly understood and which are supported by reason and evidence are far more worthy than any beliefs that could be undermined by the process of rational scrutiny.

This book is designed to provide the reader with an overview of the major issues in the philosophy of religion; with an understanding of how these issues have been addressed by both classical and contemporary philosophers; and with a sense of the direction in which this field is moving at the present time. It is intended as an aid not only to the academic study of philosophy but also to that process of personal reflection on the significance of religious beliefs and practices which is an essential part of nearly every thoughtful individual's search for meaning in life. The philosophy of religion is one of the most active and creative areas of philosophy in the closing years of the twentieth century; the 1900s have seen very substantial change — change that I believe it is proper to call progress — in this very important branch of philosophy and human thought. For this reason, although an attempt is made here to acquaint the reader with the classic tradition, special attention is devoted to the innovative interpretations of issues that twentieth-century thought has produced and to the suggested new solutions to problems brought forward by contemporary philosophers.

One area of highly creative activity in the philosophy of religion during the past few decades is the epistemology of religion: the study of how we obtain knowledge about religious matters and how our knowledge claims are justified. Chapter 1 attempts to clarify what is meant by reason and show the ways in which religious beliefs can be regarded as rational. The position taken is an empirical rationalism which attempts to take into account every possible kind of evidence that might bear on religious belief. The intention is neither to reject anything out of hand nor to accept anything uncritically at face value, but to attempt to understand how reason can make use of evidence from science, scriptural traditions, philosophy, religious experience, history, aesthetic experience — in fact, every aspect of human experience — to assess religious and philosophical claims and thus to arrive at a world view that is intelligible and rationally justified.

Because theism has been the most widely held position, particularly in the West, it is examined rather fully in this book. Chapter 2 examines the attributes traditionally ascribed to God; Chapter 3 assesses the arguments in support of theism; and Chapter 4 examines the objections to theism. These are topics that every complete survey of the philosophy of religion must treat; indeed, many such texts deal almost exclusively with theism. But a significant number of people in the modern world are finding theism no longer plausible or acceptable. Thus — and this is an innovative feature of this book — Chapter 5 is devoted to an examination of several alternative world views as well as to the question of whether or not theism is the most plausible position.

Many religious devotees maintain that a philosophical approach to religion is merely theoretical and cannot get at the essence of religion. If there is to be real understanding, they argue, it must come through personal experience. Chapter 6 examines the claims made on behalf of religious and mystical experience, conceding that such experiences, if they can be known to be genuine, must be regarded as valuable sources of knowledge about religious matters, but insisting at the same time that such claims must be subjected to rational scrutiny.

Chapter 7 examines the relationship between religion and ethics, taking the position that, despite the widespread assumption that religion is the source of moral truths, ethics is actually independent of religion. The truths of morality, like the truths of logic and mathematics, are matters discovered and authenticated by reason, not derived from the arbitrary decrees of God or from divine revelation. Religion can serve as an important interpreter of morality and especially as a source of motivation to live the moral life. But if the moral teachings of a religious tradition require devotees to behave in ways that are inconsistent with rational morality, the sectarian teachings must yield to the more universally applicable requirements of philosophical morality.

The single most important development in the philosophy of religion in our time is the confrontation of the religions of Western culture with the other great religions of the world. This phenomenon reflects the very significant changes in travel, communication, news reporting, and political and economic interaction occurring among nearly all of the nations of our small planet. The former isolation of one people from another, an insularity of cultures that resulted in very little mutual contact between persons of different religious traditions, meant that until very recently the various religions of the world impinged on one another hardly at all. There has been a nearly universal assumption, particularly in the West, that the religions of the rest of the world were crude, primitive, and simple minded — if not outright heathen. The provincialism of Westerners has been particularly conspicuous with regard to religion.

But it is no longer possible to be isolated, or to ignore the cultures of the rest of the world. Not only do citizens of every nation travel to every other nation for the purpose of tourism or business; they live in close interaction with one another in their own cities and towns. America has been a pluralistic nation from its very beginning, but today our pluralism involves people from virtually every part of the world. They have brought with them their art, music, literature, cuisine, festivals, social practices — and their religions. Where once there were only churches and an occasional synagogue, there are now also mosques and temples representing all the major religions of the world.

Religion has also come to play an increasingly crucial role in the complicated balance of world political and economic power. In the confrontation of nation with nation, differences of religion often are a powerful factor; *within* nations, the strife between religious communities threatens to fracture and destroy the state. No longer can we afford to pay attention only to our own traditions and ignore the others. If we are to live together in pluralistic communities — and we must; it is no longer avoidable — it is imperative that we understand the beliefs and practices that play such a central role in the lives of the people of those other communities.

Only very recently have these issues begun to find their way into books on the philosophy of religion, and mostly in minimal ways. An innovative feature of this book is its extensive recognition of religious pluralism. Chapter 8 examines the philosophical teachings of five of the great world religions and the question of how philosophy should deal with pluralism in a world where religions live in daily contact with one another. Philosophers attempt to approach religious teachings from an objective stance that does not presuppose the validity or preferability of any one tradition. They seek criteria and points of comparison in terms of which the teachings of the several traditions can be judged more or less adequate. They raise questions about the extent to which religions might profitably learn from one another, and whether there should be mutual sharing, or perhaps even mutual transformation of some traditions by others. These issues, integral to the discussion in every chapter, are brought to a special focus in Chapter 8.

The last chapter of the book treats the relationship of religion to the question of the meaning of life. It is a topic often neglected and even sometimes scorned by philosophers in the past. But in the last few decades philosophers have begun increasingly to recognize the opportunity, and accept the responsibility, of engaging in rational reflection about how life might be lived most significantly. Throughout human history, probably most persons have found their life-meaning through religion, but there are other paths to meaning as well. Chapter 9 examines some of these alternatives and raises the question whether religion is the only satisfactory, or the most plausible, source of meaning.

A word about gender and language in referring to the deity may be in order here. In the West, the concept of God as father and king has been nearly universal, and male pronouns have nearly always been used. There are religious traditions, particularly Hinduism, in which the feminine aspects of deity have been given an important place. It is clearly time for Westerners to outgrow the outmoded masculine image of God. To this end, several of the Christian churches have changed the wording of their liturgy to avoid gender-specific references, and a new rendering of the Bible also involves more inclusive language. In this book, the masculine pronoun has been used occasionally when the only possible alternative construction would have been awkward or distracting. Persons who believe in God and believe that God is a personal being should be mindful that the image of God as mother is just as appropriate as that of God as father.

Some of the issues philosophers of religion take up, and some of the arguments and theories by means of which they address these issues, are complex. To appreciate the problems and to understand the theories is sometimes challenging. An effort has been made here to minimize complexity without oversimplifying the issues, to avoid unnecessary use of technical jargon, and to present these materials in as accessible and attractive a way as possible. An extensive glossary has been included to help with vocabulary that may not be familiar. It is the author's sincere hope that the intrinsic excitement and importance of these matters will help to sustain the reader's interest in those places where an effort is required to follow the argument of the book. When such an effort gives rise to genuine new insight and understanding, the result can be deeply gratifying. For those who have not previously had the experience of thinking through their religious beliefs, such an activity, undertaken in the right spirit, can be an exciting adventure. Blessed are they who open their minds to new understanding; great will be their reward!

ACKNOWLEDGMENTS

A book reflects, in a way, its author's whole life experience. There are debts to everyone with whom one has had any significant intellectual relationships. To acknowledge all the persons who have contributed to my fascination with philosophy and religion, and all from whom I have learned about these subjects, would be impossible. The list would certainly have to include, among many others, most of my teachers, and definitely many of the very large number of students I have taught in my philosophy classes over nearly thirty years. But it is appropriate, and a welcome opportunity, to mention by name a few individuals whose help has been very direct and substantial. Several student workers did a great deal of leg work between my office and the library: Stephen Hord and Bill Priestly served as able research assistants, Gina Rogers and Mike Sulski proofread, and Toby Yos did outstanding work on a wide variety of tasks, including particularly the Annotated Guides to Further Readings and the index.

I gratefully acknowledge the helpful suggestions of my reviewers: Bond Harris, Eastern Kentucky University; Mark Lenssen, Ohio Northern University; David Lee Miller, University of Wisconsin—La Crosse; Robert Miller, Eastern Kentucky University; Thandeka, San Francisco State University; R. Duane Thompson, Indiana Wesleyan University. They helped me avoid a number of blunders and infelicities and offered insightful suggestions that enabled me to strengthen many parts of the book. Professor Michael Carlsen-Jones offered particularly helpful commentary on the entire manuscript. James Bull, philosophy editor for Mayfield, has been unfailingly helpful and encouraging. I am very grateful to Colby College for reducing my teaching load during two semesters while I was working on this book, for providing funding to support research assistance, and for offering an intellectual climate conducive to creative research.

My wife, to whom this book is dedicated, has been an unflagging companion, offering encouragement and constructive criticism at every stage of the work and reading the entire manuscript through three times ("Greater love hath no one than this . . ."). And so my greatest expression of appreciation is to her.

For Louise

THE
PHILOSOPHY
OF
RELIGION

1

The Philosophical Study of Religion

RELIGION

Religion is one of the oldest, most natural, and most persuasive activities of human life. Philosophy, by contrast, is a more recent, more artificially contrived, and more critical endeavor. Whereas most people naturally tend to be religious in some sense, most people do not naturally tend also to be philosophical until a self-reflective attitude leads some to a conscious questioning or rejection of religion. In other words, the philosophical attitude is something that is achieved rather than something that comes naturally to us. The philosophy of religion is an attempt to achieve the philosophical attitude toward religious beliefs and phenomena.

Before we can understand very clearly what the philosophy of religion is, we need to examine the concepts of *religion* and *philosophy*. Both are difficult to define with any precision, but for different reasons: religion because this pervasive dimension of human life takes such diverse forms in different times and places, and philosophy because it pertains to so many different areas of human life, and pertains to them in such different ways. We tend to assume that we have a clear understanding of their meaning. Many persons beginning a study of the philosophy of religion, however, may not have had a previous opportunity to reflect carefully and objectively about these terms, and when we attempt to offer clear definitions we may discover that our own understanding is actually rather vague.

We will also discover that ordinary dictionary definitions of many of the terms used in the philosophy of religion are too general; they fail to provide the degree of clarity that a close scrutiny of the subject demands. When we begin to reflect on our own understanding of the meaning of the term *religion,* the definitions that come to mind tend to connect most closely with the religious tradition we know best. Westerners, who are most familiar with the religions of Judaism and Christianity, are likely to begin their explanations of religion by mentioning belief in God. But if we are seeking a definition that applies to all instances of religion, this won't do. Some major world religions—Theravada Buddhism, for example— explicitly reject belief in a divine being. As Westerners, we are likely also to assume that religion is founded on the teaching of some great prophet, incarnate deity, or avatar, such as Moses, Jesus, or Muhammad, but at least one major world religion, Hinduism, has no such founder—although it does recognize many human teachers as avatars. We similarly tend to assume that religion is grounded in a body of sacred writings handed down through the ages and believed originally to have been revealed to humankind by the deity through a human prophet, patriarch, or apostle. But we make this assumption because the religions we know best are "religions of the book," as the Moslems call them. Not all religions look to a single, authoritative body of holy writings or scriptures. This is particularly true of the religions of preliterate people, but it was even characteristic of the ancient Greeks, who frequently quoted their own poets Homer and Hesiod, but did not regard their accounts of gods and goddesses authoritative scriptures as Jews do their Bible or Christians theirs.

So many of the traits we most naturally assume to characterize religion turn out to apply to only some and not all religions. An adequate definition, if one is to be found, must apply to any set of beliefs and practices that is properly called a religion and must not apply to any set of beliefs and practices that is not a religion. When we begin to recognize the limited and ethnically bound nature of our ordinary conceptions of religion, our quest for a more universal definition begins. The nineteenth-century sociologist Herbert Spencer says that "Religion is the recognition that all things are manifestations of a Power which transcends our knowledge." This definition represents an effort to move away from the concept of a God or gods that some religions don't recognize, but it is so general that it does not distinguish religion from science or any other secular philosophical belief in the powers of nature. The great Indian poet and philosopher Rabindranath Tagore offers several attempts at defining religion. He tells us that the ancient Zoroastrians taught that "religion is a knowledge or learning, a science of what is true."[1] Certainly, religion has often been regarded as knowledge or teachings that are true, but clearly this is only one dimension; religion also involves feeling, will, worship, morality. Tagore himself recognizes this when he says: "Our religion is the inner principle that comprehends those endeavors and expressions and dreams through which we approach Him in whose image we are made."[2] But this definition again involves the presumption of a God. The philosopher Harold Hoffding says, "The essence of religion is a belief in the persistency of value in the world,"[3] and Matthew Arnold says, "Religion is ethics heightened, enkindled, lit up by feeling."[4] These statements recognize the importance of morality to religion but err by leaving out nearly everything else.

Many other definitions of religion offered by writers on philosophy and religion also fall short of what we are seeking. In his article in the *Encyclopedia of Philosophy*,[5] William P. Alston quotes a dozen prominent scholars, pointing out how each definition offered fails to state the necessary and sufficient conditions for calling any set of beliefs and practices a religion. The failure of persistent efforts to produce a satisfactory formulation has led twentieth-century philosophers to conclude that a different approach is called for. John Hick suggests[6] that we take a cue from Wittgenstein, who pointed out that many words defy definition because the things to which they refer are not simple and uniform. Wittgenstein suggested that, instead of searching for a set of characteristics common to all, we think rather in terms of "family resemblances" shared by the things a word names. Alston proposes a similar idea, offering a set of what he calls "religion-making characteristics":

1. Belief in supernatural beings (gods).
2. A distinction between sacred and profane objects.
3. Ritual acts focused on sacred objects.
4. A moral code believed to be sanctioned by the gods.
5. Characteristically religious feelings (awe, sense of mystery, sense of guilt, adoration) that tend to be aroused in the presence of sacred objects and during the practice of ritual . . .
6. Prayer and other forms of communication with gods.
7. A world view, or a general picture of the world as a whole and the place of the individual therein . . .
8. A more or less total organization of one's life based on the world view.
9. A social group bound together by the above.[7]

If we accept these attributes as religion-making characteristics, we can say, not that everything called a religion has all of them; not even that every religion must have certain key ones or at least a certain number. Rather, according to Alston, we can say that "when enough of these characteristics are present to a sufficient degree, we have a religion."[8] But how many are enough and how much is a sufficient degree? Perhaps we cannot give a general answer. There are, however, clear, unquestioned examples, what we call paradigm cases, that everyone admits to be religions: for example, Hinduism, Christianity, Islam, Judaism. There are also borderline cases that leave room for dispute about whether or not they are true religions: for

example, humanism, naturalism, communism. The latter resemble acknowledged religions in certain ways and fail to resemble them in others.
The more closely the borderline cases resemble the paradigm cases — that
is, cases about which we have no doubt — and the more of the so-called
"religion-making characteristics" they have, the more ready we will be to
call them religions; the further they depart from these criteria, the more
hesitant we will be to call them religions.

PHILOSOPHY

In our attempt to understand what the term *philosophy* means, a good place
to begin is William James's statement that philosophy is the attempt to
think without arbitrariness or dogmatism about the fundamental issues.
Even though this definition is too general and fails to distinguish philosophy from other human activities, it does indicate several things about philosophy that are very important. First, it makes clear that philosophy represents an *activity*, an attempt to think things through and discover the living
truth. Philosophy is not a static body of beliefs; rather, it is a process
through which we think about our beliefs, subject them to the most honest
and careful scrutiny, and modify both our beliefs and our behavior on the
basis of what we have discovered. This is why philosophy is such an exciting and important activity. It has to do not with the merely abstract and
the theoretical, but rather with our beliefs about who we are, why we are
here, and what our ultimate destiny may be as individuals and as a species;
it has also to do with how we live our lives from day to day. Far from being
an idle pastime, philosophy is an attempt to find our place and our way in a
world that sometimes overwhelms us with its mystery.

   This is why what we think and how we think matter so much. This is
why James urges us to think without arbitrariness or dogmatism. The arbitrary is the capricious, the whimsical, the unjustified, that for which there
is no reason. To think without arbitrariness is to attempt to ground what
one thinks in evidence or reason rather than simply taking its truth for
granted, accepting without question what one may have been taught or
clinging to the belief that happens to please one. To think without dogmatism is to steer clear of the adamantly asserted opinion, to recognize the
possible fallibility of even the most authoritative belief; to "sit humbly like
a child at the feet of the facts." Taking a philosophical attitude involves
approaching any subject with as few presuppositions as possible and making
a conscious effort to submit every belief to the bar of rational scrutiny.

   Philosophy is a quest for *rational* beliefs, which means a search for
beliefs that human reason can understand and that are supported by the
best available evidence. It is sometimes alleged that religious truths are
mysterious, paradoxical, and beyond the power of human reason or under-

standing; that it would be impious or even blasphemous to question revealed religious truths, as if we humans believed that our reason is competent to test the word of God. The philosopher, however, insists that it is not the word of God that she or he is questioning, but rather the human expression of that word. Many authorities, after all, claim to speak for God without expressing a single or consistent message. The philosopher insists that no knowledge claim is entitled to be accepted merely on the basis of authority. To do so would be arbitrary because it would involve choosing one authority over another without rational justification.

In the course of growing up, we inevitably absorb a large number of beliefs that we have never thought to question. Some we have been explicitly taught, some we have adopted more or less deliberately, but most have simply invaded or infested our minds without invitation. When we are called on to justify them, we feel sure that they are true, that every right-thinking person must believe them, but we often cannot say why. Many are dear to us, and we are loath even to consider that rational examination might require giving them up.

But if we reflect on the beliefs prevalent a hundred, five hundred, or a thousand years ago, we recognize at once that in the past nearly everyone believed many things that were not true. In 1490, most people in Europe firmly believed that the earth was flat; a few years earlier, nearly everyone believed that the sun revolved around the earth; and until fairly recently, most people believed that the atom could not be split. It is common knowledge to everyone today that these beliefs were mistaken, and they are only three of many. The progress of human thought discovers new truths that inevitably overturn old beliefs. Most of the beliefs of antiquity about nature and the physical world were either mistaken or seriously inadequate. Similarly, our descendents looking back upon our beliefs from the perspective of a hundred or a thousand years will recognize that a very large part of what seems most obviously true to us will have turned out to be mistaken.

This fact brings home to us clearly the importance of James's plea that we think without arbitrariness or dogmatism. We do not suppose that any of our beliefs are false; if we did, we would not believe them. But the Europeans of 1490 did not think that their belief about the shape of the earth was false, either. Recognizing that many of our opinions — much of what we call knowledge — will ultimately be discovered to be faulty helps us to understand why there is so little justification for adamantly held opinions in any age.

The general philosophical question here is this: How do we know what we claim to know? The branch of philosophy called **epistemology** has to do with the sources of knowledge and the techniques for seeking, testing, and validating knowledge claims. Epistemology concerns itself with the way in which our sense impressions and our thoughts contribute to the opinions we believe to be true; it is also concerned with how we can tell whether a proposition is true. Although we cannot examine in any detail here the issues that emerge from epistemology, we will deal with some of them as they relate to knowledge claims about various aspects of religion and how we decide whether or not we are justified in accepting such claims.

There are many different kinds of knowledge claims, and the criteria by which we decide their validity vary from one type to another. For example, if the claim consists of the sum of a column of figures, only an indisputable certainty based on the principles of arithmetic will be satisfactory. If the claim is that the truth of a certain statement follows logically from others, the criteria will be those of valid logical inference. Mathematical and logical knowledge claims of this kind show a high degree of reliability—indeed, we are often justified in claiming that we know the truth of the claim with absolute certainty. But such certainty is rare. In the realm of the empirical world, the world of nature and science, our beliefs are based on sense impressions, repeated observations, and reasoning that never achieves the level of certainty characteristic of logic or mathematics. We are all too aware that our senses sometimes deceive us; that things are not always exactly as they seem; and thus that our beliefs based on observation may turn out to be mistaken. We have only to listen to the multiple reports of several witnesses to an auto accident to realize that people do not always see things the same way; where testimony differs, there is always reasonable doubt. Even in the realm of science, where the ordinary nonexpert tends to be highly trusting of the claims of the experts, we soon become aware that on many issues the experts themselves disagree because the evidence is equivocal. The moral of the story is that we really know very little with any substantial degree of certainty. Thus we must practice a measure of humility in making knowledge claims, recognizing that much we think we know could turn out to be mistaken.

Philosophy is an attitude, then, and a methodology that makes a deliberate effort to avoid holding unjustified beliefs. It attempts to approach every topic with an open mind and a readiness, at least for the time being, to set aside accepted beliefs in order to consider honestly and objectively any alternative idea, however new or surprising. It involves the recognition that we cannot be confident about beliefs we have not analyzed, clarified, and validated. Thus, philosophy inevitably involves a certain measure of practiced skepticism. This does not mean that we attempt to avoid holding beliefs, that we turn aside evidence in favor of not believing, or that we hold that beliefs never can be justified. Quite the contrary. But the careful philosopher, like the careful scientist, regards every belief as "guilty until proven innocent" or, to speak less metaphorically, as dubitable until proven indubitable. And since, as we have seen, only a very few of our beliefs can ever be proven indubitable, we will always hold most of our opinions tentatively, acting with appropriate confidence on the truth we have, but ready, when the accumulation of evidence requires, to alter our beliefs to conform with new truth.

This attitude of the philosopher is, of course, a matter of degree. Certain thinkers have taken the extreme position that no one is entitled to hold any beliefs without subjecting them successfully to philosophical scrutiny. William Clifford claims that holding opinions is a matter of morality not unlike our other deliberate actions. Thus he proposes the fundamental principle of what he calls the ethics of belief: "It is wrong always, everywhere, and for anyone to believe anything on insufficient evidence."[9] This is a very high ideal, one to which it is unlikely that any of us can ever fully conform. We all hold innumerable unquestioned beliefs, and we simply do not have the occasion or the leisure to examine every single one of them. Indeed, we would not live long enough to finish. The tacit beliefs that the floor will support us, our food will not poison us, the sky will not fall on us, or our friend will not betray us — all of them beliefs about whose truth we are not in a position to be certain — might just as well be accepted without spending the time and effort necessary to provide justification. Clifford is too scrupulous if he intends to insist that we are morally blameworthy in doing so. But he is surely right in making us aware that there are moral implications in accepting certain kinds of beliefs and that we are thus morally irresponsible to accept them uncritically. Our moral, political, religious, social, scientific, educational beliefs affect the way that we behave and consequently the impact of our behavior on other persons. We do have a moral obligation to base our behavior on informed opinion, not on prejudices or unthinking presuppositions.

We have said that philosophy is the quest for rational beliefs. The whole question of what constitutes rationality is a complicated one for which it may not be possible to offer a mechanical formula. But rationality certainly involves such traits as open-mindedness; dedication to the truth, even at the expense of one's cherished opinions; concern for objectivity; and an honest search for, and a serious taking account of, appropriate evidence. The ideal objective of the rational person is to hold her or his beliefs with a degree of conviction equal to the strength of the evidence. Such a person actively seeks and considers evidence on all sides of the issue and is always ready to adjust or revise beliefs in the light of new evidence. That person certainly conforms also to William James's ideal of thinking without arbitrariness or dogmatism about the fundamental issues. To engage in such an honest and forthright activity is to set off on an adventure, for it is impossible to know ahead of time where the process will lead. It involves the risk of exposing and possibly losing even one's most cherished beliefs. It requires courage to expose every belief to the glaring light of reason, to hold back nothing, and to follow with complete integrity wherever reason may lead. It may mean arriving at a radically different set of beliefs and possibly a significantly different way of living one's life, since our beliefs place demands on how we live. This is the adventure that waits when one honestly sets out to philosophize. Many have found it the most awesome and gratifying experience they have ever gone through.

PHILOSOPHY OF RELIGION VERSUS THEOLOGY

The terms *philosophy of religion* and *theology* are sometimes used as if they were interchangeable. But there is actually a very important distinction which should not go unnoticed. **Theology** is the interpretation, and some-times the advocacy, of a specific religious tradition. The philosophy of religion, on the other hand, is an attempt to study religious teachings and phenomena objectively, that is, not from the perspective of any particular tradition. Thus we properly speak of Christian theology or Moslem theol-ogy, but we do not properly speak of Christian philosophy of religion or Moslem philosophy of religion. Of course, the philosopher of religion may be a member of a given religious community, just as a theologian may; the difference has to do with the perspective and the stance. The philosophy of religion requires an objectivity that is not always easy to achieve, partic-ularly if the individual has strong religious convictions, and yet it is abso-lutely essential to the discipline. The person who fails to be objective and functions in fact as a partisan is not really a philosopher of religion. Perhaps we all fail in some measure, but it is of the utmost importance to hold the ideal of the objective, external perspective as primary.

The philosopher of religion uses the techniques of philosophical analy-sis to clarify the special terms used by religious thinkers and to establish both the appropriate logical procedures for testing the validity of arguments and the suitable epistemological methods for evaluating evidence and truth claims. She or he brings these techniques to bear on the doctrines and the activities, not just of one, but all the world religions.

We may say that the philosophy of religion is the nondogmatic study of religious dogma and behavior. The teachings or doctrines of a religious tradition are often called **dogma** in a technical and nonpejorative sense: The professor of dogmatics in a denominational theological seminary is not necessarily a dogmatic person in the sense that James urges us to avoid — although he or she might be presumed to be a partisan. Church dogmatics simply means church teachings, and the professor of dogmatics is the ex-pert in the church's received doctrine. The philosopher of religion applies his or her critical skills to dogmatics or doctrine in this sense of the word — namely, the teachings of the various religions.

The theologian, in contrast, asserts and interprets the doctrines that have the authoritative sanction of the religion; the theologian may even attempt to offer evidence and arguments in support of these doctrines. Thomas Aquinas, for example, devotes a great deal of effort and energy to providing support for Christian dogma. But the theologian operates from within a tradition and normally begins the process of analysis and evalua-tion with the presumption that the doctrines of the tradition are true, examining evidence or arguments against the received beliefs mainly for the purpose of refuting them. The function of the rational theologian is not to question or to attempt to decide the truth of the doctrines. Their truth is assumed by virtue of the authority of the religion itself or, in some cases, the allegation that the doctrines are divinely revealed. The theologian attempts to make the received doctrines more intelligible, to explain what they mean — or that they are mysteries not intended to be understood — and to support them with arguments.

The philosopher of religion, on the other hand, attempts to presuppose nothing about the truth of any set of doctrines. The philosopher of religion analyzes and interprets the doctrines, not of just one but of the various world religions and attempts to make them more intelligible. He or she also examines evidence and arguments for and against the claims of the various traditions, not to refute some and support others, but to assess as objectively and accurately as possible the strength of the arguments, and thus the plausibility or strength of the teachings. And although the philosopher of religion also analyzes the **phenomenology** of a religious tradition — that is, the things the people do as well as what they say and believe — she or he is interested in phenomenology only indirectly insofar as it provides evidence for teachings or truth claims. Thus a religion's institutional, political, ecclesiological, or liturgical details are not areas of concern for the philosopher of religion.

TYPES OF RELIGIONS

As a useful device for understanding religions, it has become customary to classify them into several types. Such classification is intellectually imposed; religions don't come self-labeled. And the types are never pure. Every religion contains elements of every type, intermingled, but it is sometimes illuminating to notice that a segment of one religious tradition belongs primarily to one type rather than another.

There are several ways in which religious phenomena can be classified, and thus several schemes of types are possible. The great twentieth-century theologian Paul Tillich (1886–1965), who defines religion (what he calls faith) as ultimate concern about whatever we take to be ultimate, classifies religions in terms of the dominant response of the faithful to the ultimate. If a religion's primary preoccupation is with the ultimate itself, its being and the human encounter with it, it belongs to what Tillich calls the *ontological* type of religion or faith.[10] Tillich describes two subtypes of this major type, the *sacramental* and the *mystical.* If a religion's primary preoccupation is not with the being, or the encounter with, the object of ultimate concern, but with our sense of the demands that the holy nature of that object places on us, it belongs to what Tillich calls the *moral* type.

William Alston suggests a classification of religions into three types: the sacramental, the prophetic, and the mystical.[11] Obviously these two sets of classifications overlap and are simply different ways of talking about many of the same major attributes of religion. I will use Alston's scheme of types, but not necessarily in exactly the way that he does.

The *sacramental* type of religion is characterized by the recognition of, or the sense of an encounter with, whatever is thought to be ultimate or holy as embodied or manifested in some object, place, being, or action. Most religions have an element of sacramentalism, although the word **sacrament** may not be used; some are predominantly sacramental. Westerners are likely to be most familiar with sacramentalism through the system of sacraments in the Christian religion. The Catholic branches of Christianity recognize seven sacraments: baptism, confirmation, Eucharist, penance, marriage, holy orders, and anointing of the sick. Many of the Protestant denominations recognize only two: baptism and Eucharist (or holy communion, as some call it). What makes these activities sacraments is not primarily a belief that the divine or the ultimate is present in, or represented by, the sacred objects—the bread and wine, the holy water, the consecrated oil—but the tendency actually to experience a sense of the presence of ultimacy or holiness in and through these objects.

Many of the so-called primitive religions are predominantly sacramental, encountering holiness or the sacred through the totems of the tribe; through sacred trees, stones, or other parts of nature; or through such ritualized sacramental acts as the sacred dance. In Judaism the ritual of bar mitzvah is a sacramental act; so is the act of carrying the Torah in procession through the congregation. In Islam, the pilgrimage to Mecca and many of the rituals connected with Ramadan, the month of fasting, are sacraments. Hindus are performing a sacrament when they bathe and feed the image of the god or goddess. And although the Buddha attempted to eliminate the kinds of rituals that tend to take on a sacramental nature, the various branches of Buddhism, in differing degrees, have evolved more or less elaborate sacramental rituals; a conspicuous example is the elaborate set of rituals performed in connection with the sacred tooth relic and the sacred Boddhi tree in Sri Lanka.

Those who place the most emphasis on the sacramental tend to pay the least attention to the moral dimensions of religion. Indeed, among some of the so-called primitive peoples, no connection is made between religion and morality. Even the great prophets of ancient Israel believed that the Hebrews were entirely too involved in the sacramental practices of sacrifices and burnt offerings; they chided the priests of the people for substituting religious ritual for justice and righteousness.

The *prophetic* type of religion presupposes the intervention of the divine in human affairs through the actions of human prophets or through the purported incarnation of deity in human form as an **avatar**. Christians regard Jesus Christ to be an incarnation; in Hinduism there are many avatars, including Krishna and Buddha. Thus prophetic religion is concerned not so much with any direct human-divine encounter as with the event or events through which the ultimate intervenes, and the implications of that intervention. This often takes the form of a teaching or a body of truth delivered to a people, and it usually places obligations on the receivers of the **prophecy** or revelation. The teachings revealed through the avatar or the prophet are usually reduced to writing, and the result is a body of holy scriptures that becomes the foundation of a new religious community and sometimes a new society or nation.

The revelations prophets receive often contain instructions concerning rituals that are to be performed and duties to be paid to the deity, and these rituals and duties become the basis of a sacramental tradition. The revelations also frequently involve teachings concerning the nature and origin of the cosmos, the source and status of humans, and the relation of the divine power to man and nature. But moral, social, even political teachings and commandments are usually the most prominent features, accompanied by beliefs about the way in which divine power affects the political and ethical affairs of humankind. For this reason prophetic religion tends to be preoccupied with morality and to place a high premium on accepting — that is, believing and obeying — the teaching. Much energy goes into understanding just what the teaching means, and these efforts often give rise to a large body of interpretative writings. Competing or even conflicting schools of interpretation tend to develop, often resulting in schism. Orthodoxy becomes a matter of great importance and wrong belief (*orthodoxy* literally means "straight belief," or right belief) becomes a serious fault or sin. The moralist members of a religion tend to scorn those who place any great importance on ritual, maintaining that the ethical life, and complete fidelity to moral demands, is of singular importance.

There is a very strong prophetic strand in Judaism, exemplified by Moses, who received commandments from God, and by the many teachers who are explicitly called prophets in the Hebrew Bible, where their prophecies are recorded. The singular avatar or divine representative on earth in Islam was Muhammad and his sacred title was Prophet; the Qur'an is the record of the prophetic message he brought to his people. Moslems place a strong emphasis on obedience to the word, both the ritual word, which represents the sacramental side of Islam, and the moral word, which imposes strict ethical regulations on Moslem behavior. In the Christian tradition, Jesus is regarded as the incarnation of deity, and the Bible as the authoritative teaching. But this religious tradition is split into factions; the Catholics represent much more strongly the sacramental type, and many of the Protestant groups represent the prophetic type. Among many Protestants, the teaching of the Word and the moral rules loom largest. There is a tendency to play down the importance of rituals and sacraments — the Protestant recognition of only two rather than seven is just one evidence of this — and emphasize in their place social reform and individual morality.

Though Judaism, Islam, and Christianity are the major religious traditions incorporating the prophetic type, it is also to be seen in Sikhism and, through the avatar tradition, to some degree in Hinduism.

The central feature of the *mystical* type of religion is its preoccupation with a direct encounter with the ultimate or the divine, not through sacred objects or sacramental acts, but through the mystical experience. The mystical experience is the experience of the presence of deity or the holy in the very depths of being in such a way that a unity of the human and the divine is realized. The mystic often claims that every barrier of separation dissolves, that the membranes of separation between oneself and the holy disappears, that one literally becomes God. Instances of mysticism apart from theism have also been reported. In those cases, mystics may or not talk about God, but what they experience is not so much a divine being as a sense of unity with nature or being itself. The nineteenth-century poet/philosopher Ralph Waldo Emerson expounds what might be called a kind of nature mysticism in his famous essay "Nature":

> In the woods, we return to reason and to faith. There I feel that nothing can befall me in life, — no disgrace, no calamity (leaving me my eyes), which nature cannot repair. Standing on the bare ground, — my head bathed by the blithe air and uplifted into space, — all mean egotism vanishes. I become a transparent eyeball; I am nothing; I see all; the currents of the Universal Being circulate through me; I am part and parcel of God. [12]

It is characteristic of the mystical type of religion, whether theistic or not, to be preoccupied with the experience itself of union with the divine, regarding doctrines as unimportant and even playing down or ignoring morality. The mystical experience is held to be indescribable and uncommunicable to anyone who has not had it; for the mystic, it is entirely self-certifying. It puts a person in touch with — indeed, it makes her or him one with — the ultimate. When a person becomes identical with the ultimate reality and knows it by direct acquaintance, all else is unimportant. Since the essence of truth apprehended through the experience cannot be expressed in words, little importance is placed on the creeds or doctrinal statements that might attempt to communicate such truth. Morality becomes a relatively trivial concern if all things are one; distinctions of good and bad, moral and immoral disappear during the mystical experience.

Mystics seem to be a brotherhood and a sisterhood of all times and places. Whether they are Sufi Moslems, Christian nuns, Hindu sanayasi, or Buddhist monks, and whether they live in the sixth century before the common era, the Middle Ages, or the twentieth century, they say remarkably similar things about their experiences. The mystical experience, however, is fleeting, and once gone is often very difficult to recapture. Mystics spend long stretches of their lives practicing the austerities they believe will summon the experience again, and sometimes they feel a bleak sense of doubt and despair in this quest.

None of the great world religions belongs completely to one type to the exclusion of the others. Traces of each type are present in every religion. But there are tendencies that distinguish one religion from another or that mark off one branch or wing of one religious tradition from another. The recognition of types illuminates similarities and differences and is a useful tool as we attempt to understand what is essential to human religious life and to evaluate the beliefs and behaviors characteristic of the various religions.

RATIONALITY AND RELIGIOUS BELIEF

Although religion is one of the most pervasive phenomena of human life and culture in every age, taken for granted by nearly everyone without serious questioning, there have always been some who have regarded it with suspicion. This attitude has been particularly widespread in the West during the present century, when no features of religion have escaped skepticism and doubt. In the course of our discussion we will often have occasion to judge the plausibility of claims, the strength of arguments, and the probable truth of teachings. Every claim that presents itself must be ready to demonstrate what we might call its epistemological credentials — that is, the evidence and support that justify accepting it. Much of the work of theology over the ages has been directed against skepticism that has threatened religious doctrines, one by one. Recent times, however, have witnessed attacks on religious belief of a much more basic sort, attacks that strike at the very foundation, not of a given religious teaching, belief, or tradition, but of the entire religious enterprise. If the skeptical claims of certain recent philosophical movements are correct, the philosophy of religion is a pointless endeavor. If the validity of these skeptical arguments were to be established, religious belief and activity might undoubtedly persist as nonrational features of the uneducated masses, but the supposition that religion could be understood or justified in rational terms would have to be abandoned. Before proceeding further, then, we must first examine these fundamental and sweeping charges that purport to undermine entirely the rational study of religion.

The indictments are of two major kinds. One is the general claim that it is irrational to hold any religious beliefs. To evaluate this claim, we must first examine the meaning of rationality so that we may determine what it means to designate a belief or the holding of a belief as rational or irrational. The other, even more basic, charge against the philosophy of religion as a reasonable undertaking is the claim that the very language in which religious ideas are expressed is unintelligible, that it fails to communicate anything that can be thought or understood. The most extreme form of this accusation comes from a brash book by A. J. Ayer, *Language, Truth, and Logic,* [13] which asserts that religious sentences are literally non-sense. We will examine first the issues related to religious language and then the nature of rationality and whether or not religious beliefs can ever be considered rational.

Religious Language, Meaning, and Verification

It was primarily the logical positivists, a group of philosophers who were attempting in the early decades of the twentieth century to transform philosophy into a kind of scientific enterprise, who made concern about the meaning or possible meaninglessness of religious language a major issue in the philosophy of religion. They felt that philosophy had been engaged for centuries in arguing the same issues without making progress toward resolving them, and that this lack of success was caused in large part by the lack of precision and clarity in the language philosophers used. The positivists believed that if progress was to be made in philosophy as it had been in science, the discipline needed a way to discern, with a degree of precision comparable to that which characterizes scientific statements, just what philosophical propositions mean. They further asserted that if it was not possible to ascertain with precision what a statement means, that statement must be regarded as not having any meaning at all. If a meaningful claim is made, it must make some empirically discernable difference. If the truth or falsity of a sentence makes absolutely no difference, that is, if no empirical situation is relevant to detecting whether it is true or false, then the sentence does not say anything—it is vacuous, a pseudo-statement, a sequence of words superficially resembling a proposition but actually making no intelligible assertion at all.

If a claim makes such a difference, however, it must be detectable. Thus the meaning of the statement must involve something relevant to our ability to discern whether or not the statement is true. The positivists were fond of quoting statements from philosophical writings on metaphysics as horrible examples of pseudo-statements that, they insisted, said nothing at all. One of Ayer's favorite examples comes from the British philosopher F. H. Bradley: "The Absolute enters into, but is itself incapable of, evolution and progress."[14] What possible difference could it make if this statement were true or not true? Ayer claimed that there is nothing that conceivably might happen which would enable us to ascertain whether or not **the Absolute** "entered into" evolution. He was convinced that the same thing could be said of statements about God. Such statements, argued Ayer, are compatible with any conceivable state of affairs. Thus they say nothing that makes any discernable difference or whose truth or falsity could be detected by any set of circumstances.

Out of deliberations such as these the conviction emerged among the logical positivists that a stringent theory of meaning must be formulated. The central ingredient in such a theory would be a criterion of the meaningfulness of alleged propositions — what the positivists called the **verifiability criterion.** This standard would define with complete precision what counted as a meaningful proposition, and statements would be recognized as having meaning only if in some sense they were verifiable.

The logical positivists' theory is firmly rooted in the empiricist tradition of such philosophers as John Locke and David Hume, which looks to sense experience as the primary source of knowledge. David Hume (1711–1776) proposed the skeleton of the theory of meaning in his claim that there are two kinds of meaningful propositions: statements that assert what he called the relations of ideas, and statements that affirm matters of fact. The first category consists of such propositions as, "All white horses are horses," "If A is greater than B, and B is greater than C, then A is greater than C," and "Bachelors are unmarried men." These are statements whose truth or falsity does not depend on empirical information about horses or bachelors. We do not need to conduct a survey of bachelors to find out whether or not any of them are married; anyone who understands the word *bachelor* already knows that no one can be a bachelor unless he is unmarried. (Immanuel Kant called such statements analytic, arguing that the predicate is "contained in," and needs only be analyzed out of, the subject.) Many of the basic principles of logic and mathematics fall into this category. Of such statements we say that they tell us nothing about matters of fact; they only tell us about how concepts relate to one another. They can be verified merely by thinking about the concepts they contain or by consulting a dictionary; empirical observation is totally irrelevant.

The other kind of meaningful statements, according to the empiricist tradition, is statements of matters of fact. "The wall is green," "Cigarette smoking causes lung cancer," and "The ozone layer in the upper atmosphere is being depleted by human products such as chlorofluorocarbons" are examples. One can be quite well acquainted with the terms occurring in these propositions without having any notion about whether or not they are true. To check on the truth or falsity of these statements, we need more than an understanding of the concepts; we must also have some information about what actually happens in the world. To find out if the wall is green, we must visually inspect the wall in suitable light. To find out if cigarette smoking causes lung cancer, we must accumulate statistics about cancer patients and their smoking habits.

Based on these empiricist assumptions about what sorts of propositions could be meaningful, the logical positivists set out to formulate their criterion. Many attempts were made to enunciate a principle that captured their sense of what was and was not meaningful, none of them ever quite successful. Basically they held that all meaningful propositions must be of one or other of the two kinds Hume had discussed. There was little controversy about the first type of statements. The trouble came with the second kind—and with the claim that any purported statement that is not of either kind is nonsense.

The problem lay, for the positivists, in determining what counted as a factual statement. If propositions that state matters of fact must be empirically verifiable, what actually constitutes empirical verification? At first the positivists insisted that such propositions were to be counted as meaningful only if they were conclusively verifiable through sense experience. But this claim was immediately seen to have absurd implications: Only a very small number of scientific propositions, if any, can be conclusively verified. The whole concept of conclusive verification presupposed a completely unsound doctrine about the nature of human knowledge—that empirical knowledge claims can be established with something approaching certainty, that they can be settled once and for all, and that no further progress will ever bring entrenched scientific principles or ordinary empirical beliefs into question again. Surely it would be absurd to say that "All animals are mortal" is a meaningless proposition. And yet it is not conclusively verifiable as long as even one animal—for example, the human who is attempting to verify it—is alive.

So the positivists revised the principle and proposed weaker versions. A sentence, they suggested, would be regarded as asserting a meaningful proposition in case some empirical evidence could be discovered that would show that it was at least verifiable in principle. The statement, "There is intelligent life on planets in other galaxies," seems entirely intelligible, but at the present time we do not have any way of verifying it. It might, however, be verifiable in principle. If we were to detect radio signals from the direction of some galaxy with certain characteristics suggesting that they might have been sent out by intelligent beings, that would count as some small bit of evidence for the claim and thus suffice to make the statement meaningful according to the weaker criterion. But suppose that there is a galaxy many light centuries[15] distant from us traveling away from us at a speed only slightly slower than the speed of light. I might claim that a planet in that galaxy, contemporary with the present era on earth, has beautiful sunsets. It is plain that we all understand what such a claim means, but it does not seem possible even in principle to verify the claim.

We need not trace all the tortured turnings in the paths taken by the positivists in their effort to produce a viable criterion of verification. It has long since become abundantly clear that the project was ill begotten. Every new formulation, when examined closely, turned out either to rule out statements that were obviously meaningful or not to rule out any statements at all. Two other even more disturbing features also became clear. One was that the positivists' program was not a disinterested effort to seek out the truth, to discover which statements really were and were not meaningful; it was, rather, a partisan effort to dismiss, or expel from philosophical respectability, statements pertaining to branches of philosophy that the positivists did not favor. The lack of objectivity was not even disguised in many of their writings. For example, Ayer's discussion of metaphysics in *Language, Truth, and Logic* is titled simply, "The Elimination of Metaphysics."[16]

It became clear that the positivists held certain doctrines — we may without exaggeration call them dogmas — about the nature of philosophy, and they set out to eliminate from philosophy whatever did not conform to their creed. The verifiability criterion was supposed to be the surgical implement with which they would amputate the disfavored branches of the discipline, namely, metaphysics, ethics, aesthetics, and philosophy of religion. Critics attempting to explain their motivation have accused them of "physics envy" (the punlike reference, obviously, is to Freud's concept of "penis envy"). Wanting to bestow on philosophy some of the prestige and honor gained by science, the positivists wanted to eliminate those branches of philosophy they thought could not be made sciencelike. They did not realize or concede that it is neither possible nor desirable to make philosophy resemble science. William James would have been quick to point out that they were thinking with *both* arbitrariness and dogmatism.

The other point is equally damaging. The verifiability criterion asserted that the only meaningful propositions were those that were either analytic or verifiable empirically; all other sentences were pseudostatements and thus literally nonsense. Sentences such as, "The Absolute enters into the process of evolution," or "God loves his children," were said not to be verifiable in either way. According to the positivists, they were not real statements but literal nonsense. But then, someone asked, what kind of proposition is the verifiability criterion itself? Clearly it is not of the first sort: It is not an analytic statement like "Bachelors are unmarried." But neither is it empirically verifiable. It follows, then, that the verifiability criterion is a principle that convicts itself of meaninglessness. It is, by its own standard, nonsense.

The failure to find a workable verifiability principle led some philosophers to attempt a theory of meaning based not on verifiability but on falsifiability or disconfirmability. If a claim is to be meaningful, they suggested, there must be something that, if it were to occur, would count in some measure to disconfirm the claim. If the claim could not conceivably be disconfirmed regardless of what might happen — that is, if those who assert the claim would not acknowledge that anything could count against the belief — we would be justified in regarding it as an empty piety.

Disconfirmability appeared at first to be a less caustic solvent than verifiability, and thus less likely to dissolve legitimately meaningful statements into the category of meaninglessness. As it turned out, however, this concept too is not without its problems. Consider the instance pointed out by John Hick: "There are three successive sevens in the decimal determination of π."[17] There is no question that this statement is meaningful and that we understand what it means, and yet it is not even in principle disconfirmable. It is confirmable in principle, although it has not yet been confirmed. If the computation of the decimal equivalent of π were further extended, it might happen that at some point three sevens would occur in succession, thus decisively confirming the claim. But there is no way, no matter how far the computation might be continued, that it might be disconfirmed.

The notion of **eschatological** verification illustrates again the impossibility of disconfirming statements which we all take to be intelligible. Consider the claim, "After bodily death, there is a continued existence of the person that involves ongoing consciousness and continuity of memory." If this statement is true, then its truth will be confirmed after death. But its disconfirmation, even its eschatological disconfirmation, is impossible even in principle because its falsity implies that the individual will not exist to be aware that the claim is false. The conclusion is that we do not have a satisfactory criterion of meaning either in the form of a principle of verification or a principle of disconfirmation.

And yet the sense persists that, apart from some standard of meaning, there are no reasonable restraints against even the wildest and most preposterous doctrines presenting themselves as serious and sound philosophy. The need is illustrated graphically in a parable recounted by Antony Flew, based on a story originally told by John Wisdom.[18] Two men come on a clearing in the jungle where rows of plants grow and flower amid a considerable infestation of weeds. One man remarks that some gardener must come from time to time to tend the plot; the other is convinced that there is no gardener. They keep a watch over the plot, they post bloodhounds to detect the scent of the gardener, they put up an electric fence, but no gardener is ever detected. Still, the first man insists that there must be a gardener — perhaps one that cannot be seen in any ordinary way; one who has no scent that bloodhounds can detect; one who can get through an electric fence — and this gardener comes to care for the garden he loves. But his skeptical companion argues that this alleged gardener who makes no detectable difference is significantly like no gardener at all. The believer seems determined to hold onto his belief regardless of the lack of any supporting evidence and in the face of all sorts of tests that count against the belief. Flew suggests that the claim that a gardener comes just *means* that someone who continuously watches will see the gardener, or that bloodhounds will detect a scent, or that something will be different because of his coming than would have been the case if no gardener came. Thus the believer cannot mean by his claim that a gardener, in any ordinary sense of that word, comes, because in that sense gardeners can be seen and detected. What, then, could he mean? Nothing, it seems.

Just this sort of problem arises when religious people make claims that cannot be either verified or disconfirmed. If their claims are meaningful, it must be possible to specify what they mean. If the claim is consistent with every conceivable state of affairs, then it has no intelligible meaning. And this is the problem, some would say, with much talk in religion and the philosophy of religion. Religious people make such statements as, "God loves his children." But when it is pointed out that children suffer and die in horrible ways and God does not intervene to help them, when it is suggested that such calamities as the Holocaust seem inconsistent with God's love, the believers nonetheless persist in holding to the claim. Such a statement would seem to become, then, like the claim about the invisible gardener: a pious utterance with no discernible or specifiable meaning.

There is, then, a very serious problem with the use of religious language, but efforts to deal with this problem by means of sharply crafted principles of verifiability or disconfirmability have not proven successful. Language is an astonishingly powerful, versatile, abounding instrument; when you think about it, it seems unrealistic to expect to capture it in some small net. The empiricist attempt to reduce all the functions of language to two types of meaningful statements tested by a mechanical rule of meaning proves to be inexcusably narrow and arbitrary.

The question of how words and sentences mean what they do requires specialized answers depending on the kind of use to which they are put. The standards appropriate for the explication of a claim in sociology will not be the same as those appropriate for geometry or physics. And deciding whether or not a sentence expresses an intelligible or meaningful claim is not as simple as holding up to it some generic yardstick intended to serve equally well for biology, history, and aesthetics. Discerning meaningfulness — and ascertaining what, if anything, is meant — is a retail, not a wholesale, enterprise. We must look at sentences one by one, and we must bring to bear on them all the techniques, mechanical and intuitive, that enable us to detect meaning. Several times in the course of our discussion of positivism we have said of some statement, "It is clear that this has meaning and that we know what it means." Indeed, it is in terms of our native ability to detect meaning — what we might call, without any suggestion of anything mysterious, our intuitive capability to recognize meaning — that we judge the verifiability and the disconfirmability criteria unsatisfactory. We do so simply because these criteria rule out statements that we know clearly do have meaning. Since the persistent efforts of a substantial number of able and dedicated philosophers during more than a generation have failed to produce a rule that captures our sense of meaning, it seems that we will have to make do with that sense itself. In most cases we can tell fairly readily whether a sentence expresses anything intelligible and, if so, what it expresses. And there are abundant ironclad examples that can serve as paradigms when we come across a doubtful case.

What is really at issue, under the guise of meaning, is a willingness to submit our claims to scrutiny; to allow evidence to count, for whatever it is worth, for or against these claims; and to give up our tendency to reserve the right to believe certain cherished notions despite the evidence or lack of it. To this attitude the positivists were right to object. They simply objected in the wrong way. The verifiability criterion was an attempt, however clumsy and ill expressed, to denounce any claim that its advocates hold to be above the reach of evidence; the disconfirmability principle was an effort, though not directly conceived as such, to convince dogmatists that they could not fly in the face of reason with impunity. The point is not to call a claim meaningless, but to bring to bear on it all the clarifying techniques of analysis, and particularly to test it against every relevant sort of evidence and the most careful arguments of reason that can contribute toward ascertaining whether or not it is true. This is exactly what we do with sentences in the field of science or any other area of intellectual endeavor.

As a result, we will sometimes have to decide whether or not to believe a religious assertion in the absence of clear-cut evidence. But religious claims are not essentially different from most other kinds. We believe, or do not believe, that a product is safe, or economical, or effective on the basis of fragmentary information or in the face of conflicting evidence from different studies. We make some of our most important life decisions without nearly as much evidence as we need. We invest our life savings on the advice of an investment counselor who has a vague sense, based on certain ambiguous signs in the market, that the price of a stock will rise. We enter a marriage without any guarantee of our prediction that it will be a happy match.

A reasonable person, however, does not adopt beliefs about serious matters without considering how weighty the evidence is, or how good the reasons may be, for believing and for not believing. And by the same token a reasonable person does not reserve the right to hold beliefs above, or out of the reach of, evidence. To do so is not, as the positivists wanted to claim, to assert something meaningless; it is rather to reject the process that offers our very best hope of obtaining truth rather than comfortable fictions. The question is not whether the claims of religion and the philosophy of religion are meaningless. A few may be, but close analysis will determine this. The question is rather whether they are true — or at least whether there is any justification, in the form of evidence or good reasons, for believing them.

An important word remains to be said, however, about holding firmly to a belief in the face of opposition. Basil Mitchell[19] offers an illuminating parable: Suppose that during the war you meet and spend a single day with a charismatic stranger who assures you that he is on your side. He impresses you as completely trustworthy and of exemplary character, and he urges you to have faith in him no matter what happens. You never see him alone again. In the subsequent days and weeks you see him doing things that sometimes clearly seem consistent with your cause, and you say to your companions, "He is on our side." Sometimes you see him do things that appear contrary to your cause, but you say to your companions, "He has his reasons."

It may never be possible to discover with certainty whether the stranger really is on your side. If you were sufficiently convinced of his sincerity and integrity, you will trust him despite considerable suspicious evidence. But the point is this: Your trust need not be total and blind. There are things the stranger could do that, if you are rational in your beliefs, would finally convince you to abandon your faith in him. Mitchell suggests that rational religious believers may be in a similar situation. They trust the integrity of their religious beliefs. They will continue to believe that God loves them or that in the end things work out well for God's children, even though they suffer and in the short run things go badly. But the important distinction between rational believers and irrational dogmatists is that rational believers, however willing they may be to trust in the face of compromising evidence, do not disregard evidence or reject sound arguments, and they do not insist that nothing that conceivably might happen could count against their belief. They recognize, for example, that evil is evidence against their faith in the existence of a good and caring God. They also see the good things that happen to them as evidence on the other side. And they may realize that only eschatological evidence can be decisive.

In the practical affairs of our lives, we must often act more decisively than the available evidence can justify. We carry or do not carry an umbrella, we marry or do not marry a certain individual, we join or do not join a certain political party or religious group. But in our role as philosophers of religion, we must attempt as much as we can to hold no beliefs above the reach of evidence, to seek out every attainable scrap of evidence of every conceivable sort, to discover and formulate the strongest and soundest arguments of every kind that relate to our questions, and then to follow where the evidence leads and adjust our conclusions and the strength with which we hold them accordingly.

Before we leave our examination of religious language, one further point should be noted. Although the philosopher is usually more directly concerned with the literal meaning of sentences, he or she must also recognize other important, nonliteral functions of language. If the poets have taught us anything, it is that words and sentences can be made to carry far greater and richer meaning than they literally express. This is particularly true of our deepest feelings and our strongest values. When it comes to communicating our joyous feeling toward someone we love, the breathtaking experience of a resplendent sunset, or the crushing shock of a devastating loss, we understand all too poignantly the poverty of language. Many of our most moving and significant experiences are simply not expressible through language in its mundane and literal sense. Mystics, as we will have occasion to see, frequently say that their experiences are ineffable, inexpressible in language. To express such experiences we resort to other modes of expressions — music, art, and poetry. These media stretch and tax sound, color, and words to make them say what they will not otherwise say. The language of poetry is metaphor, allegory, simile, figure of speech, symbol, allusion, imagery. By these devices the poet is able to convey at least fragments of the inexpressible and thus to communicate something of what is beyond words.

When philosophers and philosophers of religion grasp after a sense of the ultimate, of greatness infinitely beyond the mundane, of reality in its final and complete sense, they too experience the poverty of literal language. Some theologians, such as Paul Tillich (1886–1965), emphasize very strongly the necessity, in attempting to think and to talk about what is ultimate, of recognizing and utilizing the symbolic power of language. Indeed, Tillich maintains that the language of religion is symbols and myths. [20] We have already had occasion in this chapter to cite several parables offered by philosophers not merely to illustrate but actually to convey meanings not easily expressed in literal language. Our attempts to say what we need to say would be immeasurably poorer if we did not have access to the mind-stretching power and the language-enriching potency of poetic expression.

A serious word of caution, however, is essential here. Poetic expression is not nearly as susceptible to the controls and restraints of reason as is literal language. When an assertion is intended to be taken literally, the techniques of philosophical analysis can determine just how much is being claimed and of what sort of claim it is. The claim can be subjected to the rigorous standards of evidence and reasoning that are essential if philosophy of religion is to be intellectually sound. For the purpose of expressing our most important insights, we must be free to draw upon all of the implements of poetry. But the flourishes of poetic expression and the flights of symbolic imagery must always be kept anchored — however long we permit the tether to become — to fact, evidence, argument, documentation. And although apprehension and expression of the inexpressible is an important alleged function of religion, comprehension and authentication of cognitive claims is the business of philosophy. In the final analysis, even if religion has to do with the ultimate, the divine, and the beyond, the philosopher of religion can be satisfied only with what can be understood in human terms, expressed in rational terms, and justified by humanly intelligible evidence and reason.

The Rationality of Religious Belief

After our excursion into the realm of religious language, it is time to return to the general charge sometimes leveled against religion that religious belief is, by its very nature, irrational and that there can consequently be no such thing as rational religious belief.

It is not a new claim and, indeed, not only the enemies of religion have put it forward. The irrationality of religious belief was advanced as a proud item of orthodox theology in the Christian tradition by such fathers of the Church as St. Tertullian (c. 160–c. 220 C.E.[21]). Tertullian and others like him were convinced that human reason is a very feeble and fallible instrument that is not to be trusted in deciding matters of great moment. This belief was grounded in the teaching about the fall of humankind and the doctrine of original sin. According to one of the biblical accounts of creation, found in the second and third chapters of the book of Genesis,[22] Adam and Eve, the first man and woman, originally created perfect and in the image of God, sinned by disobeying God and eating the forbidden fruit. This ancient myth was interpreted by Christians as teaching that the result of the sin was the loss of the image of God and the tainting and damaging of human nature, an effect that passed from parents to children through all generations from Adam and Eve to the present day.

Thus, as Tertullian saw it, human faculties such as reason have been damaged by the fall. Infected as it is by the result of the original sin of our first parents, reason cannot be expected to understand the great mysteries of divine truth. In a famous and oft-cited passage, Tertullian makes clear his attitude toward reason and his own devotion to the unintelligible revelation of the Christian religion. "What hath Athens to do with Jerusalem? What concord is there between the Academy and the Church? what between heretics and Christians? . . . With our faith, we desire no further belief."[23] It is even said that he claimed he believed the Christian faith because it was absurd. Athens, the symbol in the ancient world of philosophical reasoning, is the temple of what Tertullian liked to call "bastard reason." Jerusalem is the center of that holy irrationality, that mysterious revelation which, in the eyes of arrogant human reason, seemed absurd but is in truth the wisdom of God.

According to Tertullian, then, it is far better to believe what we cannot understand — what indeed human intellect perceives as utter folly because it is the gift of God's revealed truth, far too high and unattainable to the human mind — than to add to our already mighty sum of sin by pompous intellectual pretensions. Thus, because our reason is so befouled and tainted, the very absurd appearance of Christian revelation bears witness to its truth. Religious belief cannot be and ought not to attempt to be rational, for the rational is the fruit of presumptuous, sin-ruined reason. The teachings of true faith are irrational, mysterious, and beyond the feeble powers of the human mind.

There has always been a streak of such anti-intellectualism in Christian teachings.[24] It was already present in the writings of St. Paul, who suggests that the idea that a crucified criminal could actually be God incarnate seemed absurd to outsiders but was actually the highest wisdom of God.

The word of the cross is folly to those who are perishing, but to us who are being saved it is the power of God. . . . Has not God made foolish the wisdom of the world? . . . we preach Christ crucified, a stumbling block to Jews and folly to Gentiles, but to those who are called, both Jews and Greeks, Christ the power of God and the wisdom of God. For the foolishness of God is wiser than men.[25]

The distrust of human reason is to be detected in some of the ongoing practices of the Church such as censorship, prohibition of certain books, resistance to translation of the Bible into the vernacular languages and, when translations could no longer be prevented, the careful annotation of certain passages designed to make sure that reason did not make unorthodox interpretations. St. Augustine taught that we should believe before we seek to understand, and that ordinary persons should not attempt the understanding of the high theological mysteries at all, leaving this task instead to authorized and properly educated doctors of the Church.

At the same time a strong countervailing trend in Christian history has argued that human reason is a gift of God and thus intended by its maker to be used to seek understanding, a process that, it was alleged, amounts to thinking God's thoughts after him. Though not denying the doctrine of original sin, this view held that human reason was not utterly ruined and could function as God intended it to do in finding out truths about God and his world. The great thirteenth-century theologian St. Thomas Aquinas took this approach, making very extensive use of reason to provide arguments in support of the Church's teachings.

Thomas insisted that there is no quarrel between faith and reason, nor any inconsistency between divine revelation and rationally discovered truth, and his ingenious scheme for reconciling reason and revelation became fixed Church doctrine. There are many things which our reason can find out, Thomas maintained, but there are also some things that exceed the power of reason. Thus God has seen fit to reveal to us through scripture and the authoritative teachings of the Church those high truths that are necessary for our salvation. He also tells us that God has revealed some things that we can independently discover through the use of our reason. God did so to provide us with an opportunity to test our reason and learn to use it properly. For example, God's existence is clearly revealed to us through scripture. But it is also possible, Thomas insisted, to prove God's existence by human reason. Indeed, Thomas provided us with five proofs, the famous **five ways**, each of which by itself allegedly suffices to prove the existence of God. This overlapping of what we can find out for ourselves and what God reveals serves a function somewhat like that of the answers placed at the end of logic and mathematic textbooks. After the students have done the calculations, they can look up the answer to make sure that they did it correctly. Similarly, when we exercise our reason to prove things for ourselves that have also been revealed by God, we can test and improve our reasoning skills.

The conclusion that Thomas eagerly desired to establish is that religious belief is not irrational. To be sure, there are certain truths we need to know that reason is not powerful enough to find out for itself — for example, the fact that God is a Trinity, or the miracle of transubstantiation in the mass — but these truths are not irrational. God's reason, to which ours bears a similarity, does understand them. Such beliefs are not unintelligible or contradictory to reason, as Tertullian believed; rather, they merely exceed the power of our reason in ways similar to that in which an educated king's understanding of the economy of a great political realm exceeds the simple peasant's understanding of economy in terms of his small household accounts. Thus Thomas supports the position that religious beliefs can be and ought to be rational.

When we look a bit more closely at what it means to say that a belief is rational or irrational, we discover that the distinction is not as simple as it may appear at first. Rationality is not a concept created arbitrarily by the mathematician or logician to serve some narrow purpose. Rather, it represents the pattern or the structure according to which the normal, mature mind operates, and we find it natural to believe that rationality also represents the pattern of the world as well. There is an objectivity and necessity about rationality that the informed and unclouded mind cannot avoid.

It is this necessity that coerces us when we think logically and mathematically. When we understand what the expressions *2*, *plus*, *equals*, and *4* mean, it is impossible (that is, irrational) for us to think that $2 + 2 = 4$ is false. The mind is built in such a way that we cannot avoid believing the conclusion of a mathematical sum or of a logical argument. It is not merely difficult, it is literally impossible to understand "All men are mortal" and "Socrates is a man" without believing "Socrates is mortal." In cases such as these, where the requirements of reason are so luminous and obvious, the mind finds itself definitely unable to believe in an irrational conclusion. In order to accept irrational beliefs, it is necessary for us not to see the irrationality. We do sometimes hold mutually contradictory beliefs, but only if we do not notice that they are contradictory. As soon as their inconsistency is pointed out, we undergo the curious experience of finding that we simply cannot any longer accept both beliefs. Among the large number of beliefs that we accept, there are bound to be inconsistencies that go unnoticed; we do not always bring to bear on a belief the evidence we may have that, if juxtaposed with the belief, would force us to abandon it.

When religious leaders urge the faithful to accept beliefs that are irrational in the sense of being contradictory or inconsistent with other things we know to be true, they often make use of devices to obscure the fact that the beliefs are irrational. Political leaders follow a similar strategy. This is undoubtedly the reason that religious authorities have often discouraged laypersons from attempting to understand or reason about the articles of faith. Doctrines are called mysterious and above reason, and sometimes teachings that seem distinctly contradictory — such as the claim that God can be three and at the same time one — are called *paradoxes*, a word intended to designate teachings that appear to be contradictory but that allegedly, at a deeper or more sacred level, are not.

Thus, to say of a belief that it is irrational is to denounce it in the strongest possible way. It is a very serious matter to say that religious beliefs are not or cannot be rational. This means that if the people who hold such beliefs really understood them and the evidence related to them, they would not be able to accept them. It means, in other words, that persons could be religious only if they were very ignorant or very dishonest — willing to hide from themselves the truths that undermine their beliefs.

Is religion actually rendered untenable by reason when it is clearly examined and fully understood? It is quite likely that some of the teachings of the various religions are indeed irrational. Many of the tenets put forward by religious teachers incorporate the current scientific or common-sense beliefs of the era in which the teacher lived. The progress of human knowledge reveals that these opinions are false, but because they have become part of sacred writings, the defenders of the religion often feel that they must continue to present these opinions as revealed truth. This is the most serious epistemological fault[26] of fundamentalism, whether Christian, Moslem, Buddhist, or Hindu.

One of the important tasks that many modern theologians assign themselves is that of separating such unessential, time-bound, empirical or commonsense teachings that do not pertain to the spiritual core of the religious revelation from the essential religious teachings that pertain to every era. The fact that religious scriptures or doctrines have in them such time-bound beliefs means that some religious teachings are indeed irrational. But the charge that all religious belief is irrational is based on a mistaken and too simple-minded understanding of the meaning of rationality and irrationality, an understanding that assumes that every belief is either required by reason or forbidden by reason. But the two classes "forbidden by reason" and "required by reason" do not exhaust all of the possibilities. Some beliefs — indeed, the great majority — are neither forbidden nor required by reason.

Reason requires us to believe that bachelors are unmarried men, that a whole is greater than any one of its parts, that two plus seven is nine. It also requires us to believe, apart from distorting or deceiving circumstances, that what we see before us is approximately as it appears to be; it even requires us to believe with a considerable degree of confidence various scientific and commonsense claims for which there is very strong appropriate evidence: that smoking causes lung cancer, that the material things in the world are all made of various combinations of approximately 100 basic elements, that the sun produces energy by fusing hydrogen atoms into helium, that racial and ethnic prejudice are fairly widespread in the world in the twentieth century, and so on. Reason forbids us to believe that there are any five-sided triangles, that by the year 2000 the world will have existed for a shorter period of time than it had existed in 1900, that three times three is eleven, or that a man could be his grandfather's sister. Reason also forbids us to believe with any substantial degree of conviction that there is no connection between serum cholesterol and heart disease, that the moon is made of a substance totally different from what constitutes the earth, or that it is safe to expose humans to very high levels of radioactivity.

When we talk about the beliefs that reason requires and the beliefs that reason forbids, we speak of the areas of well- or of relatively well-established human knowledge. But there is much that we do not yet know. There is some justification for believing that a vaccine effective in preventing AIDS will be discovered before the year 2015, but there are also substantial reasons for believing that this will not happen. Evidence suggests that the mean temperature of the earth is rising very gradually; but this evidence is far from conclusive. Reason neither requires nor forbids us to believe these and a very large number of similar claims. About such beliefs we say that there is room for reasonable doubt and reasonable disagreement. It is not irrational to believe; neither is it irrational to disbelieve. Indeed, we actually find numbers of very reasonable persons on both sides of many of these issues.

We must conclude, therefore, that the question of rationality involves not just two but three categories: (1) "required by reason," (2) "forbidden by reason," and a third that is neither required nor forbidden but is rather (3) "permitted by reason." Now it is clear that persons would be irrational if they adopted beliefs forbidden by reason and rational if they adopted beliefs required by reason. But what about the very large category of beliefs about which the sum of our evidence is insufficient to enable us to say that they are either required or forbidden? Certainly it would not be irrational to believe them, since the evidence is inconclusive and thus they might be true. Likewise, it would not be irrational to disbelieve them for a similar reason. We must say of those beliefs that are "permitted by reason" that it is rational to believe them *and* that it is rational not to believe them.

We may summarize our findings, therefore, by saying that when we call a belief irrational, we mean that it is forbidden by reason. That means that the belief is known to be false or that the evidence against it is strong enough that no reasonable person could be justified in accepting the belief. But when we say that a belief is rational, we mean not necessarily that it is required by reason, but perhaps that it is permitted by reason. In other words, the class of rational beliefs includes those that are required and also those that are permitted by reason. Perhaps a diagram will help:

Irrational Beliefs	Rational Beliefs	
Beliefs forbidden by reason	Beliefs permitted by reason	Beliefs required by reason

But where, in this framework, do religious beliefs fall? Clearly the positivists believed that religious beliefs were excluded from the whole scheme of classification because they are not true assertions and thus do not count as beliefs at all. But we have already seen that the positivists were not justified in that position. We must find the proper place, then, for religious assertions that make genuine claims.

It is clear that some religious beliefs are required by reason, particularly those whose truth is determined exclusively by the meaning of their terms: for example, "God is the creator of the world according to Christian doctrine," or "The Buddha is the enlightened one." And any parallel claims that are false by virtue of the meaning of their constituent terms are forbidden by reason: for example, "God is a created being according to Christian doctrine" or "An avatar is not an incarnate deity." The overwhelming majority of religious claims, however, are neither forbidden nor required by reason. "God exists" is supported by certain plausible arguments, but there are also substantial counterarguments. "God is omnipotent" is maintained by Christians on fairly convincing grounds, but opponents have brought forward strong objections. "Mystical experiences are merely abnormal psychological states with no religious significance" has been argued with a certain plausibility, but there are good reasons on the other side. Thus, these claims may not be either required nor forbidden by reason. This means that such beliefs are permitted by reason: It is reasonable to believe them; it is also reasonable to disbelieve them. But we must be very careful not to become lax in weighing the evidence. Only those beliefs concerning which the available evidence is quite evenly balanced can be considered in this sense rational to believe. Those for which there is even a small balance of negative over affirmative evidence cannot be affirmed rationally.

Beliefs that are permitted by reason are not irrational. They are, in fact, one of the categories of rational beliefs. It follows, therefore, that it is not irrational to hold some religious beliefs or, stated another way, that some religious beliefs can be rational. But we must remember that this is not a very strong claim about religious beliefs. It does not amount to saying that any religious beliefs are true; that is an entirely separate question. Many beliefs that it is rational to hold may turn out to be false. Of course, once we discover that they are false, it is no longer rational to hold them. Indeed, as soon as there is a preponderance of evidence against a belief, it ceases to be rational to hold it.

Many religious beliefs, however, have strong arguments in their favor that many honest and careful thinkers find convincing. The business of the philosophy of religion is to examine the claims made in the name of religion. In so doing, we must keep in mind at all times William James's injunction to think without arbitrariness or dogmatism. Thus we will give rank or privilege to no belief, whether favorable to, or critical of, religion, but will attempt to place all on an equal footing, demanding of every one satisfactory epistemological credentials and standing ready to reject any that do not pass muster. We will make use of all the tools of evidence and reasoning and will hope for illuminating results. But whether our conclusions are meager or substantial, we will learn in the process a great deal about religion, philosophy, and perhaps also ourselves.

ANNOTATED GUIDE TO FURTHER READINGS

Abernethy, George L., and Langford, Thomas A., ed. *Philosophy of Religion.* New York: Macmillan, 1962.

A collection of short essays offering a wide variety of viewpoints; authors include Kant, James, Aquinas, and Tillich. Chapter 1 discusses the nature of religion; chapter 2, the relationship between the philosophy of religion and theology; chapter 5, religious language,

Clifford, William K. "The Ethics of Belief." In *Philosophy of Religion: Selected Readings,* 2nd ed., edited by William L. Rowe and William J. Wainwright. New York: Harcourt Brace Jovanovich, 1989.

Clifford argues that we are morally obligated to believe only what is supported by the evidence. A belief not backed up in such a manner should, according to morality, be rejected. Other readings in this section, "Faith and The Need For Evidence," are by Aquinas, James, Plantinga, and Wykstra.

Delaney, C. F., ed. *Rationality and Religious Belief.* Notre Dame: University of Notre Dame Press, 1979.

Eight essays dealing with the link between rationality and religious belief. There are two central themes: (1) the concept of rationality must be scrutinized and not blindly accepted, and (2) religion is more than a mere assortment of beliefs, it plays an inseparable role in how we define ourselves.

Flew, Antony, Hare, R. M., and Mitchell, Basil. "Theology and Falsification," In *New Essays in Philosophical Theology,* edited by Antony Flew and Alasdair MacIntyre. London: SCM Press, 1955.

To what extent are theological utterances assertions or explanations? Flew, Hare, and Mitchell address this question, along with that of maintaining faith when faced with evidence that may make this faith seem irrational. Each thinker uses a parable to clarify his position, a format that makes the argument highly readable.

Hick, John H. *Philosophy of Religion*. Englewood Cliffs, N. J.: Prentice-Hall, 1983.

> *Hick's introduction attempts a definition of the philosophy of religion. Chapters 6 and 7 deal with religious language. Presenting various viewpoints, Hick examines the question of whether or not religious statements should be seen as assertions of truth. The idea that religious language should be regarded as symbolic rather than literal is presented by an analysis of the theories of Paul Tillich and J. H. Randall, Jr.*

Pojman, Louis P. "Can Religious Belief Be Rational?" In *Philosophy of Religion: An Anthology*, edited by Louis P. Pojman. Belmont, Calif.: Wadsworth, 1987.

> *In this excellent essay Pojman argues that religious beliefs are a part of a larger, interconnected network of beliefs. When deciding on the merits of a religious belief, an individual should attempt to be impartial and to judge rationally the evidence presented. But this is not an entirely objective process because personal experiences will influence such an analysis. Also included in this section of Pojman's text (VII.D, "Rationality and Justified Religious Belief") are passages by John Hick, Alvin Plantinga, and Philip Quinn.*

NOTES

1. Rabindranath Tagore, *The Religion of Man* (Boston: Beacon Press, 1931),p. 77.

2. Ibid., p. 126.

3. Quoted in William P. Alston, "Religion," *The Encyclopedia of Philosophy*, ed. Paul Edwards (New York: Macmillan, 1967), vol. 7, pp. 140ff.

4. Quoted in John Hick, *The Philosophy of Religion*, 3rd ed. (Englewood Cliffs, N.J.: Prentice-Hall, 1983), p. 2.

5. Alston, "Religion," vol. 7, pp. 140ff.

6. Hick, *Philosophy of Religion*, p. 2.

7. Alston, "Religion," pp. 141f.

8. Ibid.

9. William K. Clifford, *Lectures and Essays* (New York: Macmillan, 1901), vol. 2, p. 175.

10. Paul Tillich, *Dynamics of Faith* (New York: Harper & Row, 1957), pp. 55ff.

11. Alston, "Religion," vol. 7, pp. 143ff.

12. Ralph Waldo Emerson, "Nature," *Essays, First Series*, from *The Complete Writings of Ralph Waldo Emerson* (New York: William H. Wise, 1985, 1929), p. 2.

13. A. J. Ayer, *Language, Truth and Logic* (New York: Dover Books, 1946).

14. F. H. Bradley, *Appearance and Reality*, quoted in ibid., p. 36.

15. A light century is the distance light travels in 100 years.

16. Ayer, *Language, Truth and Logic*, chapter 1.

17. John Hick, "Theology and Verification," *Theology Today* 7, 1 (April 1960): 16.

18. Antony Flew, R. M. Hare, and Basil Mitchell, "Theology and Falsification," in *New Essays in Philosophical Theology,* edited by Antony Flew and Alasdair MacIntyre (London: SCM Press, 1955).

19. Ibid.

20. Tillich, *Dynamics of Faith.*

21. The expressions "C.E." (Common Era) and "B.C.E." (Before the Common Era) will be used in this book instead of "A.D." (which abbreviates the Latin for "in the year of our Lord) and "B.C." (Before Christ) because the latter expressions are specific to Christianity, whereas the others are not religion-specific.

22. It is worth noting that the opening chapters of Genesis present two distinct accounts of creation with very important differences in tone and teaching. Most contemporary biblical scholars believe that they were written by different persons at different times and merged into a continuous account much later by yet another person. The account in the first chapter presents humankind and all things created as good, depicts man and woman as having been created simultaneously, and says nothing about sin or the fall. The doctrine of the fall and the concept of original sin are based on the second creation account, which is much more moralistic in tone, which depicts woman as created later than man and from one of his ribs, and which lacks the phrase, oft-repeated in the first account, "and God saw that it was good."

23. *De Præscriptione Hœreticorum,* in Alexander Roberts and James Donaldson, editors, *The Ante-Nicene Fathers* (Buffalo: Christian Literature Publishing Company, 1887–96), vol. 3, p. 246.

24. Examples of anti-intellectualism could also be cited from other religious traditions, such as Islam and Hinduism.

25. I Corinthians 1:18–25.

26. There are grave moral flaws that flow from this epistemological mistake. We will discuss fundamentalism in more detail in Chapter 4.

2

Theism: The Perfections of God

THEISM AND WESTERN RELIGION

Theism is the doctrine that there is one God, the creator and ruler of the
universe, who is perfect in every way, personal, worthy of worship, separate
from the world, and concerned with human affairs. It is to be distinguished
from **atheism**, the denial of the existence of God, from **pantheism**, which
regards God as identical with the world, and from **deism**, which teaches
that God created the world in the beginning but is no longer involved with
it. Although Western philosophers have examined and sometimes advocated a variety of other doctrines about God, clearly theism has been most
widely considered and accepted during the past two thousand years. Many
of the most important theological and philosophical disputes have focused
on questions about the nature of God and arguments for and against God's
existence. Theism is not the central focus of several of the world religions,
as we will see in a later chapter. Because it has preoccupied Westerners to
such an extent, however, we will devote four chapters to issues related to
theism. In this chapter we will analyze the major characteristics or perfections usually attributed to the theistic God. Our concern here is not with
whether or not any deity exists; rather, we will ask what characteristics a
God, if one turns out to exist, would have. Chapter 3 examines the major
arguments for the existence of God; Chapter 4, the major objections to

theism. Chapter 5 looks at several of the alternative ways of accounting for the world and humankind that leave God out of account.

Before we turn to a detailed examination of the most important characteristics usually attributed to God, it may be useful to note that the concept of theism is an achievement of human thought, evolved from other less sophisticated and mostly less philosophically respectable positions. Although religion seems to have been present in human society from the very earliest times, early religion is not usually theistic. Our human ancestors developed religious responses to various aspects of their experience involving the recognition of superior powers that had to be dealt with and placated. Most often, these powers were conceptualized not as one but several or many, and the appropriate response frequently involved a substantial element of magic as well as religion. Indeed, vestigial traces of magic are still to be seen in some of the religious practices of the most highly developed religions.

The most characteristic difference between a magical and a religious response to the forces that affect us is that magic attempts to coerce the beings or powers to do our bidding whereas religion seeks to persuade, please, and find favor. The forms that early religion has taken are almost as varied as the groups that developed them, although there are certain similarities. There is nearly always a sense of awe, often accompanied by fear, toward whatever is regarded as sacred. Virtually every object in the material world that has ever existed or been imagined has been treated as sacred by one group or another.

A fairly widespread type of early religion is called **animism**. This involves the belief that spirits inhabit various objects, animate and inanimate, in the world. Diverse functions are assigned to the different spirits, and thus an assortment of rituals is required to badger benefits or to curry favor. Sometimes rituals, such as rain dances, act out the effect desired; sometimes they imitate the object of concern, behaving like the animal to be hunted or making images and dressing, feeding, bathing them or (conversely) stabbing or mutilating them; sometimes prayers are offered containing elements of bargaining with the powers to do favors in exchange for offerings; sometimes sacrifices are given to please the spirits or to pay them for favors granted.

Humans have always felt powerless in the face of the great sources of danger, need, and suffering that animate nature. Natural catastrophes such as flood, drought, disease, storms, famine, and death have inspired awe and an effort to understand the forces responsible for these life-threatening and destructive events. Religion has nearly always addressed the need to deal with these mighty forces; to control or ward off the grave danger; and to ensure the fertility of the earth, of the animals needed for food, and of human beings themselves in their procreative functions. Many have included a belief in some continued existence after bodily death, with rituals devised to ensure a safe and comfortable journey to the next world and graves furnished with offerings of objects thought to be needed in the next life.

As the vague powers and spirits thought to be in control of humankind's destiny take on personalities, we observe a transition from animism to **polytheism**, the belief in many gods. The various gods were believed to have different functions, one sending or withholding rain, another afflicting with disease or curing, still another making the seeds germinate and yield their increase. An interesting variation on polytheism can be observed in the historical evolution of Hebrew religion during a phase called **henotheism**. This is the belief that each tribe or people has its own god, local to a particular territory and responsible for the well-being of its own people. In the Hebrew scriptures, these gods are depicted as fighting against one another when the tribes go to war. The Hebrew religion itself was a moralistic one, in which the god laid down a system of moral law and rewarded or punished the people in proportion to their conformity to the law, often by granting them victory over, or bringing on them defeat at the hands of, their enemies.

The evolution from polytheism and henotheism to theism, sometimes called **monotheism** to contrast it with polytheism (*mono* = one; *poly* = many), is distinctly visible in the literature of the Hebrew Bible as a gradual recognition that the many gods with their various functions, and the several gods of the different tribes of people, are really diverse ways of seeing or thinking about what is just one God, the God whose power embraces all the tasks of creation and control in the world and who is actually the creator and lord of all peoples.

This step represented a very large and important transition in the moral and religious thinking of humankind, achieved in different eras by different peoples yet, at the same time, never fully assimilated into the emotional dimension of human thought. A recognition that there is but one God who created all tribes and peoples carries the implication that all humans belong to the same family. This was, and still is, a concept that many find very difficult to accept. It seems to be characteristic of humans to see persons not of their own tribe or clan as radically different from themselves — often as greatly inferior or even subhuman. Modern sociologists call this universal human tendency **ethnocentrism** and biologists give the name *xenophobia* (literally, "fear of strangers") to its extreme form. Ethnocentrism is indelibly marked in the thought and feelings of the human race, showing up unmistakably in the very terms human groups use to distinguish themselves from out-groups. The Greeks divided the human race into two types of people: Greeks and barbarians. The Hebrews similarly distinguished between Jews and Gentiles; Christians divided humankind into Christians and pagans or heathens. The word *Eskimo* is said to mean "the people," suggesting that anyone not an Eskimo is not quite human. In contrast, the recognition of one deity to whom all humans relate in the same way has egalitarian implications often expressed in terms of "the fatherhood of God and the brotherhood of man" (today we would speak of God as the parent and all humans as siblings).

It is not surprising, then, that the transition from polytheism to monotheism occurred earliest and most fully in the context of a religion that placed great emphasis on God's moral nature and the ethical demands God places on human beings. The Hebrew people had been as ethnocentric as any, their religious teachings had been explicitly henotheistic during one stage of development, and they had even believed themselves to be the chosen people of God, God's favorites, we might say. And although such a concept of a God who chooses a particular people is not very egalitarian — it seems that the ancient Hebrew God was not an equal opportunity God — the teaching already contained an implicit suggestion that the Gentiles were also God's children, even if not the most favored ones. Gradually the Hebrews evolved a theistic doctrine with explicit egalitarian and universalist implications, a position that historians have often called **ethical monotheism**. Important ingredients of this doctrine were carried over into Judaism's two major offshoot religions, Islam and Christianity, both of which emphasize the oneness of God and God's moral demands. Indeed, the central item in the Moslem creed is the belief that God is one: "There is no God but Allah." Christians also affirm a belief in monotheism, though overtones of polytheism crept into the Christian creed by way of the doctrine of the Trinity: that the one God is somehow three — Father, Son, and Holy Spirit.

In Hinduism, the affirmation of an ultimate monotheism coexists fairly comfortably with a lavish polytheism that affirms 330 million gods — all said by the philosophers of Hinduism to be ways of conceiving the one ultimate deity, Brahma. But the monotheistic dimension of Hinduism is not a true theism in the Western sense because Brahma is conceived not as a personal deity but as an impersonal force. Hinduism is not monotheistic, believing in one god, but **monistic**, teaching that all reality, the impersonal deity as well as the material world, are one being. This aspect of Hinduism is more like the teaching of certain Western philosophers called absolute idealists, who speak not of one God but of the Absolute, which is the ground and source of all things, and of which all things are parts. This way of conceiving the ultimate often takes on explicit pantheistic characteristics among both the absolute idealist philosophers of the West and the philosophers of Hinduism. Buddhism, partly in order to escape the exuberant proliferation of gods and godlings so characteristic of Hinduism, denied the existence of God altogether. Over the centuries, certain branches of Buddhism have shown a tendency to deify or make a god of Gautama the Buddha — as many would say the Christians did with the man, Jesus Christ — but theologically Buddhism remains mostly atheistic or nontheistic.

Thus theism, in its most characteristic form, is a feature primarily of Western religion[1] and particularly of Judaism and Christianity. It is this expression of theism that will primarily concern us in the next few chapters. Once the notion of one God, creator and governor of the whole world, had become firmly established in the mind of Western religious thinkers, they devoted the major portion of their energy to attempting to figure out just what this great God must be like. The result has been the evolution of a set of characteristics usually attributed to God, together with an extensive discussion of what the attributes of God entail and whether they are all compatible with one another. These discussions have been concerned also with other issues, such as why a perfect God would create the material world and human beings and whether this God of perfection could be identified with the God revealed through Moses, Jesus, and Mohammed. We turn now to examine several of the most important qualities attributed to the God of theism.

OMNIPOTENCE

The Meaning of Omnipotence

Theism conceives of God as the supreme being, unsurpassed in greatness, the one in whom all perfections meet in perfect harmony. One perfection that such a god must have is power. Thus God is said to be almighty, possessed of all power. The label philosophers and theologians have used to name God's supreme power is **omnipotence**. The word comes from two Latin words: *omnis*, meaning "all," and *potens*, meaning "to be able." Thus, an omnipotent being must be able to do all. It has often been said that nothing is impossible to God; that God is all powerful; that God can do anything. God is the creator of the universe, having depended on nothing other than his own creative power to make all things. Theism usually teaches that God creates *ex nihilo*, that is, out of nothing. This means there was no preexisting matter or substance out of which God created; rather, God created both the order the universe manifests and the substance it is made of. Whatever exists in the created realm depends for its original creation on the exercise of divine power; indeed, according to many theologians, God's creative power is exercised in every moment in such a way that the continued existence of everything in the universe depends on the ongoing, sustaining creative power of God. Such a vision of the divine power suggests that there is no power anywhere that is not ultimately the power of the omnipotent God and that God is able to exercise that power in any way he chooses, without limit.

When these claims are examined more closely, however, it soon becomes evident that they raise very serious problems. One of the most famous ways of posing the problems, a way that provoked considerable theological controversy during the Middle Ages, was by means of the question: Can God create a stone so heavy that God cannot lift it? This puzzle seemed to show, no matter how it was answered, that God is not almighty in the sense of being able to "do" literally anything. For if God created a stone he subsequently could not lift, there would be at least one thing he could not do, namely, lift the stone. On the other hand, to say that God could not create such a stone was to admit from the very start that there was something God could not do. Either the claim that God is omnipotent must be false, or else omnipotence must mean something other than the ability to do anything at all. Thus, it becomes necessary to examine more closely the notion of omnipotence to discover whether it has a rational meaning that can be applied to God.

In light of these problems, more careful and modest interpretations of the word *omnipotence* have been attempted. Instead of saying that God can do anything at all, it may be more reasonable to say that God can do anything that is possible. After all, even an omnipotent being should not perhaps be expected to do impossible things. Surely the inability to do things that cannot be done is no diminution of God's omnipotence. Thus we may define **omnipotence** to mean the ability to do whatever is possible. When we speak of God's omnipotence in connection with his creative power, we may say that omnipotence means the ability to actualize any possible and every **compossible** state of affairs (that is, any set of states of affairs that are not mutually incompatible).

Contemporary philosophers speak of **possible worlds**, meaning worlds consisting of mutually compatible states of affairs. Obviously the world that actually exists is a possible world, but we may say that there are many other possible worlds as well. For example, in the actual world there is an island called Greenland between the North American continent and northern Europe, but it would have been possible for the world to exist without Greenland. We express this by saying that there is a possible world in which no such island exists. There is also a possible world that contains a whole string of islands stretching from Greenland to the equator. In the actual world, Ludwig von Beethoven was a great musician, but there is a possible world in which Ludwig von Beethoven was tone deaf. Obviously, there are a very large number and perhaps an infinite number of possible worlds.

So when we define omnipotence in possible world language, we say that an omnipotent being is able to create or actualize any possible world. It is obvious, however, that this way of defining omnipotence already involves a substantial backing off from the most supreme claims about God's power by acknowledging that some things are impossible. Some philosophers have been unwilling to make this step, even though without it there seems to be no way to avoid contradictory or irrational claims. When we said that a possible world is a world consisting of some mutually compatible state of affairs, we were saying that a world involving incompatible or contradictory states of affairs is not a possible world.

Some philosophers, however, would say that for God even worlds involving inconsistencies and contradictions are possible worlds. Those who take this position maintain that God's logic is above ours; that what appears impossible to human reason is not impossible to God. We have already seen in Chapter 1, however, that such a position implies the abandonment of any attempt to understand religious claims. It reduces religion to arbitrary assertion; it embraces irrationality; and it makes of the various religions of the world alternative declarations of belief to which it is impossible to apply any criteria of truth, plausibility, or rationality. It even licenses the assertion of, and the attempt to believe, what is unintelligible. To take such a position is to abandon the philosophy of religion and to join the ranks of believers like Tertullian, who glory in irrationality. If we are to engage in reasoning about religion, we must analyze the concept of omnipotence and the other perfections alleged to characterize God and attempt to find rational interpretations. We will see that such an analysis discovers that certain things are impossible. Not every world is a possible world, even for God. In light of this discovery, it will eventually be necessary either to define omnipotence in terms that recognize the distinction between what is and what is not possible, or else to abandon the claim that God is omnipotent.

Challenges to Omnipotence: What Can an Omnipotent Being Not Do?

When we interpret omnipotence in terms of what is possible or of possible worlds, the first question is: What sorts of things are impossible, and what makes them impossible? We will examine five types of alleged impossibilities. The five are not completely distinct—there is some overlapping—but they can be treated most clearly by separating them in this way. We will also discuss the so-called "paradox of omnipotence." And we will conclude by examining the question of whether these purported impossibilities threaten God's status as omnipotent.

Logical Impossibility. When we think about the kinds of things that exist in the world, it soon becomes evident that many things do not exist that might have existed. For example, there are no unicorns, but this seems to be an accidental matter; there does not seem to be any necessary reason why there might not have been some unicorns. In some possible worlds very much like the actual world unicorns might exist. But among the things that do not exist are some that, when we think about them, we realize could not have existed, for the very good reason that they are impossible. For example, there are not any square circles. And this is no accident. It seems clear that if God had decided to create unicorns, assuming that God created the things that do exist, God could have created unicorns. But it seems equally clear that if God had decided to create a square circle, he would not have been able to do so. The reason is easy enough to see: Square circles are impossible. The very name is contradictory and fails to name anything that can be consistently conceptualized. There is no possible world in which square circles exist. Many other instances of the same sort could be cited: God could not have made $2 + 3 = 8$. God could not make yesterday later than tomorrow. God could not make a part of a thing larger than the whole thing.[2] The issue involved in all these examples is that of logical or mathematical impossibility. It is logically impossible, and therefore impossible even for God, to make a certain true statement be at the same time false.

The question all of this raises is whether God creates and controls the laws of logic and mathematics, or whether these fundamental laws are in some sense antecedent to God; whether they are principles which God himself must obey. Descartes, who insists that an omnipotent being can do anything, maintains that God must be the creator of logical and mathematical laws, and thus able, if he chose, to alter them. But this amounts to saying that impossible things are possible. To be sure, God might bring it about that 2 means this many: I I I; and that 3 means this many I I I I I; in which case $2 + 3 = 8$ would be true (assuming that 8 means I I I I I I I I). But this is no great feat requiring the power of an omnipotent being; we could do the same thing ourselves. If we agree to the redefinition of the values of the figures involved, we ourselves could make $2 + 3 = 8$. Indeed, if the figures are redefined in the way suggested, it becomes impossible for either God or humankind to make $2 + 3$ equal anything but 8. And this latter fact of impossibility clearly shows that no alteration or violation of mathematical laws is involved. The relationships of numerical quantities remain the same, no matter how we redefine the names we give to such numbers. Something objective about arithmetic coerces anyone who thinks, whether human or divine. We can *say* that $2 + 2 = 7$, but there is no way that we can *make* $2 + 2 = 7$. Indeed, if we insist on saying it, we do not alter or even violate the laws of logic or mathematics; rather we illustrate them by showing that when we say things contrary to them we merely show ourselves to be talking nonsense. The laws of logic and mathematics are not like civil statutes that can be altered by the requisite authority. It does not matter who makes a contradictory claim, God or man; the result is the same: unintelligible nonsense or falsehood. If God were to attempt to promulgate laws contrary to the principle of identity or the principle of contradiction,[3] God would be faced with the necessity of exemplifying these principles in his speech, for if he attempted to do otherwise, nothing intelligible would be communicated.

It is for reasons such as these that most thinkers have conceded that not even an omnipotent God can change or act in a way contrary to the fundamental laws of logic and mathematics. There may be room for dispute about the ultimate source of the laws themselves. Some would say that these laws are in some sense antecedent to God himself; others such as Edgar S. Brightman would say that they are simply an unalterable part of the divine nature — what Brightman calls God's "rational given."[4] But the practical implication is the same; in either case, the laws bind God. To violate or change them is not possible even for an omnipotent being.

Time-Bound Matters: Altering the Past and Determining the Future. Changing the laws of logic is not the only kind of impossible thing. Another group of problems raised by the claim that an omnipotent being can do anything at all relates to such matters as changing the past and determining future contingent events. A special category of future contingents is those events that relate to God's promises and the question whether, once God has made a promise, his power is limited by the obligation to fulfill that promise. And this raises a more general problem, called the *paradox of omnipotence,* the question, namely, of whether any being, even one that might initially have been omnipotent, can continue to be omnipotent over time.

Changing the Past. A few philosophers — Peter Damian is one example — have maintained that God can alter the past, but the clear majority has conceded that altering the past is impossible even for an omnipotent being. The specific example so often discussed in the Middle Ages is whether God can restore the virginity of a woman who has lost it. The issue is complicated by the claim put forward by some thinkers to the effect that God is timeless, that God transcends time, or that what happens in a temporal sequence from our point of view is actually present to God in an eternal, unchanging present experience. This claim will be examined later in this chapter. But Anselm, Jerome, Aquinas, and many other Christian thinkers concluded that although God might have prevented the loss of virginity before it was lost (this claim relates, as we will soon see, to the question of determining future contingent events; it also relates to controlling the free acts of other agents), once it had been lost it could not be restored, even by God.

It is not difficult to see that there is something compellingly unidirectional about time. It moves forward, not backward. A decision by an agent, human or divine, to act in a certain way — say, to paint the wall green or create a world containing unicorns at some future time — can be a decisive factor in bringing about one state of affairs rather than another in that future time. But a decision by an agent to act in a certain way in the past — say, to speak a kind word to a certain person or to prevent the loss of a certain woman's virginity — cannot bring about a different state of affairs in that past time. Indeed, it does not even make sense to say that a person can decide to behave in a certain way in the past. We can wish that we had said a kind word instead of an angry word; we can be glad about or regret what we did yesterday; but we cannot decide to behave differently *then,* much less actually change the way we behaved. This unbending character of time is the subject of many soliloquies of sorrow and regret — would that we could change some things about the past! But this is clearly impossible. And it is just as impossible for God as it is for us. Once an event has happened, it will be true for all eternity that it has happened. We may forget what happened; we may come to believe that things were different than the way they actually were; but that does not change how they actually were. Once a thing has been done, it cannot be undone. The passing of the present moment locks up forever the events that occur and the deeds we do. Not even God has a key to the lock that binds the past. The past is fixed, and not even an omnipotent being can change it.

Future Contingent Events. But the future, apparently, is another matter. Until a moment has passed, until an event has happened, until a deed has been done, the deliberate choices of agents, human and divine, appear to be effective in determining which of the possibilities will be actualized. It seems to be up to me whether I will go to work today or stay in bed on the pretense of being ill. Many things are clearly *not* up to me, but in the context of a belief system that affirms an omnipotent deity, it seems to be up to God whether or not those things happen. Even if an omnipotent being cannot now determine the past, surely that being can now determine the future.

God's Promises. Theism nearly always involves the belief that God is involved in the affairs of human history, calling certain peoples to tasks connected with the divine plan, making moral demands, helping those who respond and frustrating those who do not. In the process, God is said to make promises. For example, according to the Hebrew scriptures God called Abraham and commanded him to leave the land of his birth and to journey to a new land that God promised to give him. Thus God made a covenant with a chosen people, a covenant that placed certain obligations on the Hebrew people and in turn placed certain obligations on God.

The belief that God makes covenants and promises, however, raises problems concerning the claim that God is omnipotent. For once a promise has been made, God is under a moral obligation that limits his power in the future. The limiting nature of promises and vows is widely recognized even in human situations, particularly those involving persons with great power. In the scriptures of Judaism there are instances of human kings and judges making promises that become inflexibly binding and must be kept, even when the outcome is unexpected or tragic. For example, the judge Jepthah vowed to sacrifice the first thing that came out of his house when he returned from battle and was thus obliged to give his daughter and only child as a burnt offering to keep the vow.[5] If God does indeed make promises — for example, to lead Israel out of slavery in Egypt or to send a Messiah (and we assume that morality is another binding attribute of God) — it would appear that once the promise has been made, God is no longer truly omnipotent, for now there are things that God (consistent with a moral nature) cannot do.

The Paradox of Omnipotence. Making promises is not the only thing an omnipotent being might do that would limit that being's future power. The possibility of such limiting actions by an omnipotent being has been called by Mackie the "paradox of omnipotence."[6] It is a paradox because it seems to imply that, even if some being might be initially omnipotent, no being can be permanently omnipotent. If we admit that an omnipotent being can perform actions that limit its future power, we concede that, after the actions have been performed, the being is no longer omnipotent. But if we deny that any such future-limiting actions are possible, we grant that the being is limited from the start. Mackie compares the situation with that of a political sovereign, a king or a parliament, confronting what he calls the "paradox of sovereignty." If the king or the parliament is initially sovereign, then he or it can make laws that limit this sovereignty; if he cannot make such laws, he was not sovereign to begin with. Either way he cannot have a permanent, complete sovereignty.

Attempts to solve the paradox of omnipotence have referred to the other divine characteristics or perfections, such as wisdom and goodness. It might be said that because God is omnipotent, he can indeed do things which would attenuate his future power by placing moral obligations on him, but he is wise enough to know all the potential consequences of any actions and benevolent enough to will only what is good for the whole creation. Thus he would never do any of those things that, although he is certainly able to do them, would compromise in disabling ways his power to perform his proper divine functions. Just as a wise parliament would limit its own future power only in ways consistent with the best interests of the nation, it might be argued, so also God would act only in ways consistent with the future well-being of all of his creatures.

This answer sounds reassuring, but it is also sufficiently vague to obscure the details of what it does and does not recognize as possible. It does not remove the paradox altogether. The assumption of God's moral nature is what gives rise to these problems. The only way that God could avoid limiting his own future power while remaining a morally scrupulous being would be to refrain from any act that would obligate him in the future. But to be under the necessity of avoiding such a vast range of actions would itself substantially attenuate his power. Not only would it be impossible for him to make any promises; he could not even create an orderly and ongoing world. For if God creates an orderly world, whether the orderly laws of nature are themselves his own creation or are antecedent to him, these laws bind his future behavior if the world is to continue. In other words, just as promises place obligations and thus limitations on anyone who makes promises, so also do many other actions, such as the act of creating a universe. Thus, even if God might initially have been omnipotent, the paradox shows that God cannot long continue to be so.

This places the claim that God controls all future events in quite a different light. For if the created world is under the complete control of a set of laws of nature that God himself does not now have the power to change, the notion of future contingent events disappears. All future events are thus under a rigid **determinism** imposed either by the laws that God created along with the world, or else by laws that already existed and regulated God's own process of creation. Of course many persons believe in determinism on scientific grounds quite apart from religious considerations. We may be willing to concede that the laws of nature are such that, given a certain state of affairs in the universe at a stated time, every future state of affairs necessarily follows. Such a teaching appears to be inconsistent with the belief in miracles, but even religious persons are sometimes willing to give up miracles that would require that God alter the laws of nature. (We will discuss miracles in some detail in Chapter 4.) It also seems to imply a theology closer to deism than to theism. An even more serious problem about the belief that God determines all future events, or that all future events are determined by unalterable natural law, is that such a teaching seems to deprive humans of any measure of free will.

The Free Acts of Human Agents. Humans have a very strong impression that at least some of their actions are performed freely, as the result of deliberation and choice. It is quite easy to see that the extent of free control that we have over our actions is limited. Any person who has tried to stop smoking or to break some other ingrained habit knows very well that an act of choice or volition is not always all it takes to determine how we will behave. But there are many other instances when alternative courses of behavior seem open to us and our choice to do one rather than the other immediately produces the selected action. So the strongest evidence we have for the belief that at least sometimes we act freely is the feeling, the impression, the experience of choosing and acting freely. To be sure, strong impressions can and sometimes are mistaken — just as strong sense perceptions can on occasion turn out to be illusory. Apart from compelling reasons for doubting such impressions, however, we accept them, and we are convinced that we are nearly always justified in doing so.

This direct sense of choosing and acting freely is not the only evidence we have that human actions are sometimes free. We can see as well that the whole system of morality that is such an important part of our human nature also implies that we are able to control or determine our own actions. For if we are not free, then what we do does not really amount to our own actions. But persons cannot be held responsible for actions that are not their own. If my actions are in fact determined by God, then they are God's actions, not mine. If I do evil under those circumstances, it is not I who am to blame, but God. Thus, if God is omnipotent in the sense of determining all the actions of human agents, whether directly through special volitions or generally through inflexible natural law, then morality is a great system of illusions.

Not every philosopher or theologian agrees with this claim. One traditional position in Western Christian theology, known as **predestination**, has maintained that God predetermines all human behavior and that humans are nonetheless responsible for what they do. The so-called "predestinarians" believe that omnipotence means possessed of all power. And since they take the position that God is omnipotent in this sense of the word, it follows that all the power there is must be in God's hands and thus none of it can be in the hands of humans. Genuine human free will would imply a limitation on God's power; there would be some things that God could not do, and thus God would not be omnipotent. Therefore God must control the actions of human agents.

The predestinarians have often recognized the problem this position raises concerning human moral responsibility but have attempted to justify holding humans responsible for their deeds while affirming God's determinative power over human behavior. A group of twentieth-century philosophers, arguing in terms of determinism rather than predestination, takes what amounts to a very similar stance. They maintain that determinism, often construed in terms of the deterministic laws of nature rather than the predestining power of God, is compatible with human free will and thus human moral responsibility.

The efforts of both the predestinarians and these **compatibilists** to have their cake and eat it, too — that is, to preserve both the strong sense of God's omnipotence and human moral responsibility — place serious strains on their theory and result in sometimes complex doctrines designed to show that the teachings are only apparently and not actually contradictory. One among many examples is the position taken by the great American Puritan theologian, Jonathan Edwards.[7] Edwards conceded that the human will must be free if there is to be moral responsibility, but he also insisted on God's absolutely sovereign and unlimited power. Thus Edwards taught that, in a certain sense, humans are free to do as they will and thus are morally responsible. To the question, "Could Adam have refrained from eating the forbidden fruit?" Edwards answers that he could have refrained if he had willed to refrain. But the catch is that the will itself is determined by God's foreordaining power. Adam could have acted differently if he had willed to act differently; but since his will itself was determined by God, he could not have willed differently. This distinction, Edwards believed, makes a place for both human moral responsibility and absolute divine omnipotence. Because being free to do as we will is what makes us morally responsible, Adam was responsible for his sin of disobedience to God: He was *culpable,* as we say. On the other hand, to guarantee God's omnipotence it is necessary for God to have all power, and this is accomplished by the fact that God has the power to determine how humans shall will. Thus, he argued, the total sovereignty and almighty power of God is preserved and so is the moral responsibility of humankind.

To many philosophers, such a move appears as just so much fast philosophical footwork. It only creates the illusion of reconciling extreme omnipotence with human moral responsibility. In the final accounting, Edwards's theology still implies that God is responsible for Adam's sin and for all other human actions. The separation of the act of willing, which determines the action, from the event that determines what will be willed only inserts a step into the process that makes God's relation to the action slightly more indirect. If I force someone else to commit a crime, I am just as responsible for the crime as if I had committed it directly. Similarly, if God determines Adam's will to eat the forbidden fruit, it is God and not Adam who is to blame if eating the fruit is culpable. The numerous and varied efforts of the predestinarians and the compatibilists, ingenious and crafty as they have been, do not succeed in removing the problem. Either human beings are genuinely free and therefore morally responsible — in which case God does not determine the free acts of human agents and thus is not omnipotent in the strongest sense of the word — or else human wills and behavior are determined — in which case God holds onto total power but gains with it culpability for any wrongdoing that occurs.

When this argument is combined with the powerful support from the direct sense of freedom we often experience, the case for human free will is strong indeed. We can add to this, our very strong direct feeling of moral obligation, the experience, in some ways comparable with sense impressions, that we ought to do certain things and that we ought not to do others. Some philosophers have called this human awareness of moral obligation our moral sense. Because our sense of freedom and our sense of morality are so direct and strong, any theory that denies these compelling feelings is highly implausible and, unless supported by overwhelming arguments, unacceptable.

The position of the predestinarians and the compatibilists not only lacks the strong support of plausible argument, it even puts forward claims that come close to being unintelligible or irrational. This can be expressed another way in logical terms. The compatibilists sometimes urge that divine omnipotence means that God determines the free acts of other agents. But an examination of the very meaning of the claim turns up inconsistency. The term *agent* means one who acts freely and uncoerced; *free acts* mean acts determined by the individual who performs them and by no one else. To say that humans are agents but that their actions are determined (whether directly or indirectly) by God is to say that persons whose actions are determined by no one but themselves have their actions determined by someone else, and this is an explicit contradiction. To say that free acts are determined amounts to saying that free acts are not free and the discrepancy becomes blatant. Even an omnipotent being cannot determine the free acts of other agents. The remaining question is: Are there any free acts of human agents? The arguments we have just examined strongly support the claim that there are.

Compatibility with Impeccability: Can God Sin? If God's omnipotence means that God can do anything at all, then apparently this would imply that God could do evil things. But besides omnipotence, one of God's perfections is **impeccability**: God is not only almighty but also morally flawless. This entails that it would be impossible for God to do anything morally questionable or sinful. The question that arises, then, is whether or not omnipotence is compatible with impeccability. If God cannot sin or do evil things, God's power is to that extent limited. But if God can sin or do evil things, then God is not morally perfect.

There are several ways that this dilemma might be solved. If the question is stated just in theological terms—that is, if what is asked is whether or not God can sin—it might be argued that sinning means doing what is contrary to the will of God. Surely God could not do what is contrary to his own will. But just as surely it is no limit on God's power to be unable to do what he does not will to do. Because God can do whatever he wills, God is free and powerful without limit. But his impeccability is also intact, because he cannot sin.

A problem with this solution is that it identifies sinfulness and sinlessness with what God wills, suggesting that right and wrong are merely the arbitrary inclination of the divine mind or will. Such an identification raises serious issues about the relation of religion to ethics. This topic is the subject of Chapter 7 and cannot be discussed in detail here. We must note briefly, however, that a matter as weighty as morality must have firmer ontological grounding than arbitrary whim, even if it is the whim of an omnipotent being. Indeed, whimsy is all the more dangerous the more powerful the being whose fancy it is. Furthermore, our moral sense intuits quite clearly that certain actions are wrong, regardless of who wills them or performs them. Pointless severe cruelty inflicted on an innocent person is wrong no matter who does it, whether God or man. Its wrongfulness is not a matter of opinion; not a debatable point; not something that differences of culture or religious belief might alter. It is wrong by virtue of its nature and by virtue of the nature of human beings, who are capable of understanding both moral imperatives and suffering.

What this means is that the validity of fundamental moral principles is analogous to the validity of basic logical principles. They are objective and valid quite apart from what anyone thinks, or wishes, or wills. And this entails that the fundamental rules of morality are not derived from the divine will and subject to change merely by an act of that will. Rather, they are binding on God's will in such a way that if God should inflict pointless cruelty on an innocent person, God himself would have done wrong.

Thus, if God is omnipotent in the strongest sense, then God is able to do what is evil. If in order to be impeccable God must be unable to do evil, then an impeccable God is not omnipotent in this sense. When the dilemma is put this way, it might be suggested that the solution is to be found in God's moral character. God's power is unlimited in the sense that God is able to do evil, but at the same time God's moral character is such that he never would actually exercise the power to do evil. This amounts to recognizing that morality is independent of God's will, a point that reason seems to require. This move appears to preserve both omnipotence and impeccability. Of course, the claim that God's power enables him to do evil is never proven as long as he never actually does an evil act. The claim becomes incapable of either verification or disconfirmation. Still, it is a claim that we can understand and one we may be willing to regard at least tentatively as plausible. If, on the other hand, our consideration of the problem of evil should convince us that God causes, or at least permits, the existence of avoidable evil, the claim of impeccability would fall on these other grounds.

Universals: Does God Create the Possibilities or Create Within the Limits They Impose?   As long ago as the time of Plato (c. 427–347 B.C.E.), philosophers were already arguing that God is limited by antecedent possibilities; that is, that there are eternal forms or universals that define what can and cannot exist and that impose restrictions on the process of creation. Plato's own view of creation was that the creator (whom he called *demiurge,* from a Greek word that means something like "tinkerer") found preexisting blueprints, patterns, or universals, and preexisting matter, and that he created the world by imposing the preexisting patterns on matter. The implication is that God could only create things for which there were patterns. Thus the forms or universals, as they were called, constituted the complete set of possibilities and everything else was impossible. The issue, which really embraces and summarizes all the other questions about omnipotence, is whether God creates the possibilities or whether he creates within limits imposed by universals that are antecedent to God's creative activity. Those who hold to an extreme interpretation of omnipotence maintain that with God, literally, all things are possible.

We have already noted that there are certain fundamental principles such as the laws of logic, mathematics, and morality, which do not have their source in the divine will but are in some sense antecedent to, and binding on, God's will. We have argued that if God were to attempt to revoke the law of contradiction, all he would be able to accomplish would be to illustrate the impossibility of even communicating anything intelligible apart from that law. And we have noted that if God should decide to inflict needless cruelty on an innocent person, he would not abolish the moral law but instead convict himself of immorality. The basic principles of logic, mathematics, and morality set limits on what anyone can do, whether human or God. It was this discovery that led us to move away from defining omnipotence as the ability to do anything at all toward interpreting it as the ability to do anything that is possible. The claim is that certain things are not possible, even for an omnipotent being.

This claim is easy enough to see, and difficult to deny, in logic and mathematics, and as we shall see in Chapter 7, likewise in morality. But Plato's philosophy implies that the realm of the possible is more extensive than just logic, mathematics, and morality. Certain beings and situations in the realm of nature are possible and others seem to be impossible. We have also noted that there does not seem to be any necessary reason why God should not have created unicorns or, in other words, that a world containing unicorns seems to be a possible world. But what about centaurs or mermaids? Perhaps there is something intrinsic in the nature of a horse and a man, or in the nature of a fish and a woman, that makes it impossible for there to be a creature that combines those natures in the ways depicted in mythology. Why do fish have gills instead of lungs? Perhaps because lungs are just not the sorts of equipment that make it possible for an animal to live in water. The more closely we examine the phenomena that exist and happen in nature, the more the suggestion presses itself on us that some things *are* impossible — perhaps not logically impossible, but impossible nonetheless. If God had wanted to create a world in which pure water could serve as a combustion fuel for internal combustion engines, he would not have been able to do so, because the chemistry of it just does not work.

We can see that not all things are possible, but we see also clearly that many things are possible that are not actual. If God wanted to create a material world in which there could be living organisms, he might have done so in several ways. Perhaps a life form could have been created that made use of silicon as one of its principle ingredients instead of the carbon that actual living organisms on earth use. The chemistry would have been different, but it might have been possible. Some contemporary modal logicians seem to construe the concept of possibility so widely that anything that can be named, apparently even what is logically contradictory, is regarded as possible; they claim that there are "possible worlds" in which each of such things or situations might be, or might have been, exemplified. Peter Geach has some appropriately harsh things to say about those who attempt thus to overstep the bounds of the laws of logic in their talk about possible worlds.[8] The issue is precisely the one we have been discussing: whether there are any limits on what God might create or whether literally all things are possible. The conclusion that reason seems to support is this: Just as the laws of logic, mathematics, and morality are not the product of God's will but rather laws to which God himself must conform,

God creates within the constraints of an additional set—a very large one, no doubt, but definitely a finite set—of possibilities that he does not determine but that determine what he and all others can and cannot do.

In light of all these types of limits on what an omnipotent being can do, is it still proper to say that God is omnipotent? That depends partly on how one is willing to use the word. If we accept the definition of omnipotence in terms of possibility—that omnipotence means the ability to do whatever is possible or to actualize any possible and every compossible state of affairs—then we can still attribute omnipotence to God. Defining omnipotence in terms of possibility amounts to recognizing that there are many things that an omnipotent being cannot do, because we have discovered that there are a great many things that are not possible. An omnipotent being cannot do the logically impossible, cannot change the past, cannot create an ongoing orderly world without attenuating its own power, cannot make morally binding promises without limiting its power, cannot determine the free acts of other agents, and cannot determine the set of possibilities within which it acts.

We might be inclined to say that a being with all of these disabilities ought not to be called omnipotent. Perhaps in the last accounting it is not of utmost importance whether we use this word for God or not. Certainly God, if we find reason to believe that there is such a being, can do a very great many important things. God, if one exists and possesses all of the characteristics that reason permits us to attribute, can create the universe, can inspire humankind with the ideals of morality, can equip us with sensitivity to beauty and goodness, can call us to deeds of heroism and compassion—can, to say it briefly, possess the qualities that make God worthy of worship and devotion. Such a being retains all its greatness whether we decide to designate it omnipotent or not.

OMNISCIENCE

The Meaning of Omniscience

The second great characteristic or perfection usually attributed to the theistic God, that being in whom all perfections merge in perfect harmony, is knowledge or wisdom. The word used to express this quality is **omniscience**. It comes from two Latin words, *omnis,* which means "all," and *scientia,* meaning "to know." Thus the omniscient being is the all-knowing being, the one who knows everything.

But just as we found that the naive, literal meaning of omnipotence raises problems that require a more guarded interpretation, there also turn out to be problems with a literal understanding of omniscience. If God is omniscient and omniscience means knowing everything, then God must know the numerical value of the square root of − 1; God must know the answer to the question, "How many are 3 times tomorrow afternoon?"; and God must know the exact date on which God will die. But it is clear that God cannot know any of these things for the simple reason that there are no such things. God does not know what square circles look like or what the largest whole number is.

Just as God cannot do certain things because it is impossible for them to be done, so also God cannot know certain things because it is impossible for them to be known. Thus, just as we found it necessary to pull back from the straightforward, literal interpretation of omnipotence as the ability to do anything at all (saying instead that omnipotence is the ability to do anything that can be done), so also it seems necessary to withdraw to the position of defining omniscience as knowing everything that can be known — and even that will turn out to be too strong a claim.

Omniscience and Time

The inability to know nonsense things or things that are unintelligible does not appear to be a very serious limitation of omniscience. The most important problems raised by claims of omniscience have to do with God's relationship to time, particularly to the future. Two significant issues are involved here, namely, future contingent events and the future free acts of other agents. As we discuss these topics, we will see that they relate to certain points already made in our examination of the question of God's power over future contingent events and the free acts of other agents.

God's Knowledge of Future Contingent Events. Theists have usually assumed that an omniscient being not only knows everything that has happened in the past but also has foreknowledge of everything that will happen in the future. But they have also believed, as most of us do, that there is at least a measure of contingency about the future. As Wainwright puts it, "while the past history of the universe and the laws that govern it block out the rough shape of the future, the finishing strokes must be supplied by future decisions."[9] Indeed, such future decisions play a very significant role in what the future will be like — whether the world will be engulfed in disastrous war, for example, or whether growing pollution of the environment will eventually render the planet uninhabitable. But it is not possible for anyone to know what those decisions will be until they have been made. How, then, can an omnipotent being have foreknowledge of the future?

Nevertheless, many theists have insisted that in fact God does know the future in just as complete detail as he knows the past. But this claim raises very serious problems about the assumption that future events are in any measure contingent. For if God is omniscient, what God knows must be true. And if God knows the things that will happen in the future, then they certainly will happen. This seems to imply that the future is as rigidly determined in every detail as is the past. The appearance of contingency must be illusory.

Indeed, some interpreters of the doctrine have suggested that God's foreknowledge amounts to determining the future in the sense of being the cause of what will happen. But to know what will happen is not the same thing as causing it to happen. Of course what God knows to be true about the future must be true, but this is so partly because of the logic of the word "know." Indeed, whatever anyone *knows* is in fact true, because if it were not true it would not be correct to say that he or she *knows* it. Now it has conventionally been accepted that there is a difference in the logic of "know" and "believe" as they apply to humans, but not as they apply to God. If I may properly say that I *know* that I have 30 cents in my pocket, then it must be true that I have 30 cents; but if I say that I *believe* that I have 30 cents, it need not be true. But this distinction allegedly does not apply to God. The beliefs of an omniscient being can no more be false than its knowledge can be false, according to many theologians. I will argue that God, like humans, may hold justified beliefs about the future which need not be true.

If omniscience thus means knowing whatever can be known, then our question is: What can be known about the future? Certainly an omniscient being knows the meaning of every true proposition and knows, further, that it is true; such a being also knows the meaning of every false proposition and knows that it is false. Are all meaningful propositions either true or false? And, in particular, are all propositions about the future either true or false? The answer seems to be that propositions about contingent future events are neither true nor false until such time as they are no longer contingent. Thus, if there really are contingent future events, if anything about the future is not already predetermined, then there are propositions about these events that are not yet either true or false. But it is impossible to know the truth value of a proposition that does not yet have a truth value, although we can often be justified in holding beliefs about the truth value it will eventually have. A complete knowledge of the state of the universe at the present moment, and of the laws of nature, can give an omniscient being much knowledge about what will happen in the future. But if some details about the future depend on human decisions, not even an omniscient being can know those details until the decisions have been made. God certainly knows I might go to work tomorrow or might stay in bed; God even knows that it is very likely (and thus God justifiably believes) that I will go since I rarely miss a day even when I am not feeling well; but until I decide which to do, or until the set of circumstances, if there is such a set, that will determine which I will do (and that, if I really am free, will include my decision), occurs, the proposition, "I will stay in bed tomorrow," is neither true nor false. Thus no one, neither God nor human, could know its truth value.

God's Knowledge of the Future Acts of Other Agents. Theists have often believed that God knows the secrets of every human heart and the details of every choice and action every creature will ever make. Indeed, the predestinarians taught that before the creation of the world God predestined some humans to be saved in paradise and others to be condemned to eternal punishment. These theologians often claimed that God's election of those to be saved was based on God's foreknowledge of the kinds of lives the individuals would live, their choices and actions. But the same kinds of problems arise with these claims as we have already seen with claims about God's knowing contingent future events. Indeed, the most important contingent future events, and perhaps the only future events that really are contingent, are just those that human agents determine by their free choices. But if God omnisciently — infallibly — knows ahead of time what choice I will make, then I must make just that choice. God's foreknowledge of my actions seems incompatible with my acting freely. To be sure, God might infer on the basis of an intimate knowledge of my character and past behavior that I am likely to go to work tomorrow and not call in sick, and might therefore have a justified belief about what I will do. But that does not constitute knowledge of my future action since, if I am genuinely free even in some small measure, I might sometimes act out of character. The statement, "I will go to work tomorrow," is neither true nor false until I actually decide to go, and do go. But no one can know the truth value of a statement that does not yet have a truth value.

Thus, either there is no such thing as human free will, or else God's omniscience does not include knowing the future acts of other agents. And, as we saw in the previous section, this is not because knowing what will happen is the same thing as causing what will happen. God might know what I will do without causing me to do it by knowing the set of circumstances that inevitably will cause me to do it. But in that case, what I do is not done freely. The argument presented earlier about omnipotence and the free acts of other agents applies here as well. The strong evidence that there is at least a measure of human free will implies that even an omniscient being cannot know the future free acts of humans.

An important word of caution is necessary here. The claim that statements about future contingent events are neither true nor false until they are no longer contingent does not in any sense imply that we cannot make judgments about the future, hold justified beliefs about the future, or be held responsible for choices that will affect the future. Many of our beliefs about the future are based on inductive inferences, and these are often justified. The claim that it is wrong for me to pollute a community's water supply because the statement, "Drinking polluted water will make people sick or kill them," has no truth value until it is no longer contingent is a serious, indeed ludicrous, misunderstanding. It is not unlike the actual arguments coming from cigarette manufacturers, which claim that we do not know that smoking cigarettes causes lung cancer and many other horrible ills. In fact, we do know that smoking causes lung cancer, and this knowledge is as justified as much of our scientific knowledge. Of course, we do not know that "If some individual T smokes twenty-seven cigarettes per day for twenty years, T will develop lung cancer" is true (because it is not true [or false] until what it claims is no longer future). But we certainly are justified in believing that he will suffer that or some of the other ills connected with smoking. This means that promoting cigarette smoking is morally culpable. It also means that every individual is responsible to act on what she or he justifiably believes about the future, even though the propositions describing the believed-in state of affairs are not true or false ahead of time.

Transcendence of Time: Does God Know All Time is an Eternal Now?   One way that many theists have attempted to preserve God's complete omniscience in the face of such objections is to claim that God transcends time and thus that everything we experience as past, present, and future is experienced by God simultaneously in a great eternal Now. The claim that God knows ahead of time what will happen and what other agents will do seemed to imply that there can be no contingent future events and no genuinely free acts. According to this doctrine, God does not know these things ahead of time because God is not immersed in time but stands above it and views the whole sweep of history from the perspective of eternity. Thus God may be seen as the impassive observer, seeing all the events of creation stretched out, as it were, on a screen to be taken in at a glance, or eternally observed all at once from start to finish. The omniscient observer does not affect in any way the course of events but knows eternally what all these events are — that is, what, from our finite perspective, they are, were, and will be. But the initial impression that this ingenious doctrine saves omniscience, contingency, and freedom turns out to be illusory.

One of the most commonplace problems with such a conception of omniscience is that it implies that God does not know many things that most humans know. A simple example: According to this doctrine, God could not even know what time it is.[10] God could know what happens on earth at 8:39 P.M. Eastern Standard Time, on January 17, 2097 C.E. and at every place in the universe at every other moment in the sweep of time. Indeed, God's knowledge of the entire span of history might be likened to that of a playwright who knows every detail of her play, including not only the dialogue but the set, the lighting, the sequence of gestures and expressions of every actor, and every bit of stage business. But despite all this knowledge, the playwright who is not seeing the play in real time cannot know which scene is in progress *now,* something that everyone in the audience knows. Many other examples might be cited. A timeless being cannot know what the passing of time feels like; what it is to remember or anticipate; what it is to forget or to wonder what will happen. These and many other things that every human knows a God who transcends time cannot know.

Furthermore, the concept of timelessness does not seem to avoid the problem of determinism. If God timelessly knows the entire sweep of history, past, present, and future, this means there can be no real contingency in the process and, further, that the choices or decisions of human agents cannot make a difference. The analogy of the playwright and her knowledge of the play is apt here: If the playwright really knows every detail of the play both as written and as performed, then there is no room whatever for surprises or changes in it. Indeed, the history of the world, and every detail of how it is played out, must have been "written" or determined from all eternity, otherwise the details would not be there for God to know. If there is any contingency about the future, and if human will has any modicum of freedom, it is impossible for anyone to know the whole stretch of events at once, for the part of the screen pertaining to the future must be blank until time reaches it.

Finally, we must examine the claim that God transcends time and attempt to understand what such a claim could mean. Presumably it makes sense to say that the number 7 transcends time in the sense that it is not affected by the passing of time. The number 7 is, in the words sometimes attributed by theists to God, the same yesterday, today, and forever. But it is not at all clear what we would mean by saying that a personal, powerful, knowledgeable being such as God transcends time. It might mean that God continues to exist through all time, does not pass away, and does not acquire or lose major character traits because of the passing of time. But if God is omnipotent in the sense already discussed, he must exercise his power by creating and sustaining the material universe; if God is involved in the affairs of human history, as most theists maintain — for example, if God speaks by the prophets, is incarnate in Christ, or takes on human form in Krishna — then God cannot be timeless in the sense of transcending time, being unaffected by the passing of time, or being a passive observer of the whole sweep of time. If the claim that God transcends time is taken quite literally, it must mean that God is totally aloof, separate from, and out of touch with, everything in the temporal realm. But if God is timeless in this sense, he could neither be known by temporal beings nor could he know anything about the world of time.

We must conclude either that the notion of God as transcending time is unintelligible or else that it is a metaphorical way of saying that God lasts through all time and does not grow old and die. In either case, the teaching will not save the concept of omniscience from the contingency of future events and the free choices of human agents. If we are to say that God is omniscient, we must modify and limit the meaning of that term in ways similar to, but also different from, the way we modified and limited the concept of omnipotence. Indeed, the case is much more difficult with omniscience. Even if we define omniscience in terms of what it is possible to know, we still cannot say that God is omniscient, because there are things that each human individual can know but no one else, not even God, can know. Consider two things that I know: (1) Hudson is writing this chapter; and (2) I am writing this chapter. Clearly God can know (1), but no one but me can know (2). There are many such statements that each person can make and that only that person can know.[11] An adequate definition of omniscience, then, would have to say finally not just that an omniscient being knows everything that can be known, but that such a being knows everything that can be known except the first-person knowledge of other persons—a definition that begins to sound cumbersome enough even to smack of the ad hoc. Perhaps an adequate definition will be found that does not seem so patched up. But we may appropriately observe, as we did earlier, that the greatness of God does not depend on whether or not this or that venerable term can be attributed to him. The concern of the philosopher of religion is not to save or overturn a vocabulary, but to understand the ideas the terms were invented to convey and to discover to what extent these ideas stand up to the disinterested scrutiny of reason.

Knowledge and Wisdom. It may plausibly be argued that theists have been so preoccupied with defending omniscience in the sense of showing that God possesses absolutely every scrap of information that they have neglected what may be a much more important meaning of omniscience, one that emphasizes not knowledge but wisdom. There is an important difference between these terms, and on reflection it seems clear that it is wisdom that really constitutes what we might call the highest epistemological perfection. We know well that it is possible to possess vast stores of information and thus, in this sense of the word, to be knowledgeable, but at the same time to be very sadly lacking in wisdom. Alfred North Whitehead (1861–1947)[12] remarked, "A merely well-informed man is the most useless bore on God's earth." Perhaps we might add: in God's heaven, too.

The emphasis on omniscience as encyclopedic knowledge of every tidbit of information about everything in the universe has overtones of the snoop or the busybody. Surely this is not what is important in the concept of God as omniscient. A person, human or divine, can be wise without being all knowing in the sense of a know-it-all. Wisdom has to do not merely with how much is known but with how one's knowledge is held, managed, understood, used, appreciated. Wisdom involves good judgment, prudence, discretion, understanding of the significance of what is known, synoptic perspective on what is known, insight into what it all means. Wisdom is also inseparably connected with consideration, gentleness, beneficence, forbearance, tolerance, kindliness, magnanimity, humaneness, goodness.

Knowledge in the sense of information has no necessary connection with any of these qualities, qualities that theists have surely meant to signal when they have said that God is omniscient. And if we are willing to define omniscience in terms of wisdom, then it becomes plausible again to say that God is omniscient. This involves the understanding that one cannot be wise who does not have a very great deal (although not necessarily every little scrap) of knowledge. It also involves the recognition that knowledge is only a necessary and not a sufficient condition of being wise. For surely the greatness of God that the theists envisioned, and that made them seek out superlative expressions to describe or characterize God, pertained to a being supremely wise and thus possessed of all those ancillary features that constitute wisdom. This, then, is what we must intend when we call God omniscient.

DIVINE GOODNESS

Besides being powerful and wise, the God of traditional theism is said to be perfectly good. The theological term often used to express this attribute is **omnibenevolent,** coming from three Latin words — *omnis,* which means "all," *bene,* meaning "well," and *volentis,* meaning to wish or to will. An omnibenevolent being, then, is one that wills the well-being of all. Clearly this is the central and most important characteristic of God, according to theism. It is curious, then, that those who have written on theism tend to take the divine goodness for granted and say little or nothing about it. Nearly every study of the philosophy of religion has a chapter or at least a section of a chapter on omnipotence and another on omniscience. Most also treat other divine attributes such as eternity, immutability, simplicity, and impassibility. But most of these same books only mention omnibenevolence in passing; virtually none devote a section to divine goodness. And yet perfect goodness is the characteristic most theists would regard as absolutely fundamental — in the political language of argument, we might say that it is the most clearly nonnegotiable quality.

Some theists, confronted by the difficulty of explicating and defending omnipotence and especially threatened by the issues raised by the problem of evil, have been willing to concede that perhaps God is not omnipotent, at least not in the strongest sense of the word. Others have been impressed with the difficulty of reconciling **impassibility,** God's complete independence, and **immutability,** God's unchangeability, with certain doctrines of Christianity and Judaism and have been willing to compromise those perfections. But perfect goodness is a fixed characteristic, not to be negotiated, compromised, or attenuated. Whatever else can be said about God,

God is supremely good. Perhaps it is because goodness is thought to be an essential, defining characteristic of deity that few philosophers argue it. For the theist, God *means* good.

The goodness of God is elaborated in the scriptures of Judaism and Christianity, however. In Jewish thought it involves the notion of fidelity and concern for one's own. God has chosen the Jews to be his special people, and this means that they can count on God to care for them and to be faithful to them. In the thinking of both Jews and Christians, the concept of power has often colored the vision of divine goodness. God was called king and lord, and thus his goodness was that of a powerful ruler who, despite his great power and the demands that he placed on his people, was also merciful and compassionate. This combination of power and compassion is expressed in mature and late Hebrew literature by likening God to a father. Still, it is a stern and fear-inspiring father that is depicted: "As a father pitieth his children, so the Lord pities those who fear him."[13]

Jesus made the father image central in describing the divine nature, abandoning the stern and fearful aspect and interpreting fatherliness in a very intimate way. Jesus depicts God as a being who loves his human creatures the way a human father loves his children. Thus the concept of love becomes integral to the Christian vision of God. The goodness of God means God's loving nature. It is not the stern love of a potentate, not the merely reciprocated love of one who loves those who honor and obey him; rather, it is an unconditional love that remains steady and unblemished even when the beloved children disobey, dishonor, and rebel. It is a love that stops at nothing in its effort to assure the well-being of the children, not counting any cost too great. In Christian scriptures, God is depicted as taking human form and enduring suffering and death as an expression of his goodness and love: "For God so loved the world that he gave his only son, that whoever believes in him should not perish but have eternal life."[14] The great Indian philosopher-poet of the twentieth century, Rabindranath Tagore,[15] representing the theistic strand of Hinduism, has also portrayed God in intimate terms as the lover, longing for his beloved humans, searching them out, and presenting himself at their door seeking an offering. The goodness of God, in theistic teachings, means God's lovingkindness, for as the Christian scriptures sum it up: "God is love."[16]

Perfection and Creation: Why Would a Perfect Being Create a World?

If God is a being who is perfect in every way, why would he create a material world? It cannot be to satisfy some need that God has, because a perfect being does not need anything. Furthermore, before creation — if there was a time before creation — presumably nothing imperfect existed. But the world that God created is imperfect. It would have been better, it seems at first, if the world had not been created.

This problem presents in bold relief the tensions that exist between the religious teachings of such religions as Judaism and Christianity on one hand, and philosophical theism on the other. Philosophical theism is an effort to work out a consistent, coherent set of beliefs about the nature of God, the one powerful, wise, eternal, immutable, and supremely good deity of all creation. But the religions themselves are based on reports of the experiences that nonphilosophers such as prophets and priests have had. Philosophical theism, in its effort to depict a deity that is absolutely supreme and perfect in every way, tends to generate a portrait of a being above human concerns, aloof, imperturbable, unchanging, and untarnished by the imperfections of mundane existence. But such a picture does not go well with human religious experiences of an intimate, loving, suffering God. We will see that these tensions become even more severe when theists put forth their teachings about the so-called "metaphysical" characteristics of God.

The religious answer to the question of why God creates a universe is distinctly **anthropomorphic** — that is, it makes God appear humanlike. This shows up nicely in the poetry of James Johnson:

> And God stepped out on space,
> And he looked around and said:
> I'm lonely —
> I'll make me a world. [17]

According to much in the Jewish and Christian traditions, God created a world because God wanted companions. If God's need and longing for someone to love is inconsistent with certain of God's metaphysical attributes, then so much the worse for those attributes. Theists who have not been willing to admit that a perfect being could have needs and desires have explained creation instead in terms of God's overflowing goodness. Even if God was not lonely, even if God did not need companionship, still God's goodness and love are so abundant that they overflow into creation, expressing themselves generously by giving existence to the world. Thus the world is seen as an expression of God's goodness. This is suggested in one of the Hebrew scriptural creation stories: "And God saw everything that he had made, and behold, it was very good."[18]

But all this leaves unanswered the problem about a perfect God creating an imperfect world. For the theist it is a very serious problem. The first thing that might be said in an effort to diminish the problem is that any created world is necessarily imperfect. A created world is a finite world, and whatever is finite is by its very nature imperfect. Among the impossible things that even an omnipotent being cannot do is to create a material world that is perfect. God's choice therefore was not between creating a perfect world or an imperfect world, but between creating an imperfect world or not creating a world at all. The question becomes, then, not why God created a world that is less than perfect, but rather, why God created *this* world. And in the present context, that question implies yet another: Is the world as it exists consistent with divine goodness? The actual world seems to be not merely imperfect but seriously infected with problems that yield substantial evil and suffering. Would it have been better if no world had been created at all? We will examine this question in more detail in Chapter 4 when we address the infamous problem of evil. Unless a satisfactory answer can be found that reconciles God's goodness with the kind of world we find, then theism will have to be judged an inadequate, if not a positively irrational, position.

Some philosophers who have discussed this point have maintained that this is the best of possible worlds — namely, that of the many possible worlds that God might have created, this one is the best, and that is why God created this one. The notion, championed by such philosophers as Leibniz (1646–1716), was equally satirized and ridiculed by Voltaire (1694–1778). In *Candide*, Voltaire depicts a believer in the "best of possible worlds" theory clinging to this belief in the face of a cascade of catastrophes. [19]

As we will see, the occurrence of evil and suffering in the world constitutes what may well be the most serious challenge to the notion of the goodness of God. Still, the idea that this world — flawed though it may be — is the best of possible worlds is not to be refuted by satire. We have seen reasons to believe that the number of possible worlds, although perhaps very large indeed, is finite. If among that number of possible worlds one is best, then it would appear that God as a supremely good being would be under an obligation to create the best one if he were to create a world at all. Of course, among the possible worlds there may be no single best one. Several, or even many, may be equally good. Perhaps none is without substantial quantities of evil. In that case, morality would leave it open to God to decide which of the several top possibilities should be created, if one is to be created at all. It is a clear teaching of theism that God created the world because of God's goodness and as an expression of love. This amounts to a claim by theism that our world is such that a loving God could be morally justified in creating it. But only if the evidence supporting theism turns out to be quite strong, and the large problem that the flawed nature of the world raises against theism proves manageable, will we be justified in believing that God had morally sufficient reasons for selecting this world as the one to create, or for choosing to create a world at all. Otherwise the existence of such a world would have to count as strong evidence against either the goodness or the power of God.

Divine Goodness and Human Standards of Value

In ascribing goodness to God, say some, we are actually using a term derived from our human understanding of value that cannot really be applied to God, whose standard of goodness is not even on the same scale as that of humans. Thus, it has been suggested, we cannot judge the world that God has created or God's motives in creating the world according to human standards because divine goodness is something infinitely above, and thus entirely different from, human goodness. A bit of thought will discover this stance to be a part of that whole approach to theology which denies humans the right to inquire into the divine nature and which shrouds things divine in a dark cloak of mystery. It is a position that would simply rule out the philosophy of religion as a permissible intellectual activity.

John Stuart Mill (1806–1873) faced and answered this Tertullian-like position. He argued that the claim that God's goodness is totally above anything that humans can understand, or anything that we name when we characterize something human as good, amounts to saying that God is not good. When we call God supremely good, we mean, unless we are just talking nonsense, that God has characteristics like those that we call good in humans, but to a far higher degree. Mill rejects in the strongest terms any effort to call God good while admitting that God's goodness is totally different from human goodness.

> If . . . I am informed that the world is ruled by a being whose attributes are infinite, but what they are we cannot learn . . . except that "the highest human morality which we are capable of conceiving" does not sanction them; convince me of it, and I will bear my fate as I may. But when I am told that I must . . . at the same time call this being by names which express and affirm the highest human morality, I say in plain terms that I will not. Whatever power such a being may have over me, there is one thing which he shall not do: he shall not compel me to worship him. I will call no being good, who is not what I mean when I apply that epithet to my fellow-creature; and if such a being can sentence me to hell for not so calling him, to hell I will go.[20]

If we are to reason about any of God's attributes, we must do so in terms that humans can understand. This means that, however much greater than any human we conceive God to be, we must still use the same standards of judgment that apply to human affairs. The implication is that if God does something that, by human standards, is bad, then God is bad. And if any actions of God's that appear morally questionable are not to convict God of wrongdoing, then God must be morally justified for those actions in ways analogous to those that would be required to justify humans for doing similar things. There is in the world only one standard of truth, one standard of rationality, and one standard of goodness. The attribute of God that theists have nearly always considered to be the most essential is goodness. But it must be clearly understood that divine goodness is not something wholly other than human goodness — and certainly not something contrary to the human standards of goodness. When rational theists say that God is supremely good or that God is omnibenevolent, they speak of a single standard of goodness that applies to anything of which we may say that it is good. We have seen that there are some things an omnipotent being cannot do and some things an omniscient being cannot know. We now must conclude that there are some things a supremely good being *must* not do. If the evidence shows that God does these things, we must conclude that God is not supremely good. Or if the world turns out not to be the kind that a supremely good God could have created, the implication is either that there is no such God or that God is not supremely good. An informed judgment about these issues will have to wait until we have examined the arguments for the existence of God and such counterarguments as the problem of evil.

ETERNITY, SIMPLICITY, AND IMMUTABILITY

A number of the so-called "metaphysical" attributes of God come explicitly from theological discussions expressed in the language of Aristotle's philosophy. Thus, in order to understand the terminology in which arguments about these attributes are couched, it is necessary to look briefly at some of the most important of these Aristotelian concepts.

The Aristotelian Framework

According to Aristotle, everything that exists in the mundane realm, the realm of time and change, consists of some combination of two things: matter and form. Matter is what Aristotle calls the principle of potentiality and form is the principle of actuality. If we wish to understand anything fully, we must know about all of its four "causes": the material, the formal, the efficient, and the final. The *material cause* of anything is simply the matter of which it consists; the *formal cause* is the form it exemplifies: its shape, its pattern, or the blueprint from the realm of possibility that characterizes it. Its *efficient cause* is the power that impresses the form on the matter, and the *final cause* is the purpose it serves. For example, the statue of a soldier in the park can be explained in these terms. Its material cause is the bronze of which it is cast; its formal cause is the shape or form it exemplifies — that of a man or a soldier; its efficient cause is the labor of the sculptor, which gave the bronze the form it has; and the final cause is the purpose it serves: to decorate a park or to commemorate the memory of patriotic soldiers. Everything that exists can be understood in these terms.

Indeed, the whole realm of existence consists, according to Aristotle, of a hierarchy of beings ranked according to the principles of potentiality and actuality. Whatever has the most potentiality has at the same time the least actuality and thus ranks lowest in the hierarchy. The classification of all existing things according to this scheme came to be conceptualized by later Christian thinkers as the **Great Chain of Being**. It can be characterized thus:

God	Pure actuality without any potentiality
Seraphim	
Cherubim	
Archangels	
Angels	
Humans	The highest embodied and lowest spiritual being
Animals	
Plants	
Elementary life forms	Pure potentiality with virtually no
Matter	actuality

Everything in the created realm is compounded of matter and form. Even matter itself has some form, although only a very elementary form. A given thing changes as it actualizes its potential, becoming, so to speak, more fully what it really is or is destined to be. Thus a seed actualizes its potential to be a well-developed tree or a child grows into a mature adult. But whatever is compounded of matter and form, whatever is partly potential and only partly actual, is subject not only to growth but also to decay. Even the various ranks of angels and archangels, whose matter is spiritual rather than gross material substance, are in some measure subject to change and decay — as shown in Christian theology by the doctrine of Satan, the sinful, fallen angel.

The Metaphysical Attributes

The metaphysical attributes of God are those perfections that God has by virtue of the fact that God is pure actuality with no tainting admixture of matter or potentiality. This amounts to the claim that God already is all that God can be. God is not imperfectly actualized, as humans and other created beings are. Thus God is eternal, timeless, simple, immutable, impassive, independent. God's simplicity means that God is not compounded of matter and form; that God is not partly potential and partly actual. God is fully and simply what he is; his existence is identical with his essence. God is impassive in the sense of not needing or desiring anything and not suffering any pain, regret or any other passion. To speak of God's independence is another way of saying that God has no needs, does not depend on anything other than himself for anything. Even God's knowledge is independent of sense impressions, unlike that of humans and other animals. All things depend on God, but God does not depend on anything else.

We have already discussed in connection with omniscience the claim that God is timeless, that is, that God is above time or that God transcends time. Now we can see that the motive of that teaching is to place God beyond the reach of change and decay. Whatever is perfect, according to the Aristotelian scheme, already has actualized every possibility. Thus for a perfect being to change in any way or degree would be to move away from perfection to imperfection. A perfect being must therefore be in every way the same yesterday, today, and forever. The only way that a being can be thus unchanging—and this is the major meaning of the attribute of immutability—is to be outside the whole course of time, for time is inextricably bound up with change. So timelessness and immutability are attributes with essentially the same objective—to exempt the deity from change.

In our earlier discussion of the claim that God is timelessly transcendent of all temporal events, we argued that such a claim would imply that God could have no relation to, or involvement with, the process of the universe. Such an immutable, time-transcendent being could not create a changing world, much less be involved in the details of its progress through interacting with religious prophets or incarnating in a messiah or an avatar. The very act of creating a world would surely seem to involve substantial change in the divine nature. Defenders of immutability have argued that no such change in God's essence is involved because God eternally willed that in the fullness of time the world should come into being. Opponents have sometimes pointed out that even the coming into existence of a universe eternally willed by God implies a change in God, because even if God is no different in himself after than before creation, at least he would be different in his relations.

The defenders have been loath to concede the point, sometimes saying that changes in relations are not changes in the being itself, but their argument seems unconvincing. A substantial portion of what makes anything what it is is its relations with other things. God's relation to the universe makes God the creator; God's love for human creatures, according to theism, constitutes God's goodness. All theists seem to agree that God is eternal, but the notion of timelessness is hard to make intelligible. And, as many have pointed out, immutability is incompatible with many aspects of the experience and teachings of the actual religious practitioners who would call themselves theists. This point lies at the core of criticisms of theism based on the Aristotelian scheme.

GOD AS PERSONAL

In discussing the divine attributes, philosophers of religion have not usually included the attribute of personality. This is curious in a way, because the theistic religions have nearly always depicted God as personal. The

Hebrew scriptures show us a God who interacts in personal ways with his chosen people by making promises to them, giving them commandments, and guiding them in their daily lives. Sometimes we see a God who is a stern king, sometimes a demanding father, and sometimes a very loving, compassionate, and forgiving being—but always a personal God. The Christian God is depicted as a tender, loving father, one who loves his people so much that he sent his son, incarnate as a human person, to save them from their sins. Although the dominant view in Hinduism is that the supreme Brahman is without attributes and impersonal, its theistic branches depict Brahman as incarnate in forms many of which are explicitly personal. To be adequate to the religious theism actually believed and practiced, a philosophical theism must take into account the fact that God is apprehended as personal by theistic worshippers, and thus we must examine the concept of personality as an attribute of God. Because personality is not static and changeless but dynamic and full of life, some contemporary philosophers believe that an adequate theism that recognizes God as personal must give up its identification with static substance philosophy and embrace process philosophy.

Substance Philosophy Versus Process Philosophy

Aristotle's philosophy might be called *substance philosophy* because its primary concern is the substance of which things consist. Substance philosophy holds that the enduring is central and change is secondary. Indeed, in what we might call *substance theology* (and most theologians in the West have been of this type) stability, permanence, and changelessness are seen as the important and desirable qualities. Reality is conceived as substantial, enduring, and characterized in only a secondary way by the process of change. History is the progression of the subordinate, created world. The eternal world of God is timeless, aloof, and changeless. Change is seen as an imperfection or flaw.

In **process philosophy**, however, change or process is the key concept, and substances are seen as temporary pauses and hesitations in the fundamentally dynamic progression of reality. Process philosophy is not new in our era. In ancient Greece, Heraclitus taught a dynamic philosophy that held change and not permanence to be fundamental. In the past century the concept of evolution, derived from biology but generalized as a principle manifested in the whole cosmos, brought the notion of an active, growing, and changing world back into the focus of Western thought. The British philosopher Alfred North Whitehead (1861–1947) elaborated a systematic process philosophy and his followers, particularly Charles Hartshorne (1897–   ), developed it into a theology in which God himself, understood in personal terms, participates in the history of the cosmos as creator, preserver, and redeemer.

Process philosophy, in contrast to substance philosophy, depicts reality as a dynamic process of growth and progress. All things are a part of the lively process through which reality moves; nothing is entirely exempt from change. The substantial and enduring things are episodes more or less long lasting in the progression of reality, temporary pauses or hesitations in the ongoing life of the world. The primary concept is not thing but event. Change is therefore not an imperfection; rather, the unchanging appears as stagnant, dead, moribund.

When the world is conceived in this way, the so-called metaphysical attributes of God appear in quite a different light. Immutability and timelessness, understood in terms of aloofness and changelessness, no longer appear to be such desirable characteristics for the deity. Similarly, independence appears much less a perfection and more nearly a synonym for irrevelance.

Is Personality a Characteristic a Perfect Being Could Have?

It is curious that Western theologians of theism have rarely listed or given any substantial prominence to the characteristic of personality in discussing the attributes of God. Perhaps it is because the notion of God as personal appears difficult to harmonize with the other attributes, particularly impassibility, immutability, and independence. There was also the fear that a God conceived in personal terms would appear too anthropomorphic — too much like a larger-than-life human being. And yet the major theistic religions, especially Judaism and Christianity, have always conceived of God as a personal deity. The God who spoke with Adam and Eve in the garden in the cool of the evening; the God who called Abraham to the promised land; the God who led the children of Israel out of Egypt; the God whom Jesus frequently addressed as father was a very great being, far above the merely human, and yet thoroughly and entirely a person. Indeed, the majority of the traits often regarded as most important are personal. A person thinks in orderly and rational terms; a person appreciates beauty and recognizes and acknowledges moral value; a person understands the needs, the sorrows, the joys, the aspirations of other persons; a person cares about other persons, shares their hopes and fears, and loves them. These are the most important qualities that Christians and Jews have believed their God possesses, and we might say that they are the religiously important ones.

Some of these personal qualities, however, are hard to reconcile with the abstract perfections that the philosophers of theism have been convinced must be attributed to God. If God is intimately involved in the day-to-day affairs of humans, this involvement necessarily means change and thus he cannot be immutable. If God feels our pain and is grieved by our sufferings, then he cannot be impassive. If what God does depends on what we do—for example, if our needs affect God's actions; if our prayers are heard and answered—then God cannot be independent. Conversely, if God is impassive, then the religious belief that God cares about human suffering cannot be true, and if God is immutable, then the sense that God understands our human situations and offers help and guidance is false.

Certain philosophers have said that if the so-called metaphysical attributes are inconsistent with God as personal—that is, with God as we actually experience God to be—so much the worse for the metaphysical attributes. One of the most vocal members of this group is the process theologian Charles Hartshorne, who reminds us that a supreme religious value in the theistic conception of God is that God is a social being, one who relates in personal ways to human beings. But social beings are affected, conditioned, changed by the social relations in which they are involved with others.

> What is God if not the supreme case of personality? Those who deny this have yet to succeed in distinguishing their position from atheism, as Hume pointedly noted. Either God really does love all beings . . . or religion is a vast fraud.[21]

The defenders of theism, Hartshorne goes on to suggest, have insisted on all that cluster of divine characteristics which have been referred to as absoluteness or supreme perfection because they were thought to be essential if God is to fulfill the functions of a supreme deity. Our thinking about God has been much colored by analogies to earthly rulers and potentates. We have seen the dangers of rulers whose power was not sufficient to enable them to protect their people, whose life span was not long enough to make possible the completion of important projects, whose mental stability or moral resolve was not firm enough to avoid vacillation, failed promises, or even treachery. Thus God must be omnipotent in order not to lack power in any measure; God must be eternal so that God's policies can be depended on for all time; God must be immutable, impassive, independent in order not to be diverted from a steady moral course by any distractions or emotions. Hartshorne is convinced, however, that the abstract absolutes of theism, with their incompatibilities with logic and reason and particularly with the social and personal nature of God that religious persons claim to experience, are hindrances rather than aids to a philosophically coherent and religiously adequate conception of deity. "The common query 'Can the Absolute or Perfect being be personal or social?' should really run 'In what sense, if any, can a social [and personal] being be absolute or perfect?'"[22]

We have already seen how most of the supreme attributes have had to be redefined, modified, and restricted to make them intellectually consistent and intelligible. We have remarked that what is important are the actual characteristics that reason and religious experience discover deity to have and that the actual greatness of God is not in any measure diminished if we no longer use the time-honored titles. What we recognize, as Hartshorne points out, is that "God is not under the sentence of death, cannot decay; and his covenant abides, nor is his wisdom ever clouded by storms of blind passion, the effects of strong drink or disease."[23] The metaphysical attributes are intended as banners marking this steadiness, dependability, and trustworthiness of deity. Taken literally, they lead to contradiction and incoherence. If we continue to use these attributes to characterize deity, we must be careful to remember their metaphorical nature and to keep in mind what that metaphorical dimension is really intended to declare.

CONCLUSIONS

We have examined the majority of the important characteristics that religious and philosophical theists have traditionally attributed to God. In all but one case (divine goodness or omnibenevolence), we have found it necessary to refine the naive understanding of the word used to name the supreme attribute. We have seen that omnipotence cannot be attributed to God if omnipotence is taken to mean "able to do anything at all" and that omniscience cannot be attributed to God if omniscience means "knows everything." There are some things God cannot do because they are impossible in one or another of the various senses of "impossible" that we examined. Yet there is justification for attributing very great power to God, perhaps supreme power if that is understood in terms of our discussion of possibility.

Equally, there are some things God cannot know, because they are unknowable, impossible for anyone to know, and some things God cannot know because they can only be known by other individuals. But there is no impediment to attributing very great knowledge to God, and in particular for construing omniscience in terms more of wisdom than simply of knowing every scrap of information. And it must be said that we cannot attribute supreme goodness to God, if supreme divine goodness means possessing qualities that contradict the standards of goodness that apply to people and the created world. Perhaps it is a modification of the naive sense of omnibenevolence when we discover that divine goodness is not something of an entirely different sort or something on a totally different scale from human goodness. Goodness is clearly the central and most indispensable characteristic of the theistic God. Whatever is not good is not God; in saying that God is good, we mean supremely good. But that supreme goodness is not of a type different than human goodness and certainly not anything inconsistent with the standards of goodness that apply alike to all things human and divine.

We also discovered another attribute of God that is almost as important as goodness and that is inconsistent with the so-called metaphysical attributes, if they are interpreted in the naive sense. Religious, and most philosophical, theists have nearly always regarded God as personal. But a personal being cannot be absolutely immutable, independent, or impassive. And although God, existing forever, has no temporal beginning or end, this does not mean that God is timeless or transcendent of time in the sense of being unaffected by, or uninvolved in, the course of events that happen in time.

The attributes of supreme greatness that have been central to the theistic conception of God, when understood appropriately, seem consistent and intelligible. There is no intellectual impediment to regarding God as extremely powerful, wise, and good; as eternal; and as so steady and stable in moral character and resolve as to be utterly dependable. It is perhaps not ultimately important whether we continue to use the traditional vocabulary of theism, but it is important that we recognize and remember what our analysis of that vocabulary has shown. God's greatness — if there turns out to be rational justification for believing in the existence of a theistic God — seems ample to satisfy the needs of the religious person for a being to worship, and of the philosopher for a being in terms of which to explain the order and grandeur of the world. It is time now to turn our attention to the arguments for and against the existence of such a being.

ANNOTATED GUIDE TO FURTHER READINGS

Creel, Richard E. *Divine Impassibility.* Cambridge: Cambridge University Press, 1986.

> *A thorough discussion of the metaphysical attribute of impassibility. Creel closely examines the meaning of this attribute and concludes that it has four facets. He also treats some of the other divine attributes as they relate to impassibility.*

Crombie, I. M. "Eternity and Omnitemporality." In *The Rationality of Religious Belief,* edited by William J. Abraham and Steven W. Holtzer. Oxford: The Clarendon Press, 1987.

> *Deals with the debate over God's relationship with time. Some say that God resides outside of time; others maintain that God exists forever within time. Crombie points out that the finite human being's comprehension of time may differ from God's understanding of the nature of time.*

Geach, Peter. "Omnipotence and Almightiness." In *Philosophy of Religion: An Anthology,* edited by Louis P. Pojman. Belmont, Calif.: Wadsworth, 1987.

> *Makes a distinction between the terms* omnipotent *and* almighty: *An omnipotent God can do anything, even contradictory things; an almighty God has power over all things. God, Geach claims, is the latter rather than the former. This text includes other articles that deal with omnipotence, omniscience, and God's relationship to time.*

Kenny, Anthony. *The God of the Philosophers*. Oxford: Clarendon Press, 1979.

Omniscience and omnipotence are the subjects of this book. Kenny examines in considerable depth the problems and ramifications that arise when these attributes are assigned to God. Special attention is given to the topic of divine foreknowledge.

Kvanivig, Jonathan L. *The Possibility of an All-Knowing God*. New York: St. Martin's Press, 1986.

A defense of the traditional conception of omniscience. It is not only possible, but even necessary, Kvanivig argues, for an omniscient being to know the future. Kvanivig attempts to resolve the dilemma raised by his stance: If God has knowledge of the future, how then can there be free human action?

Langston, Douglas C. *God's Willing Knowledge*. University Park: The Pennsylvania State University Press, 1986.

The attribute of omniscience analyzed in the writings of John Duns Scotus, along with the conflict between humankind's free will and God's omniscience. Writings of Molina, Leibniz, Pike, and Plantinga on omniscience are also examined.

Rowe, William L., and Wainwright, William J., ed. *Philosophy of Religion: Selected Readings*, 2nd ed. New York: Harcourt Brace Jovanovich, 1989.

A useful general examination of the various characteristics attributed to God: omniscience, omnipotence, the metaphysical characteristics, along with their accompanying problems and inconsistencies, as attributes of God. An article by Charles Hartshorne addresses the conflict between a personal God who loves people and an impassive, immutable God.

Swinburne, Richard. *The Coherence of Theism*. Oxford: Clarendon Press, 1977.

An excellent source that not only discusses several of the characteristics commonly attributed to God, but also explains how these characteristics can coexist together in God. Also deals with the question of whether or not God is perfectly good and, if so, whether this is compatible with the other attributes.

NOTES

1. The expression "Western religion" is misleading. Strictly speaking, there is no such thing as Western religion since all the great religions of the world come from the East. When we speak of Western religion, we usually mean Judaism and Christianity and sometimes Islam as well.

2. We will argue in Chapter 7 that God could not have made it morally right for us to inflict needless suffering on innocent persons because it is logically impossible for such actions to be morally right.

3. The principles of identity and contradiction are considered to be the most fundamental laws of thought and perhaps of existence. The principle of identity states: "If any statement is true, then it is true," or, "A thing is identical with itself; it is what it is and not something else," or, "A word means just what it means and not something else." The principle of contradiction states: "No statement can be both true and false," or, "No thing can both exist and not exist." Failure to conform to these fundamental laws produces unintelligible nonsense. An amusing example of this is to be found in

Lewis Carroll's *Through the Looking Glass* [Chapter 6] where the character Humpty Dumpty uses a word in a way which Alice thinks makes no sense and she challenges him. Humpty Dumpty replies that when he uses a word, that word means just what he chooses it to mean then and there, nothing more or less. Alice says, the question is whether one can do such things with words. Alice is wise beyond her years. That is the question indeed! And in fact, it is not really a question. It is quite clear that one cannot.

4. Edgar S. Brightman, *Person and Reality* (New York: Ronald Press, 1958).

5. Judges 11:30–35.

6. J. L. Mackie, "Evil and Omnipotence," *Mind* 64, 200 (1955): 211f.

7. See *The Freedom of the Will*, edited by Paul Ramsey, vol. 1 in Jonathan Edwards, *The Works of President Edwards*, S. E. Dwight, editor (New York, 1829–1830).

8. Peter Geach, "Omnipotence," *Philosophy* 48 (1973).

9. William J. Wainwright, *Philosophy of Religion* (Belmont, Calif.: Wadsworth, 1988), p. 22.

10. See Norman Kretzmann, "Omniscience and Immutability," *Journal of Philosophy* 63, 14 (July 14, 1966): 490f.

11. See ibid.

12. Alfred North Whitehead, *The Aims of Education and Other Essays* (New York: Macmillan, 1929), p. 1.

13. Psalms 103:13.

14. John 3:16.

15. Rabindranath Tagore, *The Religion of Man* (Boston: Beacon Press, 1931).

16. I John 4:8; 16.

17. James Weldon Johnson, *God's Trombones: Seven Negro Sermons in Verse* (New York: Viking Press, 1927), p. 17.

18. Genesis 1:31.

19. See Voltaire's *Candide* (Geneva: Cramer, 1759; New York: Grosset and Dunlap, 1931).

20. John Stuart Mill, *An Examination of Sir William Hamilton's Philosophy* (London: Longmans, Green & Company, 1865), from chapter 7.

21. Charles Hartshorne, *The Divine Relativity* (New Haven: Yale University Press, 1948), p. 25.

22. Ibid.

23. Ibid., p. 26.

3

The Arguments for Theism

We have examined some of the major attributes the God of traditional theism has been assigned. We have attempted to sort out some of the most important of the problems that the attribution of these "omnicharacteristics" raises. And we have concluded tentatively (pending a further examination of the problem of creation and especially the problem of evil in Chapter 4) that it seems possible to work out a coherent conception of deity that preserves many, if not all, of the features of the God of Western theism. If the concept of God is not in itself incoherent or the attributes mutually contradictory, the way is left open to conclude that the God of theism *might* exist. But many things might exist that actually do not exist. The question we must now address is: Granted the possibility of a theistic deity, are we justified in believing such a God actually does exist?

THE PLACE OF RATIONAL PROOFS

It has often been said that belief in God is a matter either of experience or of faith, and not a matter of proof. For many religious people — and many not so religious — this is undoubtedly true. Many people who believe, and many people who do not, hold their beliefs without grounding these beliefs in reason. But philosophers of religion and theologians are — or, at least if the arguments of Chapter 1 are sound, ought to be — committed to the proposition that we should seek rational grounding for our beliefs and should proportion our examined beliefs to the strength of that rational support. If we are to affirm the existence of God, it ought to be only because we have reasons that support and justify that belief, and these reasons must outweigh any counterarguments that would undermine belief. Likewise, if we are to refuse to believe, it should be because we have assessed the arguments pro and con and have honestly arrived at the conclusion that belief is not justified by the evidence. Thus theistic philosophers and theologians, especially when faced with the skepticism of nonbelievers, have usually thought it appropriate to support their theism with arguments designed to prove that God exists or to provide strong reasons for believing.

Some thinkers, such as Thomas Aquinas, have asserted that the existence of God can be proven. This is a very strong claim. Other thinkers have more modestly suggested that belief is justified by arguments that fall short of conclusive demonstration of God's existence but that nevertheless marshal a preponderance of evidence in support. Conversely, some have claimed that the nonexistence of God can be proved, whereas others have said that although a positive proof is wanting, the weight of evidence is against theism. We must now examine the arguments pro and con in an effort to evaluate their relative strengths. This chapter will investigate the arguments in support of theism; Chapter 4 will examine and assess the antitheistic arguments.

In the strictest sense of the word, a **proof** may be defined as a valid argument whose premises are known to be true. A proof is a very special kind of argument, one that provides us with conclusive evidence. Perhaps the so-called ontological argument, which we will examine in the next section, is the only one that can be considered a proof in this most stringent sense, and there are as we shall see very serious questions about its validity. The other traditional arguments have sometimes been called proofs even though, however strong and valuable they may turn out to be, it seems clear that they cannot provide hard evidence for their conclusions.

It is perhaps wiser to speak not of proofs but of arguments. We justifiably accept many beliefs not because we have proofs that they are true, but because we have good reasons to believe them. An **argument** is a series of statements related to one another in such a way that some, called the premises, provide evidence or reasons for accepting another, called the conclusion. There are two major types of arguments, deductive and inductive. In each kind, the premises support the conclusion or offer justification for our believing the truth of the conclusion, but they differ significantly. **Deductive arguments** provide conclusive evidence for their conclusions, whereas **inductive arguments** offer some amount of support short of conclusive evidence. We judge deductive arguments to be *valid* or *invalid;* we do not apply the valid/invalid distinction to inductive arguments. Instead, they are judged *sound* or *unsound,* or they are evaluated in terms of how strong or how weak the support is which they provide for their conclusion; a sound inductive argument shows that the conclusion is *probably* true. There are, of course, differing degrees of probability, although it may seldom be possible to assign an exact numerical value to the degree.

A deductive argument is valid if accepting the premises as true requires us to accept the conclusion as true — that is, if it is impossible for the premises to be true without the conclusion also being true. A deductive argument is thus *coercive:* If it really is valid and its premises are known to be true, it becomes impossible to reject the conclusion; the truth of the conclusion is established with certainty.

But this is not nearly as simple a matter as it may sound. It is relatively easy to discover whether or not an argument is valid — that is the business of logic. But even if a deductive argument is known to be valid, the conclusion may still turn out to be false, for the premises may not be true. And many of the claims made in support of theism are such that it is difficult, if not impossible, for us humans to know for sure that they are true. Thus it is by no means easy to be confident that any of the arguments for the existence of God succeed in establishing what they set out to prove. We must now examine the major arguments brought forward in support of, and against, theism and ask ourselves whether or not any of them provide us with a mass of evidence strong enough to justify affirming or denying God's existence.

THE ONTOLOGICAL ARGUMENT

The **ontological argument** for the existence of God attempts to demonstrate that the existence of God is a necessary truth on grounds that the denial of God's existence is self-contradictory. What is perhaps most distinctive about the **ontological argument** is that it is alleged to be an *a priori* argument. That means that the proponents of the argument claim that it does not depend in any way on empirical evidence. Since many philosophers, especially those before the twentieth century, have shown considerable suspicion about sense impressions and the evidence they provide, the fact that this argument does not depend on such evidence has been regarded as a very great advantage. The ontological argument is also supposed to be deductive, the kind of argument that, if it is valid and its premises are true, provides conclusive evidence for the truth of its conclusion. Thus it would appear to be the ideal kind of argument for the theist. Yet, as we will see, it has also been one of the most controversial.

The Claim That God Does Not Exist Is Self-Contradictory

The ontological argument has been formulated in a variety of ways. Indeed, it might be better to say that a cluster of arguments with certain similarities are collectively referred to as the ontological argument. Some thinkers, Descartes for example, have said that the argument amounts to pointing out that the claim that God does not exist is contradictory. *God* means "the supremely perfect being." But to deny that such a being exists is like saying, "The supremely perfect being lacks a perfection." Stated in this way, the contradiction becomes blatant. Another way of putting it is to say that God is a being whose essence includes existence; to deny the existence of such a being is to contradict oneself. God allegedly is the kind of being who could not possibly not exist — whose nonexistence is inconceivable. We know that there are some kinds of things whose existence is inconceivable and that therefore do not exist because it is impossible for them to exist. For example, no square circles exist because there could not be any; the very concept is contradictory, the nature of such a thing is inconceivable, and its existence is impossible. Conversely, so the argument goes, God is the sort of thing that could not fail to exist. The very concept of God includes the notion of existence as the concept of square circle includes nonexistence. Thus the nonexistence of God is inconceivable and God's actual nonexistence is impossible.

Existence Is Inseparable from God's Essence

René Descartes (1596–1650) argues that existence is an inseparable part of the essence of God and for this reason God must exist.

> I find it manifest that we can no more separate the existence of God from his essence than we can separate from the essence of a triangle the fact that the size of its three angles equals two right angles. . . . It is no less self-contradictory to conceive of a God, a supremely perfect Being, who lacks existence — that is, who lacks some perfection — than it is to conceive of a mountain for which there is no valley.[1]

This argument does not prove that triangles or mountains must exist, but only that they must have all the features that are parts of their essence. It does, so it is claimed, prove that God must exist, because existence *is* a part of God's essence. To be a triangle means to have the sum of internal angles add up to 180 degrees; similarly to be God means to exist. Thus "God does not exist" is as much a self-contradiction as "A triangle has internal angles that add up to more than two right angles," or "There is a mountain with no valley."

Anselm's "Something Than Which No Greater Can Be Conceived"

The classic statement of the ontological argument comes from St. Anselm (1033–1109), although it was Immanuel Kant who gave the argument its name. Anselm tells us that God means that than which nothing greater can be conceived. We understand something by that expression, and thus that being exists in our thought. But a being that exists only in thought is less great than a being that exists in thought and in reality. To deny that this being exists in reality is to say, in effect, that the being than which no greater can be conceived is not as great as another that can be conceived (the one existing both in thought and reality). That is clearly a contradiction. Thus God must exist not only in thought but also in reality.

Anselm argues further that a being than which no greater can be conceived cannot be conceived as nonexistent. This means that God is a necessary being, one that could not possibly fail to exist — or, in the parlance of contemporary philosophy, one that exists in every possible world. Clearly a being that only happens to exist but that might not have existed — that is, a being that is contingent or that exists in some but not all possible worlds — is less great or less perfect than one that exists necessarily in every possible world. So the existence of God is not contingent like that of a human or a horse; rather, God's existence is necessary. Indeed, as some theologians expressed it, God *is* his existence just as God *is* his goodness, his power, and all of the other aspects of his essence.

Criticisms of the Ontological Argument

The ontological argument has had a checkered career. Some have regarded it as the decisive argument that succeeds in proving conclusively the existence of God. Others have thought it little better than sophistry. But there is something intriguing about this position, and philosophers have returned to it again and again to see whether it might not be made to do what it is supposed to do — or to see whether it might be turned against itself to prove that God does not, or even could not, exist. It is the traditional argument to which scholars in the twentieth century have probably devoted most attention.

St. Thomas Aquinas (1225–1275) held that it was a valid argument but that only God could realize that it is a proof in the strict sense, for only an omniscient being could possess the knowledge necessary to know that the premises of the argument are true. Finite humans cannot know the essence of God; the ontological argument turns on claims about God's essence; thus only God and not humans can know the truths that make the ontological argument a conclusive proof. Aquinas elected as a consequence to rely on other arguments than the ontological.

One of the most formidable critics of the ontological argument was Immanuel Kant (1724–1804). One of the objections that Kant pressed against Anselm's version had already been raised by Gaunilo, a contemporary of Anselm. Gaunilo argued that if Anselm's argument was valid, it could be used to prove the existence of any conceivable excellent thing. For example, we can conceive of an island idyllic in every way, an island paradise "than which no greater could be conceived." Because we understand the description, the island exists in our minds. But this island "than which no greater could be conceived" must also exist in reality; otherwise, we could conceive of a greater one existing both in thought and in reality, an obvious contradiction. Thus this most excellent island — or anything else conceived along similar lines — must exist. But an argument that proves the existence of all sorts of absurd things is not a sound argument. Thus Gaunilo insisted that the ontological argument fails.

A possible reply to Gaunilo, one that Anselm himself attempted in part, is to insist that God is the only being to whom the title "that than which nothing greater can be conceived" applies. It is a mistake to suppose that we could conceive an island that is supremely idyllic in every way. No matter how many varieties of luscious fruit it might have, we could always imagine adding one more or improving the flavor slightly. But God is the supremely perfect being in the sense that every perfection is actualized fully and harmonized completely in God's essence. God is not merely a being than whom feeble human intellect cannot think of a better; God is *the* being than which a greater is inconceivable. Thus God is the only being for which the ontological argument works.

Kant was not impressed by this response. He raises two objections to the ontological argument. One, which resembles Gaunilo's, is that Anselm mistakenly assumes that existence is a real predicate. A *predicate* is a word that attributes some property or characteristic to a subject. When we say that God is powerful, we predicate the property of power to God. But when we say that God exists, we do not attribute a property, for existence is not a property a subject can or cannot have. We would make a similar error if we think that in saying, "American eagles are rare," we are attributing a property to eagles. What we are actually saying is that there are not very many American eagles. Descartes makes the same error when he argues that God must exist because to deny that God exists is to say that the supremely perfect being lacks a perfection. But existence is not a perfection that can be added to or subtracted from the other perfections or properties that something may have. To say that something exists is not to say that it has some additional characteristic, existence, but rather to say that there is such a thing, that the subject named or described is present in the real world.

Kant puts it this way: "A hundred real dollars do not contain one penny more than a hundred imaginary dollars."[2] No doubt we prefer the real to the imaginary dollars, but that is beside the point; the essential nature of the two is in no way different. And this, according to Kant, is the error of the ontological argument. If existence is not an attribute that a subject can either have or fail to have, then it cannot be argued that God must exist because existence is an inseparable aspect or perfection of God's essence. Given the coherence of the *notion* of a supremely perfect being (a point not everyone would grant), like that of an idyllic island or a hundred dollars, the question remains whether or not any of them exists. The existence of God can no more be inferred from God's definition as the supremely perfect being than can that of the island from its definition as the island than which no greater can be imagined.

Kant's other major objection to this argument is grounded in the claim that no existential proposition is logically necessary. The ontological argument attempts to derive the existence of God from the definition of God, by way of the claim that a being so defined is a necessary being, but Kant is convinced that no such derivation is possible. Necessity applies to propositions and not to beings. Every existential proposition — that is, every proposition that asserts the existence of something — must be grounded on empirical evidence. Thus Kant rejects the whole notion of necessary being as incoherent.

It seems, however, that the nonexistence of some things can be derived from their definition and thus that some sense can be given to the notion of necessary nonbeing. The nonexistence of four-sided triangles can be derived from their definition as four-sided plane figures that have three sides, because such a definition is incoherent. Thus we say not just that such things do not exist, as we claim that unicorns do not exist; rather, we say that they *necessarily* do not exist. The proposition, "Four-sided triangles do not exist," seems to be an existential proposition that is logically necessary. Richard Swinburne claims that there are also affirmative existential propositions that are logically necessary or, in other words, that there are some things that necessarily exist. "There exists a number greater than one million — and it is a logically necessary truth that there does."[3] We might say that a plain figure with more sides than anyone has ever counted exists or that the ratio between two numbers larger than anyone has ever calculated exists, and so on. Thus it seems to be too much to claim that no existential proposition can be logically necessary or that the concept of necessary existence is incoherent.

It might be claimed that an eternal being is a necessary being because such a being could not begin to exist or cease to exist. Such a beginning or ending is inconsistent with the meaning of "eternal being." But this necessity is not quite like the kind of necessity we have been discussing. Even if we admit that it is proper to designate such a being as necessary, we are still justified in asking whether or not any such being exists. The statement, "Eternal beings are necessary beings," can thus be understood to mean not, "There are eternal beings that are necessary beings," but rather, "If anything is an eternal being, then it is a necessary being." Similarly, the ontological argument may be taken to mean not "God exists," but rather, "If anything is God, then it exists." Granted, if there is an eternal being, it is a necessary being, but to call it necessary does not prove that it exists. Likewise, we may grant that if there is a God, that is, a supremely perfect being — if anything answers to that description — then it exists. The question is whether or not there is anything that answers to the description. We will look more closely at the concept of necessary being when we examine the so-called ontological disproof later in this chapter.

The Modal Version of the Ontological Argument

The most popular formulation of the ontological argument among contemporary philosophers, advanced by such thinkers as Charles Hartshorne,[4] Norman Malcolm,[5] and Alvin Plantinga,[6] is grounded in **modal logic**, the logic of necessity, possibility, and impossibility, and is usually stated in possible world language. Its various advocates state it in slightly different ways, but all versions seem to have essentially the same strengths and weaknesses.

The modal version of the ontological argument attempts to infer God's existence from the claim that God's existence is logically possible, together with certain allegedly necessary truths about God's nature and the laws of modal logic. It is the assertion of the possibility of God's existence that sharply differentiates this from the classic versions of the ontological argument, which argued from the definition or from certain allegedly necessary traits of God without explicitly asserting that a being with those traits was possible.

It is a principle of modal logic that contingent truths vary from one possible world to another, but that necessary truths obtain in every possible world. This means that contingent truths such as "Horses exist" and "Logicians are fond of verbal puzzles" could not be necessary truths in any possible world, but that necessary truths such as "Unicorns have one horn" and "It is false that $2 + 2 = 7$" are necessarily true in every possible world. This is another way of saying that the modal status — whether something is necessary or possible — is a universal fact and not one that applies only to specific worlds. Unicorns may exist in one world and not in another, but in every possible world they have a single horn, that is, their existence is contingent, but their nature is not contingent. If we can say of anything that its existence is necessary, then it must exist in every possible world.

The argument begins, then, with the claim that if it is possible that God's existence is necessary, then God exists in every possible world, including the actual world. But is it possible? That it is allegedly follows from the nature of God. God is defined by certain contemporary philosophers of religion as a maximally great or maximally perfect being. It seems to be possible that such a being exists; that is, it seems that there is a possible world in which a maximally perfect being exists, even if we think this being does not exist in the actual world. But a being that exists in every possible world is more perfect than a being that exists in only one or some possible worlds. Indeed, to be maximally perfect means to exist in every possible world or, in other words, to be a necessary being. Thus if it is possible for a maximally perfect being to exist — that is, if God exists in some possible world — then it is necessarily true that God exists — that is, that God exists in every possible world. But we have already remarked that the existence of a maximally perfect being seems to be possible. There is nothing contradictory in the notion and no absurdity seems to follow from it. The conclusion is that "God exists" is necessarily true, that is, true not just in some possible world but in every possible world. But the actual world is one possible world. From all this it follows that "God exists" is true of the actual world or, in other words, that God actually does exist.

The modal argument is more complex than the earlier versions of the ontological argument. It can be stated in several different ways, and some constructions of the argument are more intuitively appealing than others. There is fairly widespread agreement among contemporary modal logicians that at least some versions of the argument are valid. But considerable disagreement remains concerning what the argument, even if it is valid, proves. One of the most serious problems lies in the premise that asserts that the existence of a maximally perfect being is possible. Some philosophers believe that perfection or greatness is like numbers; there is no such thing as a maximum. Just as there is no highest number than which none higher is possible; just as there is no island so perfect that some alteration cannot improve it; so there may be no coherent concept of a being than which no greater can be conceived. Thus if there is no such conceivable thing as a maximally perfect being, the existence of such a being is not possible. In that case, since the modal argument depends on the assumption that the existence of God is possible, it fails to establish its conclusion not because it is invalid, but because one of its premises is false.

Even if the situation is not quite this bad for the argument, we may still not be justified in claiming that the argument proves that God exists, because even if it is valid and even if all its premises are true, it may not be possible for any humans to know that the premises are true. This was St. Thomas's point about the ontological argument. He maintained that the argument is valid and that its premises are true, and thus God can recognize that it establishes its conclusion, but we humans cannot have sufficient knowledge of the characteristics of God to justify our making any confident use of the argument. Even Alvin Plantinga, one of the most able contemporary defenders of the argument, is unwilling to claim that it proves the existence of God. "What I claim for this argument, therefore, is that it establishes, not the *truth* of theism, but its rational acceptability."[7] Even that is a lot to claim, and a great many contemporary philosophers would insist that it is too much.

The So-Called Ontological Disproof

We have examined briefly the argument by which Gaunilo attempted by a **reductio ad absurdum** to refute the ontological argument by showing that, taken to its logical conclusion, it implied an absurdity. Gaunilo and Kant both tried to discredit the argument by demonstrating that parallel reasoning could establish the existence of anything that we wish to conceive of as perfect, such as the perfect island. In recent times even more radical responses to this argument have appeared. We will briefly examine just one,[8] by David and Marjorie Haight,[9] that purports to use the ontological argument to prove the existence of a devil.

The Haight argument is similar to Gaunilo's except that it parodies the ontological argument by arguing for the existence of a supremely evil being rather than an idyllic island. We have a concept of a being than which no worse can be conceived. If this being did not actually exist, it would not be that than which no worse could be conceived, since we could conceive such a being as existing, and this being would clearly be worse. Now this being than which a worse is inconceivable is called the devil. Therefore the devil exists.

The Haights point out that this argument is exactly parallel to the ontological argument. If the ontological argument is valid, so must this one be; if it establishes the existence of God, this one must establish the existence of the devil. They suggest that what the argument really proves, if it proves anything at all, is the existence of one greatest thing that might be called either God or devil. The argument, as stated by Anselm, does not prove that the being than which no greater can be conceived is a good being, unless an implicit assumption has been made identifying greatness with goodness or including goodness in greatness. But such an assumption would be question begging. And if the argument is formulated in such a way that the conception on which it turns is of a supremely perfect being, the counterargument might be made to hinge on the concept of a supremely imperfect being and the parallel would still obtain.

If the ontological argument is to work and also avoid criticisms like those of Gaunilo and the Haights, it must be supplemented somehow to show that God is the only being to which such an argument can apply. This Anselm attempted to do in his reply to Gaunilo. He first argued that any being that can be conceived to exist but does not exist can be conceived as having a beginning. But any being that can be conceived as having a beginning or an end is not that being than which a greater is inconceivable. Now an island, however perfect, or anything else whose nonexistence is conceivable, can be conceived as having a beginning. Thus the argument does not prove the existence of imagined perfect things such as islands or hundred dollars, but does prove the existence of the one thing than which no greater is conceivable, namely, God.

But this response will not work against the Haight argument. For the devil, as the supremely evil being, is a being that need not be conceived as having a beginning or an end. Indeed, his chief difference from God is only that he is evil and God is good. Anselm maintains that his argument can apply only to the one thing than which any greater is inconceivable. If God is conceived as the greatest good being and the devil as the greatest evil being, the question would still need to be raised of which is the greater of these two, that is, the single being than which no greater is conceivable. Perhaps a case could be made for the claim that to be good is greater than to be evil, but it would require an additional argument, one that Anselm does not supply and one that does not readily present itself. Wanting such an argument, the claim that to be good is greater than to be evil becomes question begging, assuming without supplying grounds a point that need not be accepted unless grounds are supplied.

The upshot of the dispute between Anselm and the Haights seems to be that the ontological argument might establish the existence of some supreme being but leave us uncertain whether it is God or the devil. This is what the Haights themselves suggest. Many theists would be pleased to welcome this concession and would regard this outcome of the Haights' argument as friendly rather than hostile to theism. These theists would then resort to empirical arguments, such as the argument from design and beauty in the world, to support their further contention that the being whose existence the ontological argument has been conceded to establish is God and not the devil. They would have to face, however, a potentially formidable counterargument based on the existence of evil in the world.

What seems really to be at issue with the ontological argument and its counterarguments, the so-called **ontological disproofs**, is the question of whether the concept of a necessary being or a maximally great being is intelligible and whether any proposition asserting the existence of such a being can be necessarily, and not merely contingently, true. The conventional view of necessity follows Hume and Kant in the assumption that no existential statement can be necessary. All existential propositions are regarded as contingent, empirical claims, and all necessary propositions as nonexistential. If "God exists" were a necessary proposition, then it could not be about existence — a patent absurdity. And if it is to be about existence, then it will be contingent or nonnecessary.

We have already questioned the claim that no necessity proposition can make an assertion about what exists. We noted that propositions such as "No four-sided triangles exist" seem to be both necessary and existential.

If these are indeed examples of propositions that are both existential and necessary, they would seem to be just the kind of proposition one would need to formulate an ontological proof or disproof successfully. An ontological disproof claims to be an analogue of the ontological proof that attempts to establish the existence of God on the basis of an analysis of the concept's meaning. An ontological disproof therefore would proceed by analyzing the concept of God and showing that it is incoherent — from which the disproof would infer that no such being could exist. If, for example, an analysis of the attributes of God like that we undertook in the previous chapter turned up convincing reasons to believe that these attributes are mutually inconsistent, and if no consistent set of modified or attenuated attributes still compatible with the notion of deity could be discovered, we would have to conclude that the concept of God is incoherent.

Now if the concept of a necessary being or a supremely perfect being really is incoherent — like the concept of a seven-sided square — the ontological disproof would seem to be successful. We believe that when we show that the concept of a seven-sided square is self-contradictory, we demonstrate not only that the concept is incoherent but also that no seven-sided squares could possibly exist. In other words, we acknowledge that such statements are both necessary and existential. An appropriate proposition of this sort about God is just what an advocate of an ontological disproof needs. If we recognize that there can be necessary existential propositions, this opens up the possibility of an ontological disproof. But we must notice that such a recognition cuts both ways: It also opens up the possibility of an ontological proof. This is the possibility that such contemporary supporters of the ontological argument as Swinburne seek to exploit.

Are we in a position to draw any conclusions about the ontological argument? One seems to be that the advocates of the ontological argument have not been able by means of the argument to demonstrate the existence of God. Another is that its critics have equally failed to demonstrate God's nonexistence and have not even been able to show decisively that the ontological argument itself completely fails. Indeed, the Haights interpret the argument in a way that amounts to a substantial concession to the theist. Many would say that theirs is much too much of a concession.

Perhaps one of the most important things we have discovered in examining the ontological argument is the plausibility of the claim that necessary judgments can have existential import. If such necessary propositions as the basic laws of logic and mathematics are admitted to have implications about what cannot exist, why may not certain necessary propositions have implications about what can or must exist? But if this point clears the way for either an ontological proof or an ontological disproof, at the same time a fully satisfactory formulation of either of these arguments remains to be discovered. The ontological argument continues to exert great powers of fascination, however. There can be little doubt that philosophers will continue to refine it and to attempt to find new ways to formulate it in hope of making it work. Up to this time, however, it seems not yet to have contributed in any substantial way to settling the question whether or not God exists. Let us now turn our attention to the empirical arguments to see whether they offer more substantial support for theism.

THE COSMOLOGICAL ARGUMENT

The ontological argument claims to be an *a priori* **argument,** one that does not depend on empirical evidence but operates exclusively from definitions and assertions whose truth can be ascertained by examining the meaning of the terms. By contrast, both the cosmological and the teleological arguments are explicitly empirical, drawing on premises about what can be observed in the world of sense experience. Because the most serious difficulties encountered by the ontological argument are related to its nonempirical nature — its attempt to infer existence from a definition, or actuality from possibility — perhaps the prospects for the empirical arguments are more hopeful.

The Argument to a First Uncaused Cause

The **cosmological argument** may be formulated in various ways. One version states that when a thing moves, it is moved by another thing, arguing that there must ultimately be something that moves other things but is itself self-moved and requires nothing else to move it; and this thing is God. Another version points to a succession of causes and effects, arguing that there must eventually be a first uncaused cause that accounts for the succession of causation; and this is God. Still another notes that contingent things exist in the world whose existence is not self-explanatory. A contingent thing is one that did not have to exist, one that depends on something else for its existence. The shoes and ships and sealing wax and cabbages and kings that inhabit the empirical world are, all of them, contingent. None is necessary. Each might never have existed.

But if something exists that did not have to exist, if something moves that did not move itself, if something is an effect not self-caused, we are impelled to ask why these things exist or happen. This is the demand for an explanation or a reason. Thus the second step in the cosmological argument is what philosophers call the **principle of sufficient reason**, the principle that states that for anything to exist or any event to occur, there must be a reason that it exists, or something adequate to cause it. It seems natural to believe that there must be a reason for whatever happens. Presumably there would be no contingent beings at all unless something created them or caused them to exist. If anything comes into existence, it must do so because something else that already existed caused it. If some things are contingent, then there must be something that is not contingent on which the contingent things depend.

Thus we explain the existence of some contingent being by pointing to some previously existing being. But each time we offer such an explanation, the question arises again about the earlier contingent being. For example, we explain the existence of a person by referring to her parents. But their existence requires an explanation as much as hers. We soon find ourselves talking about grandparents and great-grandparents; before long it becomes evident that we have involved ourselves in a regress of explanations to which we can see no end. Each new explanation simply raises anew the problem it was cited to solve. Each antecedent cause requires another cause to explain it. So the theists who make use of the cosmological argument point out that as long as we continue to make use of contingent things as explanations, no sufficient reason has been given. The only really sufficient explanation for the existence of contingent things is one that does not itself require yet another explanation. We arrive therefore at the third premise of the argument: the claim that an **infinite regression** of contingent causes does not constitute a sufficient explanation. What is required, they tell us, is an explanation in terms of a being that is not itself contingent but necessary. In other words, contingency entails necessity. Thus, so the argument goes, explanation must eventually arrive at a first cause whose cause is not another contingent being but a necessary being whose existence requires no further explanation. This necessary being that is the first cause, says the argument, is God.

Obviously this argument has a number of problems. One has to do with the principle of sufficient reason, whose status has been a matter of considerable controversy among philosophers. Another problem is the claim that the existence of contingent things cannot be sufficiently explained by an infinite regression of contingent causes. The claim that everything requires a cause or a sufficient reason for its existence is contradicted by the assumption that God does not require such a cause or explanation. If everything requires a cause, then why not God; or if God does not, then why do all other things? Finally, it has been suggested that even if the argument succeeds in establishing the existence of a necessary first cause of the contingent world, that cause might not be God. We must examine these objections one by one.

The Principle of Sufficient Reason

The so-called principle of sufficient reason is perhaps the most controversial premise of the argument. Some philosophers regard it as an intuitively self-evident law of reason practically on a par with the law of contradiction or the law of identity. At the other extreme, some think that it is merely an empirical generalization, an assumption that there are explanations for everything, based on the success we have had, particularly in the sciences, in finding explanations of some things. Furthermore, some formulations of the principle of sufficient reason appear to be inconsistent with human free will and even with the belief that God's creation of the world involves free choice.

Initially the principle certainly has an intuitive ring of authenticity. Denying it seems to amount to the claim that some things might happen for no reason at all, that they might pop into and out of existence quite fortuitously, and this appears very implausible. Most people do seem to have a very strong, nearly irresistible, propensity to believe that there are causes, reasons, explanations for whatever happens. Indeed, the suggestion that some things might be uncaused or just a matter of chance strikes us as unscientific, even superstitious or irrational. Even if we have no notion of what the cause or the explanation of something might be, we nonetheless are convinced that one must exist.

And yet if the principle of sufficient reason is intuitively self-evident in the same way that the law of contradiction is thought to be, it is surprising that a number of people do not recognize it as such. This objection is not decisive, of course. Not everyone recognizes the intuitive certainty of the basic laws of logic or mathematics — in some cases because of lack of knowledge about what is relevant to understanding them, but in other cases because of a commitment to empiricist principles that interpret them as generalizations from sense observations. Still, the laws of logic and mathematics come much closer to being universally recognized as necessary truths than does the principle of sufficient reason, and some people who are convinced that it is a necessary truth admit that it is not as intuitively evident or as fundamental as those other principles.

Part of the disagreement about the status of the principle probably rests on the fact that it can be formulated and understood in strikingly different ways. Interpreted in the strictest sense, it makes a very strong claim, one that has rigidly deterministic implications incompatible with free will, either human or divine. If it is literally true that there must be a *sufficient* reason for the occurrence of whatever happens, then everything that happens happens necessarily. For by this definition the sufficient condition for an occurrence is the set of conditions in the presence of which it *must* occur. If there is a sufficient reason for everything, then there are no contingent beings or events; whatever exists exists necessarily. Some philosophers have accepted the principle thus strictly interpreted, along with its deterministic implications (it plays a critical role, for example, in Leibniz's argument that this is the best of all possible worlds).

When we notice the extravagant implications of this most stringent interpretation of the principle, it appears much less convincing. Our intuition of the plausibility of the principle, our conviction that things do not exist fortuitously or happen for no reason at all, does not amount to the sense that everything is rigidly determined by some web of causes or some set of sufficient conditions such that, given these conditions, no person, human or divine, could ever have acted differently in the slightest detail from the way he or she did act.

A part of the problem may relate to an ambiguity in the word *sufficient* in the principle. In speaking of a sufficient condition, perhaps what we mean is simply that the cause must not be too weak to bring about the effect, or the explanation too feeble to account for what it is supposed to explain. If someone attempts to explain why a large boulder went flying through the air by saying that a child flicked it into the air with her finger, we are likely to think that the explanation is not sufficient because the alleged cause is not powerful enough to bring about such an effect.

A cause may be sufficient in this sense without being sufficient in the deterministic sense, however. I may be strong enough to lift a certain weight — and thus the force of my muscles might be cited as a sufficient reason that the weight rises — but that does not mean I have no choice about whether or not I do lift it. Perhaps, in recognizing that things do not exist for no reason at all, we actually mean to affirm our intuition that certain conditions are *necessary* for the existence of certain things or the occurrence of certain events. A necessary condition for the existence of anything is a condition in the absence of which the thing does not exist. Oxygen and combustible materials are necessary conditions for fire. The conditions, in themselves contingent, are necessary *for the existence of the thing in question.* They are not necessary in themselves in the sense that God allegedly is a necessary being. The cosmological argument states further that a set of such contingent causes or conditions, or even an infinite succession of contingent causes, is not all that is necessary to explain the existence of the world as it is today. Only a being that exists necessarily in itself and not contingently would, according to the argument, suffice to account for the existence of the universe of contingent beings.

If such a thing as free choice, either human or divine, is to exist, then there never can be, in the strictest deterministic sense of the term, a sufficient reason for the free action of a person. Thus the claim that there is a sufficient reason for everything seems not only not a necessary truth, but no truth at all. That is, for an action freely chosen there *is* no sufficient reason, unless we construe the expression differently. There are necessary reasons, of course — namely, the set of conditions in the world on which the agent acts to bring about the outcome. Over and above these conditions, however, is the undetermined, free decision to act one way rather than another. It may be less confusing, then, to say that when we speak of the sufficient reason for a freely chosen action, what we actually mean is the antecedent necessary or requisite conditions *plus* the free act of will that, together, suffices to bring about what happens. If we are careful to remember that this is how we are using the word *sufficient* in the principle, it may be possible to reconcile our intuition of the plausibility of the principle with our portent of the falsity of determinism.

These considerations, important as they are, do not materially damage the principle of sufficient reason as it functions in the cosmological argument. The argument amounts to the claim that the existence of a world of contingent things and events requires an explanation and that the complete set of contingent conditions or the complete chain of contingent causes that constitutes the world does not add up to a sufficient explanation without the addition of the volition of a freely acting creative agent, God. Whether God is required to provide a sufficient explanation is a matter we have yet to examine, but the point that an explanation does seem to be needed appears clear enough. And this amounts to recognizing the primary claim embodied in the principle of sufficient reason. If the cosmological argument fails, then, the fault seems not to be with the principle of sufficient reason.

An Infinite Regression of Contingent Causes

Even if the existence of contingent beings does require explaining, however, might not the explanation be provided without resorting to extramundane causes such as God? The candidate most readily at hand is the succession of causal events we actually discover in nature. We do succeed in explaining the existence of many things by noting their relations to certain antecedent things. We explain the existence of an individual by pointing to his parents or the existence of a disease by showing that a certain microorganism is present. To be sure, we may ask what caused each of these things or events, but we are usually able to answer that question with another similar account. If we are to explain the existence of the whole world rather than simply some very local object in the world, we may say that the world as it exists today was caused by the world as it was yesterday, that world by its antecedent, and so on. Such a way of explaining seems to leave nothing unexplained, since an answer can be given each time the question "But what caused that?" is raised. Why is this explanation not enough?

And yet philosophers have resolutely insisted that an infinite regression of causes does not constitute a sufficient explanation. Many seem to think that an event is not fully explained until it has been traced to a cause that does not itself need explaining. St. Thomas Aquinas, who formulated three versions of the cosmological argument, insistently rejected the infinite regression of causes. He explains it thus:

> Now in efficient causes it is not possible to go on to infinity, because in all efficient causes following in order, the first is the cause of the intermediate cause, and the intermediate is the cause of the ultimate

cause, whether the immediate cause be several, or only one. Now to take away the cause is to take away the effect. Therefore, if there be no first cause among efficient causes, there will be no ultimate, nor any intermediate cause. But if in efficient causes it is possible to go on to infinity, there will be no first efficient cause, neither will there be an ultimate effect, nor any intermediate efficient causes; all of which is plainly false. Therefore it is necessary to admit a first efficient cause, to which everyone gives the name of God. [10]

An ambiguity is present here that Thomas apparently did not notice. It pertains to the meaning of *first cause*. Thomas tells us that if we take away the first cause, we take away the intermediate and thus the ultimate causes. In affirming an infinite regress of causes, however, and thus denying that there is a first cause, we are not taking away any cause. All we are doing is removing the status of first cause from some given cause. We can deny that any event or any state of the world at any given moment is the first cause by pointing to an earlier cause. If the succession is infinite, we never reach a first cause, but neither do we run out of causes. To be sure, if a very long chain is hanging by its first or top link and we "take away" that link, the rest of the chain will fall. But if the chain is of infinite length, no single link will have the status of first or top link, yet every link will be supported by another one farther back. So Thomas's objection seems ill founded. He has not demonstrated that there must be a first cause.

Contingency Entails Necessity

Still another reason has been put forward for insisting that there must be an extramundane necessary cause. Even if the succession of causes and effects is acknowledged to be infinite, the argument goes, it remains a contingent series. The world may have existed forever and its condition at any selected moment may be explicable by reference to an earlier moment, but it is still a contingent world and thus we may legitimately ask what explains the existence of the entire series. This is the sense of the claim made by advocates of the cosmological argument that "Contingency entails necessity; dependence entails independence, relativity entails absoluteness." If an infinite series is contingent, so they argue, it is contingent *on* something, and that something must not itself be contingent.

This way of putting the case was attacked in a celebrated argument by Paul Edwards,[11] who maintained that after every item in a set has been explained it is unreasonable to demand a further explanation of the set. Suppose we see five Eskimos standing on a street corner in New York and someone asks why they are there. We may discover that the first came to escape the extreme climate of the Arctic; the second is the spouse of the first and wanted to live where that person did; the third is the infant son of the first two; the fourth came to seek employment as a television actor; the fifth is a detective hired to watch the fourth. Thus we have explained why each Eskimo is in New York. But if someone, unsatisfied, insists on asking why the whole group is there, Edwards maintains that this would be unreasonable. When we have explained why each one is there, there is nothing more to explain.

Edwards makes a similar point elsewhere by referring to an infinitely tall stack of books. We explain what holds up a book by pointing to the book underneath it. In this way an explanation can be offered for any book selected. But it would be unreasonable, having shown what supports each book, to be asked to explain what holds up the whole stack. In explaining what holds up each book, we have provided all the explanation we need; there is nothing more to explain. Edwards believes that his examples provide arguments parallel to the cosmological argument so that by analogy we may say, when we have shown that the existence of all of the things that occur in the world can be explained by reference to their antecedent circumstances, it is unreasonable to insist that our explanation is incomplete because we have not provided a separate explanation of why there should be a world at all.

Some have found this conclusion unconvincing, claiming that the analogies are not really parallel. The example explains why each Eskimo is in New York, and so it would indeed be unreasonable to demand an additional explanation for why the whole group is there. But the example does not explain why there are Eskimos or books at all and that question, so the argument goes, is more nearly parallel to the question the cosmological argument attempts to answer.

Consider another example. Astronomers explain our solar system by reference to a cloud of gas that condensed into a sun and planets. The cloud of gas is explained as having precipitated out of a larger swirl constituting our galaxy through forces such as gravity. The process of explanation continues until the astronomers arrive at last at the hypothesis of a great explosion, the so-called "Big Bang," from which the gases that became ingredients in galaxies, solar systems, stars, and planets are thought to have come. When someone asks why there was a Big Bang, science finds itself up against a limit beyond which it cannot go. So far as empirical science can determine, there is no answer. We just do not know what existed before the Big Bang or why the great explosion occurred. But we do not conclude that it happened for no reason at all. The Big Bang may have been the beginning of the existence of the universe of contingent things, or it may not have. Whichever the case, we are forced to recognize the world as contingent and the Big Bang itself as just one contingent event in that series which constitutes the world.

Such a contingent world demands an explanation. Imagine that science were to become so prodigiously successful that it mapped out connections tracing each thing in the world to some antecedent causal conditions. In actual fact, science is very far from that point, but it represents the theoretical presumption of Edwards's analogies. Even if such a goal were to be achieved, however, this kind of connecting would allegedly still fall far short of providing the kind of explanation needed.

So the argument maintains that Edwards's examples just fail to meet the cosmological argument's most cogent point, that the existence of any contingent beings entails the existence of some being that is necessary and not contingent. And the failure of this argument is all the more evident when we notice that the appeal to an infinite regression clashes with scientific theory, which terminates in a first event that is itself contingent and quite unable to serve as a sufficient reason or explanation of the existence of the world. The Big Bang theory inevitably points beyond itself for a further explanation, and theists insist that that explanation must be a necessary and not a contingent being. There must, after all, be a sufficient reason or a first cause, they maintain, and it can only be God.

Is the First Cause God?

This attempt to turn back Edwards's attack on the cosmological argument is not without weight, but in the final analysis it does not seem to be decisive. His argument turns on the presumption that we never reach an event or state of affairs that cannot be explained by reference to another antecedent one. The theists, on the other hand, assume that the Big Bang is an event that cannot be referred to any antecedent event or state of affairs in the material world and that therefore must be explained by reference to something supermundane. But, this, in fact is not the only possibility. As we will see in Chapter 5, there are philosophical positions that postulate the eternal existence of the material world and propose explanatory principles that are completely naturalistic and make no appeal to anything supermundane. In the world depicted by such naturalistic philosophies, the succession of states of affairs would be genuinely infinite and thus Edwards's argument would work. If the material world is indeed eternal, then there would have been states of affairs antecedent to the Big Bang and we can explain it by reference to them.

In other words, if the cosmological argument succeeds in showing that the existence of a contingent world demands an explanation in terms of a sufficient reason — and we have found it plausible to concede that it does — it still does not show that the sufficient reason has to be a God. If by God we mean a being that is omnipotent, omniscient, morally perfect, and personal, the cosmological argument does not seem adequate to prove the existence of such a being. The first cause would certainly have to be powerful, and it is perhaps not implausible to suppose that it would need to be omnipotent, at least in the somewhat restricted sense of that term at which we arrived in Chapter 2. In the abstract, without considering the nature of the created world, it seems to remain an open question whether the sufficient reason for the existence of any contingent world needs to be wise, good, personal, or even a conscious being. We have not yet examined arguments that would undertake to rule out those characteristics, but it would certainly be too much to say that the cosmological argument by itself warrants affirming them. If naturalism turns out to be a plausible philosophical position, it may be just as reasonable to affirm that the universe itself is a necessary being—an eternally existing being not caused by anything else—as it is to make that claim about God.

Why Is God's Existence Not Also Contingent?

A final objection to the cosmological argument claims that it is contradictory to maintain on one hand that there must be a sufficient reason for the existence of whatever exists and then to say that no sufficient reason is required for God's existence. It might be alleged that this objection results from a lack of clarity about the meaning of the principle of sufficient reason. We have already discussed the ambiguity in the word *sufficient* and have stipulated a meaning designed to avoid the implications of determinism. Here the problem may possibly be avoided if we make explicit the meaning of *necessary existence* by formulating the principle thus: For the existence of everything there must be a sufficient reason, either intrinsic to it (in the case of a necessary being) or extrinsic to it (in the case of a contingent being).

It is the existence of contingent beings that demands explaining, not the existence of a necessary being. To say that a being is necessary means that it could not fail to exist. Its existence is not contingent and thus not contingent *on* something else; rather, the reason for its existence is intrinsic to it rather than extrinsic. This means that it depends only on itself for its existence or that it is independent of all other existing things. The medievals had an expression for it: God was said to be *causa sui*, the cause of itself. This means that God is the cause of itself not in the sense of having brought itself into existence, but in the sense of having existed eternally. Unlike all the other things that happen to exist but might not have existed and whose existence is contingent on the existence of something else, God's existence is necessary and not contingent on anything else. The first cause, then, is the kind of being that cannot fail to exist, whose nonexistence is impossible, and that in this sense is called *causa sui*. Thus, according to those who take this position, we may say in a certain sense that there is a sufficient reason for the existence of God, just as there is for the existence of contingent things, except that in the case of God the sufficient reason is to be found not in some other being but in the very nature of God itself.

The whole concept of a necessary being bristles with difficulties, as we have seen in our discussion of the ontological argument. But if we take it to mean *causa sui*, then the argument with which the previous section concluded becomes even more urgent. If the cosmological argument does indeed show us that there must be a sufficient explanation for the existence of the world and if it is a sufficient explanation of the existence of God to say that God is *causa sui*, why may we not say of the world itself that it is *causa sui*? If theism plausibly postulates that God has existed forever and is self-caused or not contingent on anything but itself, why may not the naturalist say the same of the world? It is an explanation that has the advantage of simplicity because, unlike theism, it does not involve the postulation of another being such as God.

To be sure, the claim that the world is eternal and that each temporal state of affairs in the world is explained by reference to an antecedent one does not explain why there is a world at all or why anything exists rather than nothing. But the theist position does not explain why there is a God. The question, "Why is there anything rather than nothing at all?" seems to be one that neither theism nor naturalism answers satisfactorily. The theist claims to have an answer: God's existence is self-explanatory. That explanation might be clear enough to God, but it does not help mere humans. Each approach ultimately reaches a limiting "why" question, and neither really has an answer. This means that the cosmological argument, even though it does show that there must be an explanation or sufficient reason for the existence of the world, does not succeed in establishing that that explanation must be God.

Summary

Before we turn to the teleological argument it may be helpful briefly to summarize our discussion. The cosmological argument rests on three main premises, namely, (1) the affirmation of the existence of contingent beings, (2) the principle of sufficient reason, and (3) the claim that the existence of a contingent world cannot be sufficiently explained by an infinite regression of contingent causes. The second and third of these premises raise serious problems. We have suggested, however, that the principle of sufficient reason can be understood in a way that avoids the objections usually brought against it by opponents of the cosmological argument, thereby clearing the way for acceptance of a clarified version of the principle. It follows that we must acknowledge the claim of the cosmological argument that the existence of a contingent world does demand an explanation.

The third premise does not fare as well. Edwards's analogies show that the objections against an infinite regression of causes are not insurmountable. Each contingent thing can be explained adequately if the material world is eternal and the regression truly infinite. The cosmological argument can be made to work, if at all, only if it can be shown that the universe is not eternal, for only then would some causal agency over and above the succession of contingent states of affairs be required to explain the beginning of the universe. Scientific theories about a Big Bang do not succeed in showing that the universe did actually have a beginning in time. Although we do not know that a succession of states of material affairs existed prior to the Big Bang, which could be cited as its cause, that supposition seems no less plausible than the theistic claim that a supernatural deity exists as the explanation. Thus the cosmological argument establishes the need for an explanation or a sufficient reason for the existence of the world, but it does not show that the explanation must be God.

THE TELEOLOGICAL ARGUMENT

We have seen that the ontological argument attempts to prove the existence of God from definitions and logical principles alone, without the use of empirical premises. The cosmological argument begins with an empirical premise — the claim that contingent things exist — but it is a claim that applies to any possible world and that does not depend on specific observations about the nature of the actual world. In a sense, then, the **teleological argument** is more thoroughly empirical, because it appeals to claims about observed regularities and order in our experience of the existing world. These observed regularities are used to argue that the world must be the product of an intelligent being who arranged the order for a purpose or to achieve an end. The name comes from the Greek concept of *telos,* which means end, goal, or purpose. Like the other arguments, the teleological argument has been put forward in a variety of forms. We may classify these many forms into two major types, one deductive and others inductive.

The Deductive Form

Some scholars, influenced especially by the philosophy of Aristotle, have distinguished a deductive and an inductive form of the teleological argument. Thomas Aquinas gives us the deductive form as his "fifth way."

> We see that things which lack knowledge, such as natural bodies, act for an end. . . . It is plain that they achieve their end, not fortuitously, but designedly. Now whatever lacks knowledge cannot move

toward an end, unless it be directed by some being endowed with
knowledge and intelligence; as the arrow is directed by the archer.
Therefore some intelligent being exists by whom all natural things
are directed to their ends; and this being we call God.[12]

Such nonsentient beings as acorns move resolutely and efficiently toward
becoming oak trees with no knowledge of what they are doing. Yet they
follow an orderly pattern that seems to mark out the one correct path
rather than any of the innumerable false paths that might have been taken.
This highly ordered pattern of growth certainly appears to be aimed toward
achieving the goal — of becoming an oak tree. Something other than the
acorn itself, that is, something that is conscious of the goal and of the path
that leads to the goal, must direct the development. This being that guides
nonsentient beings along correct, efficient paths to certain goals, the argument maintains, must be God.

The Inductive Forms

The inductive formulations of the teleological argument usually take the
form of an argument from analogy. The world is said to resemble in some
significant way an object known to be the product of intelligent creative
design. William Paley (1743–1805) and other eighteenth-century thinkers
liked to draw analogies between the orderly nature of the universe and such
deliberately designed artifacts as watches, weaving shuttles, and other
complex machines. Imagine, Paley suggests, that we are walking on some
island thought never before to have been visited by humans and we come
across a watch lying on the beach. It is a natural, virtually unavoidable,
inference that the watch was lost there by some human who had visited the
place before us. If someone were to suggest that on this island watches
occurred naturally, growing on trees or coming up out of the ground, surely
no one would give the suggestion a moment's consideration. Watches are
made by watchmakers; their many parts are all made and fitted together by
express forethought and design with the distinct purpose of constructing a
machine that will measure the time. Now the whole universe, the argument continues, bears a remarkable similarity to a watch; it, too, consists
of many parts, all of which fit together to form a pattern and design — and
one that is indeed vastly more intricate and astonishing than a watch's. It is
easy to read in the providential features of this order the purpose of providing a congenial place for human beings to live. Must we not infer that the
universe is likewise the product of intelligent design, and therefore that a
great "cosmic watchmaker," so to speak, a being like human designers but
much greater, exists as the creator of the world?

The argument has been elaborated in a variety of ways. Many other
objects besides watches have been cited as examples of intricate contriv-

ance and design and then used to argue for a divine designer. The eye is a favorite choice. The eye consists of many parts fitted together and made to mesh not only with one another but also both with the rest of the body and the world in which seeing animals live. It would strain credulity to the breaking point to suggest that the eye was not designed for the purpose of seeing. The eye, moreover, is only one of innumerable parts of the body, each of which might similarly be examined to discover the ingenious delicacy of contrivance in its structure and the marvelous ways in which it fits with other parts of the body and the environment to achieve certain goals or purposes. The suggestion that this entire order, these instances of parts fitted together into increasingly complex arrangements all cooperating to the attainment of ends, might be accidental or unconscious smacks of mystery or miracle mongering. The only reasonable explanation, the argument concludes, is that an intelligent being with objectives and goals in mind created the world, contriving both the orderly parts and the scheme they fit within to achieve those goals.

As we have seen, advocates of the teleological argument are fond of conjuring up imaginary scenarios whose consideration is supposed to convince us that the rejection of the notion of purpose and creative design is absurd. Imagine, they suggest, a thousand monkeys seated at a thousand typewriters for a thousand years. Pecking away with no knowledge of what they were doing and no purpose in mind, they would never produce so much as one of Shakespeare's sonnets, much less one of his plays or the whole corpus of his works. Yet the world is a corpus whose scale and grandeur dwarf Shakespeare's productions. Are we to admit that great creative genius was required to write Shakespeare's works and then assert that the universe just happened by chance, without conscious design or creative purpose? Is it not far more likely, these philosophers ask, that we could expect one of Plato's dialogues to be produced accidently by repeatedly tossing up boxes of printer's type than to imagine that the whole vast, intricate, composition that is the world could arise from the random, unguided, bouncing together of material particles? Not even a short poem or a simple story can be produced without design. Clearly the universe itself could never have arisen without a powerful and highly intelligent designer.

Hume's Devastating Criticisms

The teleological argument has traditionally been highly favored in the West, and it has not aroused the same levels of suspicion provoked by the ontological and, to a certain extent, the cosmological arguments. The argument is to be found in very rudimentary form in the Bible.[13] It also appears in the writings of such ancient authors as Cicero and Plato, in the works of St. Thomas and others in the Middle Ages, and in the thought of such persons as William Paley in the eighteenth, F. R. Tennant in the nineteenth, and Richard Swinburne in the twentieth centuries. But the teleological argument has also been the target of forceful attack.

Perhaps the most sustained and devastating criticism is to be found in the writings of David Hume (1711–1776). Hume brought to bear on the argument not only a very astute philosophical mind but also a keen and sprightly wit. The piquant humor with which he expressed his criticisms may initially obscure his objective to the uninitiated reader, but it also has the long-term effect of making the arguments seem even more powerful.[14]

The fundamental point of the several critical arguments offered by Hume is the weakness of all empirical arguments and particularly of arguments from analogy. Even the strongest argument based on generalization from sense experience falls short of demonstration. So the very best we can expect from the teleological argument, under the ideal circumstances, is a degree of probability. And if the empirical evidence is slim or the analogy remote, the degree will be very small. Hume's way of expressing this general point is as follows:

> Our ideas reach no farther than our experience. We have no experience of divine attributes and operations. I need not conclude my syllogism. You can draw the inference yourself.[15]

The inference, obviously, is that we have no ideas or knowledge of divine attributes and operations. It is a skeptical position that would tend to undermine all empirical arguments; indeed, Hume would be inclined to apply it to all theistic arguments. It does not demonstrate that God does not or could not exist. What it does attempt to show is that we never can have the kinds of experiences — experiences of divine attributes and operations — that would be necessary if we were to be justified in claiming to know that God exists.

But the teleological argument points to certain experiences that all humans do have, and it maintains that these experiences do constitute evidence that justifies inferring the existence of God. We all witness the order in nature, the ingenious contrivances of its various parts fitted together into a great machine operating in ways that unavoidably call to mind the deliberately designed machines that human intelligence creates. The analogy is so strong, proponents of the argument maintain, that we can hardly avoid inferring a divine designer as the creator of the world.

Hume attacks this inference from analogy with a series of counterarguments. He points out that the similarity between a watch and the whole universe is not, after all, very great. And because the analogy is so weak, the inference is likewise very weak. Furthermore, he reminds us, we are acquainted with only a tiny corner of the vast universe and quite imperfectly with that. Even if this small neighborhood of the cosmos that is our home is characterized by order suggesting an intelligent designer, may we validly infer from a tiny part to the whole? For all we know, other parts of the universe may not manifest order at all. At best, an inference from a small part to the whole is extremely hazardous and carries very little weight.

Moreover, Hume continues, when we do successfully argue from analogy, we do so on the basis of repeated observations of sequences of conjoined events. We notice that some one phenomenon is always accompanied by some other phenomenon, and then when we see the one before we see the other, we assume that it is there. But this cannot be done when we attempt to argue from apparent design in the universe to a designer. We have seen many watches or spinning shuttles, and we have seen them being made by human designers. But the universe is unique. We have not seen other universes, nor have we witnessed the creation of universes by gods. Only if we had would we be justified in inferring that this universe was created by a god.

But even if we grant the claim that the part of the universe that we observe does appear to have an order that suggests a designer, we are nonetheless not justified in inferring a designer that is God. Our conclusion should not exceed the evidence provided by the premises. The cause we infer on the basis of the observed effect cannot justifiably be greater than what would be required to produce the effect. The creation of the world we observe, however, does not seem to require an omnipotent, omniscient, morally perfect deity. Indeed, if we are to argue from analogy, we should infer a cause as much as possible like the causes involved in the analogy. We know that machines, ships, houses, and other products of intelligent human contrivance are often the product of many laborers working together. Perhaps, then, the teleological argument supports polytheism rather than monotheism. The world might be the project of a team of gods or godlings working together. Besides, we observe machines and other contrived objects being built by rather stupid workmen who imitate the work of earlier builders and whose ingenious machines are actually the result of a series of minor improvements introduced by various workers during many years of the evolution of machine making. Hume suggests that

> many worlds might have been botched and bungled, throughout an eternity, ere this system was struck out; much labor lost; many fruitless trials made; and a slow but continued improvement carried on during infinite ages in the art of world-making.[16]

Why may we not therefore be justified in inferring, he asks, that this universe might have been created by a rather dull-witted deity who learned his craft from other universe builders, who in turn evolved the art of building worlds by tiny accidental innovations over aeons of time? And if the analogy is to be a good one, Hume reminds us, the more similar the things compared, the better. Like effects argue like causes, he points out; thus, the liker the effects, the liker must be the causes. So if we argue from human creations like machines to the divine creation, the universe, we ought to suppose that the deity is very much like a human. This would mean a god with a body, faulty memory, a bent to sinning, and all the other features that humans, the cause of humanly designed machines, have.

Hume then takes a different tack, pointing out that design is only one of the causes of order in our experience. To be sure, human designers confer order on the machines they build by deliberate planning. But there are other examples of order in the world that display no signs of direct planning or designing. For example, a plant or animal confers order on its offspring, not through the process of design, but by procreating through vegetative or animate generation. Organisms confer order, the order of their own cells and organs, on the food they ingest by a process of digestion. These seem to be natural processes involving no forethought or design.

With this argument Hume to some degree anticipates a nineteenth-century argument derived from the Darwinian theory of natural selection. Before Darwin's time, it had often been argued that although an existing animal or plant might bestow on its progeny an order like its own through procreation, the existence of animals and plants in the first place is left entirely unexplained. Even if the biological world could sustain itself without extramundane care once it came into existence, nothing short of deity can adequately explain the creation of plants, animals, and humans in the first place. This argument was grounded in the belief that all species are fixed and never change.

Darwin showed us, however, that this is not true. More complex organisms arise through a gradual process of mutation and natural selection so that over long periods of time the nature of the organic world changes very substantially. The theory of evolution further reveals how the first, simplest organisms probably arose through modification by means of natural processes from inorganic substance. No extramundane deity is needed to explain the order that organisms confer on their progeny; and Darwin's findings seem to indicate that no deity is required to explain the origin of species or even the origin of life itself. This argument constitutes a challenge not only to the inductive, but particularly also to the deductive, form of the cosmological argument.

In a flash of wit Hume suggests that perhaps the universe is a vegetable that has sprouted from the seed of another vegetative universe; or that the world is a great animal brought into existence through a process of animal procreation. To be sure, the universe does not look very much like a vegetable or an animal — but then it does not look very much like a house or a watch, either. If we infer by means of remote and highly questionable analogies, we do not seem to be very greatly constrained in the conclusions we reach. But if the world has received such order as it has through some natural process analogous to vegetable or animal procreation — and Hume would certainly have mentioned natural selection if the process had been

known in his day — there is no need to infer the existence of a supermundane or divine cause. An axiom of philosophy, sometimes known
as *Ockham's razor* (from the work of William of Ockham, a thirteenth-
century British Franciscan philosopher), states that we should not multiply
causes beyond necessity or offer explanations that are more complex or that
postulate greater causes than needed to explain the phenomena in question. The suggestion that the order we notice in the world was conferred on
it by some natural process such as procreation appears to be a simpler hypothesis than the claim that an unknown supernatural divine being is the
cause.

Moreover, Hume reminds us, for all we know there may be a natural
principle of order in the world that functions without intelligent foresight
or supermundane intervention. It was formerly supposed that nothing
would ever move unless something else moved it — this was a premise of
one version of the cosmological argument. But now we know that there are
forces in nature, such as gravity and magnetism, that make bodies move,
and that organisms possess the power to move as a part of their nature. Is it
more extravagant to suggest that matter has within it a power of motion or
a principle of order than to introduce from outside the universe the notion
of an omnipotent deity? Indeed, Hume says, if the universe consists of a
finite number of particles, self-agitated in constant motion through infinite
time, they would necessarily take on every possible arrangement, including
the order that we now witness in the world. In fact, this given arrangement
of the world would arise, flourish, perish, and arise again an unlimited
number of times in the timeless swirl of the ingredients of the universe.
Even if this supposition is precluded by the existence of an infinite number
of particles or a finite stretch of time, the possibility remains that the order
we observe is the result of natural processes rather than supernatural design, and that suggestion has the advantage of simplicity.

Finally, Hume points out that order is not the only feature we observe
in the world. There is a very substantial and quite distressing amount of
disorder. Mechanisms operating in the world do mesh to provide conditions conducive to the existence of intelligent beings and the realization
of their values. But there are other mechanisms that operate in just the opposite direction, hindering, frustrating, hurting, and destroying. Here
Hume is raising the famous problem of evil, a matter of such seriousness
that we must set it aside until we can give it a detailed examination in
Chapter 4.

If the presence of order argues the existence of a designer, perhaps the
presence of disorder argues that no such designer exists; indeed, the widespread presence of evil at best seems to imply that no god exists and at worst
that the creator of the universe is a morally indifferent or even a wicked
deity. Or the admixture of order and disorder that seems so characteristic of
the world might suggest the work of an incompetent deity.

This world, for aught we know, is very faulty and imperfect, compared to a superior standard; and was only the first rude essay of some
infant deity who afterwards abandoned it, ashamed of his lame performance. It is the work only of some dependent, inferior deity, and is
the object of derision to his superiors. It is the production of old age
and dotage in some superannuated deity; and ever since his death has
run on at adventures.[17]

At the conclusion of a playful presentation of a series of very serious
philosophical arguments, Hume reflects on the outcome and concludes
that "the whole of natural theology . . . resolves itself into one simple . . .
proposition, *That the cause or causes of order in the universe probably bear
some remote analogy to human intelligence.*"[18] This outcome of natural theology, and of the teleological argument in particular, provides at best a modicum of support for theism, but the availability of other explanations for
order in the universe makes that evidence weak and indecisive.

What Can Argument from Analogy Prove?

Hume's formidable attack left the teleological argument severely battered,
and subsequent philosophers have been reluctant to put much trust in it.
The added force of Darwinian evolutionary theory virtually drove the argument from the field. It has remained for a few twentieth-century philosophers, such as Richard Swinburne, to attempt its rehabilitation.[19] A first
step toward an objective reassessment of the argument might be to notice
the extent to which Hume's arguments gain plausibility by the use of satire.
Many of his proposed counterexplanations of the order in the world are
clearly not serious suggestions. We cannot believe that Hume himself seriously thought that the universe might be a vegetable or an animal, that it
might have sprouted from a seed shed by another universe, or that it might
be the product of eons of universe making by dim-witted godlings gradually
improving their technique through trial and error. Neither should we fall
for the intimation that such proposals are really no more absurd than the
proposal that a divine person created the world and its order. Hume's attack
does raise some very serious and difficult objections against the teleological
argument, but its destructive effect is somewhat exaggerated by the rheto-
ric through which it is presented. Let us attempt to separate substance from
style and see what the major philosophical points are.

The fundamental objection that the teleological argument is weak because it is based on fallible empirical evidence is certainly a proper caveat,
but it applies to a large portion of what we call knowledge, including the
findings of science. Hume was aware of the wide net that his skeptical
philosophy cast — that it constituted a major attack on the methodology of
science, for example. The outcome has been a more careful approach to

empirical or inductive reasoning generally by both philosophers and scientists. Hume's principle that remote analogies serve to prove little is well taken, and his point that the analogy between a watch or a house and the whole universe is really not very close is an important one. But his skepticism has not undermined the progress of science nor convinced us that arguments based on empirical premises are of no worth at all. Instead, it has helped us to recognize the fallibility of much of our purported knowledge and the need to be modest and restrained about what we claim and pretend to know. Thus we recognize that inductive arguments based on empirical premises never yield absolute certainty, either in science or in theology. But at the same time we also recognize that they can and do contribute support for claims in a greater or lesser measure, depending on the type and amount of empirical evidence and the way in which that evidence fits together into more or less coherent explanatory schemes. Science is a fabric woven of just such evidence.

Indeed, a substantial portion of science is vulnerable to Hume's criticism about the uniqueness of the universe and the absence of repeated observations of patterns of phenomena. Hume's point is that we infer the presence of some unseen phenomenon on the basis of other observed phenomena because we have frequently seen the two conjoined in the past. We have seen lightning strike trees and leave a burned scar running down the trunk to the ground; when we see a tree with such a burned scar, therefore, we infer that it was caused by a lightning strike, even though we were not there to observe the strike. We have seen a certain set of symptoms accompanied by the presence of a certain microorganism in the person's physical system; when we see that set of symptoms again, we infer that the microorganism must be present. But we have not seen universes being designed and created by a god. The universe is unique, Hume points out; we cannot make any inference about how it came into existence because we have no previous experience of the creation of universes on which to base the inference. The fact that some parts of the universe look more or less vaguely like things whose design and creation we have observed is not sufficient to justify the inference.

Much of the content of several important branches of natural science, however, depends on inferences of just this sort. Geologists have not seen the drift of continents, the collision of land masses, nor the thrusting up of mountains by such forces, yet they infer that the continents have the shape they have and the mountains are there because of forces of this kind. Astronomers have not observed the several-million-year process of the condensation of clouds of gas into stars and solar systems, yet the most widely accepted theories make use of such reasoning. Biologists have not witnessed the evolution of complex life forms from simpler ones or the synthesis of simple organisms from inorganic materials, but we are convinced that this process actually took place.

If such inferences are justified in the sciences, then, why are they to be rejected in theology? To be sure, many scientific theories are less sweeping than the hypothesis of theism—although some of the most fundamental theories in astronomy approach it in magnitude. The evidence used by geology and biology may plausibly be said to be more detailed and less impressionistic than that cited by theists, but many persons find the similarities striking. If these several sciences are justified in reaching their conclusions on the basis of empirical arguments of this kind, by parity of reasoning it appears that theology is justified in reaching its conclusions.

Of course, Hume's point about the fallibility of empirical evidence applies to both fields. The findings of science are established with varying degrees of probability, not with certainty. Since the evidence used by the teleological argument may be said to be vaguer, more sweeping, less detailed, and less subject to the various controls used by science, its conclusion must certainly be conceded as undemonstrated, and even as weaker than some of the findings of science. But even granting all this, some philosophers believe that a residue of evidential support remains that, as Swinburne puts it, "increases significantly the probability that there is a God, even if it does not by itself render it probable."[20] When this evidence is combined with evidence from other arguments, Swinburne thinks it may add up at the very least to a justification of the claim that the existence of God is in some measure probable.

But two other of Hume's objections remain: the suggestion that the universe may contain its own natural principle of order and thus require no supernatural designer, and the point that even if an extramundane cause is required, it need not be God. Unfortunately, Hume's version of the first objection is badly stated and amounts to little more than an argument from ignorance.

> We dare not affirm that we know all the qualities of matter; and, for aught we can determine, it may contain some qualities which, were they known, would make its non-existence appear as great a contradiction as that twice two is five.[21]

This, however, is almost like impugning a person's character by arguing that although he was never known to have committed any indiscretion, his personality might, "for aught we can determine," contain some qualities that, were they known, would make us ready to accuse him. Perhaps, "for aught we can determine," the world may exist necessarily and require no cause, or may contain within it the principle of order that would account for the order we observe.

To argue from the supposition that the world may exist necessarily to the claim that an alternative explanation is unjustified is at least as promiscuous a mode of inference as that involved in the teleological argument. Hume himself elsewhere condemns arguments of this kind. To say that the universe manifests order because it contains within it a principle of order is not unlike saying that a sleeping pill induces sleep by a soporific power that is part of its nature. This amounts not to an explanation, but merely to using big words to say what has already been said in small ones. Perhaps the universe does indeed exist necessarily, "for aught we know." Perhaps the order we observe is only the result of a natural principle of order in the universe. But the suggestion is no more than a supposition, and we are entitled to ask what reason, if any, there is for thinking that it is true. A certain newly discovered illness might, "for aught we know," be caused by demon possession. But the alternative explanation that it is probably caused by a virus or a bacterium is surely more plausible in the absence of some evidence for demon possession. Similarly, many theists argue, the suggestion that the universe and the order it contains are caused by a being who planned and intended to cause it seems more plausible, even though its truth cannot be demonstrated with certainty, than Hume's alternative suggestion.

Even so, Hume's position asks, must that being be God? Perhaps the existence of a material universe, even a fairly impressive one characterized by ingenious patterns of order and planning, would not require as its cause a being who is omnipotent, omniscient, and morally perfect. On this point Hume seems to be right. The teleological argument by itself, even if it does provide a measure of support for belief in an extramundane cause of the universe's existence and order, does not seem to require that we infer a being with all of the divine attributes. Indeed, it might not even require a conscious being at all. If the being whose existence theism sets out to establish is God, theism will have to call on evidence beyond that provided by the teleological argument to prove that point. Perhaps what this argument does demonstrate is not that the existence of the God of theism has been shown to be probable, but rather that theism has been shown to be a plausible hypothesis in conjunction with alternative naturalistic hypotheses that grow out of science. The plausibility of the alternatives remains to be examined, however, and is one of the subjects of Chapter 5. Whether Hume's point about disorder and evil in the world is serious enough to rule out a creator who is God will be considered when we turn our attention to the problem of evil in Chapter 4.

THE MORAL ARGUMENT

The German philosopher Immanuel Kant argued that the existence of God cannot be demonstrated and that the arguments designed to prove God's existence lead to inconsistencies. He further suggested, however, that although we cannot know whether or not God exists, the postulation of a divine being can make intelligible certain aspects of human experience, particularly our experience of moral obligation, that would otherwise be a mystery. The suggestion came to be regarded as an argument for the existence of God, and it enjoyed special popularity among theistic philosophers, who found themselves unable to trust the traditional arguments in the face of Hume's criticisms.

This **moral argument** was given several formulations by its supporters. One argues from the presupposed existence of objective moral law to the existence of a divine lawgiver. Another states that if the moral perfection to which our moral sense or conscience unavoidably calls us is to be realizable, the universe must have a moral order and a moral sponsor. A third form argues that humans in all ages and all parts of the world, despite great differences in their living circumstances, agree in certain fundamental ways about what morality demands, and that such concord can only be explained by the existence of a divine being that communicates a universal moral law to all.

The absolute and uncompromising nature of moral principles is sometimes cited as evidence that they must come from a source beyond human authority. Conscience sometimes summons us to oppose the laws of human society, the expectations of public opinion, even the moral teachings of one's own religion. But no human source is authoritative enough justifiably to make such demands. Thus, the argument concludes, the voice of conscience must be the voice of God. The clear summons of moral law points to a supreme moral lawgiver and judge.

Moreover, the demands of morality that our moral sense presses unavoidably on us are so great that they could never be realized in the short span of a lifetime spent in a world such as ours, where the correlation of moral good and evil with consequences in the lives of the moral agents is so imperfect. Morality calls us to strive for nothing less than the moral perfection of ourselves and of the world. If the mundane world is the sum total of reality, that call is a mocking summons to futility. But humankind's moral sensitivity is its most exalted capacity, and we cannot believe that the highest ideals to which morality beckons us are empty fantasies. It follows that there must be another life beyond this one in which our struggles toward moral perfection meet more dependably and regularly with success and where the vision of a creation made whole can become a reality. This means that in the long run the universe itself must support morality as it does not always seem to do in this life. And that requires a moral governor who watches over the process and guarantees that, ultimately, wrongs are righted and the fruition of moral striving achieved.

Finally, widespread human concord on the basic demands of morality strongly suggests that these demands issue from a common source, a divine being who is moral teacher as well as governor and judge. The tremendous range of variation of customs, beliefs, languages, religion, social structure, and cultural practices that characterizes the human race would lead us to expect an equally wide range of moral beliefs. Surprisingly, this is not what we find. Although a superficial view of human societies might suggest widely differing moral expectations, closer scrutiny reveals remarkable similarities about the central issues of morality. The most plausible explanation of this similarity, amid the diversity of other beliefs and practices, is a divine being who communicates the demands of morality to all peoples. Any small measure of variation can be explained by suggesting that not all peoples understand equally well the divine commands and by pointing to the convergence toward agreement among those who take the trouble to reflect carefully on moral questions.

Few, if any, philosophers have regarded the moral argument as a totally compelling one. Most have agreed that at best it offers a measure of support for theism. Critics of the moral argument have found it very weak, some suggesting that it would appeal only to those who already believed in God for other reasons. The presupposition of the objective existence of morality on which the argument is based has been seriously questioned by persons who believe that morality is subjective, the expression merely of cultural or personal preferences. The form of the argument that hinges on the alleged remarkable similarity of moral beliefs in all ages and societies is rejected by many, who claim that diversity and not similarity is the most characteristic feature of moral belief and practice. The defiance of all human laws and institutions to which morality allegedly sometimes calls might be no more than a stubborn illusion grounded in the conviction that our beliefs are right and everyone else's wrong. After all, persons sometimes justify blatantly immoral behavior by claiming to have heard the voice of God, when the most enlightened moral reasoning convinces us that it is the voice of the devil—or, to speak less metaphorically, the voice of a mistaken or demented human mind.

Further, the claim that the universe must support the human demand for moral perfection has been characterized by critics as wishful thinking not justified by actual experience. An even more serious objection to what has been called the "divine command" theory of morality states that it either reduces God to an arbitrary tyrant or else renders the claim that God is good unintelligible. These two criticisms must await the more detailed examination of the relation of religion to ethics in Chapter 7.

The fact that all humans appear to be basically alike in their physical constitution, that all share certain fundamental needs, and that their physical and mental capacities in every age and place seem to be essentially similar might suffice to account for the fact that all human societies recognize moral demands and for such moral similarity as we find from one society to another. We do not appeal to a divine lawgiver to explain the fact that humans everywhere discover the same laws of mathematics and logic. If there are universal moral principles analogous to the universal laws of mathematics and logic—and there is good reason to believe that there are—perhaps this likewise requires no divine explanation. If the other arguments suffice to convince us that God's existence is probable, the moral argument may add a measure of strength to our conviction, since our experience of morality is certainly compatible with theism and meshes nicely with it, but for persons not already otherwise convinced, this argument will probably not suffice.

THE PRAGMATIC ARGUMENT

The **pragmatic argument**, which is basically a voluntaristic position, has been advanced particularly by the French philosopher Blaise Pascal (1623–1662) and the American psychologist and philosopher William James (1842–1910). It is not so much an argument designed to establish the truth of the claim that God exists as it is an attempt to provide justification for choosing to adopt a belief in God.

Pascal's Wager

Pascal is convinced that reason is quite unable to discover by its own powers anything about the nature or the existence of God. The traditional proofs prove nothing, either affirmatively or negatively. But he is equally convinced that it is not possible simply to leave the question undecided. We must make a wager, he tells us. It is not optional. Thus Pascal urges us to decide the matter in a practical way by calculating the potential gains and losses which might accompany each choice. If we believe in God and the belief is true, our gain is infinite felicity and bliss, for if God exists and we believe in him, he will grant us eternal salvation. If we believe and the belief is false, the loss is minimal. On the other hand, if we refuse to believe and turn out to be wrong, our loss is infinite since eternal salvation is forfeited, whereas if we refuse to believe and turn out to be right our gain is trivial. We have, in other words, everything to gain and nothing to lose by believing. We are therefore well advised to make the wager and believe.

Pascal recognizes that we cannot always induce belief by merely deciding to do so, so he proceeds to make some suggestions concerning what we may do to get ourselves to believe. He recommends that we behave as if we did believe, by "taking the holy water and having masses said, etc."[22] And he assures us that we will come to a saving knowledge of God by these means, as so many other Christians have before us.

James's Will to Believe

William James agrees with Pascal that we have everything to gain and nothing to lose by believing. James distinguishes several kinds of belief options that we face. Some options are relatively trivial, others are momentous. For any given person some are living options—options that appeal as real possibilities—and some are dead. And some options are forced—that is, you must make a choice since refusal to choose constitutes a negative choice—whereas others are avoidable. An option that is living, forced, and momentous is a *genuine* option, James says. The option presented to us by theism, he further states, is a genuine one. It represents for us a real possibility, one about which we cannot remain neutral since not to choose God is to reject him. And it is momentous because the potential gains and losses are infinite.

James is careful to point out that he is not arguing that we have the right to believe anything that makes us feel good. When options can be decided on the basis of evidence, we must believe what the evidence supports, whether it is decisive or only slightly stronger on one side than the other. When options are not genuine ones, if the evidence is evenly balanced we are justified in suspending belief and waiting until more evidence accumulates. But the choice between believing or not believing in God is forced, living, and momentous; it is a genuine option. We cannot suspend judgment. Neither, as it turns out, can we simply follow the evidence, because the evidence is fairly evenly balanced. In such situations, James urges, we are entitled to consult our feelings, what he calls our "passional nature," in deciding what we will believe, choosing the belief that will have the most beneficial consequences for our lives:

> The thesis I defend is... this: *Our passional nature not only lawfully may, but must, decide an option between propositions, whenever it is a genuine option that cannot by its nature be decided on intellectual grounds.* [23]

James is aware that some persons regard such a procedure as morally objectionable. He refers to W. K. Clifford's insistent claim that we can never, under any circumstances, be morally justified in believing anything on insufficient evidence. But Clifford's obsessive fear of error, James suggests, leads him to such a cautious attitude toward belief that he makes himself vulnerable to a loss of much truth. James points out that we will inevitably believe a lot of things that are not true simply because the reach of our understanding is so small and so many things remain to be found out. We should therefore take a rather more lighthearted attitude toward error. Far better to bet on the side of a belief that, if it turned out to be true, would bring great benefit, than to risk losing that benefit for the sake of avoiding possible error. Thus when the option is genuine and the evidence is indecisive, we are justified in exercising what James calls our *will to believe* on the side of the belief most beneficial to us.

Clearly, the pragmatic approach is not an additional argument for the existence of God parallel to the others we have been considering. It is not designed to support the truth of the claim that God exists. Rather, the pragmatic approach is an attempt to show that even if God's existence cannot be proved, we may still justifiably believe in God. But the critics of the argument claim that it fails even to justify belief. It amounts, they say, merely to an assertion, not a proof, that belief is justified. Yet Pascal's approach is more explicitly nonrational than James's: Pascal denies that reason is capable of dealing with the question of God's nature or existence and thus concludes that evidence and reasoning are irrelevant to the issue. James, on the other hand, recognizes that there is evidence to support belief in God but points out that there is equal evidence to support nonbelief. If one side could show even a tiny surplus of evidence over the other, James would insist that our belief be determined by that evidence. It is because the evidence is so evenly balanced and thus not capable of determining our belief that we are justified in following our "passional" feelings, rather than our rational nature, in this case. Nevertheless, James's pragmatic argument does not constitute support for the truth of theism. The best that it can do is provide some measure of justification for a decision to hold a belief even though that belief is not upheld by the evidence.

CONCLUSION

We have examined the major philosophical arguments that theists have usually used to support their position. All except the pragmatic approach are rational arguments intended to prove or to support the claim that God exists. The pragmatic position is not so much a theistic argument as an attempt to justify adopting theism on other than rational grounds. Three other kinds of arguments supporting theism will be briefly mentioned here, pending more detailed discussion in later chapters: religious experience, revelation, and miracle.

Other Theistic Arguments

The argument from **religious experience** is another empirical argument that attempts to infer the existence of God from certain aspects of human experience — but in this case, experiences alleged to be of a very special kind. Sometimes the claim is made that certain individuals have direct encounters with God and thus know God, as it were, face to face. Such experiences are very powerful and tend to be completely self-certifying for those who have them. Even religious or mystical experiences that involve no direct encounter with God often seem to provide unmistakable evidence for God's existence to the persons who have them. Certainly, if such experiences are literally what the persons who have them believe they are, they do constitute very powerful evidence for theism — or for some kind of God belief, such as pantheism, when the experiences are of certain kinds.

These experiences, however, are private, and the persons who have them uniformly tell the rest of us that they cannot really be communicated to persons who have not had them. And the experiences themselves are capable of being interpreted in several different ways, not all of them supportive of theism. Because these experiences have played such an important role in most of the major religions of the world, they will be given detailed and careful treatment in Chapter 6.

Several of the great religions of the world point to sacred writings or scriptures containing the core of their teachings that are alleged to have been communicated to humans by divine revelation. The Qur'an, the holy scriptures of Islam, is supposed to have been revealed by Allah to Muhammad, who wrote down and preserved the sacred revealed truths. The Hebrew and Christian scriptures are also alleged to be revelations of divine truth, although not dictated all at once to a single person. Some believers make very strong claims about their holy writings: that they are literally the words of God and that they are literally true in every detail. Others make more moderate, but still strong, claims: that their scriptures were written by humans inspired by God or guided by the Holy Spirit of God. Still others regard the holy writings as materials that reveal through metaphor or myth important truths about reality that justify our holding an attitude of reverence toward creation or a belief that there is a divine dimension or quality in the world. Many of these claims, if they could be authenticated, would provide evidence stronger or weaker in support of theism. Because revelation in most of its forms is actually a special kind of religious experience, we will have a closer look at it in Chapter 6.

Miracles have also often been cited as evidence for the existence of God. **Miracles** are supposed to be events that deviate from, or violate, the normal routines of nature, that are the sorts of things which only a deity could cause. Clearly, any such occurrence would be very strong evidence for the existence of God. But the claims made about miracles have serious problems that need to be examined in more detail. This we will do in connection with our discussion of religion and science in Chapter 4.

Assessing the Arguments

We began by noting that some thinkers insist that the existence of God can be proved, using the word *proof* in the very strict sense of a valid argument whose premises are known to be true. Our examination of the so-called proofs or arguments for theism seems to lead to the conclusion that none of them amounts to a proof in that strict sense. We found it more profitable to speak, not of strict proofs, but of good reasons that support or justify accepting or rejecting beliefs.

St. Thomas held that the ontological argument is a proof in the very strictest sense, but he said that only God could know that the premises are true and therefore that it is such a proof. Other critics of the ontological argument urged plausibly that we never can prove the existence of anything by arguing only from its definition and that arguments with existential conclusions must have at least one existential premise. Rejecting this position, as some thinkers do, opens up the possibility for an ontological proof, and equally for an ontological disproof—but neither seems yet to have received a satisfactory formulation. Thus, though the ontological argument remains a matter of fascination for many philosophers, it also remains a matter of dispute. For that reason we cannot look to it for any substantial help in establishing the truth of theism.

The cosmological argument includes a general existential premise about the contingent nature of any possible world and attempts to argue to a necessary being as the cause—or at least to an actually existing being as the ultimate cause. But problems with the notion of necessary being, and the argument that the universe could be an infinite series of causal conditions that might require no extramundane cause, weakened the argument considerably. At the very best, the cosmological argument shows that the world requires an explanation and that the theistic explanation might be a plausible one, but since plausible naturalistic alternatives also exist that the argument is unable to eliminate, it fails to establish the existence of God.

The teleological argument, because it is empirical, suffers from the weaknesses that characterize all empirical arguments. Certain of its advocates, however, have succeeded in putting it forward in plausible forms and in defending it from the most devastating of Hume's criticisms. The argument certainly does not prove the existence of God, but it does make plausible the claim that the universe is characterized by a measure of design, and this suggests that an extramundane explanation of the cosmic order might be a reasonable supposition. We noted, however, that this design could be explained without postulating a being possessing all of the characteristics of God, and thus that the argument would need supplementing if the cause of the universe is to be shown to be God. Indeed, the evidence brought forward by the teleological argument seems to be consistent with naturalistic explanations that make no use of any postulated supernatural being. The plausibility of these explanations will be discussed in Chapter 6.

The moral argument turned out not to be a very strong one for establishing the claim that God exists, but the points which it brings forward are compatible with theism. They harmonize with theistic teachings and render them more intelligible—perhaps in a small measure more plausible—provided those teachings have been accepted on other grounds.

The pragmatic argument does nothing to strengthen the theistic position, but it does support taking a religious attitude of faith toward theism. For the religious person it may be valuable; for the philosopher seeking to prove God's existence it offers little help.

Once we have examined religious experience, revelation, and miracles more closely, we will be in a better position to judge whether or not any of them offers support for theistic claims. For now, however, we must conclude that no proof of God's existence has been discovered and that the arguments we have thus far considered leave theism at best only very tenuously supported. Certainly none shows that theism is required by reason. If it is proper at this point to say that theism is a reasonable belief, it is only in the sense that thus far we have also not encountered an argument showing that theism is forbidden by reason. We turn now to an examination of the arguments raised against theism.

ANNOTATED GUIDE TO FURTHER READINGS

General

Mackie, J. L. *The Miracle of Theism.* Oxford: Clarendon Press, 1982.

A comprehensive survey of the arguments for the existence of God. Hume, Descartes, Berkeley, and Swinburne among others are given special attention. Mackie's own position is skeptical.

Rowe, William L., and Wainwright, William J., ed. *Philosophy of Religion: Selected Readings*, 2nd ed. New York: Harcourt Brace Jovanovich, 1989.

Contains an excellent collection of readings dealing with the ontological, cosmological, teleological, and moral arguments. The section on the ontological argument provides a particularly good introduction; it contains Anselm's argument and Gaunilo's response, selections from Descartes and Plantinga, and Kant's attack upon the argument.

Swinburne, Richard, *The Existence of God.* Oxford: Clarendon Press, 1979.

A somewhat technical analysis of the topic. Swinburne thoroughly examines the evidence for the existence of God, including traditional proofs as well as arguments based on historical and religious experience.

The Ontological Argument

Hartshorne, Charles. *The Logic of Perfection.* La Salle, Ill.: Open Court, 1962.

Chapter 2 of this book extensively examines various forms of the ontological argument. Hartshorne's analysis, although somewhat technical at times, is excellent; he thoroughly discusses most of the arguments and counterarguments.

Hick, John, and McGill, Arthur C., ed. *The Many-Faced Argument.* New York: Macmillan, 1967.

This comprehensive study of the traditional ontological argument focuses on the writings of St. Anselm but also deals with the more recent reformulations of the argument.

Plantinga, Alvin. *The Nature of Necessity.* Oxford: Clarendon Press, 1974.

Plantinga looks at the concept of necessity in this challenging book. Through such means as the notion of possible worlds, Plantinga creates a solid foundation for the understanding of the term necessity, *using this framework to examine the ontological argument.*

Plantinga, Alvin, ed. *The Ontological Argument.* Garden City, N.Y.: Doubleday, 1965.

A collection of essays tracing the ontological argument from its beginnings (Anselm, Aquinas, and Descartes) through contemporary times (Moore, Alston, Hartshorne, Malcolm). Especially intriguing is the piece by J. N. Findlay, in which he tries to disprove the existence of God by turning the ontological argument back on itself.

The Cosmological Argument

Craig, William Lane, *The Cosmological Argument from Plato to Leibniz.* New York: Barnes and Noble, 1980.

Craig gives a comprehensive history of the cosmological argument, then distinguishes arguments of three different types: those based on the principle of determination, those based on the principle of causality, and those based on the principle of sufficient reason.

Kenny, Anthony. *The Five Ways.* Notre Dame, Ind.: University of Notre Dame Press, 1969.

Kenny recounts and analyzes Aquinas's five ways to prove the existence of God: The first four of these ways are forms of the cosmological argument and the fifth is the deductive form of the teleological argument. Aquinas's writings form a vital part of the basic historical foundation of the cosmological argument and are important to the study of the argument.

Rowe, William L. *The Cosmological Argument.* Princeton, N.J.: Princeton University Press, 1975.

An excellent source for analysis. Rowe first discusses the various forms of the argument and then examines some of its faults.

The Teleological Argument

Hume, David. *Dialogues Concerning Natural Religion,* edited by John Valdimir Price. Oxford: Clarendon Press, 1976.

In this classic contribution to the philosophy of religion, Hume levels devastating criticism against the teleological and cosmological arguments.

Paley, William. "The Watch and the Watchmaker." In *Philosophy of Religion: An Anthology,* edited by Louis P. Pojman. Belmont, Calif.: Wadsworth, 1987.

Paley's famous analogy. This section of Pojman's text also has a fine article by Swinburne and an excerpt from Hume.

The Moral Argument

Adams, Robert Merrihew. "Moral Arguments for Theistic Belief." In *Rationality and Religious Belief*, edited by C. F. Delaney. Notre Dame, Ind.: University of Notre Dame Press, 1979.

> *Through the framework of the divine command theory, Adams discusses the existence and nature of God. He talks about two types of moral arguments for the existence of God, the theoretical (which tries to prove that God exists) and the practical (which seeks to show that it is morally desirable to believe in God).*

Kant, Immanuel, *Critique of Practical Reason*. New York: Bobbs-Merrill, 1956.

> *In book II, chapter II, Kant explains the role his dialectic of pure practical reason plays in establishing the concept of a highest good, and then interprets the highest good as God. Although God's existence cannot be proven, if we postulate that God exists we are able to understand morality as commanded and made possible by God.*

The Pragmatic Argument

Cargile, James. "Pascal's Wager." In *Contemporary Philosophy of Religion*, edited by Steven M. Cahn and David Shatz. New York: Oxford University Press, 1982.

> *Cargile denigrates the importance of Pascal's pragmatic argument for religious belief by saying that realistically it probably will not sway anyone's opinion.*

James, William. "The Will to Believe," in *The Will to Believe and Other Essays*. New York: Dover Publications, 1956.

> *In this famous essay James argues that, in cases where a decision has to be made about a very important issue and the evidence is evenly balanced, we are entitled to exercise our "will to believe" and affirm the belief that is more encouraging or more consistent with our desires. When the evidence is stronger on one side or the other, we must follow the evidence in our believing.*

NOTES

1. René Descartes, *Meditations on First Philosophy*, in *Discourse on Method and Meditations*, trans. by Laurence J. Lafleur (Indianapolis: Bobbs-Merrill, 1960), p. 121.

2. Immanuel Kant, *Critique of Pure Reason*, trans. by N. K. Smith (London: Random House, 1964), p. 503.

3. Richard Swinburne, *The Coherence of Theism* (Oxford: Clarendon Press, 1977), p. 27.

4. See Charles Hartshorne, *Anselm's Discovery* (La Salle, Ill.: Open Court, 1965) and *The Logic of Perfection* (La Salle, Ill.: Open Court, 1962).

5. Norman Malcolm, "Anselm's Ontological Arguments," *The Philosophical Review* (January 1960), reprinted in John Hick, ed., *The Existence of God* (New York: Macmillan, 1964).

6. Alvin Plantinga, *The Nature of Necessity* (Oxford: Clarendon Press, 1974).

7. Alvin Plantinga, *God, Freedom and Evil* (New York: Harper & Row, 1974), p. 112.

8. A celebrated argument, put forward by J. N. Findlay, attempted to turn the ontological argument on its head and prove the nonexistence of God. Although the argument enjoyed great currency for a while, it is now regarded as seriously faulty (some would say simply a piece of sophistry) and decisively refuted. See Findlay's presentation of the argument: "Can God's Existence Be Disproved?" in Antony Flew and Alasdair MacIntyre, eds., *New Essays in Philosophical Theology* (London: SCM Press, 1955), p. 48. This book also contains some of the counterarguments that finally convinced Findlay that his argument does not work.

9. David and Marjorie Haight, "An Ontological Argument for the Devil," *The Monist* 54 (1970): p. 218–20.

10. St. Thomas Aquinas, *Summa Theologica,* from *The Basic Writings of Saint Thomas Aquinas,* edited by Anton C. Pegis (New York: Random House, 1945), part I, question 2.

11. Paul Edwards, *The Cosmological Argument* (New York: Doubleday, 1967), pp. 113f. Originally published in *The Rationalist Annual,* 1959.

12. St. Thomas Aquinas, *Summa Theologica.*

13. E.g., Jeremiah 33:25ff; Romans 1:20.

14. See especially David Hume, *Dialogues Concerning Natural Religion* (Indianapolis: Hackett, 1980), one of the most brilliant and amusing pieces to be found among the writings of philosophers.

15. Ibid., p. 15.

16. Ibid., p. 36.

17. Ibid., p. 37.

18. Ibid., p. 88. Hume's italics.

19. See, for example, Richard Swinburne, *The Existence of God* (London: Oxford University Press, 1979).

20. Ibid., p. 150.

21. Hume, *Dialogues Concerning Natural Religion,* p. 56.

22. Blaise Pascal, *Pensées,* trans. A. J. Krailsheimer (New York: Penguin Books, 1968), p. 152.

23. William James, *The Will to Believe and Other Essays* (New York: Dover, 1956), p. 11. James's italics.

4

Objections to Theism

Our examination of theism in the previous two chapters has covered the major characteristics usually attributed to God by theists and the principal arguments usually put forward to support the claim that the God of theism actually exists. We have also made note of some counterarguments against the theistic arguments. We will now consider three of the most serious and threatening types of objections raised against the claim that such a being as God exists.

THE PROBLEM OF EVIL

Nearly everyone, theist and nontheist alike, recognizes that evil and suffering, so pervasive in human life, constitute a very grave threat to the rational acceptability of theism. Some are convinced that there is simply no way to reconcile the great-making attributes of God with a world filled with suffering. Even those who hold fast to a belief in a powerful and morally perfect deity recognize that evil requires an explanation that exonerates God and preserves the divine character. If theism is to present itself as a position acceptable to reasonable persons, it must confront and answer the **problem of evil**.

The Allegedly Inconsistent Tetrad

The problem of evil can be stated in its starkest form by means of an *inconsistent tetrad*,[1] a set of four propositions all of which a theist would seem obliged to accept but that seem to involve a contradiction. The first three propositions simply affirm the three central great-making attributes of God that we examined in Chapter 2, and the fourth points out and affirms the existence of evil.

1. God is omnipotent.
2. God is omniscient.
3. God is morally perfect.
4. Evil exists.

If God is omnipotent, then God should be able to prevent evil if he knows about it and wishes to do so. If God is omniscient, then God knows about evil. If God is morally perfect, God would prevent evil if he could. And yet there plainly is evil in the world. Any three of the propositions can be affirmed, but the affirmation of any three implies the falsity of the other one. The assertion of 1, 2, and 3 seems to imply the falsity of 4; the assertion of 1, 2, and 4 seems to imply the falsity of 3; the assertion of 1, 3, and 4 seems to imply the falsity of 2; and so on. If God is omnipotent, omniscient, and morally perfect, then the world God would create should contain no evil. If the world created by a God who is all powerful and all knowing contains evil, then that God must not be morally perfect. It seems impossible for all four statements to be true at the same time, but traditional theism affirms the first three and can hardly avoid acknowledging the fourth. The conclusion some philosophers draw from this problem is that theism is false and therefore that God does not exist.

Theists usually try to show that the tetrad is not inconsistent by devising a way of reconciling the four statements. Their opponents, however, insist that such a move is impossible. Contradictory statements cannot, by some clever device or argument, be made not to contradict one another. Of course, there is a very easy way to solve the problem, namely, by giving up one or another of the statements, but most theists are unwilling to do this. If it were conceded that God is not omnipotent, then the existence of evil could be explained by saying that God is not powerful enough to prevent it. Or if God is not omniscient, evil might exist because God did not know about it or did not know how to prevent it. God might even deliberately cause evil to exist, but this seems to imply that God is not morally perfect.

Some theists have been willing to give up the fourth proposition. If no evil exists, then no problem of evil exists. St. Augustine (354–430), who saw the problem of evil as the death knell for theism unless it could be answered, argued that we should recognize that evil is not anything real but is only the privation of good. Just as there is no such real thing as darkness, there is no such real thing as evil. Darkness is nothing more than the

absence of light; evil, nothing more than the absence of good. Every existing thing that God has created, Augustine insisted, is good. What we call
evil is not some real thing God has created but is simply the absence or the
privation of good.

Other thinkers have taken an even more extreme position. It has
sometimes been argued that what we call evil is an illusion, a result of the
finiteness of human understanding, or a blindness caused by human sin.
The concept of *maya* in Hinduism involves the notion that certain human
beliefs and perceptions are actually illusory and that the quest for enlightenment or salvation consists in an effort to overcome illusion and see reality as it really is. Success in that effort yields the realization that there really
is no evil; that evil, suffering, and the separation of human from divine are
all errors or illusory perceptions. It is not that we need to destroy evil and
strive for the perfection of the world; the world is already perfectly good.
What we need to do is to overcome our ignorance, which misleads us into
thinking that there is evil, so that we can actually recognize the reality of
the perfection that already exists. Christian Science seems to teach a somewhat similar doctrine: that disease is unreal, the result of ignorance or
imperfect understanding and that we should not attempt to cure disease
with medicine but strive instead for the insight that only health is real.
Since everything real is good, whatever is evil must not be real but the
result of illusion or misunderstanding.

But such efforts to argue evil and suffering away by attributing them to
ignorance or illusion are not very convincing. If, as Augustine suggests,
what we call evil is privation of good, we may still appropriately ask why
God allows such privation; why God does not fill the world with goodness.
Even if we accept the teaching that evil is only ignorance and illusion,
surely we must recognize that such ignorance and illusion themselves remain as real evils that cannot be dismissed in the same way. To many
people it seems at best highly naive and at worst callous, insensitive, and
uncaring to write off suffering as not ultimately real. To tell a person in the
throes of great misfortune that her troubles are illusory or, worse yet, the
result of her own ignorance, seems not only inexcusably insensitive but
quite wrong headed. Anyone who is willing to be candid, to face the world
without the protecting screen of a preconceived, rose-colored religious fil-
ter, cannot avoid seeing that evil and suffering are rife, that they pervade
the lives of a great proportion of humanity, and that their grinding and
unrelenting torment renders the lives of many humans a dreary, bleak,
hungry, empty, drudgery, or even worse, a pain- and sorrow-racked ordeal.
Indeed, so impressed and appalled was Gautama (c. 566–480 B.C.E.) with
the all-pervasive weight of human suffering that he made the recognition of
this human condition the prime item in the Buddhist teaching, and the
escape from it the central objective of the Buddhist life. "Life is *dukka*,
suffering, craving." To live is to suffer; this is the first of the Buddha's four
noble truths. The eightfold path is the path to liberation from *dukka*.

To the privileged few—that tiny fraction of the human population who live in comfort, plenty, security, health, freedom, even luxury—the poignant descriptions of human suffering may seem overplayed, an echo of some far away and greatly exaggerated situation having little reality or relevance for their lives. But even their lives are not untouched by loneliness, rejection, disease, broken homes, drug and alcohol abuse, parental neglect or abuse, and sometimes a sense of the emptiness and futility of life. And even the privileged or fortunate few must expect eventually to face the debilities of old age, disease, and death. Those who write about human ills seem all to agree that material prosperity is a protection only from the grosser, but in the long run less important, forms of human suffering.

Suffering, in short, is not the exclusive province or destiny of any one class, although each class perhaps has its own special forms of wretchedness. Starvation is a constant threat to many and a fact of life that flares into sickening prevalence every few years when flood, drought, or war disturbs the fragile web of life support. Natural disasters such as earthquakes, hurricanes, weather-precipitated famine, and disease are widespread, appalling, and oppressive. But even worse are the savage cruelties that humans persistently perpetrate on one another, whether through physical abuse, psychological intimidation, robbery, rape, and murder or through the broader social vehicles of political exploitation, economic repression, social and racial oppression, and the inconceivably diabolical deeds and events of war.

When we look evil straight in the face, the question of how a powerful and loving God could create such a world becomes insistently disturbing. The problem of evil can be solved by giving up any one of the propositions in the tetrad. Clearly, though, there can be no justification for giving up number 4.

Yet it is not possible to give up any of the other propositions and remain a theist in the standard sense. As we have seen in Chapter 2, omnipotence, omniscience, and moral perfection are precisely the attributes that theists insist God must have. To admit that God is not omnipotent, omniscient, or morally perfect is to abandon theism. Thus theists have made many attempts to show that the existence of evil is compatible with the existence of a God who has these perfections—an effort that amounts to attempting to show that the tetrad, rightly understood, is not really inconsistent. What this usually involves is an attempted reinterpretation of one or another of the great-making attributes.

Natural Versus Moral Evil

One way that theists have attempted at least to reduce the quantity of evil for which God might be held responsible is to point out the difference between natural evil and moral evil. Some of the evil in the world is the direct consequence of human choice, whereas some results from natural phenomena over which humans have no power. The evil for which human choice is responsible is called **moral evil**; that which results from natural, nonhuman processes in the world is called **natural evil**. God, who is presumed to have created nature, would seem to be responsible for the flaws or defects in it that contribute to suffering, but it would not be fair to blame God for evils that humans bring about.

The distinction between natural and moral evil seems to shift the responsibility for much evil from God to humans, making the task of justifying evil in a world created by a morally perfect God a smaller one. Indeed, many people would say that an overwhelming proportion of evil is actually moral evil for which God cannot be held responsible. A few have even gone so far as to attempt to attribute all evil to human sin. For example, Leslie Weatherhead (1893–1976),[2] a British clergyman, offers an argument based on the extent to which mental attitude contributes to the course of a human illness. Psychosomatic medicine has discovered, he points out, that negative, fearful, hostile, angry, suspicious attitudes can actually cause serious physical illness. May it not be, he asks, that disease-causing bacteria are actually organisms that once lived harmlessly in our bodies, but that, through the influence of human chemistry brought on by sinful attitudes, were transformed into harmful creatures? By arguments analogous to this various thinkers have attempted to increase the number of ills for which humans can be held responsible and decrease the number of those that could be blamed on God, ideally to the point that God might be exonerated of all evil.

Critics have parodied these attempts as human efforts to become God's savior and redeemer by taking on themselves the sins of God. It certainly is true that a very large proportion of our troubles are of our own making. Of all the evils from which we suffer, very many are moral evils attributable directly or indirectly to human ignorance or perversity. Even much of what at first looks like natural evil does indeed have a human cause — for example, deforestation, which contributes to floods and droughts, and smoking, which causes cancer and myriad other ills. Even so, when humans have done their best to take on themselves as many as possible of the sins of creation, a great deal of evil seems to remain for which they cannot plausibly be blamed. If a large part of our misery is of our own doing, it is also true that there is much natural evil for which we cannot reasonably be held responsible.

Furthermore, according to theism, God not only created the natural world; God also created us. And if God is omnipotent, God should be able to control what we do. If God knows that I am about to commit an evil act that will cause very great suffering to others, and if God has the power to prevent me from doing it, how can God be cleared of responsibility if God does not prevent it? Moreover, if I am a person able and inclined to do evil,

God must have created me that way. It would appear, then, that not I but God is responsible for my wrongdoing.

The Christian doctrine of the fall, based on the first several chapters of the book of Genesis, supposedly provides an answer to this problem and exonerates God. According to Christian teachings, God created the world and human beings perfectly good. Humans are said to have been created in the image of God. It was human perversity, the deliberate disobedience of God, that resulted in the loss of the image of God and the tainting or ruining of human nature. Thus the sinful nature of man and the sufferings that flow from the expression of that nature cannot be blamed on God. The blame must stand squarely against humankind. But the doctrine thus stated fails to take account of the fact that God created a being capable of sinning; one apparently inclined toward sinning. If human nature were indeed perfect, like God's, whence came the perversity that resulted in human disobedience of God? And, according to the biblical myth, God created a situation that tempted humans to sin — by placing a very alluring but forbidden fruit tree in the garden. An omnipotent, morally perfect God, it would seem, should have created a being less susceptible to temptation, and such a God certainly should not deliberately have thrown temptation our way. The response to this challenge takes the form of what is called the free will argument. In due course we will examine the argument in detail.

Can the Existence of Natural Evil Be Justified?

Many arguments have been devised to show that natural evil is not incompatible with the existence of the God of theism. We will examine several of the more important ones.

Evil Is the Result of the Operation of the Laws of Nature.   The existence of an orderly and intelligible world is possible only if certain laws invariably obtain. Without them, creation would be a chaos in which such things as plants, animals, and humans could not live. The existence and flourishing of living things depends first on soil, water, sunshine, and myriad other factors and second on these things having steady and unvarying qualities. In a world without orderly laws, the nutrients on which plants depend might sometimes nourish them but other times poison them. In a world without dependable laws, a person might sometimes safely walk along the surface of the earth but other times sink into the ground and be swallowed up or float away into space. Moreover, human knowledge would be impossible in a nonlaw-abiding world. Knowledge about the physical world consists of a grasp of the invariable ways in which objects and events behave. If there were no natural laws, objects and events would not behave dependably, and thus we could never have any knowledge about them.

The theist willingly admits that the invariability of natural law does result sometimes in suffering, but insists that that suffering is the unavoidable price for the existence of human beings, of knowledge, beauty, morality, and value of all kinds. To call it unavoidable amounts to claiming that there are some things that even an omnipotent being cannot do. Perhaps a world governed by natural law in which sentient beings never suffer as a consequence of the operation of that law is simply not possible. If we are to enjoy the positive benefits that result from the operation of natural law, certain dangers inevitably accompany them. If storms did not occur in the earth's atmosphere to stir gases and drive off the harmful vapors, humans would suffocate in the stagnant air. Storms also pick up moisture from the oceans and lakes and transport it in the form of rain and snow to inland areas that, without such precipitation, would dry up and become deserts. To be sure, sometimes humans or animals suffer harm or even death from storms, but the consequences would be vastly worse if there were no storms to bring their beneficent effects.

Opponents to theism usually agree that the laws of nature are necessary, but they often argue that a god as great as God is supposed to be would surely have been able to devise a world regulated by a set of laws that provided the benefits but only very rarely caused evil and suffering. Surely a God who is all powerful, all knowing, and all loving could have devised a way to provide the forces of nature in a more balanced and less violent way. Even a very carefully and skillfully designed universe governed with delicately adjusted natural laws might result in some suffering when humans and animals run afoul of winds, storms, or other forces, but such suffering would be minimized. In the actual world the forces of nature run amuck so frequently and so wildly as to suggest that they are at best rather crudely adjusted and by no means the best we could expect of the kind of God the theists promote.

It is easy to see that a major part of the dispute here has to do with a disagreement about the meaning of omnipotence. The nontheists, assuming that an omnipotent being can do anything at all, argue that an omnipotent God should have been able to create a world governed by natural law that nevertheless involves little or no suffering. Since the world does involve much suffering, God must not be omnipotent or else there is no God. But the theists insist that omnipotence does not mean the ability to do anything at all, but only the ability to do what is possible. They maintain that it is not possible to create a world governed by natural laws, with all of the benefits such a world brings, without the possibility that sentient beings such as humans and animals will run afoul of nature's processes and be hurt. Natural evil is the unavoidable consequence—unavoidable even for an omnipotent being—of the beneficial order that natural law makes possible.

In Chapter 2 we discussed the question of what sorts of things an omnipotent being can and cannot do, and we discovered there that not all things are possible even for God. Clearly, God cannot be blamed for not doing what not even an omnipotent being can do. Thus the theists' argument about evil resulting from the operation of natural law does seem to have weight. It appears to be true that it is just not possible for God to convey the benefits of a naturally orderly world and also prevent the suffering that results when humans run afoul of natural law. But the counterargument is forceful. A world like ours in which evil is so very pervasive and devastating is certainly not the kind we would expect a loving and powerful God to create. Even if some evil is the inevitable consequence of natural law, it is not clear that all of the natural evil that occurs is genuinely unavoidable by such a God. If the argument based on the laws of nature diminishes in some measure the sting of the problem of evil, it does not seem to constitute a complete answer.

Good Is Impossible, or Impossible to Appreciate, Without Evil. Pleasure can be known only by contrast with pain, the argument goes. If there were no evil, we would not be able to recognize good. If we can imagine that the whole world were green, we can see right away that we would not know what green, or any other color, means; we would not even have a word for it. Similarly, without evil to provide a contrast, we would not know what good is and would not have a word for it.

This argument shows at best that a tiny quantity of evil is necessary. To recognize the color green, all we need is a tiny spot of red. Similarly, to recognize what goodness is, all we need is a tiny bit of pain or evil. If it is true that good could not be recognized or appreciated unless there was also evil, surely we do not need the great quantity of evil that actually exists.

Moreover, there seem to be some goods that can exist without contrasting evils. It appears that physical health can exist without disease and that sanity can exist without insanity. There does not seem to be any reason why everyone could not be healthy and sane. And if it is true that we do not really appreciate our health until we have suffered from disease, then a minor bout with some illness would surely suffice. It is clearly not a situation where the amount of possible good is commensurate with the amount of evil. If the argument is that evil is a means to the existence of good, then we might expect that what would follow is: The more evil, the more good. Clearly, this is not the case. And if the claim is that God cannot create good except by using evil as a means, this amounts to acknowledging a very serious attenuation of God's power. If God does have to make use of means for the realization of the ends he envisions for the world, God ought to make use of good means, not evil ones. If certain ends can be achieved only through evil means, perhaps God should forego those ends and settle for others that do not require such means. It is a principle of human morality that good ends do not justify evil means. Surely God's standard of morality must be at least as high as humankind's.

Evil Is Punishment for Human Sin or a Warning Not to Sin. This is not a very plausible argument, because the evil does not seem to be distributed proportionately to merit. Notoriously, the righteous often suffer while the wicked prosper. And if it is suggested that such injustices will be righted in the next life, the reply is that this is an article of faith, not known to be true, and thus not available as a premise for an argument about evil as we experience it in this world. And if God intends to be using suffering as a warning to humankind, it appears that God's use of it is extremely clumsy and that it does not to any considerable extent succeed in its objective. The disproportionate distribution of suffering seems to be a serious threat to God's justice. God's use of the extreme measures of evil and suffering at all seems to call God's goodness into serious question.

The World Is Better Off with Some Evil in It. It has often been pointed out that the existence of natural evil such as famine or disease is a great stimulus to very worthy moral good in the form of human dedication to overcoming that evil. If there were no evil to strive against, what would the human character be? Where would be the opportunity for courage, unselfishness, compassion, heroism in the help of others? Indeed, human life would be colorless unless there were temptations to be overcome, sacrifices to be made, moral battles to be fought and won. The great pioneers of medicine are called to a life of heroic, life-saving, pain-easing effort just because there is sickness for them to fight. Many great engineering feats are inspired by the need to overcome natural circumstances which cause great human suffering and inconvenience. Teachers are called to lives of service because ignorance needs to be overcome. Research has been inspired in agriculture because of human hunger. The world would be a much poorer place without the greatness of character which such moral struggle builds, and evils to battle against are necessary conditions of that struggle.

We may grant all this and still argue that it does not justify all the evil and suffering in the world. A great deal of suffering seems to serve no purpose whatever in inspiring heroism or building character. Instead, it seems to crush the spirit of innumerable persons, making their lives wretched and yielding no compensating good. Is the heroism of character achieved by a small number of dedicated servants of human suffering valuable enough to counterbalance all the terrible suffering itself? Is a world in which millions suffer from disease and a few thousand achieve heroism as medical practitioners and researchers a better world than one in which everyone is healthy and no medical practice or research is needed? Given a choice between the two worlds, it seems clear which one most of us would choose. It seems clear, too, that the obvious choice is also the reasonable one.

These several arguments, designed to justify the existence of natural evil, all claim that certain very valuable types of good could not be achieved, even by an omnipotent being, without the natural evils that accompany them. Viewed in the light of the allegedly inconsistent tetrad, they are all directed toward the first proposition having to do with God's omnipotence. They do not quite concede that God is not omnipotent; rather, they modify our understanding of omnipotence by pointing out that even an omnipotent being cannot do certain things. They claim that God's existence, and what is most important about God's great-making attributes, are not threatened by the existence of evil, because, great as God is, God cannot realize these important values without also creating conditions under which some evil can occur.

However much these arguments may contribute toward justifying a measure of the evil and suffering in the world, it seems clear that they have not been able to turn back the whole force of the problem of natural evil. To the extent that they succeed in justifying the existence of evil, they do so by modifying the concept of omnipotence. If they yield too much, they have in effect abandoned theism (perhaps unwittingly embracing a finite deity). If they yield too little, the attempt to justify evil fails. Whether there is a safe path between the two extremes we will attempt to discover after we have examined the nature of moral evil.

Can the Existence of Moral Evil Be Justified?

The principal way in which theists have attempted to justify the existence of moral evil is by attributing it to human choice. But this approach can be successful only if it can be shown that God is not responsible for the choices that humans make. Theists often argue that God has given humans free will and, having done so, can no longer control what they do. But the argument for free will has certain problems, which we must now examine.

The Free Will Defense.   An omnipotent God could certainly have made all living creatures in such a way that they always do good and never do evil. But this could have been accomplished, the defenders of the **free will defense** insist, only by making humans programmed robots. What God wanted, the theists tell us, was free, intelligent beings as much as possible like himself who could themselves be rational and creative and who could enter into loving relationships not only with one another but with God. The only way that this could be achieved was by creating beings who are free in a radical sense — so free from God's control, that is, that they can, if they choose, even reject God and do evil things. For only beings able to choose in this unrestrained sense can really decide to accept God's love and to cooperate with God's plan of creation. Coerced love is not real love; friendship with beings who have no choice about it is not real friendship; and obedience from those who cannot disobey is slavery.

What the argument amounts to is the claim that free will, or the goods that are impossible without free will, are so valuable that they are worth the cost of the evil that would result from the bad choices of free creatures. One of the very highest values in the created world is morality. There can be no such thing as morality apart from free will. God could have created beings who always did the right thing without giving them free will, but they would not have been moral beings. To be a moral being means to have the power to deliberate between options and to choose, uncoerced. And this is possible only if the person is able to choose either the good or the evil alternative. No matter how nobly a person may behave, if her behavior is not under her own control, we cannot attribute morality or virtue to her. But morality is our highest human quality, a characteristic that raises us immeasurably above the level of brutes. It is what makes humans God's finest creation. Many would say that it is what constitutes the greatest created value in the universe. Because morality is so valuable, it justifies the cost of the moral evil that will occur when free humans make wrong rather than right use of their freedom.

Objections to the Free Will Defense.   The claim that human free will places many things that happen in the world outside God's control has often been cited as a serious threat to God's omnipotence. We have addressed this issue in Chapter 2 and have concluded that any conception of omnipotence that is likely to prove acceptable must allow for human free will. We discussed there the claims of the group of philosophers called compatibilists, who maintain that free will is compatible with God's determining our behavior. The double objective of their position is to preserve both human moral responsibility and God's omnipotence in the strongest sense of the word. The compatibilists argue that God cannot be held responsible for human wrongdoing because humans are free to do whatever they choose. At the same time, this is said to be no threat to God's omnipotence, because God determines the choices we make. We discovered, though, that this position disguises a contradiction and fails to allow for free will in any significant sense.

Certain philosophers such as J. L. Mackie and John McCluskey have attempted to argue that God could have created free human beings who always freely choose to do what is good.

> If God has made men such that in their free choices they sometimes prefer what is good and sometimes what is evil, why could he not have made men such that they always freely choose the good?...
> God was not... faced with a choice between making innocent automata and making beings who, in acting freely, would sometimes go wrong: there was open to him the obvious better possibility of making beings who would act freely but always go right.[3]

Now clearly if this were a possibility, namely, if God could have created free, morally autonomous, and responsible persons who would always freely choose to do good, but instead created persons like us who often do evil, God would have to be regarded as blameworthy. At first glance this proposal appears to be plausible. As Ninian Smart has shown, however, more detailed examination of the claim that God could have created free humans who are wholly good reveals it to be an illusion.

The problem with Mackie's utopian scheme is that it assumes that you can change one aspect of the world without affecting any change in anything else. But clearly this is not the case. To create humans who are wholly good would be to create beings who never yield to temptations and do wrong. But the only way to make sure that this never happened would be to create beings who never desire what they should not have, who never resent the behavior of others, who never feel any urge to assert themselves in strong competition with others, who do not feel fear in the presence of danger, and so on. We call a person good because he resists temptation, because in the face of desire for what belongs to others he refrains from taking it, because when he feels the urge to compete unjustly he restrains himself, because despite fear he still does his duty. If a being existed who was not susceptible to these temptations, desires, urges, and fears, that being certainly would not be what we normally call a human being, and it is difficult to see what sense it would make to call that being good.

Smart examines more closely some of the changes that would have to be made in human nature if humans were always freely to be perfectly good.

> Unless we were built in a certain way there would be no temptations: for example, unless we were built so that sexual gratification is normally very pleasant there would be no serious temptations to commit adultery, etc. It would appear then that the only way to ensure that people were wholly good would be to build them in such a way that they were never tempted.[4]

The only way positively to ensure that a man would never commit adultery would be to build him in such a way that one and only one woman attracted him, and she would have to be built such that he and only he attracted her. To ensure that people never cheated one another, for example, over a piece of property, they would have to be built in such a way that only one piece of property in the world was desirable to each of them and they would have no interest in the property anyone else wanted, that differences in investment value between properties were of no concern to them, and so on. Or else each person would have to be built in such a way that just knowing that a piece of property was owned or desired by someone else made it undesirable to him or her. As we think through these scenarios in detail, it becomes increasingly clear that the creature we are imagining is not a human being. So Mackie's question, "Why did not God create free humans who would be wholly good?" becomes, "Why did God create humans instead of angels or some other kind of creature?" But even angels are capable of feeling angry and jealous, of rebelling against God, of trying to take over power from God. According to Christian mythology, it was Satan, the prince of angels, who sinned most grievously against God. Thus, if angels were to be wholly good, God would have had to build them differently, too.

If created intelligent beings were to live in a created world and be wholly good, both they and the world would have to be very different from the way they are. But different in what way? When we think about the differences that would be required, we begin to realize that we are not imagining a real possibility, but only a fantasy, an impossible dream. It strikes us as plausible, stated in abstract terms, because we do not notice just what it would involve. On closer inspection, however, we see that there is no way to create free humans who are wholly good, because it would be possible to make them wholly good only by making them no longer humans or no longer free — we cannot even imagine what they would have to be like. Furthermore, to make them beings that are never tempted, never frustrated, never jealous, never needing to engage in moral struggle renders unintelligible the claim that humans are wholly good, or good in any sense.

The theists' attempt to justify moral evil through the free will defense, like their attempt to justify natural evil, is grounded in their modified understanding of omnipotence. The critics of the free will argument take omnipotence to mean able to do anything at all — able, for example, to create beings who always freely do only what is good. This is simply another version of compatibilism, the claim that human free will is compatible with God's determining what free agents do. But it is impossible for God, or anyone else, to determine the free actions of other agents, because necessarily if they are free actions, no one else determines them, and if someone else does determine them, they are not free. If the considerations we examined in Chapter 2 suffice to justify the belief that humans do sometimes act freely, then God cannot determine their actions. This seems to exonerate God of moral evil. Does it at the same time diminish God's omnipotence to the point where theism must be abandoned? If there is an adequate theodicy, it must preserve both human free will and a plausible interpretation of the great-making attributes of God. We turn now to see whether such a **theodicy** — that is, an account of God's nature that exonerates him of all evil — can be constructed out of all of these strands and others.

A Morally Justified Means to the Highest Good

When we examine it more closely, the alleged inconsistent tetrad seems actually to carry with it a tacit fifth proposition that its supporters fail to recognize, namely: (5) "God could not under any circumstances be morally justified in allowing evil to exist." But when that assumption is made explicit and examined, it does not appear to be true at all. The various arguments offered in defense of the God of theism against the problem of evil add up to the claim that this assumption is false. These arguments can be summarized thus: Evil exists because it is the necessary condition for the existence of greater good. Some natural evil exists, for example, because it makes possible an orderly, law-abiding world in which there can be living things, and knowledge, and friendship, and morality. Some moral evil exists because of human free will, and free will exists because it makes possible the kind of beings who know, understand, reason, judge, love, and practice morality. Omnipotence, as we have seen in Chapter 2, means only the ability to do what is possible, not the ability to do anything at all. Now if it is true that an omnipotent God is able to realize very great good in a created universe only at the cost of allowing the occurrence of evil, that fact may constitute the moral justification for the existence of evil, particularly if the good is of supreme importance. This is just what defenders of theism assert in response to the problem of evil.

But is the good sufficiently great to justify the cost? And is it true that the good is not possible without the possibility, or perhaps even the actuality, of evil? I wish to put forward an argument designed to support an affirmative answer to both of these questions.

The central claim of the argument is that the only intrinsic value that ever exists anywhere is located in the conscious experiences of beings I will call persons. By persons, I mean beings which enjoy and suffer, appreciate, reason, know, judge, and evaluate. Humans are persons; if there is a God, God may be a person; and if there are other conscious, knowing, rational, value-judging, and value-creating beings elsewhere in the universe, they would also properly be called persons in my sense, whether they otherwise resemble humans or not. So, the claim goes, if there were no persons in the world, there would be no intelligible distinction between good and evil.[5] Some things are good because conscious beings exist to appreciate or value them; and some things are bad because conscious beings exist who abhor or disvalue them. In a world in which no such conscious beings or persons exist, all things would be indifferent, neither beautiful nor ugly, neither noble nor base, neither good nor evil. It is, indeed, the valuing and appreciating activity of the consciousness of persons that makes valuable everything with value, good or bad.

The great Indian poet-philosopher, Rabindranath Tagore, has expressed this idea that the existence of goodness or beauty in the universe depends completely on the consciousness of persons through his sublime poem entitled "I," of which the following stanzas are excerpts:

> My consciousness has colored the emerald green,
>   the ruby red.

I opened my eyes to the heavens,
　　Light flamed up
　　In east and west.
I looked at the rose and said: "Beautiful."
　　And it became beautiful.
You will say that this is philosophy,
　　Not a poet's words.
I will say, this is true,
　　That is why it is poetry. . . .
Man's eyes on the day of his departure
　　Will wipe away all color from the universe.
Man's mind on the day of departure
　　Will strain out all of its sweetness.
The vibrations of strength will pass from sky to sky,
　　No light will burn anywhere. . . .
Then in the great universe
　　From distance in the far away eternal myriad worlds
These words will no where be heard:
　　"You are beautiful."
　　"I love you."
Will the Creator sit again in meditation?
　　Through the ages?
Will He repeat in the evening of the day of destruction,
　　"Speak, Oh speak"?
Will He say: "Say, 'You are beautiful,'"
Will He say: "Say, 'I love you'"?[6]

It is important to notice that this theory does not amount to saying that whatever any person likes or approves of is thereby made morally good, which is the position of **moral relativism**. It does not imply that the moral preferences of one individual are just as good as those of another or that the moral practices of different societies are all equally good (the position of **moral cultural relativism**). Because human nature is the same in all times and places; because all human persons have essentially the same basic needs; because rationality is a human trait common to the whole human race, there are grounds for universal moral principles. Inflicting needless suffering on innocent persons for no important reason is morally wrong without regard to time or place, and this moral fact takes precedence over any political, religious, or social teaching or custom to the contrary. To be sure, the ways in which universal moral truths find appropriate expression in moral behavior may vary from one time and place to another because the circumstances differ. The fundamental principle that the valuing activity of conscious persons creates all the value that ever exists emphatically does not imply moral relativism. These points will be explored in more detail in Chapter 7.

We have only to note also the distinction between intrinsic and instrumental value to realize that our basic principle does not imply that it is morally acceptable to seek out and enjoy just any value experiences an individual person may fancy. The **intrinsic value** of an experience is the value it has in itself without regard to any effect it may have on anything or anyone else. The **instrumental value** of an object or experience is the contribution it makes to some other value experience or situation. The enjoyable experience of listening to music or sharing with a friend is an intrinsic value, good in itself, and not merely good for the sake of some other benefit. The experience of having one's teeth drilled and filled by the dentist (an intrinsic disvalue because of the pain) is an instrumental value, contributory to future dental health and freedom from pain. Thus we may say that any instance of consciousness a person enjoys or appreciates is intrinsically good, and any instance of consciousness a person dislikes or abhors is intrinsically bad.

Some experiences that are intrinsically good for an individual may have instrumental features that are so bad that morality requires our forbidding anyone from enjoying those experiences. For example, the pleasure a sadist derives from inflicting pain on someone else is intrinsically good, as all pleasure is. But the activity that yields the pleasure has such important instrumental disvalue that rational morality forbids engaging in that activity.

Nothing is ever good or bad in itself, then, except the experiences of persons. All the value that ever occurs in the universe occurs within the conscious experience of the kinds of beings we are calling persons. Any good which material things and events have is instrumental good, and these things and events have the value that they do have because of the contributions that they make to the conscious experiences of persons. If this claim is correct, it follows that persons themselves are loci of very great value. Indeed, the greatest good in the created universe is persons and their experiences. Whatever is a necessary condition for the existence of thinking, knowing, appreciating, judging, valuing persons is a necessary condition for the existence of the greatest good—indeed, of any good at all. If it turns out, then, that the possibility of evil is a necessary condition for the existence of conscious persons, we will have discovered that the possibility of evil is a necessary condition for the existence of any and all good.

This argument brings together some of the major points made by several of the other arguments we have been considering. The attempt to justify evil as the unavoidable consequence of natural law points to the very great value of such things as life, beauty, knowledge, goodness, and the like and reminds us of the fact that only in an orderly world can such value be realized. The free will argument speaks of the great value of free moral agents and indicates that moral evil is the inevitable cost of the existence of this great value. But the argument we have just sketched shows why these other claims have the plausibility that they have: An orderly world, governed by natural law, and moral freedom are necessary conditions for, and ingredients in, what we now see to be the focal point of all the created value in the world. It is sensitive, conscious, rational, value-appreciating, and value-creating persons who bear in their nature and in their experiences the highest created goodness that exists. Indeed, it is easy to see that no created good could ever have existed if such beings did not exist. Now if God can only create and sustain such value-realizing and value-creating persons by creating circumstances that allow for evil, this would seem to show that God is in fact justified in allowing evil to exist. God is justified because it appears that there was no other way in which God could have created any good.

If the argument that we have sketched here is sound, we have grounds for rejecting the claim that the tetrad is inconsistent, because we have discovered good reasons for rejecting the tacit assumption that God could not be morally justified in allowing the existence of evil. This turns out to be a version of the claim that good cannot exist without evil. Since all good depends on the existence of conscious persons and since the existence of such persons seems to be impossible apart from circumstances that allow for evil, we may conclude that there was no way for God to create a world that would contain good without creating one that contained evil.

Even if this must be granted, the antitheists might still justifiably raise the question whether the quantity and quality of good that the existence of value-realizing and value-creating conscious persons makes possible is sufficient to justify the amount of evil which exists. This amounts to the question whether — if indeed this very great amount of evil was an unavoidable consequence — it would have been better not to create a world at all. If we could be sure that this life is not all there is to human existence; if we could be confident that individual humans continue to exist after death in a realm where evil is finally vanquished, that would surely suffice to tip the scale and convince us that all is well. We will examine the arguments pro and con concerning death and immortality in Chapter 9. For the present, we can only regard belief in such a teaching as a matter of faith and not available as a premise in an argument dealing with the problem of evil.

The argument that we have before us suffices at best to show that the allegedly inconsistent tetrad *may* not really be inconsistent; that God *may be* justified in allowing evil to exist. This is enough, perhaps, to tame some of the ferocity of the problem of evil and diminish some of its force. But even if most of its force can thus be taken away, this does not suffice to establish the truth of theism. The most such an argument can do is to show that the problem of evil does not definitively refute theism. Thus it may contribute in some measure toward establishing the rational acceptability of theism.

SOCIOLOGICAL AND PSYCHOLOGICAL OBJECTIONS: RELIGION AS PROJECTION, OPIATE, OR MASS DELUSION

The psychological and sociological objections to theism are not so much efforts to refute theism as to undermine it or to explain it away. They amount to the claim that religious beliefs are human accounts of their experiences in dealing with the powers of the world which have then been objectified and projected onto the "screen of heaven." They generally make little or no attempt to deal with the specific teachings taken as literal truth claims, but instead suggest that once we have seen how these beliefs arose and have understood the roles they play in the psychological and social life of humans, we will recognize their mythological and fictional character and no longer feel any inclination to believe them.

Sociological Objections

August Comte (1798–1857), sometimes called the father of sociology, argued that theism is a stage in the historical progression of human thought from its superstitious beginnings to its maturity in the knowledge discovered by modern science. Comte believed that our intellectual history passes through three stages, the theological, the metaphysical, and the scientific or positive. In the *theological* phase, according to Comte, we attempt to understand the world in terms first of spirits that animate nature and natural objects such as trees and streams, then through belief in many gods, and finally through the merging of the gods into the one god of monotheism. When the anthropomorphism of such beliefs begins to trouble rational thinkers, there is a shift to the *metaphysical* stage, in which explanation in terms of the will of spirits, gods, or God gives way to explanation by means of abstract concepts having to do with impersonal causes and forces, often unified by the concept of Nature. In the *scientific* or *positive* stage, abstract explanations yield to the detailed findings of science practiced through empirical observation and experimentation. Comte regarded our persistent clinging to theological or metaphysical beliefs as a hindrance to the progress of science, which he believed to be the only method for discovering what really deserves to be called knowledge.

Emile Durkheim (1858–1917), another early sociologist, suggested that the sense of awe in the presence of a higher power that is the core of religion is actually caused by the moral authority of the society that impresses itself on individuals by means of powerful rituals, customs, and taboos. Because the beliefs and practices of a society are so completely pervasive in the lives of its members, they appear to have a transcendent source. And indeed they do. But it is not a deity; it is the society itself. Because the mores of the society demand unquestioning obedience; because society's rituals are the forces which accompany, legitimate, and make possible all of life's transitions such as birth, maturity, marriage, and death; and because all persons depend on the customs and practices of society to sustain and carry them through the great crises of their lives, the belief arises that these mores, rituals, and customs are handed down by a deity often thought of as the father of the tribe or the being responsible for its creation. Theism, then, is a human invention, and God is an imaginary being, created unconsciously in the mythological evolution of the society to serve as the repository of morality and custom and as the powerful being on which the tribe can depend for its safety and well-being.

Contemporary sociologists are more wary of explaining away religion by means of theories about its origins, preferring instead to point out correlations between certain social contingencies and the rise of certain forms of religious belief and practice. A sociologist who takes this approach is Guy E. Swanson.[7] Swanson examines data from preliterate and early historical societies and reports a very high correlation between such factors as the society's abundance or scarcity of food, its position of safety or vulnerability relative to enemy tribes, its patterns of property ownership, population size, and the like and certain religious beliefs and practices. The extent to which many contemporary sociologists still regard their work as uncovering the disreputable origins of religion and thus undermining it seems to be detectable in Ronald Johnstone's comments on these findings:

> While Swanson himself admits that even strong positive correlations do not conclusively establish cause-and-effect relationships ... the relationship is strong enough to at least tempt the reader to begin thinking of talking about necessary and sufficient conditions for the development of that particular belief.[8]

The clear suggestion here, that the religious beliefs and practices correlated with certain historical contingencies are *caused* by those historical circumstances, was an explicit part of Karl Marx's (1818–1883) theory about religion. In his introduction to the *Communist Manifesto*,[9] Lenin calls this the manifesto's fundamental proposition:

> That in every historical epoch, the prevailing mode of economic production and exchange, and the social organization necessarily following from it, form the basis upon which is built up, and from which alone can be explained, the political and intellectual history of that epoch.[10]

And religion, of course, is an ingredient in human political and intellectual history. This doctrine of Marx and Engels, sometimes called **economic determinism**, amounts to the claim that human beliefs and behavior are caused by historical circumstances, particularly the economic means of production and exchange, that dominate a given era. It is usually supposed that the social, political, and religious beliefs of a people affect or even determine the way in which they set up their social institutions; we have tended to believe that our society has the structure it does *because* we hold certain beliefs. Marx insists that the causal relation runs in the opposite direction: We hold the beliefs we do *because* certain economic institutions and practices prevail. Religious beliefs and practices, far from originating from divine revelation, are merely the effects of economic forces. When certain economic arrangements prevail, certain religious beliefs and practices also prevail; when one economic situation gives way to another in the dialectic progression that is an inevitable part of the process of history, an appropriate modification of religious institutions and doctrines follows in its wake.

Marx's other major criticism of religion is that it is a tool in the hands of the ruling class for keeping the masses under control. Religion has the effect of distracting the attention of the oppressed masses from their wretchedness, of pacifying them, and thus of keeping the ruling classes in power. Thus Marx characterizes religion as the "opium of the people," and a "means of stupefying the masses."[11] Its promise of a better life in the world to come stifles discontent with oppressive government; its teaching that the powers that be are ordained of God and must be obeyed as a slave must obey his master keeps down thoughts about rebellion even against severe injustice. So religion is an enemy of the oppressed classes, a reactionary force designed to keep the masses submissive to their oppressors and to retard movement toward the revolution that leads to the classless society.

Psychological Objections

The most famous critic of religion on psychological grounds is Sigmund Freud, but he was not the first. Ludwig A. Feuerbach (1804–1872) argued that religion is a projection outward of our own self-consciousness; it is seeing ourselves in a mirror, so to speak, but not realizing that we are only seeing an image of ourselves. "Religion is the childlike condition of humanity . . . the disuniting of man from himself. . . . God is the manifested inward nature, the expressed self of a man."[12] It is thinking that our outwardly projected image of ourselves is actually something completely different from ourselves, something infinite, perfect, eternal, almighty, and holy. "It fancies its object, its ideas, to be supernatural. . . . [but] the antithesis of divine and human is altogether illusory. . . . All the attributes of the divine nature are, therefore, attributes of the human nature."[13] Feuerbach attempts to show that the various items of religious belief are actually objectifications of human needs and wishes. We are especially fond of believing in miracles, he suggests, because through miracles we get what we want immediately, without our going through the effort necessary to get it in natural ways. What we worship as gods are what Feuerbach calls *Wunsch-wesen*, "wish-beings," and our religious behavior represents the acting out of a delusion.

Sigmund Freud (1856–1939) takes up the theme of religion as wish fulfillment in his *Future of an Illusion*[14] and several other works. Freud attempted to give his claims an appearance of scientific authority, which Feuerbach's teachings lacked, by wrapping them in the cloak of psychoanalysis. But anyone who reads his works on religion can easily see that they are highly speculative—as many of his psychoanalytic theories are, too—and not very scientific in the usual sense.

Freud begins his attack on religion by arguing that human life is hard, filled with dangers and suffering imposed on us by the hazards of nature. Storms, floods, famines, disease, and death threaten us and make us keenly aware of our weakness and our vulnerability. They are mysterious, beyond our understanding; we are at a loss to know how to deal with them. Thus the first stage in religion is an attempt to domesticate the powers of nature. We know that much that happens to us is the result of the plans and schemes of other persons, and that persons can do evil things to one another. So we attribute personal spirits to the forces of nature because we understand how to deal with the anger, ire, or even the whimsy of persons.

> Life and the universe must be robbed of their terrors; moreover [human] curiosity . . . demands an answer. A great deal can be gained with the first step: the humanization of nature. . . . If everywhere in nature there are Beings around us of a kind that we know in our society, then we can breathe freely, can feel at home in the uncanny and can deal by psychical means with our senseless anxiety. . . . We can apply the same methods against these violent supermen outside that we employ in our own society; we can try to adjure them, to appease them, to bribe them, and, by so influencing them, we may rob them of a part of their power.[15]

But the suffering and frustration that comes from nature is not all, nor even the worst, we have to endure. Much of what makes our lives difficult comes from other persons. In fact, the very society that we form for the purpose of immunizing ourselves against the hazards of nature itself imposes great restrictions on the pleasures and satisfactions we seek. These sacrifices are a necessary consequence of living in a civilized society. We are basically pleasure-seeking creatures, according to Freud. We do not like to work, and we are particularly intolerant of anything that frustrates our efforts to satisfy our drives and to enjoy pleasure. As everyone knows, Freud attempts to explain a large proportion of human behavior in terms of the sex drive, which places urgent and insistent demands on us for sensuous pleasure. For humans to live together in a civilized society, however, we must sacrifice much of our pleasurable activity. We cannot simply help ourselves to any potential sex object we happen to meet.

Furthermore, Freud is convinced that humans have a finite amount of energy, that sexual activity uses up considerable energy, and thus if humans are to expend their energy on the labor necessary to build and maintain a civilization, that energy must be diverted from sexual activity. So, unavoidably, the civilized person is a frustrated person, and the more complex civilization becomes, the more we will suffer frustration. Freud mentions several ways in which humans attempt to cope with this fear, anxiety, and frustration, including such activities as drug taking, becoming absorbed in one's work, or gaining substitute satisfaction through art.

Another — in Freud's judgment, thoroughly unsatisfactory — way of coping with frustration and anxiety is through religion, which is designed to provide guarantees of safety that neither the individual nor society can supply. In childhood, individuals feel safe because they believe that their father is powerful enough to protect them from all harm. As they gradually become aware of their father's finiteness, they create for themselves a Father whose power is not limited and who can be depended on to provide protection from all danger. "The derivation of religious needs from the infant's helplessness and the longing for a father aroused by it seems to me to be incontrovertible."[16]

God is a human creation, then, a projection not so much of ourselves, as Feuerbach said, or of our society, as Durkheim suggested, as of our father. Religion, however, is the direct consequence of wishes and needs that are not satisfied in the mundane realm and that require a superpowerful being to guarantee that they are to be satisfied.

> The common man cannot imagine this Providence otherwise than in the figure of an enormous exalted father. Only such a being can understand the needs of the children and be softened by their prayers and placated by the signs of remorse. The whole thing is so patently infantile, so foreign to reality, that to anyone with a friendly attitude to humanity it is painful to think that the great majority of mortals will never be able to rise above this view. It is still more humiliating to discover how large a number of people living today, who cannot but see that this religion is not tenable, nevertheless try to defend it piece by piece in a series of pitiful rearguard actions.[17]

Freud argues that this self-deception, sometimes unconscious but often deliberate, that characterizes religious belief, amounts to making religion into a psychological crutch. "Countless people find their one consolation in religious doctrines, and can only bear life with their help."[18] People attempt to gain possession of "happiness and a protection against suffering," in a world where pleasure and security are forever eluding their grasp, "through a delusional remoulding of reality. . . . [the] religions of mankind must be classed among the mass delusions of this kind."[19]

Religion and Pathology

To describe religion as delusional equates it explicitly with mental pathology, a charge even more extreme than merely calling it infantile or saying that it is grounded in desire. Freud is not the only person to allege a connection between religion and psychopathology. What is different is his claim that the practice of conventional religion and the beliefs of ordinary religious persons are delusional. The more customary attempt to associate religion with pathology has tended to focus on the spiritual leaders on whose religious experiences the great religions have been founded.

The great prophets and saints of religion, it has often been pointed out, were prone to seeing visions and hearing voices. Judaism might be said to have had its birth through what some of the psychiatric critics of religion like to call visual and auditory hallucination. This was the vision of the burning bush and the voice understood to be the voice of God that set Moses onto the path that yielded—apparently through further hallucinations—the ten commandments and the transformation of the Hebrew people into the worshippers of Yahweh. Islam also had its birth from the visions and voices allegedly experienced by Muhammad in dreams as the angel Gabriel revealed to him the message that became the Qur'an. During the nineteenth century a number of scholars who examined the records of the life and teachings of Jesus concluded that they show a pattern of pathological symptoms. David Friedrich Strauss (1808–1874) found Jesus' belief that he was the Messiah, the one foretold in the Hebrew scriptures, and his teaching about his own second coming on clouds of glory surrounded by angels to become the judge and ruler of the world, so fanatical as to amount almost to madness.[20] William Hirsch, a psychiatrist, went further, actually diagnosing Jesus with paranoia.[21] George de Loosten cites Jesus' hallucinations on the occasion of his baptism, at the time of his temptation after forty days of fasting in the wilderness, and on the mount of transfiguration, along with such irrational acts as the cursing of the fig tree and the violence committed in the Temple when Jesus took up a whip and drove out the money changers, as evidence of insanity.[22]

Indeed, so widespread did the idea of Jesus' mental pathology become during the nineteenth and the early part of the twentieth century that Albert Schweitzer (1875–1965) felt called upon to make a study of the literature that lodged the charge in order to assess the claim. Schweitzer was trained in both theology and medicine. In 1906, he had written his famous *Quest of the Historical Jesus*,[23] in which he had brought out "the apocalyptic and what in modern concepts is considered the visionary in the Nazarene's thought" to an extent that might suggest that he agreed with those who regarded Jesus as paranoid. In 1913, he published his *Psychiatric Study of Jesus*,[24] examining the views of de Loosten, Hirsch, Charles Binet-Sangle, and Emil Rasmussen. Schweitzer argued that these authors failed to understand the culture in which Jesus did his work and thus took events that were not abnormal in that culture as evidence of pathology. Since insanity and other forms of deviance are socially defined, and since the social expectations of a person's culture influence both what he or she does and whether the behavior is regarded as deviant, the question of that person's sanity can only be judged in its own social context. Schweitzer concluded that the charge of insanity had not been made good.

William James (1842–1910), celebrated American psychologist and philosopher, treated the subject of religion and psychopathology in his monumental study of religious experience. He observed that many persons deeply involved in religion do indeed show symptoms of "nervous disorders":

> There can be no doubt that...a religious life, exclusively pursued, does tend to make the person exceptional and eccentric.... Religious geniuses have often shown symptoms of nervous instability.... Religious leaders have been subject to abnormal psychical visitations.... Often they have led a discordant inner life, and had melancholy during a part of their career.... Frequently they have fallen into trances, heard voices, seen visions, and presented all sorts of peculiarities which are ordinarily classed as pathological.[25]

Citing many examples of individuals who have manifested such eccentricities and symptoms, James attributes this tendency to an unusual sensitivity and points out that it is to be found in geniuses of other sorts as well—artists, poets, even scientists.

Clearly, many of the thinkers who point out the eccentric behavior of religious leaders, and especially those who call religious leaders mad, insane, or paranoid, believe that their arguments destroy the credibility of these individuals and by implication undermine the religions they founded or led. James, as we shall see in the next section, argues that this amounts to committing the logical fallacy called *argumentum ad hominum*—the attempt to destroy a teaching not by refuting the teaching itself, but by attacking the person who puts it forth.

Assessment of These Objections

The various sociological and psychological objections to theism present many detailed problems, but because nearly all have a certain feature in common, one general grievance can be raised against them as a group. These objections to theism attempt to explain how theism must have arisen and then to assert, or at least to intimate, that this explanation in itself explains theism away. The tacit assumption seems to be that if any belief or activity has an irrational origin, if it originated from human need or desire, if it can be shown to have a connection with bodily or organic conditions, or if the individual who puts it forth has at any time exhibited a pathological state of mind, the belief is discredited. Such an assumption, William James points out, would equally condemn nearly every human activity. Science, industry, history, art—even psychoanalysis itself—originate from human need and desire; all these activities are grounded in irrational organic conditions in the human body.

> There is not a single one of our states of mind, high or low, healthy or morbid, that has not some organic process as its condition. Scientific theories are organically conditioned just as much as religious emotions are. . . . Let us play fair in this whole matter. . . . When we think certain states of mind superior to others, is it ever because of what we know about their organic antecedents? No! . . . In the natural sciences and industrial arts it never occurs to anyone to try to refute opinions by showing up their author's neurotic constitution. . . . It should be no otherwise with religious opinions.[26]

Beliefs and activities must be judged on their own merits, not on the circumstances, however humble or noble, of their birth. James insists that they must be evaluated by their fruits, not their roots. Astronomy is an outgrowth of a discredited and disreputable ancient human activity, astrology. Is it thereby discredited? Chemistry traces its ancestry to alchemy, the medieval practice of persons who were searching for the philosopher's stone, a mysterious substance that was supposed to transform base materials into gold. Does that ignominious parentage cast doubt on the worth of chemistry? James's point is that even if religion can be shown to have originated in the superstitions, fears, anxieties, and needs of humankind, that fact tells us nothing about the truth of mature religious claims any more than the fact that chemistry originated in alchemy tells us about the reliability of its mature findings.

James's argument undermines almost completely the plausibility of the sociological and psychological objections. To be sure, James has not thereby offered any argument in support of theism. Showing that objections raised against a position are unsound does not prove the position itself to be true. But the arguments in support of theism have already been examined in the previous chapter. What James has shown quite effectively is that the sociological and psychological objections, all of them, depend on an assumption that turns out to be false: that whatever originates in fear, superstition, need, desire is therefore false or unreliable.

A vague awareness of this fallacy probably motivates such sociologists as Johnstone to attempt to avoid making claims about the origins of religion or about cause-and-effect relations between social and psychological circumstances and religious belief, but it is clear that Johnstone has not succeeded in avoiding the fallacy. In a passage quoted earlier in this chapter, he admits the great temptation to speak not merely of correlations but of necessary and sufficient conditions. If sophisticated sociologists and psychologists have yielded to the temptation or have not even noticed the problem, it is not surprising that the sociological and psychological arguments have persuaded so many ordinary persons. It seems to be something approaching the conventional "wisdom" of the age in our day that religion has been discredited by the arguments of such persons as Marx and Freud. But we see plainly here that these arguments do not carry logical weight because they are based on the fallacy that James has made so plain.

Thinkers such as Feuerbach and Durkheim have formulated speculative explanations concerning how religion *might have* originated and then, without offering any evidence or support, have affirmed that that is in fact how it did originate. They have proceeded to claim that because religion originated in the fears and needs of helpless people, it can be dismissed as nothing more than fantasy. The argument is faulty in each of its two main transitions: the unsupported move from a theory that explains how religion might have originated to the assertion that that is how it did originate; and the assumption that anything that originates in fear or need is therefore not to be trusted. Not merely one but both of these moves are unjustified.

The argument based on the alleged insanity of religious people generally or of the founders of religion is similarly flawed. As James has plausibly argued, events and behavior considered insane in one culture may be regarded as normal in another. Although we might legitimately attribute insanity to a person in the twentieth century who rejected belief in bacteria and insisted that disease is caused by demon possession, we may not properly call a person insane who, in a society knowing nothing of bacteria, attributes illness to demon possession. Thus the allegations of insanity have not been proven. But even if they had, this would not undermine the doctrines. The fact that an individual suffers from a psychopathology does not show that his or her ideas are false. A theory can be refuted — or proven — only by considerations having to do with the ingredients of the theory itself. The fact that an idea is put forth by a brilliant, mentally healthy person does not suffice to show that the idea is true; and the fact that it is put forward by a mentally disturbed person is not sufficient to show that it is false. Beliefs must be judged on their own merits, without regard to their origins, the social circumstances in which they arose, or the state of health of their originators.

RELIGION AND SCIENCE

Another body of knowledge often thought to constitute a threat to theism, or to put forth teachings that contradict and undermine theism, is science. The argument is made from at least two points of view. The first begins by assuming that religion is humankind's explanation of the origin and workings of the universe and concludes that, once science has provided an alternative explanation, religion is eliminated. The other involves pointing out ways in which the findings of science allegedly conflict with or contradict specific teachings of religion, or events alleged to support religion such as miracles.

Faith and Reason

The dispute between science and religion may be seen as a new form of the conflict between faith and reason. The issue concerns the extent to which the doctrines of religion are to be regarded as authoritative and beyond the scope of rational examination. Most religious traditions consider their teachings to be based on pronouncements from superhuman sources and thereby exempt from rational criticism. In some cases reason is declared to be finite, limited, even tainted, and therefore not competent to make judgments concerning the truth of what is divinely revealed. Even if reason is not explicitly denigrated, it is often consigned to the realm of the material world and mundane human affairs, with revelation serving as the only recognized source of knowledge about spiritual matters. It is the inspired writings of religious traditions, their scriptures or holy books, that are most frequently considered to be the source of divine revelation, and the faithful are often expected simply to accept and to believe unquestioningly the teachings derived from these writings.

Thus, from this standpoint, the source of religious truths is supposed to be revelation or **faith**. When philosophers or theologians begin to raise objections to the uncritical acceptance of prescribed dogmas, their objections are usually based on the claim that reason has discovered inconsistencies in the doctrines themselves, or between religious knowledge claims and knowledge claims derived by reason from other sources. This sets the stage for battles between the supporters of faith and the advocates of reason.

In the Christian tradition during the Middle Ages this battle sometimes involved denunciations of reason by defenders of faith and, for a period of time, a consequent antiintellectualism and opposition to learning. It was from this context that the conflict of science and religion had its beginning in the Christian tradition. Thomas Aquinas attempted a reconciliation of faith and reason by insisting that because both are gifts of God, they could not possibly be in conflict. Reason, Thomas pointed out, is the highest faculty God has bestowed on humans. Surely, he argued, God intended us to develop and make good use of this, our most Godlike faculty.

Thomas thus sets forth a teaching that explains how the two faculties, faith and reason, may be regarded as mutually supplementary rather than

contradictory. There are many things that reason is competent to discover
for itself, unaided by revelation, and it is clear that God intended us to use
it for just that purpose. On the other hand, some things are beyond the
powers of reason. Among these are things that humans need to know because they are essential ingredients in the practice of religion and for human salvation. It is these things in particular that God has vouchsafed to
reveal to us through holy scriptures and the doctrines of the church.

Certain items of belief, however, come to be known to us through both
faith and reason. Thomas points out that the existence of God can be
known to us in both ways. Thomas provides us with five arguments, the so-
called "five ways," sufficient to prove through human reason that God exists. And we also know that God exists because God has revealed himself to
us through scripture, prophets, the doctrines of the church, and the incarnation. But there are certain things about God that reason cannot discover
and cannot even understand: for example, that God is a Trinity, or that
Christ is both fully human and fully divine. These we would never have
known except for revelation. Thomas concludes by suggesting that God
has provided the overlap of reason and revelation for a good and deliberate
purpose: namely, to make it possible for us to test the workings of reason as
we develop more fully its use. In everyday terms, we may compare this to
the practice of putting the answers of some of the arithmetic problems in
the back of the book, so that students, after having worked the problems,
may look up the answers to make sure that they have got them right.

Ingenious as it was, however, Thomas's solution did not really reconcile faith and reason because its ultimate implication is that revelation
must be the final authority. Thomas claims that the two cannot ever really
conflict, yet it is clear that in any showdown reason and not revelation
must yield. Thomas declines to admit that the doctrine of the Trinity, for
example, is irrational, a violation of fundamental principles of logic and
mathematics; one cannot possibly, at the same time, be three. Rather, he
places doctrines of this sort beyond the competence of reason, and this
amounts to exempting at least some of the deliverances of revelation from
rational scrutiny.

It is clear that the first loyalty of the philosopher must be to reason,
and when alleged revelations clash with the considered findings of reason, those revelations must either be rejected outright or reinterpreted
in symbolic or mythological terms. Specific teachings such as the doctrine of the Trinity or the creation stories may be capable of mythological
interpretation so that the irrationality of what they literally claim disappears. But the literal claims of those who insist that sacred scriptures must
be accepted literally, regardless of whether or not their teachings clash
with reason or other evidence, are unambiguously irrational. Where reason and revelation contradict one another, without any question reason
must prevail.

Beliefs about the Creation and Operation of the World

One of the functions religion has usually performed is to provide human-kind with accounts, or what modern thinkers often prefer to call myths, about the origin of the natural world and the processes by which it operates. These accounts often involve gods or a God who brings the world into existence or gives it form, who creates living things with the features they have and for certain stated purposes, who makes human beings, sometimes in its own image, sometimes in several kinds or classes to correspond with the stratification of humans in a given society.

These creation stories often bear the mark of the setting, social and natural, in which they arose — it is this fact which gives such plausibility as it has to the sociological and psychological theories about the origin of religions — and the specific problems faced by the people among whom the stories are believed. For example, the Hindu myth of creation that depicts the human race as having been made from parts of the body of a god explains why it is that the Brahmins are properly regarded as superior to the Sudras. And the Jewish myth about God's condemnation of woman and man for eating the forbidden fruit explains such things as why childbirth is painful and why humans have to work so hard to survive. It is clear that the stories contain spiritual and moral teachings blended with beliefs about the origin and nature of the world.

When such accounts, usually passed down through an oral tradition for generations, come to be written down, the details take on a significance they may well not have had originally. The written documents in turn become sources for further interpretation and elaboration not only of the spiritual and moral teachings but also of beliefs about nature, about humans, and about people's place in nature.

We can see this process at work in the Christian tradition during the Middle Ages when the Ptolemaic theories of astronomy were taken over and blended with biblical ideas to generate a Christian cosmology, along with theories about humankind's place in the universe that cosmology depicted. Ptolemy, an astronomer who lived during the second century of the Common Era, depicted the earth as the center of the universe, with the moon, the planets, the sun, and the stars all revolving around the earth. The central place of importance this theory gave to man's habitat made it very attractive to Christian theologians, who incorporated it so fully into their doctrines that they soon forgot they had borrowed it from the secular science of the day.

When scientific astronomy developed in the fourteenth and fifteenth centuries, a battle in the Christian tradition began between the defenders of the now orthodox doctrine that embraced Ptolemaic astronomy and such astronomers as Copernicus (1473–1543), Kepler (1571–1630), and Galileo (1564–1642), who taught that the earth is not the center of the universe. The conflict led eventually to Galileo's being hauled before a tribunal of the Church and forced to renounce his astronomical theories. But the concerted efforts of the Church were not able to stamp out the work of the astronomers, who continued to refine their discoveries and support them with an accumulating mass of evidence.

The development of other branches of science brought forth new challenges to other dogmas the Church had affirmed. Around 1650, Archbishop James Ussher, by adding up the years the Hebrew patriarchs of the Bible were said to have lived, calculated that the world must have been created around the year 4000 B.C.[27] This chronology became very widely accepted and was even printed in the marginal notes of many editions of the Bible. But the scientific study of the earth by the new science of geology led to discoveries supporting the belief that the earth was much older. The presence of sea fossils on mountain tops suggested that those mountains had been pushed up from the bottom of the sea, a process that would have required very long periods of time. The presence of fossils of animals now extinct not only suggested a much longer history for the earth but also clashed with the Church's assumption that all species were created at one time and remained just the same to the present day.

These and other scientific findings had profoundly disturbing effects on religious belief and were vigorously resisted by defenders of the faith, who either denounced the scientists or else attempted alternative explanations of the disturbing evidence that would allow maintaining the accepted doctrine. It was suggested, for example, that God placed the fossils there to test humankind's faith. But the greatest shock, which created a fierce and open warfare between science and religion[28] and whose effects continue to flare up today, more than a century later, was produced by Darwinian evolutionary theory.

Charles Darwin (1809–1882) became convinced that the living organisms now inhabiting the earth are the results of a long process of development and change stimulated by changes in the environment that resulted in the selective elimination of some species and the gradual evolution of others. The most startling implication of the theory was that humans were not created directly by the hand of God, as the Hebrew scriptures say, but rather evolved from other primates and ultimately from the first simple organic molecules that appeared in the primeval slime of the earth's lakes or oceans in very remote antiquity. If the Church had been able, with however great difficulty, to adjust to the loss of Ptolemaic astronomy, it appeared impossible to reconcile its teachings with modern biology, and especially with the notion that humans are merely one among the other creatures of nature who came into being through the same lengthy processes which have produced every living thing on earth. The conclusion that many persons drew was that if modern science is true, then religion is false; no one can consistently accept both. For some, that meant abandoning their faith. For others, it was a call to battle with the goal of putting down the theories of science at any cost.

Fundamentalism

Among those who took the second position a new religious movement, called **fundamentalism**, arose in the second half of the nineteenth century. In 1910, Reuben A. Torrey (1856–1928) and Amzi C. Dixon (1854–1925) began issuing a series of pamphlets titled *The Fundamentals*, which purported to set forth the basic beliefs that anyone must hold to be a Christian. Three million copies of these pamphlets were distributed free of charge to every minister, evangelist, missionary, and YMCA secretary in the United States whose address Tory and Dixon could obtain. They were able to bring together strands of opinion from religious enthusiasts in several branches and denominations of Christianity, all of whom were motivated by their common desire to refute, or at least to silence, those doctrines of science that seemed to clash with religion, above all Darwinian evolutionary theory. The teachings of the fundamentalists were summarized in five statements enunciating those religious beliefs that could not in any measure be compromised:

1. The divine inspiration, inerrancy, and infallibility of the Bible.
2. The virgin birth and complete divinity of Jesus Christ.
3. The resurrection of the same body of Jesus that was three days in the grave.
4. The substitutionary theory of atonement of Jesus for the sins of the world (i.e., that Jesus substituted for humankind by taking the punishment for our sin).
5. The bodily second coming of Jesus.[29]

These doctrinal principles drew sharply the battle lines between Christian convictions and scientific theory, particularly because the fundamentalists insisted that the Bible be understood literally, not figuratively or metaphorically, and that every sentence in it was the literal truth. Clearly, then, they intended to say that no one could be a Christian who did not believe, for example, that the world was created in six 24-hour days. This position blatantly contradicted scientific findings that the world has been in process of evolving for millions of years. Virtually every major discovery of contemporary historical geology and biology would have to be seen in the same way. There could be no compromising with science; it must be condemned as false, dangerous, perhaps even the work of the devil.

One of the more dramatic episodes in the war waged by the fundamentalists against science was the infamous trial in 1925 of a Tennessee high school teacher named John Scopes on charges of teaching evolutionary science. Although Scopes was found guilty and fined, the trial made a virtual laughingstock of fundamentalism in much of the country and contributed at least temporarily to a decline in its influence. Meanwhile, on the other side of the issue, certain liberal theologians who firmly rejected fundamentalism were busy assimilating evolutionary theory into their Christian beliefs by arguing that a God who can create a world by evolutionary means is certainly just as great as one who can call the world into existence fully formed in six days. Scripture, they maintained, could properly be regarded as holy and inspired, as the Word of God, without being interpreted literally as the *words* of God.

The radical irrationality of the fundamentalists and the relative success of liberal theologians in reconciling evolution with Christianity resulted in a waning of fundamentalism for a time. In North America, however, it has flared up again and again in the second half of the twentieth century. Fundamentalism is the motivating spirit of the widespread Christian Schools movement, which undertakes to provide education outside the framework of the public schools in a setting where evolutionary science and other aspects of science thought to be incompatible with Christian teachings can be avoided. It has also resulted in the invention of so-called "creation science," — really little more than recasting the biblical account of creation under the label of science — and an effort through litigation and other methods to force public schools to teach "creation science" as a theory alongside evolutionary theory.

To the philosopher of religion, an examination of Christian fundamentalism is important for two main reasons. In the first place, it presents in perhaps its starkest form the challenge to religion that comes from science — and an irrational, completely unphilosophical way of responding to that challenge. Second, it illuminates the meaning of fundamentalism as that concept applies to all the world religions. Clearly, Moslem fundamentalism does not teach the five so-called Christian fundamentals; nor do Buddhist or Hindu fundamentalism. All these movements, however, share with Christian fundamentalism a basic irrationality, an insistence on interpreting the scriptures and traditions of the religion in a literal way, and a total inflexibility in dealing with alternative interpretation of the religion or with anything else seen as incompatible with, or a threat to, the religion.

That fundamentalism is a gravely dangerous ingredient in any religious tradition we have seen proven over and over again in the twentieth century. Because it arises out of a complete conviction that its adherents have the absolute truth and that anything in any measure disagreeing with their beliefs is wrong, fundamentalism tends to sanction all manner of ruthlessness and brutality in dealing with its enemies and seems willing to stop at nothing in fighting for its beliefs. There seems to be no way of reasoning with its advocates, since they have renounced reason in order to maintain their beliefs. And there seems no reason to expect fundamentalism to be any less dangerous in one religion than in another; under circumstances of appropriately perceived threat to the religion, fundamentalist believers seem capable of the most extreme acts in any setting.

Separating the Spiritual from the Protoscientific Content of Scripture and Doctrine

We have already seen that science can threaten religion in two major ways: in a very general way by offering natural explanations of the origin and workings of the universe, thus making the religious explanations redundant; and in more specific ways by showing that certain events in the world actually seem to have happened in a manner inconsistent with the way that holy scriptures or religious doctrine says they happened. An example of a general threat is the so-called Big Bang theory in astronomy. An example of the second is the plate tectonics theory in geology, which implies a history of the earth so lengthy as to contradict the biblical teaching that the world was created in six days.

A possible response to these various challenges posed by science is the one that the fundamentalists, and some other less extremist conservative religious teachers, have taken: namely, to renounce science, to maintain that it is false, and to insist that the religious teachings are literally true. Religious authorities have attempted this approach again and again, only to find the evidence that supports the scientific theories accumulating and growing stronger until the effort simply to shout science down looks increasingly absurd. Where religious leaders have held substantial political power, they have succeeded in suppressing unpalatable scientific findings by threatening or persecuting the scientists, thus retarding temporarily the progress of science. But this has never been more than a temporary expedient, and it seems clear that it never can be. Because the findings of science are grounded in the rational methods that lead to truth, these findings would be rediscovered even if opponents were to succeed at some point in wiping them out.

Reactionary religion has fought a long series of unsuccessful battles against science and has consequently been forced to engage in a humiliating series of retreats and concessions in the face of the advance of science, which is an unavoidable part of the onward progress of human knowledge. It has been suggested that the unbending attitude of such literal interpreters of religious doctrine and scripture is responsible for the decline in the influence of religion in the modern world and that such an attitude makes religion no longer intellectually respectable.

Other interpreters of religion maintain that these ongoing skirmishes are quite unnecessary and actually result from an unjustified assumption about the nature of religion, and particularly of religious scripture. Such conflicts, say these interpreters, result from an uncritical failure to notice that the holy writings of the world's religions actually contain a blending of spiritual or religious materials with protoscientific beliefs about the world that happened to be current at the time that the religious doctrines were being developed. The religious writers probably did not consider what they said about the nature of the world to be a necessary part of what they were teaching, often using it only as illustrations of their religious points, but once it became enmeshed with religious teachings and enshrined in scripture, later readers came to consider this material to be as much a part of the alleged revelation as the religious teachings. To recognize this phenomenon, a measure of objectivity in examining the holy writings is necessary. It is not difficult for a Christian to see that the moral teachings of the Bhagavad Gita are presented in a setting that is probably not literally historical. Similarly, a Hindu can see the Genesis story of creation as presenting claims about God and human duty in what is basically a mythological setting. It is not as easy, however, for these two to view their own traditions with a similar objectivity and to recognize that what must be preserved in a tradition is not the time-bound shell but the timeless spiritual kernel. The shell, representing the level of secular knowledge attained at the time the scripture was written, is what clashes with science. But this shell can be discarded without loss of the central and essential religious meaning.

It is important to notice two things about scientific theories of creation such as the Big Bang hypothesis. First, even if it is redundant with the belief that God created the world, redundancy does not disprove the belief. There is nothing inconsistent in accepting the Big Bang theory and affirming that science has discovered some truths about *how* God created the world. Second, the ultimate cosmological theories generated by science do not offer any final answer to the question of where the world came from; they only offer postulated answers about how the world may have taken on the form we find that it has today. The Big Bang theory, and the other cosmologies astronomers have explored during the twentieth century, all leave unanswered the question of where the matter/energy of which the universe consists ultimately came from. If the universe as we know it began when the concentrated material of the world exploded and began the expansion that we can still observe, the question remains where the material came from, how it came to be concentrated at a single point, and why it exploded.

Scientific explanation, in short, always reaches a point beyond which it cannot go. The religious person can embrace the explanation of the scientist and suggest that perhaps God is the ultimate source; that the phenomena the scientist has discovered and described are some of the ways in which God's creative power operates in creation. Whether or not this theistic suggestion is true must be decided on other grounds, such as those we have been discussing in these chapters on theism. The point is that science does not refute or undermine theism, except a theism that insists on a literal understanding of every detail of its scriptures. If a separation between kernel and shell can be made, no conflict need arise between science and the spiritual and moral essence of religion.

Thinkers such as Paul Tillich make use of the concept of myth to show that science is not incompatible with religion. To call an account a myth is not necessarily to say that it is false; rather, it is to say that the importance of the account is to be found not in its literal but in its symbolic content. The American political tradition carries the story of George Washington cutting down the cherry tree. Some historians doubt that the incident ever happened, but that is not the point. The story survives to carry the moral teaching that truth telling is a very important thing, a value that needs to be reinforced by appropriate examples from the experiences of great heroes. If we were to discover firm evidence that George Washington never did cut down a cherry tree, would we stop having our children make axes and cherry trees from construction paper to decorate their school rooms in February when President's Day is celebrated? Not at all.

The great myths of our religions are like this, Tillich argues. The central myth of the Bhagavad Gita about the great battle fought by Arjuna with Krishna as his chariot driver may or may not echo some actual historical battle. What is important about it is not whether or not the battle really happened just as the Gita describes it, but rather the lesson about doing one's duty and keeping one's ego detached from the outcome. Tillich tell us that "historical research has discovered . . . that in their narrative parts the Old and the New Testament combine historical, legendary, and mythological elements."[30] When science discovers that the historical elements do not reflect actual history, this is quite irrelevant to the religious significance of the Bible.

> Faith can say that the Old Testament law which is given as the law of Moses has unconditional validity for those who are grasped by it, no matter how much or how little can be traced to the historical figure by that name. Faith can say that the reality which is manifest in the New Testament picture of Jesus as the Christ has saving power for those who are grasped by it, no matter how much or how little can be traced to the historical figure who is called Jesus of Nazareth.[31]

If the holy writings of the great religions are understood in Tillich's sense as myths, then the findings of science that clash with the literal sayings of these scriptures do not in any sense threaten the religion. Even the writer of the Christian epistle of Corinthians recognized something to this effect when he said, "We have this treasure in earthen vessels."[32] It is the treasure that religion cherishes; it is only the vessels that science in any sense threatens. Many of the myths and legends of the great religions cannot stand up to close scrutiny if taken literally in an age of science, but only those persons who insist that there is no distinction between treasure and vessel, between kernel and husk, are disturbed by this fact. Religion in its spiritual dimension is in no more danger of being refuted by science than science is of being crushed or extinguished by religion.

Miracles

Another area in which religion has sometimes felt threatened by the progress of science is miracles. All the great religions involve reports of miracles. These miracles have sometimes been cited as evidence of the supernatural powers of the religious figures who allegedly perform them and as proof of the truth of their teachings. Here is an example from the Christian tradition: A certain man is reported to have said to Jesus, "Rabbi, we know that you are a teacher come from God; for no one can do these signs that you do, unless God is with him."[33] (The Greek word traditionally translated as "miracle" in the Christian scriptures is *semeion*, literally "sign.")

Miracles have been regarded as divine interventions into the workings of nature; science, however, operates on the assumption that every event in the world is causally determined in ways described by laws of nature that are universal and unexceptionable. This implies that there could never be violations of those laws, which in turn implies that miracles could not happen. The extent to which this position threatens religions depends on the extent to which believers insist that miracles really have been performed by their leaders, and especially the extent to which they depend on such alleged miracles to support the truth claims of their teachings. A few religious thinkers seem willing to abandon the notion of miracles in order to enjoy peaceful relations with science. But the miracle phenomenon has been religiously significant enough throughout the history of the various great religious traditions to deserve careful examination rather than casual discarding.

The case against miracles has been pressed most enthusiastically by David Hume. He points out that experience is our source of knowledge about what ever happens, that when the evidence of experience is extensive and consistent we justifiably believe with very strong conviction, but when the evidence of experience is small or inconsistent the wise person proceeds cautiously and tailors his or her belief to the strength of the evidence. Hume defines a miracle as "a transgression of a law of nature by a particular volition of the Deity, or by the interposition of some invisible agent."[34] But the laws of nature are firmly established by unalterable experience witnessed by countless persons throughout the entire stretch of human history. Thus the evidence that a miracle has occurred, necessarily very limited because miracles are by definition unique or rare events, can never suffice to counterbalance the overwhelming evidence for natural law, unless the falsity of the testimony would be an even greater miracle than the one to which it claims to witness. This, however, is never the case.

Tales of the supernatural and the miraculous, Hume argues, abound chiefly among ignorant and barbarous peoples. "When we believe any miracle of Mohamet or his successors, we have for our warrant the testimony of a few barbarous Arabians."[35] He examines the miracle claims of various religions, and he marvels at the strength of the faith of persons who accept claims about miracles contained in writings derived not from the most enlightened but the most ancient persons of barbarous and unimproved intellect. As an example, he cites the *Pentateuch*, a portion of the Hebrew Bible cited by Christians as the word and testimony of God.

> We are first to consider a book, presented to us by a barbarous and ignorant people, written in an age when they were still more barbarous, and in all probability long after the facts which it relates, corroborated by no concurring testimony, and resembling those fabulous accounts, which every nation gives of its origin. Upon reading this book, we find it full of prodigies and miracles. It gives an account of a state of the world and of human nature entirely different from the present: Of our fall from that state: Of the age of man, extended to near a thousand years: Of the destruction of the world by a deluge: Of the arbitrary choice of one people, as the favorites of heaven; and that people the countrymen of the author: Of their deliverance from bondage by prodigies the most astonishing: I desire any one to lay his hand upon his heart, and after a serious consideration declare whether he thinks the falsehood of such a book, supported by such a testimony, would be more extraordinary and miraculous than all the miracles it relates.[36]

Hume concludes his attack on miracles by claiming that the miracles of one religion, insofar as they support the truth of the teachings of that religion, contradict the miracles and thus the teachings of the other religions. All religions make use of miracles to support their teachings. Thus the religions mutually destroy one another's credibility. Still, Hume admits, many people remain fascinated by miracles and against all reason and evidence are prone to believe them. This Hume explains by pointing to the agreeable emotion people tend to feel when they are surprised. Humans love tales of the strange and astonishing ways of persons said to have been observed in remote parts of the world. If he were writing today, Hume would undoubtedly cite the public fascination with reports of flying saucers, strange beings from other planets alleged to have visited earth, and the great number of assorted fantastic tales that make up the stock in trade of several tabloid papers. Hume suggests that the emotion such surprising fables arouse — the more fantastic the more agreeable — accounts for the widespread acceptance even in an enlightened age of reports of the miraculous, despite the overwhelming evidence against their truth.

Richard Swinburne is perhaps the most successful among those who have attempted to answer Hume's attack. He begins by refining the definition of miracle, drawing on Ninian Smart's notion of "a non-repeatable counter-instance to a law of nature."[37] Swinburne points out that a counterinstance to a law of nature is not a miracle if it is repeatable. Rather, it is an instance of a more subtle law than the one it had been thought to violate. But how could we ever be confident that an observed event was nonrepeatable? Suppose, Swinburne suggests, that we make a diligent effort to discover an appropriately simple, non–*ad hoc* law that explains everything explained by the old law plus the alleged miraculous event, and that makes predictions about new events, some of which turn out to be correct. If we succeed, we have shown that the event was repeatable and have discovered a new law of nature that explains it. If sustained effort fails to find such a new law, however, we have good reason to believe that the observed event is nonrepeatable. The possibility of such an outcome shows, Swinburne believes, that it is at least possible to demonstrate that a miracle has occurred.

Here Hume would still object that the testimony of the witnesses could not ever suffice to prove that a miracle had in fact occurred. Swinburne replies that their testimony need not be all we have by way of evidence. If a certain event really did occur, it will have an ongoing series of consequences reaching perhaps down to our own time. Just as the scientist sometimes formulates laws of nature based on detective work about what happened in the remote past through observing the remaining effects of those presumed events, so also the occurrence of an alleged miracle — that is, a nonrepeatable counterinstance of a law of nature — could be established by appropriate investigation of the surviving effects of that event.

Perhaps the question of the possibility of the occurrence of miracles can be illuminated if we draw an analogy between the actions of free human agents and the actions of God that result in what gets called a miracle. If humans do in fact have free will, as we have seen reason in an earlier part of this chapter to believe, then the results of their behavior bears a resemblance to so-called miracles in the sense that no description of antecedent conditions in the material world, by itself, suffices to explain what happened. The explanation must include not only the description of the antecedent physical circumstances *but also* the free volition of the agent.

Another way of saying the same thing is to point out that the outcome of an action by a free agent could not have been predicted on the basis of a knowledge of all the antecedent physical conditions and the relevant laws of nature. But we do not regard the action of a free agent as a miracle, or a violation of a law of nature. Rather, if we believe in human free will, we also believe that the laws of nature are structured in such a way that free human action, although not explained or predicted by these laws, is compatible with them. This is really just another way of explaining what we mean by the claim that humans have free will. If humans can act freely, however, producing results that are not fully explained or predicted by the laws of nature, it should not surprise us that God, if he is a free agent similar at least in some ways to humans, can do so as well. And if we do not call such actions a violation of a law of nature when humans perform them, then neither should we if God does. This amounts to the position that events that cannot be explained by natural law might, without supposing them to be violations of natural law, plausibly be attributed to the divine will.

Of course, it is important to remember that our understanding of the world, summarized in the science of a given historical period, is imperfect. The fact that we cannot account by scientific law for some event today does not by any means preclude the possibility that it is actually a natural phenomenon, explainable by a more developed science of the future. Still, if our account of human free will is plausible, and if God exists as a free agent, there would seem to be no reason why God might not act freely on occasion to produce effects in the world that were no more explainable exclusively in terms of natural law and antecedent physical conditions than human actions are. We should carefully heed Hume's warning that our delight in the fantastic is likely to make us all too ready to believe reports of strange and remarkable things. We should cling faithfully to the virtue of epistemological modesty, being always careful not to make extravagant knowledge claims. This virtue will make us very slow to attribute any happening to God's intervention in the world because, as Hume reminds us, such intervention, if it ever happens, is very rare. Most alleged miracles probably have natural explanations, even if we may not always be able to discover them. Still, if our analogy with human free will is sound, the claim that such intervention could never occur seems to have been turned back.

But this account seems to involve a radically different understanding of what a miracle would be. If God's intervention in the affairs of the world, if it ever occurs, is analogous to the actions of free human beings, then such intervention would not be a violation of natural law. Does such an interpretation render the concept of miracle vacuous? Theologians such as Paul Tillich definitely do not think so. Tillich suggests that the concept of miracle might appropriately be applied to astonishing experiences that awaken in us an awareness of the wonder and the mystery of reality and put us in living touch with the divine dimension of reality that is the ground of our being. If we understand the rootedness of the world and of human life in the divine, which Tillich conceives not as a being but as Being itself, then the experiences through which finite consciousness reaches ecstatically beyond itself to awaken in some measure to its kinship with its divine ground become miraculous events — not in the sense of a separate being interfering in or violating the rational process of being, but in the sense of that which is infinitely beyond human awareness entering to some extent into the finite to enlarge and empower it. These astonishing experiences become revelations of the divine, and when they are sufficiently effective in the life of a human individual, they become incarnations of deity. It is such miraculous events that give birth to a new religions — new ways of seeing and understanding deity — and to transforming reformations of old ones.

CONCLUSION

Our examination of those objections to religion, usually thought to be the most formidable, has shown that, contrary to what casual thinkers have often assumed, they do not undermine or refute theism. We have already seen that theism has not been proven true by the arguments presented in its favor, although those arguments do provide some support and, at least to the satisfaction of some, render it probable. The objections to theism, though serious and forceful, similarly do not prove it false, although they do raise serious questions which cast a shadow of doubt.

The problem of evil is a very weighty one. The pervasive existence of terrible suffering constitutes a severe challenge to the claim that the world is the creation of a deity who is both powerful and morally perfect. The attempt of some religious persons simply to dismiss evil as unreal is not convincing. And yet a close examination of the allegedly inconsistent tetrad revealed an implicit assumption — that God could not be morally justified in allowing evil to exist — and that assumption proved not to be warranted. The claim that God could have created a world with no evil and could have created humans who always freely choose the good turned out to be fanciful and unsupportable. Our analysis of the most plausible responses to the problem of evil found them able to reduce the threat to theism very substantially. The outcome seems to be that some evil is a necessary condition for the existence of good and is thus morally justified on those grounds.

What remains of the problem is the question whether the quantity and quality of good made possible by those conditions for which evil is a necessary condition are worth the cost of the evil that occurs. This amounts to the question whether, if such evil is indeed the inevitable condition of the existence of good, it would have been better not to create a world at all. The limits of human vision and our ability to judge the relative weight of good and evil makes it impossible to give a definitive answer. If the arguments for theism were a great deal stronger than we found them to be, or if we could be confident of a continued life in an evil-free realm after death, the answer would be straightforward. As it is, we find the arguments indecisive. The problem of evil, even when the counterarguments have done all that they can do, continues to cast a shadow of doubt on theism. It surely has to be conceded that the problem has not been removed altogether.

The sociological and psychological counterarguments do not set out to refute the arguments that support theism, but rather attempt to undermine theism, and religion generally, by showing that it grew out of irrational human desires and needs. But this argument turned out to tell against science and all other human activities just as strongly as against theism. Science, history, politics, art, industry, religion — indeed, all human activities — are grounded in needs, fears, and desires. Chemistry has its origins in alchemy, the misguided desires of avaricious persons to find a way to change base metals into gold. Astronomy grew out of the superstitious practices of astrology. But we do not dismiss the findings of chemistry or astronomy when we notice the disreputable nature of their ancestry. Likewise, the claims of religion are not undermined by arguing that religious beliefs are related to early human fears and superstitions. Science and religion must both be judged by their mature teachings. Neither is damaged by claims about how they originated. Thus the sociological and psychological objections to theism turn out not to have much substance.

The seriousness of the threat posed by science to theism depends on the extent to which theism is identified with specific teachings derived from time-bound scriptures or traditions that predate and thus conflict with modern science. There is no question that many statements in the traditional writings of most of the great world religions, if these statements are understood literally, are inconsistent with many of the discoveries of modern science. Thus, anyone who claims that the statements contained in scripture must be accepted literally is adopting a shaky position. The findings of science are so well documented and supported that there is no reasonable justification for rejecting them in favor of the doctrines of religion. This amounts to recognizing that no rational person can accept the findings of science — findings that every rational person must accept — and also accept certain religious teachings literally understood. Science has therefore rendered certain religious teachings unacceptable, and it is irrational to continue to hold such beliefs. This the fundamentalists of the various world religions have recognized quite clearly. But they have taken the irrational, and inevitably unsuccessful, position of denouncing science and clinging blindly to discredited beliefs.

If theism is not identified with the literal truth of some particular set of scriptures or doctrines, then science constitutes no threat at all to its truth. Many theologians in most of the major world religions have seen that there is a distinction between the spiritual and moral teachings of scriptures, on one hand, and the setting of those teachings in a context of social and protoscientific beliefs characteristic of the age. It is with the protoscientific beliefs about the natural world that the findings of modern science conflict, not with their spiritual essence. Science does not contradict the spiritual content of religion.

Neither is there a conflict between science and theism. As a philosophical position, theism is not wed to the specific doctrinal teachings of any one of the world's religions. The threat to religion from science, therefore, turns out to be only to narrowly interpreted, literal-minded, doctrinaire religion, not to theism as such. Our examination of theism has shown that the truth of theism has not been established beyond doubt. Neither has it been refuted or definitely undermined. The attributes of deity taught by theism, when carefully understood, seem not to be incompatible with one another; the arguments for theism are weighty but, in the final accounting, not decisive; and the arguments against theism, also forceful, are not conclusive. We must conclude that the evidence leaves room for reasonable doubt. Some persons, impressed by the beauty, the order, and the grandeur of creation and the joy of human life, will believe in God. Others, depressed by suffering, disorder, and human conflict in the world, will not believe.

In Chapter 1, we examined the distinction between what reason requires, what reason forbids, and what reason permits because it neither forbids nor requires. We pointed out that we properly call a belief irrational when it is forbidden by reason. But we may call a belief rational not only when reason requires it, but also when reason only permits it. When we understand rationality in this way, we must conclude that both belief and disbelief in theism are rational because the evidence is not sufficiently weighty to coerce. In an age characterized by skepticism and the unreflective assumption that religion is leftover superstition that has been discredited by the progress of human knowledge, perhaps the most interesting finding is that theism stands on firmer grounds than the conventional attitudes of our day might incline us to expect.

The question remains, however, if theism is the most plausible world view. Atheism is fairly widespread and represents a serious challenge to theism and to religious beliefs and practices based on theism. Furthermore, other philosophical alternatives to theism impress thoughtful persons as highly plausible and are perhaps more strongly supported by the whole range of evidence and arguments than theism is. It is time now to examine some of these major alternatives.

ANNOTATED GUIDE TO FURTHER READINGS

The Problem of Evil

Mackie, J.L. *The Miracle of Theism.* Oxford: Clarendon Press, 1982.

> *Mackie treats the problem of evil as a serious challenge to the rationality of traditional theistic claims. (The title of the book is a humorous allusion to Hume's claim that nothing short of a miracle could engender belief.)*

Pike, Nelson, ed. *God and Evil.* Englewood Cliffs, N.J.: Prentice-Hall, 1964.

> *An excellent source for the study of the problem of evil. An excerpt from Dostoevsky's novel* The Brothers Karamazov *provides a particularly graphic illus-*

tration of the problem of evil. Selections by Hume, Mill, Mackie, and Mc-
Closkey conclude that the existence of evil seriously compromises the theistic
God; in the final two sections Pike and Smart come to the defense of God.

Plantinga, Alvin. *God, Freedom, and Evil.* Grand Rapids, Mich.: William B.
Eerdmans, 1977.

*A sustained, somewhat technical examination of the problem of evil. The pri-
mary vehicle of Plantinga's case is the free will defense. Plantinga goes through
his argument step by step, logically progressing to his conclusion that God and
evil can indeed coexist.*

Pojman, Louis P. *Philosophy of Religion: An Anthology.* Belmont, Calif.: Wadsworth, 1987.

*Part III explains and outlines the problem of evil and then presents selections by
Hume, Hick, and Swinburne, Leibniz, Edward Madden and Peter Hare, and
D. Z. Phillips.*

Swinburne, Richard. *The Existence of God.* Oxford: Clarendon Press, 1979.

*Swinburne attempts to surmount the problem of evil by emphasizing the impor-
tance of human free will. The possibility of moral evil, he argues, is a necessary
condition of genuine human freedom; natural evil is also needed because it
allows human beings to learn about evil through experience and gives them true
free choice.*

Other Objections To Theism

Bonansea, Bernardino M. *God and Atheism.* Washington, D.C.: The Catholic
University of America Press, 1979.

Bonansea defends religion from science on the issue of creation.

Freud, Sigmund. *Civilization and Its Discontents.* New York: W. W. Norton,
1961.

*Freud theorizes that the individual is frustrated when his or her natural aggres-
sive, self-serving instincts are stifled by the restrictions and obligations created by
society. Religion is an effort to escape from the harsh realities of life by creating a
substitute father, God, who will protect the individual.*

Freud, Sigmund. *The Future of an Illusion.* Garden City, N.Y.: Anchor Books,
1961.

*Religion is a delusion created by humankind, says Freud, and as such it is a form
of psychopathology, a result of our misguided attempts to tame the uncontrolla-
ble aspects of the environment.*

Rolston, Holmes. *Science and Religion.* New York: Random House, 1987.

*A thorough study of the relation of religion to science, with an interesting for-
mat: Rolston takes specific examples from various natural and social sciences
and examines how they relate to religion.*

Tillich, Paul. *Dynamics of Faith*. New York: Harper and Brothers, 1957.

Tillich finds that there is, in fact, no real dispute between science and faith because they belong to different spheres of understanding, a viewpoint that derives from Tillich's belief that religious teachings should not be taken literally.

Trueblood, David Elton. *Philosophy of Religion*. New York: Harper and Brothers, 1957.

Part III of this text, "Challenges to Faith," includes a section on the Marxian objections to religion.

NOTES

1. Many philosophers set up the argument as a triad or a tetrad. See, for example, David Stewart, *Exploring the Philosophy of Religion* (Englewood Cliffs, N.J.: Prentice-Hall, 1980), p. 245; William J. Wainwright, *Philosophy of Religion* (Belmont, Calif.: Wadsworth, 1988), p. 69; J. L. Mackie, "Evil and Omnipotence," in Basil Mitchell, ed., *The Philosophy of Religion* (Oxford: Oxford University Press, 1971), p. 92; Nelson Pike, "Hume on Evil," in Nelson Pike, ed., *God and Evil* (Englewood Cliffs, N.J.: Prentice-Hall, 1964), p.87ff.

2. See, for example, Leslie Weatherhead, *Psychology, Religion and Healing* (New York: Abingdon, Cokesbury Press, 1951).

3. J. L. Mackie, "Evil and Omnipotence," *Mind* 64, 254 (1955), reprinted in Nelson Pike, *God and Evil* (Englewood Cliffs, N.J.: Prentice-Hall, 1954), p. 56.

4. Ninian Smart, "Omnipotence, Evil and Supermen," *Philosophy* 36, 137 (1961), reprinted in Pike, *God and Evil*, p. 105.

5. Some nonhuman animals on earth, and perhaps elsewhere in the universe, possess in diminished degree some of the attributes of persons; thus a measure of value occurs in their conscious enjoyings and sufferings. This is a very important consideration for ethical theory and can easily be accommodated in the theory being developed here.

6. Rabindranath Tagore, *Shyamali* (Calcutta: Visva-Bharati Publishing, 1955), pp. 6–8.

7. See Guy E. Swanson, *The Birth of the Gods* (Ann Arbor: University of Michigan Press, 1960).

8. Ronald L. Johnstone, *Religion in Sociology: A Sociology of Religion*, 3rd ed. (Englewood Cliffs, N.J.: Prentice-Hall, 1975, 1988), p. 32.

9. Karl Marx and Friedrich Engels, *The Communist Manifesto* (New York: International Publishers, 1948), p. 6.

10. Ibid.

11. See Karl Marx and Friedrich Engels: *Religion Ist das Opium des Volks* (Zurich: Ring-Verlag, 1934).

12. Ludwig A. Feuerbach, *The Essence of Christianity*, trans. M. Evans (New York, Harper and Row, 1881, 1951) excerpted in George I. Mavrodes, *The Rationality of Belief in God* (Englewood Cliffs, N.J.: Prentice-Hall, 1970), pp. 192f.

13. Ibid., p. 193.

14. Sigmund Freud, *The Future of an Illusion* (Garden City, N.Y.: Doubleday & Company, 1961).

15. Ibid., p. 22.

16. Sigmund Freud, *Civilization and Its Discontents* (New York: W. W. Norton, 1961), p. 19.

17. Ibid., p. 21.

18. Ibid., p. 57.

19. Ibid., p. 28.

20. David Friedrich Strauss, *The Life of Jesus* (London: William and Norgate, 1879); *The Life of Jesus Revised for the People* (London: William and Norgate, 1879).

21. William Hirsch, *Conclusions of a Psychiatrist* (New York: Truth Seeker Company, 1912), p. 99.

22. George de Loosten [Dr. Georg Lomer], *Jesus Christ from the Standpoint of the Psychiatrist* (Bamburg, 1905).

23. Albert Schweitzer, *The Quest of the Historical Jesus* (New York: Macmillan, 1961) from the 1906 edition.

24. Albert Schweitzer, *The Psychiatric Study of Jesus* (Boston, Beacon Press, 1948) from the 1913 edition.

25. William James, *The Varieties of Religious Experience* (New York: Macmillan, 1961) from the 1902 edition, pp. 24f.

26. Ibid., pp. 3ff.

27. James Ussher, *Annales Veteris et Novi Testamenti* (published between 1650 and 1654).

28. See a detailed account of this warfare in Andrew Dickson White, *A History of the Warfare of Science with Theology in Christendom* (New York: D. Appleton, 1896, 1926).

29. Fundamentalism as a modern religious movement within Christianity is discussed in such sources as: J. Paul Williams, *What Americans Believe and How They Worship* (New York: Harper & Row, 1962), Winthrop S. Hudson, *Religion in America* (New York: Charles Scribner's Sons, 1981), and Dean W. Ferm, *Contemporary American Theologies: A Critical Survey* (Minneapolis, Minn.: Seabury, 1981).

30. Paul Tillich, *Dynamics of Faith* (New York: Harper & Row, 1952). p. 86f.

31. Ibid., p. 88.

32. II Corinthians 4:7.

33. John 3:2.

34. David Hume, *An Enquiry Concerning Human Understanding* (Indianapolis, Ind.: Hackett, 1977), p. 77.

35. Ibid., pp. 81f.

36. Ibid., p. 90.

37. R. G. Swinburne, "Miracles," *The Philosophical Quarterly* 18, 73 (October 1968), reprinted in William L. Rowe and William J. Wainwright, *Philosophy of Religion: Selected Readings*, 2nd ed. (New York: Harcourt Brace Jovanovich: 1989), p. 446.

5

Alternatives to Theism

The most obvious alternative to theism is atheism, the belief that there is no God or that the God of theism does not exist. The principle arguments in support of atheism are those that are put forward against theism, many of which we have already examined. A position often confused with atheism is **agnosticism**, which is actually the suspension of judgment or the refusal to affirm either theism or atheism. More radical than agnosticism is **skepticism**, which expresses doubt about the possibility of any knowledge at all — concerning religious matters or anything else. In its most extreme form, skepticism involves the claim that nothing can be known, but this is contradictory since its assertion implies both that it (the claim that nothing can be known) is known to be true and that it could not be known to be true. In its less extreme and more wholesome form, skepticism is an attitude of doubting claims that are not substantiated by evidence or of demanding good reasons before accepting claims.

Agnosticism is sometimes adopted by persons who do not want to take the trouble to think about their beliefs or to engage in the mental labor required to work out a rationally supported position. Of course, theism or atheism may also be embraced lazily and without thoughtful reflection. A responsible agnostic is one who has carefully weighed the evidence for and against theism and reached the informed, tentative conclusion that it is too evenly balanced to justify taking a stand for either side. Similarly, the responsible theist or atheist is one who has adopted this position thought-fully, based on a careful consideration of the reasons that support both points of view.

The philosopher of religion is interested in atheism as an alternative to theism principally as it is elaborated into a position that gives alternative answers to some or most of the questions that theism addresses. We will be examining here several major atheistic positions that deny the existence of God or make no place for the theistic deity. Our focus will be on their constructive teachings — what we might call their "world view" — particularly what they have to say about such ultimate matters as the origin, nature, and destiny of the world and of humankind. Some advocates give some of these positions an explicitly religious tone, encouraging an attitude of reverence toward nature or toward human values, whereas others simply attempt to provide metaphysical accounts of reality without God or any religious dimension. In addition to these philosophical alternatives to theism, certain great world religions such as Buddhism, because they are atheistic or nontheistic, also constitute alternatives to theism. We will reserve our examination of them until Chapter 8, where the philosophical teachings of several major world religions are discussed.

REDUCTIVIST MATERIALISM

Materialism is a philosophy that maintains that only the material world is real or that everything that exists is made of matter. It usually involves principles of explanation according to which those things not ordinarily thought of as material — such things as consciousness, rationality, and what religious persons call the spiritual — can be understood as manifestations or characteristics of material processes. Materialism is a very old position, taught by Greek philosophers as early as the sixth century before the Common Era, and by Indian philosophers at least that early. In its long history, the doctrine of materialism has evolved in various ways and has been given a variety of forms. As with atheism, the term has served as a label of abuse both in ancient and modern times by connection with coarse pleasure seeking or greed for material wealth.[1] But materialists are not necessarily any more "materialistic" in this crude sense than theists or anyone else.

The early materialists of both the East and the West believed that the objects we encounter in the world are configurations of material substance differing from one another because of the different quantities of the various elements and the different ways in which the elements are arranged. The **Carvakist school** of materialism in ancient India and such ancient Greek materialists as Empedocles believed in four elements, earth, water, air, and fire, from various combinations of which all things are made. Other ancient materialists, the so-called atomists, taught that the ultimate constituents of all things are tiny atoms (the Greek term means "uncuttable") that swirl, collide, stick together, and form themselves into stars, planets, plants, animals, and human beings. Whatever happens in the world, they said, is a manifestation of changes in the arrangements of the material particles. Some of the ancient materialists believed that humans have souls, but they thought that souls were simply the smoothest and most active atoms and believed that these atoms dispersed when the person died.

Modern materialism is a much more refined extension of these ancient theories. The vaguely described atoms of the ancients and the four elements of earth, water, air, and fire have been elaborated into nearly 100 so-called natural elements — that is, elements that naturally occur in physical circumstances such as exist on earth — and an as yet undetermined number of so-called artificial elements. The persistent work of the sciences has provided much more detailed and reliable knowledge about the nature of these particles, including the discovery that they are not after all uncuttable, and about the processes that blend them into the rich array of material objects from galaxies to cosmic dust, from stars to planets, from bacteria to humans. The vague suggestions about how atoms in an incessant swirl stick together, "somehow" forming all material things, have given way to detailed descriptive theories that provide increasingly plausible accounts of the mechanism of cosmic, stellar, planetary, organic, and even psychological and social development.

Materialists argue that they have succeeded, without resorting to gods, spirits, or anything supernatural, in providing relatively comprehensive and detailed explanations of reality. They point out that their theory is simpler than theism because it does not postulate intangible or mysterious beings such as a God and, unlike theism, it has the support of science. When nature is intelligible by itself, we do not need to complicate our explanation by postulating spiritual beings whose nature or existence cannot be detected by science and that themselves are quite beyond our understanding. The teachings of theism are redundant as explanations of nature, since nature can be explained in its own terms. Materialism makes clear in terms that humans can understand what reality is like; theism only plunges us into mystery and superstition.

Despite the impressive explanatory theory the materialists have provided, however, and despite the substantial and ever-increasing support that materialism seems to have received from the steady growth of scientific knowledge, they have always been hard pressed to provide satisfactory explanations of some features of human experience. Theists argue that even if the explanations of the cosmic and earthly processes that materialism derives from science are correct, several difficult questions remain unanswered. Materialism does not explain where the ultimate ingredients of matter come from; what drives the process by which these ingredients are transformed into the objects we encounter in the world; how dead matter can come to life and give rise to living organisms; or how unconscious organisms can ascend to high levels of knowledge, intelligence, aesthetic sensitivity, moral awareness, compassion, even altruism.

The explanations offered by the materialists, based on the findings of science, do account much more adequately and in gratifying detail for the mechanisms by which material objects and physical bodies come to have the features that they have. The vagueness that characterized ancient materialism in these matters returns in nineteenth- and early twentieth-century materialism in such matters as life, consciousness, self-consciousness, and all the many levels of what theists call spiritual awareness. Theism does postulate spirits that are not discoverable by science, but this does not mean that there is no reason to believe in such spirits. The concept of the divine spirit provides an explanation of where the ultimate constituents of the universe came from and the force that moves the world to ever higher and higher levels of order. These are matters that materialism ignores or glosses over. And the concept of the human spirit provides an explanation of the mental, intellectual, ethical, aesthetic, and spiritual dimensions of human experience and behavior. None of these traits is adequately explained by materialism.

Another way that criticisms of materialism have been expressed is by charging that the doctrine is reductive. This charge amounts to turning against the early twentieth-century materialists an aspect of their own explicitly enunciated goal. Many of these materialists set out to achieve the reduction of the "higher" or more complex sciences to the principles of the basic science of physics in order to achieve their goal of the unity of science. It seemed clear to these thinkers that nature is a seamless whole. But science divides nature into parts, each studied by a different field or discipline. If the results of all the compartmentalized studies of the various sciences are to find their way into a comprehensive picture of nature as a whole, a means must be found to stitch together the separate branches of science into a single fabric with no gaps or holes. This was one of the projects associated with logical empiricism during the 1930s. The theories of a unified science should cover comprehensively every aspect of the natural world.

To work toward this goal, the sciences were arranged hierarchically, with physics as the most fundamental, followed by chemistry and biology, and then by psychology, sociology, economics, politics, and the like. The unity of science was to be demonstrated by showing that the phenomena studied by chemistry are simply more complex aspects of those studied by physics; those of biology and psychology and sociology are similarly complexification of the phenomena of the next level downward. To demonstrate the connections would involve *reducing* the laws of chemistry to those of physics; the laws of biology to those of chemistry — and ultimately to those of physics, and so on. This reduction would be accomplished by restating the laws of one science in terms of the concepts and principles of the other science. The reduction of the laws of one science to those of another must in principle express completely what the laws of the more complex science expressed; nothing must be left out. Thus, for example, it must be possible to reduce psychology to biology *without residue*. And the language of biology might be regarded as a shorthand way of expressing a much longer set of principles in the language of chemistry.

This means that materialism tries to explain what is higher and more complex in terms of what is lower and simpler. But such an objective, its critics argue, inevitably just ignores and leaves out the qualities that do not lend themselves to reduction, and these are the most important ones. According to this argument, reductivism is a "nothing but" theory: Living organisms are nothing but inorganic substance rearranged, conscious persons are nothing but animals with a more complex nervous system, and so on. But this type of reasoning does not *explain* the amazing new attributes that characterize the ever higher and more complex levels of being to which nature seems forever to be striving; rather, it *explains them away*.

To be sure, a simpler theory is to be preferred to a more complicated one, *provided* both explain equally well what is to be accounted for. Theism is more complicated and does postulate things that materialism gets along without, but materialism does not get along well without them. The critics of materialism allege that theism, too, can embrace the findings of science, which materialism claims as its primary support, and can go beyond to give real explanations of things that materialism explains away. Theism explains the appearance of order, purpose, and value in the world in terms of a being who is rational and who orders and energizes the world process in order to realize a purpose and create values. Materialism is forced, according to its detractors, to regard these mental, spiritual, and value phenomena as fortuitous events occurring for no intelligible reason in a blind, unconscious, mindless universe. Some theists go farther and point out that materialism has desolate and dismal implications for the ultimate fate of humankind, since by this account the universe is a cold, uncaring, mechanical process without a God, and humans are "nothing but" small machines produced by a blind cosmic process that is unaware of their existence and that will soon swallow them up again, wiping them out as if they had never been.

This final argument has more pragmatic than rational force, since the fact that a theory is encouraging to humans does not prove that the theory is true. The ending of cosmic history might, after all, be tragic. But the other points that theist and other philosophers have raised against materialism have had a powerful effect. The "crude" materialism of the early twentieth century was vulnerable to the kind of charges that the theist persistently pressed against it. As a result, the old materialism gave way to

other nontheistic positions that claim to be able to deal more adequately
with the weaknesses of materialism, especially the charge of reductivism.
Darwinian evolutionary theory gave the cue and the impetus to the development of such theories as emergent naturalism and humanism, which are
actually refined versions of materialism. For a time, many philosophers
avoided the word *materialism* because of its widespread association with
reductivism. But recently, a group of nontheistic philosophers has developed ever more sophisticated versions of materialism and the term has once
again come very much more into favor. Before we look at these contemporary versions of materialism, however, it will be useful to examine several
forms of materialism that call themselves by other names.

EMERGENT NATURALISM

Modern types of **naturalism** are nearly all materialistic because they postulate no substance other than matter and its constituents as the stuff of
reality. They make, however, conscious attempts to avoid the charge of
reductivism and to overcome the sense that nontheistic world views have
to be dreary pictures of a cold and alien world. Most of the several varieties
of this position that developed in the West during the past hundred years
make use of the evolutionary image as a central explanatory principle,
elaborating by analogy the notion of biological evolutionary theory to apply to cosmic and historical processes. The discovery by modern physics
that matter and energy are simply different forms or states of the same
thing, and that they are mutually transformable into one another, provided
another important tool for a naturalistic account of reality. Relativity
physics and evolutionary biology made it possible plausibly to picture the
entire universe as a dynamic, energetic, emergent process and to account
for mind, value, and spirit in nonsupernatural terms.

   Modern types of naturalism begin with the assumption that nature is
all there is, and that nature is ultimately intelligible, capable of being fath-
omed and understood by rational human thought. Its proponents call their
position "naturalism" to mark their rejection of the supernatural and their
insistence that reality is identical with the realm of nature. But they differ
from materialism in one important point. The reductivism characteristic of
the cruder earlier materialism was the result of attempting to explain all the
different levels of reality by means of the most basic scientific laws. Late
nineteenth- and early twentieth-century materialism often assumed that
the explanatory principles of biology, psychology, and sociology could ultimately be reduced to those of physics. The organic and social sciences have
increasingly discovered, however, that such reduction is not possible. Each
higher or more complex level requires explanatory principles of its own that
cannot be reformulated or translated into those of the lower levels. Conse-

quently, the naturalists introduce the notion of multiple levels of nature, each "controlled by laws that are peculiar to itself."[2]

Modern naturalisms characterize humans as "children of nature," which means that the human being is "neither a child of God living in a supernatural world nor an orphan living in an 'alien world,'" but a "natural citizen of the cosmos" in which he or she is thoroughly at home. This teaching of naturalism has two effects: It "naturalizes man," but it also "humanizes nature."[3] It means that a human is not a supernatural being set apart from the natural world or a being different in kind from any other being in the world. It also means that all human characteristics, physical, mental, aesthetic, moral, spiritual, are features of the natural world, traits that nature generates and supports under appropriate circumstances. Humans cannot be explained exhaustively in terms of the basic principles of physics, as the early materialists tended to assume. There are principles unique to the organic and the mental levels of being, irreducible to the principles of physics, that complete the account of living and mental beings. But these beings are nonetheless integral parts of nature.

The Evolutionary Naturalism of Samuel Alexander

Naturalistic systems were worked out during the late nineteenth and early twentieth centuries by a number of important thinkers in the West and the East, sharing most of the same basic assumptions but differing in details. One of the most successful systems in the West was that of Samuel Alexander (1859–1938). He depicted reality as a multilevel process grounded in the most basic units of differentiation of the space-time continuum, rising through many levels to life and mind, and striving ultimately toward the creation of deity. Each new level of reality, he argued, represents a higher and more complex arrangement of some of the entities that constituted the next lower level. At the same time, each higher level also has new characteristics that cannot be explained fully in terms of the laws of the previous level, nor could they have been predicted before they arose.

The most basic unit of reality Alexander called a "point-instant of space-time." Space, undifferentiated by time, would be a total blank. Time, if it were not measured and divided into units by space, would similarly be empty. In reality, every instant of time is spread out over every point of space and every point of space streams through every instant of time. And each of the more complex objects and events we experience in the world occurs at the conjoint intersections of a group of spatial points and temporal instants and is, in a sense, only a very great complexification of those point-instants but at the same time is characterized by genuinely new features.

The motion of time, Alexander says, sustains the vibration of space in a cosmic dance that continuously creates the world. We may begin by imagining an abstract situation "before" the world began — although apart from time, there could be no "before"; thus such a situation is merely abstract and imaginary, and we must recognize that the world process had no beginning. The imaginary condition, however, enables us to picture to ourselves the process by which nature complexifies itself in its restless striving for higher levels of being. Thus we imagine time "moving over the face of space," so that empty, undifferentiated space is filled and the blank continuity of time is segmented, and there appear the most fundamental units of the world, point-instances of space-time. As the patterns of vibration induced on space by the sweep of time become more complex, some of the point-instances rise to a higher level of being and become the tiniest and simplest particles of matter, whatever those turn out to be. This level of being has new characteristics not present at the lower level. The process continues ever upward, forever generating new and more complex entities. Eventually electrons, protons, and neutrons arise with the new and unprecedented quality of electric charge. Atoms appear with their various qualities; also compounds, each new and unique.

In the long dawning of creation, these natural processes generate the galaxies and stars, the planets and planetary climates, the complex inorganic chemicals and simple organic forms, the reptiles and mammals that constitute our world. It is a process of astonishing variety, and what is most amazing is the ubiquity of newness. At every bend and turning appear new configurations of material things, each with new characteristics which no one could have imagined until it appeared. When chemical compounds reach a certain level of complexity, they suddenly begin to be characterized by the unprecedented capacity to absorb other chemicals from their surroundings and to make copies of themselves, and thus a world formerly dead comes to life. In the eons of biological evolution, again and again new complexifications arise with the capacity to absorb sunlight and synthesize energy and to move about in the environment; with new sensitivity to their surroundings by way of sense organs; with crude facilities to remember and to foresee; and eventually with refined capacities to reason, to imagine, to enjoy, to understand moral obligation, to experience aesthetic appreciation, to love, and even to worship.

It would be unpardonably crude to say that life is "nothing but" its chemical constituents or that mind is "nothing but" a complex nervous system. The unique qualities of each level are new, *emergent* qualities, grounded in the material processes above which they arise; they are even in a way products of those processes — perhaps in some sense identical with them. Life in all of its multifarious forms is an emergent quality of certain chemical compounds and material organisms. Mind is an emergent quality or set of qualities of certain central nervous systems when they reach appropriate levels of complexity and function in certain ways through interaction with their surroundings. Contemporary philosophers of mind use the expression *supervenience* in this sense. Mind is not a separate spiritual substance that somehow hovers about or infests the central nervous system, as such dualists as René Descartes believed. Rather, mind is supervenient on the central nervous system. It is, as Alexander saw it, a quality which could never have appeared if the nervous system had not evolved as it did. Neither, however, could it have been predicted on the basis of the structure and function of the nervous systems of simpler or lower organisms.

Alexander worked out his philosophy of **emergent naturalism** in his major work, *Space, Time, and Deity*.[4] His system includes the concept of deity, but certainly not in anything resembling the theistic sense. Deity is not a being antecedent to the world and responsible for its creation. Rather, deity is a quality of being, posterior to the world, emergent in the world. It is that highest level of being toward which reality is striving. Indeed, deity is a relative term, used to express the unique and unpredictable quality expected to characterize being at the level just higher than the present one. Thus from the perspective of the inorganic world, life is deity; from the perspective of what we call "brute" animals, mind is deity. The divine dimension consists of those astonishing innovations that nature generates when it leaps up to a new level of complexity and shows forth new qualities which seems almost supernatural to beings at the next lower level.

Mind is the highest level yet to appear, but there is no reason to think, says Alexander, that the process of elaboration, refinement, complication, and increasing complexity has ended with humans. Just as some living beings acquired more complex nervous systems and began to manifest the new quality of mind, it may well be that some humans, or perhaps some groups or communities of humans, are in the process of acquiring still more complex physical characteristics that, in the fullness of time, might come to manifest a new quality as different from mind, and as much higher than mind, as mind itself is above the merely organic.

Alexander explains the attitude of reverence in some humans as a dim recognition of the quality of deity with which the world is "pregnant," and which the emergent process is striving to bring to birth. Religious believers mistakenly think that their worshipful attitudes are addressed toward a being that already exists as a supernatural creator of the world. In fact, religious aspirations reach upward toward a quality of being that exists at best only implicitly and that is yet to become explicit when reality achieves the next level of being. The evolutionary process is forever deifying nature by bringing forth qualities so new and astonishing that they appear supernatural.

Just as naturalism "naturalizes man" and in the process "humanizes nature," then, so also it naturalizes God, and thus deifies nature. According to naturalism, the highest qualities we aspire to imagine and strive to realize—the qualities of justice, compassion, saintliness, and love—are not consigned to another world beyond the reach of humans. Rather, they must be recognized as natural characteristics of a human world, within the grasp of human striving, and standing as lures and challenges to our highest and most zealous efforts. Evolutionary processes gradually deify the world; in small measures human endeavor may also contribute to that process of deification.

When Alexander speaks of the creative process that so pervasively characterizes the world, he uses the expression *nisis:* The universe, he says, shows a *nisis*, a striving, a reaching forth, toward the creation of newness. It is this *nisis*, he suggests, that religious persons become aware of through religious experience. Some of his critics have suggested that the concept of *nisis* is actually Alexander's surreptitious God, designed to answer the question of what drives the process of creation and enables it to move, not downward as systems not energized from without are expected to do, but upward, against the pull of inertia, contrary to the principle of entropy, toward ever higher, more complex, and qualitatively superior levels of being. The notion of *nisis* is somewhat reminiscent of the *élan vital,* the "vital impetus," that Henri Bergson (1859–1941) credits with driving evolution to produce higher and more complex beings. Bergson presented a version of emergent naturalism, which he called creative evolution,[5] that shares many of Alexander's basic naturalistic assumptions.

Critics of both systems have suggested that although the notion of emergence does much to overcome crude materialism's problem of reductivism, it raises another problem itself, namely, that of explaining how a blind material process can achieve order and an ever-ascending progression. To say, as naturalists have sometimes tended to do, that such order and progression is part of the nature of nature is not really to explain it. It almost amounts to saying, "We don't know how it works; it just works." Similarly, charge the critics, *nisis* and *élan vital* become simply names that refer to the fact that evolution does indeed move upward. Unless they name something real, something capable of infusing a motivating energy or at least a guiding principle, they only cover up, and do not solve, the mystery.

Alexander firmly rejects the ultimate question of why there is anything rather than nothing. He recognizes that every system begins with the assumption of something already existing that has existed forever—whether it be matter or nature or God. Thus he tells us that we must accept with what he calls "natural piety" the existence of the world, and then find the best possible description of the processes of which the world consists. Our metaphysical explanations account for how and why things happen as they do *within* nature; it is presumptuous to attempt to speak of what might be before or beyond nature, where our knowledge does not reach. We must recognize that this point is well taken. But the question remains concerning whether the concepts of *nisis* and *élan vital* offer any satisfactory help in addressing the question of what drives and guides the evolutionary process in which the universe seems to be engaged.

Aurobindo's Criticism of Emergent Naturalism

The great Indian philosopher Sri Aurobindo (1872–1950) is convinced that the concepts of *nisis* and *élan vital* do not offer a satisfactory explanation of the world. Aurobindo assimilated evolutionary theory into his philosophical system, but rejected naturalism in favor of a form of supernaturalism called **absolute idealism**. According to this position, advocated in the West by such thinkers as F. H. Bradley (1846–1924) and Josiah Royce (1855–1916), ultimate reality consists of one single all-encompassing mind called the Absolute. There is a sense in which such a supernaturalism is itself an alternative to theism, since the Absolute, even though sometimes also called God, is clearly not a being like the theistic God. But Aurobindo's version of absolute idealism stands as a criticism of evolutionary naturalism because in effect it absorbs and includes the evolutionary framework of explanation for the natural world, but insists that this explanatory framework is truncated and inadequate until it is completed by the concept of a supernatural Absolute Mind.

Aurobindo finds naturalism inadequate, and the notion of *nisis* or *élan vital* unhelpful, in explaining what drives and guides evolution, the question of how the higher can arise from the lower. The only way that we can make sense of the fact that blind, dead matter gives rise to rational and spiritual mind, he insists, is to suppose that the qualities that appear in the higher levels are present in some way in the lower. And the only plausible explanation of how this can be is that a great antecedent mind should first have immersed or devolved itself into the material world. The only explanation of evolution, with its continuous creative newness, is in terms of an antecedent devolution or what Aurobindo calls "involution," a plunge of the Absolute into every part and particle of the material world.

The Absolute Mind, says Aurobindo, created the material world through a process of self-negation, self-alienation, descending from the level of superconsciousness through multiple grades of lesser consciousness eventually into the dull loss of consciousness that characterizes the dead material world. The evolution of the universe which we see today represents the reversing of this process. The divine mind is once again ascending from the depth to which it sank itself toward that ultimate unity of superconsciousness into which all reality will one day once again dissolve. Evolution can be seen to be driving material reality ever upward, generating more and more complex levels each with new qualities faintly resembling the superqualities of mind, overmind, cosmic mind, and Absolute

Mind. The *nisis* of Alexander and the *élan vital* of Bergson are the dimly apprehended but misunderstood activities of the Absolute. Aurobindo calls his fellow humans to the practice of religious disciplines, which he claims will accelerate the rise of individuals toward higher levels of mentality as a part of the long cosmic struggle toward reunion with the Absolute.

What is perhaps most remarkable about Aurobindo's system is that it is virtually a faithful copy of the philosophy of naturalism, but embedded in a larger framework of absolute idealism. With this larger framework, moreover, Aurobindo stands solidly in the Indian tradition of **Advaita Vedanta**, a philosophy that denounces dualism (*dvaita* in Sanskrit means "two" and the prefix *a* is the negation of twoness), that affirms that all reality is one, and that teaches that this single, unified reality is the Absolute Mind. Advaita Vedanta rejects theism, which it sees as postulating a dualism between God and the world. It also finds fault with theism for teaching that God is a being with a form like that of humans. Theism is anthropomorphic, making God a being among other beings and like a magnified human being. But the Absolute, which is known in the Hindu tradition as Brahman, is without form. Brahman, the Absolute, is not a being among beings, but is being itself. Everything is a part of the Absolute, and our belief that the world and the multitude of things in the world are separate is an illusion. What we see as separateness, Advaita calls *maya*, illusion.

Criticisms of absolute idealism, whether Western or Eastern, have often pointed out that the belief that reality is an Absolute Mind of which earthly things are merely undifferentiated parts denigrates the temporal process in which we all live and provides no adequate explanation of why our experiences of separation seem so vivid and real to us. This criticism Aurobindo attempts to meet by his incorporation of many of the teachings of naturalism into his system. Evolutionary theory applied to the natural world, the world of *maya*, gives a detailed account of how the temporal process moves in human experience. The evolutionary account of the mundane world in his system generates what he believes is a much more adequate version of absolute idealism by incorporating the life of the Absolute Mind, a life which he calls the Life Divine.[6] But if naturalism is taken in isolation from the framework of the Absolute, it leaves the most fundamental of questions unanswered. Not only does it simply pass over, with Alexander's "natural piety," the whole question of ultimate origins; it also leaves unanswered the question of what drives the upward progression of evolution and what gives it direction. Such concepts as *nisis* and *élan vital* do not answer this second question; instead, they betray a faint awareness in both Alexander and Bergson that a serious problem remains unaddressed.

It is clear that Aurobindo has targeted naturalism's soft spot. Naturalism certainly does a better job than the older materialism of explaining the temporal process of the world. Aurobindo's adoption of so many of the teachings of naturalism shows that he, too, finds it a very convincing account. Naturalism's recognition that the complex processes of life and mind cannot be reduced to, and explained by, the laws of particles in motion is an important step forward. The recognition of ubiquitous creativity and newness in the cosmic process makes the naturalistic explanation much more plausible than that of plain materialism. And the concept of a humanized — even a divinized — nature makes the naturalistic vision of reality equally more palatable. We can all feel more at home and happy in such a world.

But the question of how a blind process can follow such an orderly path; and of how a process not energized or fueled from without can defy the drag of entropy to soar ever upward in never ceasing complexity, creativity, and newness remains to puzzle and amaze the reflective mind. Concepts like *nisis* and *élan vital*, Aurobindo claims, merely obscure the problem, covering it with names that have no real explanatory power. In the light of the more sophisticated materialism emerging in the closing decades of our century, however, it may be appropriate to regard these concepts merely as holdovers from a period when we had not fully assimilated the naturalistic claim that nature needs no supermundane cause or explanation and that everything involved in the process can reasonably be regarded as inherent in nature.

The question we must ask of Aurobindo and of absolute idealism in general, though, is how much better the concept of the Absolute resolves the puzzle. Theists argue that we know through our own personal experience how conscious, rational, purposeful persons plan and guide processes of change. If God is such a person, it is a real explanation to say that the splendid progression of a creative world is the carrying out of a divine plan guided, energized, and nurtured by an intelligent deity. But to say that the progression of nature is the reevolution of a formless being that plunged into the material realm, losing therein all qualities of mind and now blindly striving to regain them, seems hardly a more adequate explanation than that of *nisis*.

Indeed, the picture of the Absolute Mind offered by Aurobindo and some other absolute idealists — as a formless being that includes in its nature everything that exists, in an undifferentiated whole, with finite beings mistakenly thinking they and other objects in the world are separate — impresses many as a very great deal less plausible than either theism or naturalism. Aurobindo's elaboration sits ill with the principle of simplicity. And the Absolute itself, impersonal and formless, seems hardly the kind of being that should be called a mind. When we add to this absolute idealism's seeming incompatibility with human free will and its dismissal of virtually the whole realm of human experience as *maya*, it appears to be a much less plausible alternative either to naturalism or theism than Aurobindo suggests.

The problem of how dead matter can rise to the level of life, of how mindless organisms can come to manifest consciousness, feeling, and rationality, is probably naturalism's most difficult one. But the naturalists'

response to the problem has more plausibility than many of its critics recognize. The naturalists point out that in every process of explanation we
reach a point at which we can no longer explain how something happens,
but have to note simply that it does happen and perhaps seek to discover
the circumstances which accompany it. We can analyze a chemical substance, explaining its structure by discovering the elements of which it is
composed, finding out the shapes molecules of a certain type take on, and
describing the circumstances under which certain changes occur in the
substance, but for each explanation another question can be raised. Eventually we arrive at the point of saying, "This is what happens under those
conditions," "These are the qualities such a compound has," "Compounds
of this sort change in this way under such circumstances," and so on.

The materialist comes to the aid of naturalism by arguing that our
astonishment at the new qualities amounts merely to the results of our
unfamiliarity with a segment or process of nature, of the fact that sufficiently detailed knowledge of the mechanisms elude us. Indeed, the reductivism of the old materialism is based on the assumption that our surprise
about the so-called emergent qualities would disappear if our knowledge
were sufficiently penetrating and complete and if we recognized that explanation must end at some point. Naturalism indulges, even celebrates, our
surprise by making much of the newness of emergent qualities and of the
claim that they could not have been predicted ahead of time.

What this means, however, is that objects and events in the world
have certain qualities — call them supervenient if you like — and the only
way that we can find out what qualities happen to characterize a given
object is to inspect it, unless it is so similar to something else we have
already inspected that we are justified in inferring that it probably has
somewhat similar qualities. It may be true to say that it is no explanation of
the process simply to say that it happens, to say that nature moves towards
higher levels of complexity, to say that there is a tendency or *nisis* in nature
toward higher and higher levels of being. But this is not different in principle from what we must necessarily say about much of our experience. Some
things do not seem to admit of further explanation. The theist and absolute
idealist attempt to explain natural processes by an appeal to supernatural
beings amounts to postulating something less well understood, whose existence is quite doubtful to account for things with which we are after all
fairly familiar. Naturalism offers a gratifyingly detailed and penetrating account of the world we experience, it preserves the grounds for our appreciation of the remarkable features of reality graded into a multitude of types
and levels, and it explains our own place in the entire scheme of things.
The questions naturalism does not answer, or does not answer to the theist's satisfaction, are perhaps no more serious — much less serious, many
would say — than those the theist does not answer or does not answer to the
naturalist's satisfaction.

Naturalism seems to stand, not seriously damaged by Aurobindo's criticism, as an attractive and plausible alternative to theism. It is an alternative that cannot, any more than theism itself, be proven to be true. It seems definitely superior, however, both to the older materialism and to Aurobindo's absolute idealism. Most of its ingredients seem to be widely, if unreflectively, accepted by great numbers of thoughtful persons, scientists, philosophers, plain individuals. And the central teachings of naturalism seem to be largely taken for granted in the work of contemporary philosophers of mind, many of whom embrace the name "materialist," who are attempting to generate detailed and plausible accounts of the upper end of the evolutionary scale — namely, the functioning of mind.

HUMANISM

Humanism, like naturalism, is a refined form of materialism that denies supernaturalism and finds the supreme value in human ideals and possibilities. We find thinkers in several periods of history who advocate teachings consistent with modern humanism. Among the ancient Greeks, the saying, "Man is the measure of all things," attributed to Protagoras (c. 490–421 B.C.E.), is explicitly humanistic, as are some of the teachings of Epicurus (341–270 B.C.E.) and others. The European Renaissance of the fifteenth century, which was marked by a celebration of this-worldly human values connected with the rediscovery of the philosophy of ancient Greece, was a time when humanism flourished. Erasmus (1466–1535) and Rabelais (1494–1553), both monks, eloquently expressed central humanist themes. Thomas More (1478–1535) and Michael de Montaigne (1533–1592) were among a growing number of literary figures who contributed to the spread of Renaissance humanism. And there were many others.

But the humanism of these earlier times, particularly Renaissance humanism, was as much a cultural and literary movement as it was a philosophical position. As a philosophy that counts seriously as an alternative to theism, humanism began to flourish in the nineteenth and twentieth centuries particularly as a version of materialism, often called *naturalistic humanism*. In 1933, a group of thirty-four humanists in the United States issued a document called the *Humanist Manifesto*,[7] setting forth in fourteen numbered articles what they took to be the central principles of humanism. In 1941, some members of this group began to publish a journal called *The Humanist* to promote and explore humanist themes. In 1973, forty years after the initial manifesto, 115 humanists from many nations joined in drafting and publishing *Humanist Manifesto II*,[8] which was designed to give a somewhat more detailed and updated statement of humanism. Since that time, hundreds of others have added their signatures to the manifesto and the main themes of humanism have appeared in the writings of a large

number of philosophers. One of the most prominent American philosophers in the pragmatist tradition, John Dewey, signed both of the manifestos and promoted humanist ideals in many of his philosophical writings.[9]

In the twentieth century, fundamentalist religious groups have used
the label "secular humanism" as a term of abuse, like atheism and agnosticism, sometimes suggesting that secular humanists, atheists, and agnostics
are persons of low moral character who constitute a threat to society. In
fact, humanists, like many atheists and agnostics, advocate and support
very high standards of morality and humaneness and certainly seem in no
measure more dangerous than theists or fundamentalists. Indeed, what
marks humanists off from other naturalists who might not call themselves
humanists is the supreme emphasis placed on fostering the specifically human values that support a happy, healthy, and wholesome life for all human beings of every race and nation.

Like naturalism, humanism takes as its fundamental assumption "that
Nature itself constitutes the sum total of reality, that matter and not mind
is the foundation-stuff of the universe, and that supernatural entities simply do not exist."[10] As the name indicates, humanists believe that the focus
of concern in philosophy should be on the human being, not in the sense of
regarding the human mind as a model for understanding the universe as the
idealists do, and not in the sense of considering the human person as the
object of cosmic, much less divine, purpose, but rather as the highest being
yet to emerge in the evolutionary process, the being with the greatest potential for creativity and development.

Humanists do not believe that nature cherishes humans and their
values above other things. Rather, they say, nature is quite indifferent to
man, providing conditions in which many forms of life can flourish and in
which the evolutionary process can continue to generate variety and manifest new qualities in the new life forms that arise. Human beings are almost
certainly not the final product of evolution; it seems extremely likely that
in due course other creatures will arise which surpass humans. To borrow
current terminology, we might say that humanists look on nature as an
"equal opportunity process," furnishing resources that ambitious life forms
can exploit to make for themselves a good living and a good life. In such a
world, there is ample opportunity for intelligent and imaginative humans
to construct and maintain a thoroughly human society, one in which they
can live humane, challenging, stimulating, healthy, and happy lives. For
our era at least, humans are the highest beings to arise, and it falls to us to
foster those values that, up to now, are the highest to which the world has
given birth.

What is most important to realize, the humanists insist, is that if a
world that recognizes and promotes the highest values we can imagine is to
exist, humans must build it. The greatest fault with theistic systems is that
they encourage humans to rely on supernatural forces to bring about the

transformation of the world; or, failing that, they prepare for us a fantasy world beyond this one where the wrongs of earthly life will be righted and the dream of human felicity fulfilled. This has the consequence of making our present life seem unimportant and of dismissing human efforts to improve this world as trivial or even misguided. If the wondrous new age is to come only by divine intervention and in God's own good time, there is little for humans to do but sit back and wait. And if earthly life is only a brief prelude to a paradise elsewhere and elsewhen, then the role of humans, at most, is to be vigilant or to practice religious austerities designed to prepare them for that life to come.

What is most needed, the humanists say, and what will be the most constructive — most "redemptive" or "salvific," if one wishes to use typical religious terminology — is a candid recognition that there are no gods or supernatural powers watching over us and determining our fate. The gods are creatures of human imagination, invented to provide answers to cosmological questions in a time when scientific knowledge was not yet available to answer them and to offer comfort and help to persons whose very ignorance of natural processes left them vulnerable and helpless. Dreams of a continuing life after death were perhaps needed by a people whose ability to cope with the problems of this life was so very limited by their lack of scientific understanding. But the time has arrived for human beliefs about themselves and their own destiny to come of age as our scientific beliefs have, so that we will be motivated to make the best use of the understanding and control of nature that the progress of science places at our disposal, no longer hampered or inhibited by superstitions left over from a rude and primitive age.

A recognition that humans are alone and on their own in the world need not have the effect of making nature seem bleak and threatening, as theists sometimes suggest. Rather, the humanists insist, it can offer a most exciting possible challenge and the opportunity to create the greatest kind of world and the happiest kind of life that the finest and most cultivated human imaginations can conceive. The call is to dedicated thought and energetic action — to discover or to decide what is truly the highest human good — and then to intelligent efforts to create the conditions that promote and make possible the realization of that good. Belief in gods and the supernatural promotes belief in human helplessness or a sense that it is not our place to remake the world. Belief in humanism promotes belief that only human efforts can remake the world after our mind's vision and our heart's desire. It also promotes a confidence that human effort really can harness the forces of nature, the powers of technology, and the imaginations of human beings to build a warm and comfortable home for themselves in the world and a successful, happy, and fulfilling life. Humanism is basically an optimistic philosophy that encourages humans to believe in themselves and create the very best life their hearts and minds can conceive.

The realization of this high vision of humanism requires significant changes in the ways in which humans organize their social lives and relate to one another both within the boundaries of the groups, societies, and nations with which they identify themselves and (especially) across these boundaries. Indeed, it requires the eventual removal of such boundaries and the assimilation of the entire human race into one great family. This is why the philosophy of humanism places its most important emphasis on the moral concerns of justice, equality, respect for every human person; the breaking down of all barriers of race, sex, ethnic and economic status, ideology; and any and every other distinction that divides humans from one another. Humanists believe that it is very important to recognize what a dismal role many theological teachings, and many organized religious groups that promote these teachings, have played in fostering and sustaining bigotry, in encouraging the belief that some human groups are superior to others — even the chosen people or the elect of God — and in justifying discrimination against persons of other races or religions on the basis of such claims.

Humanism is not necessarily antireligious. Indeed, one important group of humanists refer to themselves specifically as *religious* humanists. But humanism is explicitly opposed to the beliefs and policies of all religious groups that promote exclusivism, that teach that their beliefs are the only true ones and their practices the only legitimate ones, and that make use of these exclusive claims to justify discrimination against persons of other persuasions. All too often this has been precisely the way that organized religions have behaved, especially the so-called Western religions, Judaism, Christianity, and Islam, but to a certain extent also the other religions.

Nothing is more important, according to humanism, than a recognition that there is no moral, scientific, religious, or any other kind of justification for discriminatory divisions in the human race. The foundation of humanist morality is the insistence that every human being is entitled to full and complete equality of opportunity and that every individual must be recognized as having as much intrinsic worth and dignity as any other.

> Humanism believes in an ethics or morality that grounds all human values in this-earthly experiences and relationships; and holds as its highest loyalty the this-worldly happiness, freedom and progress — economic, cultural and ethical — of all mankind, irrespective of nation, race or religion. . . . Humanism believes in a far-reaching social program that stands for the establishment throughout the world of democracy and peace on the foundations of a flourishing and cooperative economic order.[11]

Humanism is convinced that its moral emphasis on the promotion of human values for all persons of every race and nation is grounded solidly on

the foundations of science and on the metaphysics of naturalistic materialism that has been developed out of the findings of science. Scientific naturalism is able to explain satisfactorily the processes of the world and human
life for which superstitious persons used to appeal to gods and spirits. The
enlarged understanding of the nature of matter energy made possible by
relativity physics and quantum mechanics, the expanded comprehension
of the workings of the organic dimensions of reality made possible by evolutionary biology, the growing grasp of the mechanisms by which neural
processes underlie mental functions being achieved by psychology and the
philosophy of mind — all these advances contribute to the cumulative plausibility of naturalistic-materialist accounts of reality. And although such
philosophies do not have specific answers that correspond to those offered
by theism for the origin of the material universe and for the rise and proliferation of the rich array of levels of reality within it, they have the advantage of simplicity in not postulating gods or supernatural processes — themselves unproven and mysterious, and perhaps more troublesome than helpful.

CONTEMPORARY MATERIALISM AND THE
PHILOSOPHY OF MIND

In the last third of the twentieth century, the most interesting issues raised
by the whole range of materialist positions are being addressed most cre-
atively by the growing branch of philosophy called the **philosophy of mind**.
The basic tenets of evolutionary naturalism are not so much advocated as
simply taken for granted by materialist philosophers of mind. Their focus of
effort is on providing a satisfactory account of mind and its relationship to
the organism on which it depends for its functioning. The reductivist
"nothing but" attitude characteristic of earlier materialism is gone. To be
sure, contemporary materialists do sometimes accuse one another of reductivism, but if any are guilty, it is for the most part inadvertent and not a
matter of announced policy, as was often the case before. The "unity of
science" effort has either faded into the background or else has been assumed to be possible without the objectionable aspects of reductivism.
Gone too are references to mysterious forces such as *élan vital* or *nisis*. A
large number of contemporary philosophers are actively engaged in the
project of accounting for the mental, moral, aesthetic, and cultural aspects
of human life in terms of a strictly scientific materialism. Their theories are
varied and far too numerous to attempt to summarize here. A brief look at
one example may serve to illustrate some of the new and attractive features
of these theories.

Joseph Margolis has developed a theory of nonreductive materialism
that might appropriately be called *personalistic materialism* (although he
does not himself make use of that name).

> We understand by materialism the theory that whatever exists . . .
> is *composed* of matter or of whatever matter itself can be reduced
> to or is suitable linked to whatever is composed of matter (as by
> embodiment).[12]

The central ingredient in Margolis's materialism is his theory of persons, since persons exemplify the highest and most complex emergent qualities the natural world has evolved. Although the persons we know about are humans, Margolis insists that other things might be or might become persons. "Chimpanzees, dolphins, Martians — may be persons or incipient persons. . . . Some advanced machines may come to exhibit the competence of persons."[13] It is also possible that some humans, such as feral children or profoundly defective infants, do not become persons.

A theory of persons is a theory of culture, because "it is only by training certain biologically gifted animals in culturally significant ways . . . that the only persons we are presently aware of actual[ly] emerge."[14] He states:

> Persons are emergent entities . . . possessing the properties of linguistic competence, other rule-following abilities, and other attributes presupposing such abilities; they possess properties essentially lacking in purely physical bodies and in mere biological organisms.[15]

Margolis explains that one particular, the person, is embodied in another particular, a physical body. But persons are not just biologically emergent beings; they are *cultural* emergents. The very existence of a person can be explained only in terms of cultural training and not in physical terms. Persons as such are not composed of material parts, although they are embodied in sentient organisms that are composed of material parts; thus in that sense persons are composed of nothing but matter.

The unique feature of Margolis's theory is his concept of embodiment, introduced to characterize the nature of the relationship of emergent entities to that from which they emerge and in which they are embodied. All cultural products are emergent entities — persons as well as the things they make. The person is an emergent entity embodied in a sentient organism in a way somewhat analogous to the way that a proposition is embodied in a certain sentence or that a poem is embodied in a series of lines of words. Language cannot be reduced to mere sounds or physical marks, yet ideas are embodied in such sounds and marks and could not exist unembodied. Similarly, persons cannot be reduced to physical organisms or nervous systems, yet they are embodied in such organisms and could not exist unembodied. Margolis is careful, therefore, to renounce reductivism. His theory involves a recognition of the essential role that culture plays in the process by which persons emerge in human organisms, and more generally the mutual interdependence of persons and culture that implies both that persons are products of culture and culture is the product of persons. Other complex social emergents, such as governments, institutions, religions, and the like, are

among the products of persons and are embodied in the groups whose functioning makes them possible.

The materialism proposed by Margolis is one example of a number of
carefully elaborated variations on the materialist theme currently being
worked out. They differ mostly in detail; they share the basic materialist
and naturalist teachings. Their growing edges are in the area of the philosophy of mind, where they labor to produce satisfactory accounts of the latest
and most complex emergent qualities and entities that characterize human
individuals and groups. As alternatives to theism, these new materialisms
have achieved a very remarkable plausibility and stand as strong and increasingly satisfactory world views.

RELIGION WITHOUT GOD

An objection often raised to all the alternatives to theism is the claim that
they undermine the spiritual dimension of human experience, kill off the
religious life that has played such a central role in the evolution of human
culture, and reduce human existence to a base level of crass utilitarianism.
It is certainly true that religion has been an important feature of every
culture and that it has been a patron of art, music, and literature, a supporter of morality, and a powerful driving force motivating the efforts and
accomplishment of multitudes of dedicated persons. At the same time, we
must not forget that the influence of religion has not always been wholesome. As has often been pointed out, few if any horrors or atrocities have
not been committed in the name of religion. The defenders of religion
argue that the Inquisition and other instances of religious persecution have
resulted from distortions or corruptions of religion, not from religion itself.
This argument has some force, yet many of the problems stirred up so often
by religion relate to the dispute over the issue of true versus corrupted
religion.

It can hardly be denied that religion, by its very nature, tends to create
divisions between the faithful and those outside and that these divisions
very frequently become the grounds, even sometimes explicitly encouraged
by the religious authorities, for discrimination and persecution. Every age
seems plagued by ethnic conflicts, and these are very often fueled and aggravated by religious bigotry. The contributions of religion to human history and civilization have been substantial, both positively and negatively.
When all the evils and all the goods to which religion has given rise have
been taken into account, it may be plausible to argue that the balance has
been on the side of the good and that the disappearance of religion — if
such a thing could ever happen — would be an unfortunate loss to human
civilization. Whether the same thing is true of theism is open to question.
It certainly appears that some of the alternatives to theism not only provide

highly plausible metaphysical accounts of reality as a whole but also offer substantial encouragement of the same impulses toward justice, morality, and humaneness that has been a part of the positive contribution of theistic religious belief.

Freud characterized religion as an illusion, expressed his distress over what he saw as the childishness of our clinging to our glorified father figure and lamented the sorry career of religion bigotry and persecution, but concluded that religion is very unlikely to disappear or be outgrown. Materialism, naturalism, and humanism agree with Freud's claim that the theistic dimensions of religion are illusions; they also agree that the evils of religion have often outweighed its beneficial effects. But these alternatives to theism argue generally that the fault is not so much with religion itself as with the superstitious, particularly the theistic, doctrines that characterize many religions. It has very often been assumed that religion is inseparable from theism. Even some Buddhists, whose founder made Buddhism explicitly a nontheistic religion, worship gods borrowed from Hinduism and have made the Buddha into a god. But many humanists, naturalists, and materialists argue that religion does not have to involve theistic beliefs. It is possible—and many would say, highly desirable—to cultivate religion without God. This is the suggestion that all the beneficial features of religion might be sustained while purging away the superstitions on which have been grounded so much of what is evil in the effects of religion.

What features of religion remain once belief in God is eliminated? In the theistic religions, God has been the focus of human feelings of reverence and awe and of their sense of the grandeur and wonder of creation. God has also provided motivation for loving and moral behavior toward fellow human beings—or at least fellow worshippers of the same god. Dostoevsky's cry, "God is dead; all is permitted," expresses the human sense that without God morality would lose its power. But others fear the loss of all of the impulses of gentleness, reverence, and wonder that seem so important in human emotional and aesthetic life. Some have said that a world without God would be a world without good, without beauty, without love, without any sense of the sacred. Such a world is indeed unattractive to contemplate.

No need to fear it, many naturalists, humanists, and materialists assure us. Nature itself, that great, vast, storehouse of power and creativity, is a suitable object, not of worship, to be sure, but certainly of reverence. It was the majestic forests that inspired awe in Ralph Waldo Emerson (1803–1882); it was the starry skies above and the moral law within which moved Immanuel Kant (1724–1804) to feelings like those of religious reverence; it was a scientific vision of the greatness of the natural world that made a religious, but not a god-believing, man of Albert Einstein (1879–1955). Humanism points out that the feelings of awe and reverence that characterize the worship dimension of religion are actually expressions not of something divine, but of the human aesthetic capacity; the sense of moral obligation, which religions have so often used the fear of God to promote and control, is itself a dimension of *human* life, a capacity and tendency to recognize obligations and to respond to ideals instead of being driven by desires. Dostoevsky's proclamation that God's death means that all things are permitted reflects a very immature understanding of morality, one that assumes that the only reason we ought to be moral is because we might be punished if we are not. The fear that without God all wonder would disappear from the world represents an equally dwarfed sense of what could be worthy of awe.

The human capacity to respond "religiously" to what is beautiful, vast, complex, creative; our tendency to respond with pity and compassion to human suffering; our ability to respond with compunction to wickedness, our own or that of others — these are all *human* faculties. They are a part of what it means to be human, aspects of the wondrous new qualities that creatures manifest in the evolutionary process when their nervous systems reach a sufficient level of complexity of structure and function. They require no deity for their creation and none to goad them into action. But they assure the continued presence of the religious or spiritual response in human sensibility even if belief in gods and the supernatural should disappear.

Some naturalists, humanists, and materialists advocate the explicit cultivation of these human capacities through activities and organizations that are distinctly religious in character, but explicitly nontheistic at the same time. There are religious naturalists who form churchlike organizations, ethical societies, and religious groups. There are religious humanists, many of whom are members of churches or other religious organizations that embrace some or all of their humanist beliefs. They gather to engage in activities that resemble in some measure those of theistic religious groups: to celebrate; to share aesthetic experiences in music, art, and literature; and to encourage and exhort one another in their efforts increasingly to live up to their ideals and to foster them in social and political life. They engage in discussions designed further to clarify and expand their understanding of the world and of the opportunities and obligations it presents to human beings. They write books, publish journals, and operate publishing houses to disseminate information and to promote the high human ideals in which they believe. Many believe that in these activities they preserve within a materialist framework all that is valid and wholesome in religion while exorcising what is false and detrimental. They find in their alternative to theism a world view that reason can support and that in its turn can support a wholesome attitude, a happy lifestyle, and a strong sense of the moral and aesthetic value dimensions of reality that make humans, not gods, the creators of the highest ideals yet to appear in the world.

IS THEISM THE MOST PLAUSIBLE WORLD VIEW?

This brings us near to the conclusion of our examination of theism. We have looked at some of the central teachings of theism (Chapter 2), some of the major arguments for and against theism (Chapters 3 and 4), and several important types of alternatives to theism (this chapter). Our discussion in Chapter 6 of religious experience and mysticism will raise the question whether experiences of this sort can offer supporting evidence for some varieties of religious beliefs, perhaps including theism. But now may be a good time to look back briefly over the ground we have covered by raising the question of how theism fares when compared with alternative philosophies.

A point on which we must all agree at the outset is that no world view can be satisfactory that does not embrace the well-established findings of modern science. Science is one of the major paths to knowledge. Any position that rejects the warranted conclusions of science thereby convicts itself of inadequacy. This means that the various sectarian versions of theism that insist that the claims of their scriptures or doctrines take precedence over scientific truth are no longer worthy of serious consideration by rational truth seekers. Materialism, naturalism, and humanism claim as a major strength that they are scientific philosophies, building on the established findings of science — and justifiably so. But theism as a philosophical position, distinguished from the versions of it advocated by partisans of particular religious sects, also claims to be able to embrace the authenticated findings of science and to have advantages over the nontheistic alternatives that, they say, are unable to do full justice to the spiritual and value dimensions of human experience.

Although the dispute here is primarily between theism on one hand and the nontheistic positions on the other, there are points of contention among the nontheists. Reductivist materialists sometimes claim that their position has an edge over naturalism and humanism because materialism sticks closest to science, insisting that all explanatory principles be describable in terms of, or be reducible to, the most fundamental principles of science, of physics in particular — the project of the unity of science. The emergent qualities that become key ingredients in the teachings of the naturalists and humanists have an odor of the mysterious, almost the supernatural, according to some materialists, and principles such as the *élan vital* or the *nisis* of Bergson and Alexander smack of what is not scientifically respectable. It is only the complexity of biological and psychological principles and the extreme complexity that would be involved in the process of reducing these to the principles of physics — indeed, the practical impossibility — that lends a measure of credibility to the claim that such a reduction is in principle impossible. Based on this argument, the naturalists and humanists go on to elaborate theories about so-called emergent qualities alleged to be genuinely new, and forces such as the *élan vital* to explain them. Each move in this direction is, according to these materialist critics, a step away from the solid ground of scientific knowledge in the direction of the mysterious or the supernatural. Theism lies but a few steps farther down the same path.

The naturalists and humanists, in contrast, insist that any reductivist materialism is fatally flawed and that although their teachings about emergent qualities and new explanatory principles are indeed several steps removed from the principles of physics, these teachings are quite consistent with the established laws of biology and psychology. They point out that practitioners of these disciplines themselves insist that their explanatory principles cannot be reduced to those of physics. It is not scientific to insist on theoretical grounds that reductive explanations are the correct ones when on empirical grounds we discover that more complex forms have emergent qualities. Our theories must explain the facts, not explain them away. The facts we discover when we scrutinize living organisms and when we explore the workings of the mind, do not submit themselves to simplistic physicalist explanations. Emergent naturalism and humanism preserve the facts and find a place and a rationale for the vast range of new features that the world begins to have when living and thinking beings appear. This capacity of naturalism and humanism to take account of the highest value dimensions of evolution constitutes their superiority over simplistic materialism.

The contemporary materialists agree that the naturalists are right in criticizing reductivism, but they also agree with the earlier materialists that the introduction of such mysterious forces as *nisis* and *élan vital* is unscientific and unsatisfactory. Carefully avoiding both weaknesses, they offer an improved and strengthened materialism that provides detailed and highly plausible accounts of the mental, the moral, the aesthetic — perhaps even what theists call the spiritual — dimensions of human life. So the new materialism claims all the advantages with none of the disadvantages of the earlier positions — and strong new advantages of its own.

The disputes among the various versions of materialism, naturalism, and humanism seems to the theists to be only denominational squabbling among positions whose differences are matters of detail and not differences in kind. The naturalists and humanists are certainly right in their claim that reductivist materialism oversimplifies and explains away, but theists believe that naturalism and humanism suffer, perhaps in a smaller degree, from the same fault. And if the new materialism succeeds in avoiding reductivism, it also abandons such potentially spiritual forces as the *élan vital*, or the residual concept of deity that characterized Alexander's position. Although some advocates of these positions talk about preserving the facts of human moral, aesthetic, and religious experience, and even sometimes engage in practices which they call religious, they leave out entirely the one necessary condition for fulfilling their objectives: God. If our experience of the world in all of its richness is to be rendered intelligible, there must be a being powerful enough to create and drive the processes of nature, intelligent enough to create the order we see being enacted, and value sensitive enough to conceive and execute those processes in the world that inspire our admiration and call us to the best we have in us. And so the rationalist theists who seek to formulate a scientific theism see their position as including but going beyond the valid insights of naturalism and materialism. They suggest that concepts such as *nisis* and *élan vital* are disguised or unconscious names for the hand of God as it works in the realm of creation. These concepts constitute the implicit admission that reality cannot really be explained in purely natural, much less purely materialistic, terms.

But the naturalists, humanists, and materialists reply that God is not really an explanation but the confession that no explanation is available. To say that God created the world and guides its evolution explains nothing, as long as the existence and nature of God is only a matter of speculation. Postulating an anthropomorphic superbeing creates many more problems than it solves. If naturalistic explanations are incomplete at the present state of our knowledge, progress in biology, psychology, and the rapidly growing area of the philosophy of mind moves us toward increasingly adequate natural explanations. Theism, in contrast, seems stagnant, remaining content to reply to all questions simply by an appeal to the will of God.

What is the outcome of all these arguments? The answer seems to be that no definitive outcome is possible. Theism can, it seems, be formulated in ways that are highly plausible. The arguments that support it are substantial, especially when it takes adequate account of the findings of science. Although the counterarguments are formidable, they never quite succeed in becoming decisive. Theism stands as a viable, rational position. It has not been proven true, but neither has it been proven false. A rational individual can justifiably affirm theism; a rational individual can justifiably reject it.

The alternatives, however, also have considerable strength. This may be the most surprising of our findings: that the strength so widely presumed to characterize theism turns out to be not nearly so great as might be expected and that the nontheistic alternative turns out to be so impressively strong and plausible. The success of naturalism, humanism, and the new materialism in giving an account of the value dimensions of reality makes them quite convincing, and the progress in psychology and the philosophy of mind in describing the mechanisms of mind-brain activity lends increasing credibility to these positions. Indeed, the work of certain materialists in developing such positions in the philosophy of mind as central state materialism, functionalism, and what we have dubbed personalistic materialism is providing growing support for the belief that a materialist view, separate from naturalism or humanism, can stand as a strong contender.[16] Nor does it seem to be true that the nontheistic positions rob human life of its sense of the sacred or its moral impulses. Thus we conclude that some one or several of the alternatives to theism that we have discussed also emerge as strong rational positions.

Some will feel disappointed that reason, and the knowledge that human thought has been able to accumulate up to this time, is unable to settle the question. As it turns out, however, most of the large questions in science, religion, and philosophy elude our quest for a final answer. This fact stands as a lure and a challenge to continued intelligent effort. And for those whose response to life is religious, theistic or nontheistic, it stands also as a challenge to commitment. The world view most worthy of our commitment is a matter each person must try honestly to judge. What is clear is that both theism and the alternatives to theism call us to bend our every effort toward the cultivation of a worthy life for all human persons and toward the creation of a world in which the values we all cherish can be enjoyed, not just by a privileged few but by all persons everywhere.

We turn now to an examination of the great variety of types of religious experience that constitute, for many persons, the most convincing kind of evidence about the nature of the world and, for some, the definitive proof of the truth of their world view. Religious beliefs most frequently arise from experiences of certain kinds. The great religions of humankind have grown out of the religious experiences of certain extraordinary individuals. And any philosophical position that fails to do justice to the religious experiences that humans actually have will convict itself, as surely as one that rejects the established findings of science, of gross inadequacy.

ANNOTATED GUIDE TO FURTHER READINGS

Materialism

Armstrong, D. M. *A Materialist Theory of the Mind*. London: Routledge and Kegan Paul, 1968.

Argues that there are no adequate reasons to reject the central-state materialist claim that the mental activities of human beings are derived from entirely physical processes.

Campbell, Keith. *Body and Mind*. Notre Dame, Indiana: University of Notre Dame Press, 1984.

Examines the major mind-body theories, such as dualism, behaviorism, central-state materialism, functionalism, and a new version of epiphenomenalism.

Margolis, Joseph. *Persons and Minds: The Prospects of Nonreductive Materialism*. Dordrecht: D. Reidel, 1978.

Margolis develops a nonreductivist materialist theory of the person as an emergent entity embodied in a sentient organism.

Naturalism

Alexander, Samuel. *Space, Time, and Deity.* New York: Dover Publications, 1966.

In this substantial two-volume work Alexander develops his theory of evolutionary naturalism as a universal evolutionary progression toward higher and higher levels of being, culminating in deity.

Hartshorne, Charles. *Beyond Humanism.* New York: Willett, Clark and Company, 1937.

Presents the theory of naturalistic theism, in which the concepts of God and nature merge, providing an alternate way of looking at the divine.

Romanell, Patrick. *Toward a Critical Naturalism.* New York: Macmillan, 1958.

Naturalism stresses the unity of humankind and nature; the importance of the natural world comes from its own intrinsic value. Naturalism and ethics are also extensively examined.

Idealism

Aurobindo, Sri. *The Life Divine.* Pondicherry, India: Sri Aurobindo Ashram, 1977.

These comprehensive writings offer the reader an alternate explanation of the nature of existence. Aurobindo teaches absolute idealism, a form of supernaturalism that holds that all being originated from one all-inclusive mind called the Absolute. Today, all being is evolving from its current state of separation to the higher level of oneness within the consciousness of the Absolute.

Hocking, William Ernest. *Types of Philosophy.* New York: Charles Scribner's Sons, 1959.

Chapters 19 through 29 of this text deal with idealism. Hocking defines and explains idealism; examines individual facets of idealism and their relation to specific issues.

Humanism

Auer, J. A. C. Fagginger, and Hartt, Julian. *Humanism versus Theism.* Ames, Iowa: Iowa State University Press, 1981.

A good source for gaining an understanding of the humanist perspective. The first section, by Auer, is an argument supporting humanism; it is followed by Hartt's rebuttal which defends theism from the humanistic claims.

Dewey, John. *A Common Faith.* New Haven: Yale University Press, 1934.

Dewey draws a distinction between religious values and religions themselves, directing his religious faith towards human civilization and ideals rather than the supernatural.

Kurtz, Paul, ed. *Humanist Manifestos I and II*. Buffalo, New York: Prometheus Books, 1973.

> *These two documents set forth the fundamental principles of the humanist philosophy, emphasizing the importance of the individual human being and affirming the interconnectedness of humankind as a whole.*

Lamont, Corliss. *Humanism as a Philosophy*. New York: Philosophical Library, 1949.

> *A thorough introduction to humanism: definition, historical background, and an examination of basic humanist contentions, such as the overriding importance of this life and this world.*

NOTES

1. One name given to materialist philosophy in ancient India is *Carvakism*, related etymologically to the Sanskrit root *carv*, meaning to chew or to eat. See R. Puligandla, *Fundamentals of Indian Philosophy* (Nashville: Abingdon Press, 1975). In the West, materialism has been associated with the "eat, drink, and be merry" attitude because of a misunderstanding of the teachings of the ancient Greek materialist, Epicurus.

2. Patrick Romanell, *Toward a Critical Naturalism* (New York: Macmillan, 1958), p. 5.

3. Ibid., pp. 12ff.

4. Samuel Alexander, *Space, Time, and Deity* (New York: Macmillan, 1920).

5. Henri Bergson, *L'Évolution créatrice* (Paris, 1907), translated by Arthur Mitchell as *Creative Evolution* (New York: 1911).

6. Sri Aurobindo, *The Life Divine* (Pondicherry: Sri Aurobindo Ashram, 1977).

7. Reprinted in Paul Kurtz, ed., *Humanist Manifestos I and II* (Buffalo, N.Y.: Prometheus Books, 1973).

8. Reprinted in ibid.

9. See, for example, John Dewey, *Experience and Nature* (La Salle, Ill: Open Court, 1925), and *A Common Faith* (New Haven: Yale University Press, 1934).

10. Corliss Lamont, *Humanism as a Philosophy* (New York: Philosophical Library, 1949), p. 145.

11. Ibid., pp. 20f.

12. Joseph Margolis: *Persons and Minds: The Prospects of Nonreductive Materialism* (Dordrecht: D. Reidel, 1978), p. 19.

13. Ibid.

14. Ibid., pp. 19f.

15. Ibid., p. 22.

16. See, for example, the work of D. M. Armstrong; e.g., his *A Materialist Theory of Mind* (London, 1968), and Joseph Margolis, *Persons and Minds: The Prospects of a Nonreductive Materialism* (Dordrecht: D. Reidel, 1978).

6

Religious Experience and Mysticism

The philosopher of religion is most interested in the doctrines or teachings of religions and the rational arguments that can be offered to support or to undermine these teachings. Religious believers, however, often regard these areas of inquiry as far less important than specific experiences they have that seem to be direct encounters with the sacred or the divine, providing immediate certification of authenticity and making doctrines and arguments unimportant or beside the point.

Most of the great religions of the world seem to have originated because their founders had such experiences. Judaism traces its roots to certain experiences of Abraham and Moses that these patriarchs believed were encounters with Yahweh, their god. Islam originated from experiences the prophet Muhammad had through which he believed that Allah revealed to him the teachings which became the Qur'an. Christianity grew out of the experiences Jesus had of a divine calling to fulfill the role of messiah or Christ and the experiences of his disciples after his crucifixion and alleged resurrection. Buddhism had its beginning in the enlightenment experience of Gautama. Many ordinary persons who do not become founders of new religions also report powerful religious experiences, and these experiences come to be so prized that techniques for their cultivation have arisen in several of the great religions.

Many people would say that experiences of this sort constitute the core of any religion and that the doctrines of the religions are simply attempts to provide a rational framework. The insights gained through these experiences are sometimes regarded as the foundational data on which doctrine must be built, grounded, and justified. So overpowering are the experiences for some of the persons who have them that they constitute for them indubitable authentication of the beliefs they engender. To entertain any doubt becomes out of the question. Thus arguments or proofs are irrelevant. The experiences are regarded as self-certifying sources of insight or understanding far more profound than anything that can be known in any other way. It is not unusual for persons who have religious experiences to say that they cannot be described in words and that the truths gained are of the nature of direct insights that have to be personally experienced to be appreciated. Yet these same persons often regard religious or mystical experiences as a source of knowledge about such things as the nature of reality, God, the human situation, and the requirements of morality.

The philosopher of religion must attempt to understand the nature of religious experience, not only because of the importance of the experiences themselves, but especially because of the cognitive claims that the experiences seem to imply and that religious persons often assert. If persons do encounter deity directly and receive divinely sanctioned teachings through religious experience, then this would seem to be one of the most important sources for the understanding of religious truth. Some say that such evidence would make rational arguments trivial or irrelevant; others say that the content of such experiences constitutes the fundamental data on which rational arguments can be founded.

The philosopher notices that such experiences are open to a variety of different interpretations and attempts carefully to distinguish the experiences themselves from the theories and the theologies that are generated to explain them. The fact that an individual has an experience that *seems* to be a direct encounter with deity does not itself prove that that is what the experience really was. Thus the philosopher attempts to examine these experiences objectively, to understand first their phenomenology and then to ask how they should properly be interpreted, in particular, whether or not they provide evidence in support of religious beliefs.

THE PHENOMENOLOGY OF RELIGIOUS EXPERIENCE

It is sometimes claimed that religious experience furnishes the fundamental data of religion, comparable to the data of sense experience or the results of experimentation in science. Scientific observations provide the foundation and the justification [or the refutation] of scientific theories. So also it might be argued that religious experiences provide the grounds and the evidence for the truth (or falsity) of religious truth claims or doctrines. The occurrence of special kinds of experiences commonly designated as religious experiences is not to be questioned. It can no more be doubted that persons actually do have religious experiences than it can be doubted that persons have sense experiences. And yet, as with the data of sense experience and experimentation, their import must be judged by reason. What the philosophers must ask concerns the meaning and the implications of such experiences.

Although all of our knowledge about the world we live in is grounded in sense experience, some sense experiences turn out to be illusions. One important function of ordinary reason and scientific method is to provide techniques for distinguishing illusory from veridical sense experiences. Analogously, the great religious systems have arisen out of the religious experiences of their founders. But the philosopher notes that just as sense experiences sometimes turn out to be illusory and must not be taken at face value without testing by means of appropriate techniques and criteria, so also religious experiences must be subjected to rational scrutiny. When many different sense observations agree, we tend to trust them; when they disagree, we conclude that at least some of them are unreliable. Similarly, it has been suggested, religious experiences can be tested in part by the extent or the degree to which they agree or disagree. Perhaps there are additional criteria by which such experiences are properly judged. If so, we must seek them.

The Varieties of Religious Experience

A point of considerable importance, which has often been noticed, is the remarkable similarity of religious experiences reported by individuals in diverse times and places and by believers from every one of the great world religions. The similarities are particularly striking in the case of mystical experience. Yet it is also true that religious experiences show very great variety not only in differing ages, nations, and religious traditions, but also within the same times, places, and belief systems. This great variety makes it difficult even to give a general definition or explanation of what counts as a religious experience. Some religious experiences are vague and unfocused; others are extremely concrete, involving particular objects, acts, events, persons, or beliefs. Some seem to have no definite connection to any religious belief system; others involve visions or voices believed to be recognized as a specific god, prophet, avatar, or saint belonging to a specific religion. Some consist mostly of certain kinds of feelings; others include what is taken to be communications of definite information or revelations. Some are so similar to aesthetic experiences, and so lacking in specific religious content, that we may be uncertain whether or not they should even be labeled as religious experiences.

Ronald Hepburn, in attempting a definition of religious experience, concludes:

> If we ask what all of them have in common, the answer must be meager in content: perhaps only a sense of momentous disclosure, the sense that the world is being apprehended and responded to according to its true colors . . . the quality of religious experience is such that it seems to imply something about the whole.[1]

A sharp definition or a definitive set of distinguishing characteristics is probably not to be found. We come to understand what is properly called a religious experience by examining paradigm instances and noting the extent to which nontypical cases resemble them.

Typical religious experiences often involve explicitly religious content or objects, frequently related to a particular religious tradition. Although the experience of Moses, as reported in the Hebrew Bible, began as simply a startling sight of a burning bush that the fire did not consume, it quickly developed into a highly specific divine-human encounter. When he approached, Moses heard a voice speaking from the bush but did not recognize who or what it was. The voice identified itself as the God of his ancestors, but Moses, still uncertain, asked for God's name. The voice gave Moses God's name[2] and a specific mission to lead the tribes of Israel out of Egypt.[3] There are many other examples of what most people would recognize as typical religious experiences in the Hebrew Bible, usually understood as direct encounters with Yahweh and often involving specific commandments from God to the human having the experience.[4]

An example from the Hindu tradition is to be found in the experiences of Arjuna recounted in the Bhagavad-Gita. It is the story of a warrior riding out to battle who, seeing among the soldiers of the opposing army persons who are his kinsmen and friends, resolves to renounce fighting. But Lord Krishna appears to him to teach him about moral duty, particularly the duty of a person of the warrior caste. Most of the book is concerned with these teachings, and in this regard it is similar to the Qur'an, the fruit of Muhammad's religious experience. We may say that virtually all of the Bhagavad-Gita is an account of a religious experience. But a section toward the end of the book describes an experience of an even more startling and intense sort, in which Arjuna prays to Krishna to reveal to him His divine forms and the awesome, wonderful, chilling, exhilarating, terrifying, inspiring vision that resulted is described.[5]

Another kind of typical religious experience is **conversion**, an occasion when a sudden transformation of an individual's life orientation occurs as the result of an intense religious experience. The most dramatic cases involve instantaneous changes of character and personality, but there are many instances of more gradual conversions as well. Usually these events involve conversion from indifference or hostility toward a certain religion or other life orientation to an acceptance, frequently a very enthusiastic advocacy of it. Sometimes, however, they involve conversion away from a particular position or belief system. The conversion experience that transformed the Jewish Pharisee, Saul, from a persecutor of Christians into the great missionary of Christianity, is found in the book of Acts in the Christian scriptures. It was so powerful a transformation of his life that it moved Saul to change his name to Paul. The account is short enough to quote.

> Saul, still breathing threats and murder against the disciples of the Lord, went to the high priest and asked him for letters to the synagogues at Damascus, so that if he found any belonging to the Way, men or women, he might bring them bound to Jerusalem. Now as he journeyed he approached Damascus, and suddenly a light from heaven flashed around him. And he fell to the ground and heard a voice saying to him, "Saul, Saul, why do you persecute me?" And he said, "Who are you, Lord?" And he said, "I am Jesus, whom you are persecuting; but rise and enter the city, and you will be told what to do." The men who were traveling with him were speechless, hearing the voice but seeing no one. Saul arose from the ground; and when his eyes were opened, he could see nothing; so they led him into Damascus. And for three days he was without sight, and neither ate nor drank.[6]

This dramatic experience was followed by a meeting with a Christian disciple and a conviction that he had been called to be a missionary to spread Christianity to the Gentiles. Thereafter, instead of persecuting Christians, Paul devoted the rest of his life, through considerable danger and hardship, to spreading the Christian Gospel throughout much of the Roman world.

Another type of religious experience, far less explicitly connected with religious beliefs or divine personages, involves instead a thrill of feeling or a sudden insight brought on by seeing some aspect of nature in a new light or by words that suddenly seem to speak directly to the individual. One example comes from the great Indian poet-philosopher Rabindranath Tagore (1861–1941), who recounts in autobiographical writings several such experiences from his childhood and youth. One was simply a thrill that he experienced when he succeeded after great effort in learning the Bengali alphabet well enough to enable him to make out the meaning of two rhyming lines from a poem.

> "It rains; the leaves tremble." I was thrilled with the delight of the picture which these words suggested to me. The fragments lost their individual isolation and my mind revelled in the unity of a vision . . . the facts of my life suddenly appeared to me in a luminous unity.[7]

He reports a similar experience from his young adulthood, when he happened to be looking out the window of his house toward the bank of a river:

> Suddenly I became conscious of a stirring of soul within me. My world
> of experience seemed to become lighted, and facts that were detached
> and dim found a great unity of meaning. The feeling that I had was
> like what a man, groping through a fog without knowing his destina-
> tion, might feel when he suddenly discovers that he stands before his
> own house.[8]

These events seem almost entirely culture independent and make reference
to nothing specific to any religious tradition — or even to anything explicitly religious. Persons from other cultures or religions might and do report
essentially similar experiences. Sometimes such an experience involves the
vague sense of an unseen presence; in some cases the presence is identified,
in others not; and it may be sensed as human, divine, or even demonic.

An example from Western literature comes from Ralph Waldo Emerson (1803–1882).

> Crossing a bare common, in snow puddles, at twilight, under a
> clouded sky, without having in my thoughts any occurrence of special
> good fortune, I have enjoyed a perfect exhilaration. I am glad to the
> brink of fear. In the woods too, a man casts off his years . . . and at
> what period soever of life, is always a child . . . In the woods, we
> return to reason and faith. There I feel that nothing can befall me in
> life, — no disgrace, no calamity (leaving me my eyes), which nature
> cannot repair. Standing on the bare ground, — my head bathed by the
> blithe air, and uplifted into infinite space, — all mean egoism van-
> ishes. I become a transparent eyeball; I am nothing; I see all; the
> currents of the Universal Being circulate through me; I am part or
> particle of God.[9]

The resemblance of such experiences to aesthetic experiences is not
hard to see, particularly when they are evoked by a fragment of poetry, a
piece of music, or a scene such as the one Tagore saw outside his window.
Organized religion has long been sensitive to the kinship of religious and
aesthetic experiences and has made extensive use of works of art to create a
setting conducive to such experiences. Much of the great music, architecture, painting, stained glass, and sculpture of many societies was created
explicitly for religious use, and much of the great literature has taken religious themes for its subject matter. Religious institutions and personages
have been among the great supporters and patrons of the arts.

The similarity of religious and aesthetic experience is often very striking. If the immediate object of sense experience is a work of art, we usually
regard it as an aesthetic experience; unless there are special reasons for
doing so, we may not think of it as having any religious dimensions. If the
context of the experience is a service of worship, such as the celebration of
the sacrament, the playing of a great piece of religious music, or a stirring
sermon, then we are very likely to designate it as religious. But if the stimulus to the experience is some aspect of nature such as a beautiful sunset, a

soaring range of snow-capped mountains, a majestic forest, or a rugged stretch of seashore, we are likely to feel more uncertain about what to call it. An experience triggered by such sights has an unmistakable aesthetic dimension, but it may also seem like an apprehension of something too grand to be merely natural.

It is not unlikely, then, that most of the experiences we find sufficiently moving to call aesthetic or religious are in fact a blending of both types. Perhaps the most useful way to think of these two kinds of experience is as ends of a continuum with a substantial overlapping area in the middle. Occasionally an aesthetic experience that is virtually or entirely lacking in anything of the religious may happen to a person; more rarely, a religious experience with little or no aesthetic dimension. It is likely, however, that nearly every such significant moving experience involves both the aesthetic and the religious.

It might be tempting to suggest that the factor distinguishing one from the other is that religious experiences, unlike aesthetic experiences, produce great changes in our lives, altering in significant ways what we believe and often moving us to adopt new lifestyles, values, and vocations. Undoubtedly powerful religious experiences do have such effects. But aesthetic experiences are themselves not without power to affect our lives, to give us important new insight into the meaning of human existence, and to move us to change our thinking and our behavior.

Pathology and Religious Experience

Another, some would say less savory, comparison is often made between religious experiences and the experiences of the mentally disturbed. Believers often claim that their religious experiences put them in touch with reality in a way far more profound than that ordinarily experienced. Critics, however, suggest that persons having such experiences are actually out of touch with reality and involved in webs of phantasy or illusion. Religious experience often involves seeing visions or hearing voices, encountering spirits, angels, demons, or gods—things that are not a part of what we ordinarily call reality and things that are often ingredients in the hallucinations and delusions of the mentally ill, whose grasp of reality is precarious. To be seriously out of touch with reality is just what it means to be insane.

The resemblance of some very intense forms of religious experience, particularly certain types of mysticism, to psychological pathology has often been cited in an effort to discredit religion. Not only are religious people inclined to bizarre kinds of experiences; even more astonishingly, critics remark, religious teachers actually point to these experiences as evidence of the authenticity of their beliefs. Rather than encouraging

devotees to try to adjust themselves to seeing the world in standard ways —
"as it really is," critics would say — religious leaders encourage persons to
report these deviant experiences and even devise techniques for teaching
persons how to have such experiences.

William James documents and analyzes such claims about religious
experience and pathology and argues against what he calls the "absurd
notion that a thing is exploded away as soon as it is classed with others."[10]
He also points out the frequent association of morbid psychological states
with genius in art, literature, music, even science. A seriousness of mind
and a keen sensitivity to evil and human suffering seem to be the qualities
that characterize human greatness in all these fields, as it does in religion.
Some persons are constitutionally cheerful, optimistic, and seemingly unaware of evil or suffering in the world, but their habitual good cheer strikes
many persons as shallow, insensitive, callous. These "healthy-minded" individuals, as James calls them — happy and fortunate as they are, in a
sense — see only one dimension of human life. Surely this is not what it
means to be in touch with reality. There is far greater depth to human
existence than the light-hearted merriment of those who cannot quite understand why their fellows find life less than perfect, filled with sorrow and
suffering, or even tragic, and perhaps not worth living. Much in life is
good; but there is also a very great deal of evil, a distressing pervasiveness of
cruelty and injustice, and a ubiquity of suffering that only the deliberately
blind can overlook.

James believes that it is the "sick souls," keenly sensitive to both the
surface and the hidden dimensions of human life, who are really in touch
with reality. It should not surprise us, he suggests, that their experiences
and their behavior should resemble that of the insane, because they are so
very sensitive to the dark side of existence. That very sensitivity, which
gives depth and seriousness to works of genius and to many religious experiences, drives some persons to madness. It motivates others to acts of valor
and heroism, to the creation of works of art that communicate a vision of
the human predicament, or to a religious life of prophesy, preaching, healing, and spiritual devotion. James argues at length for what he calls the
"reality of the unseen"[11] and suggests that if sanity means being in touch
with reality, then those who are conscious both of the surface and the
depths of reality are surely at least as sane as those who know only the
world's facade.

THE PHENOMENOLOGY OF MYSTICISM

Mystical experience is a special type of religious experience. It is not easy
to distinguish sharply between mystical experiences and other religious experiences that are not properly termed mystical. Many examples of reli-

gious experiences cannot be neatly categorized as mystical or nonmystical. Some differentiating features, however, can be named. Perhaps most characteristic is the sense of oneness that nearly all mystics report, a sense that all things, despite their multifarious appearances, are really one, and that the individual person is also one with nature or the divine. This is often accompanied by a sense of timelessness; that all things are happening in a simultaneous, timeless now. There is nearly always the claim that the experience, though of unsurpassing value, is ineffable, beyond words, inexpressible, and the consequent claim that to be understood it must be experienced. Mystical experiences are occasionally frightening but bring, in the great majority of cases, a sense of unspeakable joy and peace.

Types of Mystical Experience

Several attempts have been made to classify mystical experiences into types, none of them yielding entirely satisfactory typologies. Walter Stace (1886–1967) divides mystical experiences into the extroversive and the introversive.[12] *Extroversive* mystical experiences look outward through the physical senses at the external world, perceiving that world and everything in it, including the mystic himself or herself, as one. The multifarious things and persons seem to merge into a unity and timelessness, making them in some sense identical with one another and united in a living, conscious, joyful, holy oneness. Even commonplace things take on a momentous aspect.

Introversive mystical experiences are directed inward, toward the depths of the mystic's soul. Unlike extroversive experiences, all sense awareness disappears as the mind, emptied of ordinary contents, experiences a unitary consciousness.[13] Sensing, thinking, feeling, and striving cease, and an entirely new kind of consciousness emerges: mystical consciousness. It is a consciousness devoid of any of the separate entities that occupy our ordinary experience. It is, in a sense, contentless consciousness. Thus, it is not conscious *of* anything; yet it is not unconsciousness. Rather, it is superconscious or unitary consciousness; it is consciousness of unity, the One, Being Itself, Brahman, or God.

To give a name to the mystical consciousness, such as Brahman or God, is already to give an interpretation, to supply a theology of explanation. The experience itself carries no such name or interpretation. Nor does it involve consciousness of Being or of God as an object, but rather as a subject. The mystic *is* identical with the One, knowing It subjectively through identity with It, knowing It as oneself. Introversive mystical consciousness, like extroversive, involves timelessness, a sense of joy or bliss, and a feeling that what is apprehended or encountered is holy or divine. Stace regards extroversive mysticism as relatively less complete and less profound than introversive mysticism, which represents mysticism in its fullest and most significant sense.

Another system of classification is offered by R. C. Zaehner (1913–), who divides mystical experiences into nature mysticism, soul mysticism, and theistic mysticism.[14] *Nature mysticism*, also known as cosmic consciousness, involves experiencing nature and the soul as identical—by the soul's expansion to absorb and include all nature or by its dissolution into nature—so that the ego seems no longer separate from the world and no things in nature seem separate from one another or from oneself.[15] Nature mystical experiences provide a feeling of joy or bliss, a sense that the world is wonderfully beautiful, and a transcending of moral categories which sees reality as above distinctions of good and evil.

Soul mysticism, also called monistic mysticism, is an experience of oneself as undifferentiated from the rest of reality. It involves the loss of all body awareness and sensual, memory, or rational content of consciousness. This experience is said to be the emptiness that is fullness; an absence of all thought, feeling, or striving that sees not a multitude of beings united into one but rather that no multitude exists; that there is only One and that oneself is that One. Soul mysticism is characteristic of the Advaita Vedanta tradition of Hinduism, which understands the world as *maya*, illusion and the mystic realizes the truth that the human soul is identical with the world soul—that Atman is Brahman—not in any intellectual or theoretical sense, but through the direct experience of apprehending oneself as identical with Brahman. It is an overwhelming experience of the joyful comprehension of ultimate truth, which Advaita Vedanta calls **satchitananda** (*sat* = truth; *chit* = consciousness; *ananda* = bliss). Whereas Advaita is an interpretation, an elaborated theology of soul mysticism, the experience itself is pure awareness; it does not carry with it any interpretation.

Theistic mysticism, according to Stace, is the consummation and full completion of mystical experience, similar to soul mysticism in certain ways but going beyond the experience of peace and joy to the fulfillment of love. It involves an emptying of the consciousness and a detachment from all things worldly, but this is only the preliminary preparation for the experience of rapture that comes when the soul unites with God. Where the soul mystic tends to consider the mystical experience as a personal achievement, the theistic mystic is convinced that God empties and fills the individual spirit, purifying (to make the person worthy of becoming one with God) and possessing (infusing the person with rapturous joy and love). Nature mysticism is characterized by a sense of moral indifference as distinctions of good and evil are transcended; soul mysticism is also amoral, involving a peaceful contentment with reality that lacks feelings of desire and aversion alike. Theistic mysticism, however, involves the concepts of purification, worthiness, and holiness of life expressed through works of charity.

Stace's extroversive mysticism and Zaehner's nature mysticism show many similarities, as do Stace's introversive mysticism and Zaehner's monistic mysticism. Certain critics have suggested that Zaehner's theistic mysticism is not really a distinct type;[16] in fact, it seems to be an interpretation, a theology of mystical experience, rather than a description of the experience itself. Indeed, there is such diversity of mystical experiences, such a continuous shading of varieties, that classification becomes difficult if not sometimes arbitrary. A typology is useful for loosely grouping accounts of experiences, particularly so that experiences from different cultures and religious traditions can be compared with one another. The two factors about mystical experience that need to be kept most in mind are their richness of variety and their ubiquity in virtually every major religious tradition — even the presence of experiences of Zaehner's theistic type in nontheistic traditions such as Buddhism.

Expressing the Inexpressible

A classic and detailed study of the whole range of religious experiences was undertaken by the great American psychologist and philosopher William James (1842–1910) in his book, *The Varieties of Religious Experience* (1902). Although there have been a number of important subsequent studies of mysticism, no more thorough or extensive examination of religious experience has yet been done. James examined numerous accounts of religious experiences of every kind, bringing to bear on them the perspective of the psychologist as well as that of the philosopher. He concerned himself first with the phenomena themselves, offering an objective examination of what the individuals actually experienced and of what happens in the lives of individuals who have religious experiences. He then attempted to state how these experiences are related to the psychological state of the individual, to what extent they are culturally conditioned, how similar they are from one religious tradition to another, and particularly their implications concerning the truth of the beliefs arising from them.

James found four qualities to characterize the mystical experiences he studied: ineffability, noetic quality, transiency, and passivity.[17] Although mystics regard their experiences as the most important event that ever happened to them and thus desire to share them with others, they universally agree that such experiences cannot be communicated; they are *ineffable*. Just as the person who is tone deaf learns nothing about the delight of hearing a symphony from treatises on music; as the person who has never been in love, no matter how much he may read or hear, never knows the special feeling the lover experiences; so also the person who has never had a mystical experience learns only the external details and nothing of its essence. Nothing substitutes for the experience itself: one must surrender oneself to the power of transcendent being, and thus merge, and fuse, and coalesce into the unity of being, if one is to know what the mystical experience really is.

To those who have them, mystical experiences may be incommunicable but they are also profoundly **noetic**, or knowledge bearing: They seem to be states of knowledge that reveal deeper truths than any known by ordinary means. "They are illuminations, revelations, full of significance and importance, all inarticulate though they remain; and as a rule they carry with them a curious sense of authority for aftertime."[18] Mystical experiences are also states that cannot be sustained for very long; furthermore, they seem to come and go of their own volition. Mystics may spend years of disciplined meditation striving to achieve or repeat a mystical experience, but it comes unannounced and on its own terms.

The noetic quality of the mystic experience makes it very different from that of the prophetic experience, in which the prophet receives a message that is to be delivered to the people, often in the form of definite information carrying with it explicit commandments. There is nothing ineffable or incommunicable about this kind of experience. The messages that came out of the prophetic experiences of such Hebrew prophets as Isaiah, Jeremiah, Micah, and Hosea were entirely plain, intended to be communicated to, and understood by, the common people. And although the more lengthy message mediated through the prophetic experience of Muhammad contains passages that may be difficult to understand, the noetic aspect of this religious experience yielded explicitly communicable teaching. Furthermore, unlike the mystics, the prophets do not place the greatest importance on the experience through which the message was received. For them, the message counts, whereas for the mystics, despite their claim that the experience reveals truths of unsurpassed importance, not the message but the experience is momentous.

James tells us that mystical experiences vary in degree of intensity — from such simple feelings as the sudden sense of the deepened significance of some maxim, poem, or passage of scripture all the way to the overwhelming, sometimes delightful, sometimes terrifying experiences of seeing the very form and face of God or of being absorbed into the great ocean of Being. Obviously, the more intense experiences have usually been regarded as having the greatest religious significance. The Indian mystic Ramakrishna (1836–1886) had a succession of ever-deepening experiences as he struggled to achieve absolute union with Brahman. As a part of this attempt, Ramakrishna studied the religious teachings of several of the world's great religions, convinced they were all paths to the same destination, all great rivers that emptied at last into the same sea. During the time he studied Christianity, he read the Christian scriptures, meditated on the life and spirit of Jesus, prayed to God through Jesus, and attempted to live the life of a devoted Christian. His biographer Romain Rolland describes

Ramakrishna's quest and recounts several remarkable experiences the mystic had.

> For the first time Ramakrishna met Christ. Shortly afterwards the word was made flesh. The life of Jesus secretly pervaded him. One day when he was sitting in the room of a friend . . . he saw on the wall a picture representing the Madonna and Child. The figures became alive. Then the expected came to pass according to the invariable order of the spirit; the holy visions came close to him and entered him so that his whole being was impregnated with them. [19]

Rolland tells us that Ramakrishna's whole life was pervaded with Christ and for days thereafter all traces of his Hinduism disappeared. He could not even bring himself to go to the Kali temple where he was the priest.

> Then one afternoon in the grove of Dakshineswar he saw coming toward him a person with beautiful large eyes, a serene regard and a fair skin. . . . He drew near and a voice sang in the depths of Ramakrishna's soul: "Behold the Christ, who shed his heart's blood for the redemption of the world . . . " The Son of Man embraced the seer of India . . . and absorbed him into himself. Ramakrishna was lost in ecstasy. Once again he realized union with Brahman. [20]

Ramakrishna's experiences would probably be classified as an example of Zaehner's theistic mysticism. William James cites a milder experience of a Canadian psychiatrist, Dr. R. M. Bucke, who spoke of his transformation into an expanded form of consciousness that he called cosmic consciousness (Zaehner's alternative name for soul mysticism):

> All at once, without warning of any kind, I found myself wrapped in a flame-colored cloud. For an instant I thought of fire . . . the next, I knew that the fire was within myself. Directly afterward there came upon me a sense of exultation, of immense joyousness accompanied or immediately followed by an intellectual illumination impossible to describe. . . . I became conscious in myself of eternal life. . . . I saw that all men are immortal. . . . The vision lasted a few seconds and was gone; but the memory of it and the sense of the reality of what was taught has remained during the quarter of a century which has since elapsed. [21]

Whereas many mystical experiences are spontaneous, coming without warning or personal effort, mystics in every culture have cultivated methods of asceticism, prayer, and meditation thought to be conducive to such experiences. Among Christian mystics a meditative practice called **orison** has sometimes yielded experiences of very great intensity. St. Teresa describes one of her experiences thus:

> One day, being in orison, it was granted to me to perceive in one instant how all things are seen and contained in God. . . . It was

one of the most signal of all the graces which the Lord has granted to
me. . . . Our Lord made me to comprehend in what way it is that one
God can be three persons. He made me see it so clearly that I remained as extremely surprised as I was comforted. . . . and now, when
I think of the holy trinity, or hear It spoken of, I understand how the
three adorable Persons form only one God and I experience an unspeakable happiness. [22]

St. Teresa does not enable us to understand the mystery of the Trinity
through her description of the experience, as we would expect if she were
reporting a prophetic vision. She is convinced that she understands and
the conviction gives her great happiness. But as long as the understanding
cannot be communicated to others, it cannot count as evidence of the sort
that is useful to the philosopher.

Her account illustrates the problem of deciding whether theistic mysticism is genuinely a separate type or merely a highly theory- or theology-
laden interpretation of an experience. Clearly this is not simply reporting
an experience; Teresa is reading into it a whole system of previously learned
Christian theology. The Indian poet philosopher, Rabindranath Tagore
(1881–1941) raises this point when he discusses how mystical experiences
of union with the Absolute should be understood. [23] Tagore, speaking from
the Advaita Vedanta tradition and its emphasis on experiencing the oneness of Atman with Brahman, tells us that the nature of the mystical experience suggests that reality is ultimately a single, undifferentiated absolute
being of which each of us is an unseparated part. The mystical experience
enables us actually to *see* that the multiplicity of our ordinary experience is
maya; that there is no plurality but only the timeless, undifferentiated
One. We are drops of water immersed in the infinite ocean of being. The
mystical experience itself, then, is inherently monistic and not theistic.
This distinction may come somewhat close to an ungarnished definition of
the experience, but there is interpretation here, too, and a reading in of
previously accepted beliefs from Hinduism.

Tagore adds his own interpretation by arguing that to give depth and
significance to our earthly life, we would do well to postpone any sustained
apprehension of this ultimate truth and yield ourselves to the pervasive
illusion of separateness. For duality and separation are necessary conditions
for morality, and especially for the most important aspect of the moral life:
love for other humans, but most important, love for God. Where complete
unity exists, there is no right or wrong; where no separation exists, there is
no longing and thus no fulfillment of longing in the union of love. Human
life, however, is full of loneliness and longing, and it is wondrously punctu-
ated from time to time with the experience of fulfillment that comes
through the mutuality of love. Tagore depicts in many of his poems a deity
who is also filled with longing and who comes to our door begging for our

love. He thus points up the tension between the amoral implications of introversive or monistic mysticism on one hand and the commonplace of our daily lives when we are not undergoing mystical experience. Categories of good and evil are surpassed in the ultimate; the Great One, Brahman, is above all distinctions.

Nevertheless, we live by far the greatest part of our lives overshadowed by *maya*, the sense of separation. In a world where plurality is the dominant feature of our experience, morality is essential. Furthermore, the experience of love that characterizes ordinary life is the highest and most valuable, second only to the mystical experience itself. Indeed, Tagore is convinced that we should mostly forego enjoyment of the monistic experience — most humans during most of their lives inevitably lack such experiences anyway — in order to savor the high and sacred experience of love and the holiness of life to which the genuine love of God calls us. Thus Tagore, like many others, regards what Zaehner calls theistic mysticism as an interpretation, in terms of personalistic theistic beliefs, of an experience that amounts to direct awareness of that absolute oneness which is both ultimate reality and oneself.

James discusses an extreme form of mystical experience called by Christian mystics **raptus,** or ravishment. Apart from the separate interpretative overlays, it resembles very closely a condition called **samadhi** experienced by Indian mystics practicing the most austere form of yoga. The mystic having such an experience lapses into a state resembling unconsciousness or even death: "Breathing and circulation are so depressed that it is a question among the doctors whether the soul be or be not temporarily dissevered from the body."[24] The Sanskrit word *samadhi* and its cognates in Hindi and several other modern Indian languages also refer to death, a cemetery or cremation place. The mystic in the state of *samadhi* like the mystic in *raptus*, manifests greatly slowed body metabolism and an unresponsiveness to external stimulation so complete that it is difficult to detect signs of life. On several occasions Ramakrishna entered into *samadhi* that lasted for extended periods of time; it is reported that his body became stiff like a corpse and that his disciples had to force liquids into him to keep him from dying. Those who experience these trances insist that they were not unconscious but rather in a state of heightened superconsciousness, directly aware of the reality itself with which they had attained complete union. Such experiences illustrate Stace's introversive type in its most extreme form as well as Zaehner's monistic type of mystical experience.

The resemblance of some of the more extreme forms of mystical experience to pathological conditions is not difficult to see. James states: "Undoubtedly these pathological conditions have existed in many and possibly in all the cases, but that fact tells us nothing about the value for knowledge of the consciousness which they induce."[25] Whether or not mystical and other forms of religious experience have value for knowledge is the question of greatest interest to the philosopher of religion, but we will delay that discussion until we have looked more closely at the concept of revelation.

REVELATION

A form of religious experience that we have been calling prophetic experience is often considered to be an encounter between a human individual and God or a messenger of God for the purpose of conveying a divine revelation to humanity. Many of the great world religions, even those like Hinduism that do not trace their founding to a single prophet or incarnation, are grounded on teachings, usually contained in holy writings or scriptures, thought to be the products of such revelation experiences. We must first examine the revelation claims put forward by the advocates of the various traditions; then we must determine if there are criteria for judging the authenticity of the many revelation claims and if, as certain critics have insisted, these different revelations contradict one another and cannot therefore be regarded as sources of knowledge. The outcome of our discussion will bear on our scrutiny of the more general question: Does religious experience have epistemic value for religious belief?

Types of Revelation Claims

The concept of revelation may be understood in several ways. According to possibly the most common view, **revelation** is the process by which certain divine truths about the world and God, and certain commandments about the moral and religious behavior that God expects of us, are communicated. This way of understanding revelation has been called the *propositional* view because it holds that revelation consists of a set of truths communicated in the form of true propositions.[26] Moses' receiving of the ten commandments at Mount Sinai is a graphic example; so are some of the messages that came to several of the prophets whose teachings are found in the Hebrew Bible. Most of the contents of such books as the Qur'an and the Baghavad-Gita are also alleged revelations. Indeed, it has often been claimed that in a certain sense all holy scriptures, of whatever religion, are God's messages of revelation.

Revelation understood in this way is supposed to be accepted and believed, not because human reason recognizes it as rational, or because it meets certain human criteria, but simply because it comes from God. The authority of the prophet authenticates the revelation; we should believe it, it is often said, because of the faith we have in God or in God's messenger.

It is in this sense that scripture is often called the Word of God, meaning that scripture consists of God's actual words; even the human writers of the scriptures are supposed to be simply scribes who wrote down what they received by divine inspiration. According to Moslem teachings, for example, Allah's angelic messenger dictated the words of the Qur'an to Muhammad, who transcribed them. Those who hold this view of revelation place great authority on allegedly revealed truths and often insist that the teachings of the scriptures are literally true in every detail. It is inappropriate, they claim — indeed, presumptuous and impious — to question any detail of the revelation. Revelation is granted by a being whose knowledge and authority far exceeds that of even the wisest human, and it is granted precisely because human reason is incapable of finding out these truths. We are to believe and obey the deliverance of revelation, then, and not question it.

Another strand of theological thought, however, interprets revelation in a nonpropositional way. According to this approach, it is not a set of doctrines about God, the world, morality, and worship that is revealed, but rather the "living God": Revelation is a process of divine self-disclosure through which God enters into the affairs of human history, calls certain individuals into covenant, and watches with provident care over the destiny of individuals and nations. The scriptural tradition of the religion is thus not a transcript of the words of God communicated to humans as true propositions to be believed and obeyed; rather, it is an account of God's dealings with God's people. The Hebrew Bible, for example, may be understood as a narrative about the call of Abraham to become the father of God's chosen people and the subsequent history of the divine-human covenant that resulted from Abraham's response.

Sometimes divine self-disclosure takes place through the life of a human or divine-human individual understood to be an incarnation or avatar, revealing in his or her life and deeds the very nature, character, and purpose of God. The Christian religion is based on such a revelation. It is not so much the message or the teachings of Jesus that mediate or constitute the revelation as Jesus himself, understood as the Christ, God incarnate. Jesus, the Christ, is said to *be* the Word of God rather than being merely a messenger communicating the words of God. John's Gospel says about the birth of Jesus: "The Word became flesh and dwelt among us, full of grace and truth; we beheld his glory, glory as of the only Son from the Father."[27] The same Gospel reports that Jesus himself claimed to be this sort of revelation of God when he said, "He who has seen me has seen the Father,"[28] and "I and the Father are one."[29]

A third view of revelation, put forth by C. H. Dodd (1884–1973), interprets revelation as the product of human genius analogous to the discoveries about the natural world made by great scientists or those about the human predicament made by great writers of imaginative literature.[30]

Prophets or holy persons, says Dodd, possess a special sensitivity that enables them to see more deeply into spiritual matters than ordinary persons. Through scriptures these prophets communicate to us the insights they have derived from their religious experiences. Just as we who are not experts in physics trust the findings of those who are, recognizing that these findings must be tested by the standards that apply to all science, so too we who are not gifted with saintly vision trust the messages of those who are, realizing that the revelations are mediated through the experiences of fallible humans and must therefore be tested and not received uncritically. We bring to bear on the teachings of those persons of religious genius our own less sensitive and penetrating religious experiences and find the revelations confirmed as they resonate or "ring true" with our religious experiences.

When revelation is understood in either of the last two of these three ways, it follows that religious teachings are to be understood as human products, interpretations by fallible individuals of the historical events through which God reveals himself or through which human genius can penetrate some of the hidden truths of human spiritual life. In this view, the scriptures can be the Word of God without being God's words. It becomes important for us to seek out criteria for judging their relative truth or authenticity, particularly because there are so many different individuals and religious traditions, each claiming to mediate divine revelations and in many cases claiming that other alleged revelations are partly or entirely false.

The Cacophony of Alleged Revelations

The concept of revelation derives most explicitly from the three Middle Eastern religions Judaism, Christianity, and Islam, but attitudes typically taken toward holy writings, events, and personages in several of the other great world religions make the concept relevant in analyzing those religions, too. We will examine the claim that the scriptures and the other authoritative teachings of the world's religions are revelations as well as the claim of certain critics that these many revelations are mutually contradictory; finally we will seek to determine criteria by which the authenticity of revelation claims can be judged.

Many of the world's scriptures contain explicit claims that they are revelations from God. In numerous passages in the Hebrew scriptures, for example, we are told that God spoke directly to certain humans. The call of Abraham is recorded thus: "Now the Lord said to Abram, 'Go from your country and your kindred and your father's house to the land that I will show you. And I will make of you a great nation.'"[31] God spoke directly to Moses as well: "God called to Moses from out of the bush . . . then he said to him, 'I am the God of your father, the God of Abraham, the God of Isaac, and the God of Jacob.'"[32] Then God gave Moses instructions about leading his people out of Egypt and continued to communicate with Moses throughout most of the rest of his life. Countless other instances in the Hebrew Bible depict God speaking directly to humans, revealing himself and his commandments. The Qur'an similarly contains an account of how the angel of God came to Muhammad to communicate the message of God; and Jesus claimed that he was making God known to his people. In the Bhagavad-Gita, Lord Krishna, an incarnation of Brahman, speaks at length to Arjuna. The Roman Catholic Church makes the explicit claim that in its authoritative doctrines we receive revelation from God.

If all these varied scriptural and doctrinal traditions claim to be revelations, the question is bound to arise about which one or ones of them are genuine, particularly when people begin to compare them and notice that they do not seem consistent with one another. David Hume (1711–1776) called attention to what he took to be serious incompatibilities between alleged revelations and suggested that these contradictions cast grave doubts on all religions. Hume noted that each religion attempts to authenticate its revelation claims by alleged miracles:

> In matters of religion, whatever is different is contrary. . . . it is impossible the religions of ancient Rome, of Turkey, of Siam, and of China should, all of them, be established on any solid foundation. Every miracle, therefore, pretended to have been wrought in any of these religions (and all of them abound in miracles), as its direct scope is to establish the particular system to which it is attributed; so has it the same force, though more indirectly, to destroy every other system.[33]

Hume is by no means the only one to claim the mutual incompatibility of the various religious revelations; many devotees of the several traditions themselves make the same claim. Instead of concluding with Hume that therefore none of them can be true, however, they infer that only one revelation can be true and that the true one is their own. This line of argument is particularly characteristic of Islam and Christianity.

One of the Christian Apostles, Peter, is reported to have made the exclusivist claim that Jesus Christ is the only means by which humans might attain salvation. It was the occasion of a miraculous healing of a cripple and the disciples were asked how it had been done. Peter proclaimed that it was through the power of the name of Jesus Christ and went on to say: "There is salvation in no one else, for there is no other name under heaven given among men by which we must be saved."[34] A similar exclusivity seems implied in several scriptural passages characterizing Jesus as the "only Son of God,"[35] and more explicitly enunciated in the verse that says, "He who believes in him is not condemned; he who does not believe is condemned already, because he has not believed in the name of the only Son of God."[36]

Many passages in the Qur'an seem to involve similar exclusive claims. In the Surah (chapter) titled "The Believers" we find these words: "He who calls upon another god beside God [Allah] — a god whose being he has no evidence — his reckoning is with his Lord. Those who deny the faith will never prosper."[37] In another chapter we read, "It is those who count the revelations of God [Allah] to be falsehood who are the losers. . . . All that you do will most certainly spell futility and loss if you give to others the worship that is solely God's [Allah's]. . . . To Jahannam [hell] will those be driven in throngs who denied truth."[38] And again, "It is He [Allah] who has sent His messenger with guidance and the religion of truth, making it victorious over all religion, notwithstanding the hatred of those who worship plural gods."[39]

Both Moslems and Christians recognize that God, "the true God," revealed himself to the Jews and made a covenant with them, but both also hold that the Jews were unfaithful to the covenant and thus lost God's favor. Furthermore, each of these two groups believes that the other has lost God's favor and become apostate. Christians recognize the revelation received by the Jews — the Hebrew Bible that Christians call the Old Testament — as valid but incomplete revelation. Moslems say essentially the same thing about both Hebrew and Christian scripture. Each religion goes on to claim complete and final authority for its own revelations. The medieval saying *Extra ecclesiam nulla salus* expresses the Christian view of "no salvation outside the [Christian] church," the belief that the Church is the "only ark of salvation." When the church split, Roman Catholics understood the saying to mean "no salvation outside the Roman Catholic Church." Similar claims of exclusivity are made, explicitly or implicitly, by various sects of Protestants toward one another and toward the Roman Church; the several Moslem sects regard one another in equally exclusivist ways. This sectarianism among Christians and Moslems, a characteristic found to a lesser extent also in most other world religions, carries the implication that one's own sect mediates the only legitimate revelation. Where appeals are made to the same written body of holy writings by various sects, the implication is that the interpretation of the scriptures constitutes the revelation and that only one's own interpretation is valid.

Universalism: One Message Variously Interpreted

Claims of inconsistency and mutual contradiction among revelations are mostly based on the assumption of a propositional understanding of revelation. If revelation is a set of propositions communicated from a divine source, then any contradictions or inconsistencies present serious problems. If the propositions alleged to have been revealed to Muhammad contradict those declared to have been revealed to Jesus, then they clearly cannot all be true — unless one is willing to abandon rationality altogether. For example, the Christian tradition claims that Jesus is the Christ, the only son of God. The Moslem tradition asserts that Muhammad is the authorized prophet of God bringing the final revelation. Although the two claims do not directly contradict one another, most people would see in them clearly contradictory implications. A more conspicuous inconsistency appears between the insistent Moslem teaching of the oneness of God and the Christian conception of the divine Trinity, despite the Christian claim that the three persons of the Trinity are one. So the propositional theory of revelation, particularly in the hands of believers who are inclined to give revelation a very strict, literal interpretation, lends itself to Hume's charge that the world religions contradict one another and therefore cannot all be true. And since none brings forward convincing evidence to show that it has stronger claims to the truth than the others, Hume's inference that none should therefore be credited seems rather plausible.

These dire consequences do not necessarily follow, however, if one accepts either of the other two ways of interpreting revelation. If revelation is seen as the self-manifestation of the divine directly or through avatars or agents; or if it is understood as the discovery of aspects of the unseen world by persons of spiritual genius, then one can plausibly argue that revelation traditions are not in effect inconsistent with one another.

Movements in several parts of the world have attempted to show that all religions teach essentially the same thing. Sometimes called **universalism**, this approach concentrates on identifying similarities among traditions and attributing differences to cultural traditions and practices. According to universalism, the One Divine Reality, called by various names in many parts of the world, reveals Itself everywhere and to all peoples; but the revelation is understood differently and given different interpretations according to the cultural circumstances and expectations of the persons receiving it. The great Indian religious teacher Vivekananda (1863–1902) made the idea of universal religion a central theme of his message to the world, claiming that the God of all the religions is one, however variously conceived:

> Every vision of truth that man has, is a vision of Him and of none else. Suppose we all go with vessels in our hands to fetch water from the lake. . . . The water in each case naturally takes the form of the vessel carried by each of us. He who brought the cup has the water in the form of a cup; he who brought a jar — his water is in the shape of a jar, and so forth; but in every case, water, and nothing but water, is in the vessel. So it is in the case of religion; our minds are like those vessels, and each one of us is trying to arrive at the realization of God. God is like that water filling these different vessels, and in each vessel the vision of God comes in the form of the vessel. Yet He is One. He is God in every case.[40]

What is important, then, is to discover and emphasize the universal qualities, features such as the unity of God, the universal brother- and sisterhood of all humans, and the moral duties we all have toward universal justice and charity.

> Are all the religions of the world really contradictory? . . . I mean the internal soul of every religion. . . . I believe that they are not contradictory; they are supplementary. Each religion, as it were, takes up one part of the great universal truth, and spends its whole force embodying and typifying that part of the great truth.[41]

Vivekananda is not advocating the amalgamation of all religions into one. Each has its unique value; each expresses for those who practice it their own experiences of the divine reality. The point is to recognize that the religions are not enemies of one another, but alternative ways of worshipping the same God or of realizing the same truth. When they accept this truth, the religions will stop attacking one another, stop trying to proselytize one another's devotees, and cooperate in a spirit of charity and neighborliness.

When revelation is not conceived in a propositional way and when the claims of universalism such as those promoted by Vivekananda are understood, much of the sting is taken out of Hume's criticism. Alleged revelations from separate religious traditions are no longer contradictory but mutually supplementary. Where apparently incompatible views appear, human cultural expectations may have injected themselves, resulting in seers apprehending the revelation within their separate cultural frameworks. The concept of revelation is thus rescued from the charge of incoherence and a way is cleared toward reconciling alleged revelations. The teachings of universalism, however, turn out to be very vague. In construing revelations as the vessels that give the water various particular forms, Vivekananda claims that he is not suggesting that any form is just as adequate as any other. And yet he does not offer any concrete guidance for judging the adequacy of interpretations of revelations. Are there any such criteria?

Evaluating Alleged Revelations

Believers in revelation often suggest that attempting to judge divine revelation is the height of human presumption. Is God to be called before the feeble bar of human reason and put to the test as we test the credibility of human witnesses? Is divine revelation to be accepted or rejected in terms of whether or not it is agreeable to human reason? But this argument begs the question. No, of course, God is not to be questioned, nor divine truths doubted. What is to be questioned is whether or not a given alleged revelation really is one; whether the source that claims to speak for God really does. The question is not whether God speaks the truth, but whether God speaks through this or that prophet, saint, or book. We cannot naively accept as genuine every message that anyone puts forward as a purported revelation. We seek criteria to enable us to judge, not whether or not God speaks the truth, but whether a claim alleged to be a revelation really is one.

Any satisfactory rational set of criteria would certainly recognize that a genuine revelation must be true, and this implies that such a revelation could not involve any contradictions or inconsistencies. Neither could it be demonstrably inconsistent with other well-established truths, such as those of science. For many devotees of various religious traditions, accustomed to accepting the sayings of their scriptures at face value, these criteria would present problems. The scriptures of all major religions involve teachings that, if taken literally, appear inconsistent with one another, and most involve scriptural teachings that appear inconsistent with science. But rational theologians from St. Thomas to the present have insisted that all truth is God's truth; that the appearance of inconsistency within the teachings of the scriptures demands that we seek a more profound understanding of the teaching; and that when we find it, it will turn out not to be inconsistent.

Such a teaching inevitably drives us to figurative interpretations of much revelation or to the recognition that revelation at best is humanly mediated and thus subject to coloration as it flows through the lenses of cultural and individual presuppositions. But if we take into account these considerations, it appears possible at least in theory to refine the revelation material of a religious tradition into a consistent set of beliefs. Indeed, it appears possible to do so for several religious traditions. Perhaps this is the task of the theology of a particular tradition, if theology is understood as an attempt to generate a systematic, rational account of the teachings of the religion. When this job is done, some of the worst of the inconsistencies from one religion to another that worried Hume may have diminished or disappeared. But there is no reason to believe that the expectations of universalism will have been realized. We may still be left with several internally consistent systems of belief that are incompatible with one another. Thus we would still face the question of which one, if any, to accept. The bare criteria of noncontradiction and consistency would not suffice to settle the apparent conflict among contending revelations.

As soon as more specific criteria are sought, however, the ones we find seem to come already equipped with certain presuppositions that themselves appear problematic, or at least in need of justification. What seems usually to be involved in a discussion of revelation is the assumption that there is a divine being who, if we accept one interpretation of what revelation means, reveals information in the form of propositions and commandments or who, if we accept a different view about revelation, reveals himself or herself. On either of these two interpretations of revelation, the presupposition of the existence of such a deity needs justification itself, and even if that assumption is accepted, the criteria we will find plausible will depend on the kind of being God is antecedently assumed to be. When Christians argue that those passages in the Qur'an that authorize or encourage the torture, killing, or capture for ransom of non-Moslems are human inventions and not divine revelations, this reflects a Christian presupposition that God is the kind of being who would not approve of such immoral acts. Conversely, when Moslems argue that they are justified in killing or kidnapping Christians or Jews because the Qur'an authorizes such actions under certain circumstances, this reflects an antecedent assumption that the Qur'an is known to be an authentic divine revelation and that whatever it teaches is therefore morally acceptable because of being authorized by Allah.

Are there any criteria that do not simply reflect our presuppositions or biases? We might suggest that everyone agrees that God is good, and thus that no revelation is authentic that portrays a divine being who is not good. But this is of no help in settling the issue just cited. Christians, Jews, and Moslems all agree that God is good. Christians, however, argue that God's goodness implies that God would not approve of the killing or torture of unbelievers. Moslems assert that Allah is good, and add that harsh punishment for unbelievers is a part of God's goodness to those who believe. It appears, then, that as long as revelation is understood either in the sense of revealing propositions alleged to be true or revealing God's nature or character, there is no set of objective criteria that is not circular in the sense of involving presuppositions that themselves would have to be justified before they could be accepted.

If we take revelation in the third sense, as the discoveries of human individuals of spiritual genius, then we may be able to generate criteria that offer a measure of guidance, even if they do not sharply set off different revelation claims as true or false. Understood in this way, revelation resembles works of genius in art, literature, or music. In these departments of human experience we have vague criteria that guide us in distinguishing a superb painting from a trite or trivial one, a truly great novel from a common potboiler. Just as we can say with a measure of confidence that the vision of the human predicament given us by Dostoevsky or Hemingway is definitely superior to that offered in the typical Harlequin romance, perhaps we can also say with some assurance that the spiritual perspective offered by the Buddha, or by Moses, is definitely superior to that put forward by Norman Vincent Peale or Jimmy Swaggart. Such criteria will enable us to eliminate some revelation claims as trivial and some as demonic. They may enable us with a measure of plausibility to rank certain others as more or less insightful, uplifting, inspiring, and so on as we rank certain works of art. But we will be left in a position consistent with universalism, which recognizes the legitimacy, at least for religious purposes, of several revelation traditions, and does not attempt to take a position of exclusivist superiority on behalf of any of these.

This outcome is of limited utility for the philosopher of religion, who does not find in the content of revelation specially authenticated data, ready to be used as certified premises for supporting philosophical conclusions. The fact that individuals have experiences that they interpret as divine-human encounters of a revelatory sort must be taken into account in any adequate philosophy of religion. But the suggestion that the deliverances of revelation might serve as foundation claims for constructing a philosophy of religion, analogous to the way that sense impressions serve as basic pieces of evidence for the construction of scientific theory, seems not to stand up to scrutiny. Now we must ask whether or not the deliverances of other religious experiences fare better.

DOES RELIGIOUS EXPERIENCE PROVIDE EVIDENCE FOR THE TRUTH OF RELIGIOUS BELIEFS?

Western philosophy was dominated from the second or third century of the Common Era until the beginning of the early modern period in the late seventeenth century by the theology of Christianity. In this tradition it was taken for granted almost unquestioningly that religious experience and particularly revelation was a reliable — indeed, *the* authoritative — source of knowledge. More recently, however, at least since the time of David Hume, Western philosophy has been under the influence of empiricist epistemology, whose central claim is that all of our knowledge about matters of fact is derived from sense experience. **Empiricism** has usually involved a skeptical attitude toward religious beliefs, whatever their purported source, but especially beliefs allegedly derived from religious experience. Hume makes use of the empiricist principle in his *Dialogues Concerning Natural Religion* to argue that we cannot know anything about "divine attributes and operations." He states: "Our ideas reach no further than our experience. We have no experience of divine attributes and operations. I need not conclude my syllogism: You can draw the inference yourself."[42] Of course, the mystic would argue that we do indeed have experience of divine attributes and operations; this is precisely what mystical and other kinds of religious experiences are taken to be by persons who have them. This claim would be roundly rejected by the orthodox empiricist, who uses the term *experience* to mean "sense experience"; in the empirical view, no other kind of experience counts.

One might plausibly argue that such a position has not been established on rational grounds but is merely asserted dogmatically. Yet during much of the twentieth century, a philosophical tradition that originated in Vienna and was soon transplanted to England and America has continued to promote what might properly be called a fundamentalist empiricism, not in a spirit of disinterested inquiry, but with a preconceived design: to drive out from the field of philosophical respectability certain branches of philosophy the advocates of this empiricism did not favor. Logical positivism, later known as logical empiricism, reasserted the central theme of empiricism in analytic linguistic terms, declaring that all sequences of words that purport to say anything about the world, but that cannot be verified by reference to sense experience, are not genuine propositions but literally nonsense. Based on these doctrines, the logical positivists announced that metaphysics, ethics, aesthetics, and the philosophy of religion were, all of them, pseudodisciplines trading not in genuine philosophical merchandise but in counterfeit products — doctrines and theories that were literal nonsense.

The nouveau-empiricist project came to grief, however, when its verifiability criterion turned out to convict itself of being literal nonsense. Even more serious was the blatant arbitrariness of the scheme, which treated the narrow principles of empiricism as revealed truths beyond question or doubt. Fortunately this philosophical fanaticism is beginning to diminish in the English-speaking world and the serious epistemological questions are again being asked, questions that must be addressed if we are to discover what the legitimate sources of human knowledge are.

William James, among others, suggests that we should indeed be empiricists, but good, thoroughgoing empiricists and not narrow, dogmatic ones. To be an empiricist is to believe that experience is the source of all of our knowledge. But it is arbitrary to limit the category of experience to sense experience. If we are to be reasonable empiricists and not dogmatists, we must be ready to consider the data we derive from all kinds of experience.

Besides sense experience, humans also have aesthetic experience, moral experience, and religious experience — at least these three kinds — and each of them has noetic quality. The kind of knowledge we feel we derive from religious experience may be different from that which comes from sense experience; the way we understand true and false may not be identical as we move from aesthetic to moral experience. Yet we do apply the cognitive categories to all three kinds of experience, and we seem to be justified in doing so. For example, moral experience (which we will discuss in some detail in Chapter 7) is the sense of "oughtness" and compunction; it is the recognition that some forms of behavior are morally unacceptable and others morally worthy, and that we ought to refrain from the one and cultivate the other. This is not just the simplistic "let your conscience be your guide." We sometimes feel that an action is morally permissible that, on rational examination turns out not to be, or vice versa. In this respect, moral experience is not essentially different from sense experience. Both are corrigible; both must be tested. But we can no more doubt that we have moral experience — the sense that we have obligations, that some kinds of things are wrong, that we sometimes fail to live up to what morality demands — than that we have sense experience.

Morality is a universal feature of human social life, even if the specific acts that are apprehended as required or prohibited may differ from one culture or era to another. And it is just as obvious that religious experiences are features of human experience in every age and society. It would surely be unempirical to characterize experience as the source of all of our knowledge and then arbitrarily to accept one kind of experience and refuse even to consider the other kinds. We must assume neither that religious experience is, or is not, a valid source of knowledge about the truth of religious beliefs. What we must do — the empirical thing to do — is look and see.

The so-called *unanimity thesis* constitutes the core of the most widely accepted argument from mystical experience: This is the argument that mystical and other kinds of religious experiences provide evidence with epistemological value in the support of religious belief. Briefly stated, the unanimity thesis claims that there is unanimous agreement among mystics in every age of history and in every culture about the character of religious experience. Steven T. Katz offers three formulations of the thesis, in ascending order of sophistication:

(I) All mystical experiences are the same; even their descriptions reflect an underlying similarity which transcends cultural or religious diversity . . .
(II) All mystical experiences are the same but the mystics' *reports about* their experiences are culturally bound. Thus they use the available symbols of their cultural-religious milieu to describe their experience . . .
(III) All mystical experience can be divided into a small class of 'types' which cut across cultural boundaries. Though the language used by mystics to describe their experience is culturally bound, their experience is not.[43]

Most contemporary philosophers of religion would concede that the first, and perhaps the first two, formulations will not stand up to scrutiny. If the argument from mystical experience is to work, the unanimity thesis will have to be formulated approximately in Katz's third way.

A standard and forceful formulation of the argument was put forward by C. D. Broad (1887–1971), a religious skeptic who wrote extensively on issues in the philosophy of religion and who regarded the argument from the unanimity of religious experience as the most plausible of the theistic arguments.[44] William L. Rowe provides us with a clearly stated outline of Broad's version of the argument:

1. There is considerable agreement among mystics concerning the reality they have experienced.
2. When there is considerable agreement among observers as to what they take themselves to be experiencing, it is reasonable to

conclude that their experiences are veridical, unless there be some
positive reason to think them delusive.

3. There are no positive reasons for thinking that mystical experiences are delusive. Therefore,

4. It is reasonable to believe that mystical experiences are veridical.[45]

Premise 1 is a general version of the unanimity thesis. The argument
would be strengthened by substituting a more carefully crafted version such
as Katz's formulation III of the thesis, particularly if, after careful scrutiny,
we could be confident that it is true. Premise 2 is a general postulate that
states what we tend to assume in dealing with sense experience, the testimony of witnesses in court, and so on. It is perhaps not self-evidently true,
but it is certainly widely accepted in our common sense dealings and seems
to be a basic assumption of science as well.

Premise 3 is a claim that has been challenged by such thinkers as Bertrand Russell (1872–1970), whose argument also attempts to undermine
the cognitive respectability of premise 1. Russell claims that there are positive reasons for thinking that mystical experiences are delusive. He points
out that the delusions of serious abusers of alcohol, who see rats, snakes, or
pink elephants, agree from person to person in whatever age or culture, just
as mystical experiences do. We believe that such delusions are related to
the effects of alcohol on the drunkards' bodies and not veridical perceptions of animals actually present. But we observe that mystics also do things
that affect their bodies, such as fasting, breathing exercises, refraining from
any external sense impressions, and a variety of other ascetic practices. It
seems reasonable to suggest that the unanimity among mystics about the
character of their experiences might well be related to the bodily effects of
their asceticism as the unanimity among the drunkards about the nature of
theirs is related to alcohol. In both cases, other persons present in the same
time and place do not have the same perceptions as the mystics and the
drunkards. For reasons such as these, Russell believes that there is justification for thinking that the mystics' experiences are delusional.[46]

Broad, in counterargument, points out that rats and snakes are the
sorts of things we would expect other persons to see if they were present,
whereas the mystics experience something we would not expect other persons in an ordinary state of consciousness to experience. Therefore
Russell's analogy with the delusions of drunkenness does not constitute a
positive reason for thinking that mystical experiences are delusive.[47]

Does Broad's argument suffice to show that religious experience does
provide epistemic support for the truth of religious beliefs? Several problems remain which stand in the way of an answer. The first relates to premise 1, the unanimity thesis. We have already noted that the claim that
religious experiences are the same in all ages and all religious traditions is
unacceptably oversimple. Katz's reformulations of the unanimity thesis attempt to take into account the conspicuous fact that, despite striking sim-

ilarities, there are also substantial differences. The second formulation undertakes to distinguish the experiences themselves from the language in which they are reported, asserting that mystics resort to the myths and symbols current in their culture as media of expression for what they have experienced. Thus it claims that the experiences themselves are the same and the differences have to do only with the set of concepts available to the mystics for describing the experiences.

Yet it is all too obvious that the experience of exhilaration felt when the meaning of a poem or verse of scripture suddenly becomes illuminated is quite different from the experience of seeing and being spoken to by what one takes to be the Virgin Mary or Lord Krishna. The experience of awe and exultation a person feels when the senses are flooded with the beauty of a sunset or the grandeur of a mountain range is not very similar to the feeling of total emptiness the monistic mystic experiences when consciousness seems to merge into the great oneness of Being Itself. A conversion experience is very different from Christian *raptus* or Hindu *samadhi*. It is this very noticeable variety, this unavoidable lack of sameness, that Katz's third formulation attempts to take into account—indeed, that the whole enterprise of working out typologies seeks to address. If the argument from religious experience is designed to prove that there is a single divine being that causes all these experiences, or a single absolute reality of which all are glimpses, the fact of similarity or unanimity counts strongly in favor, but the fact of dissimilarity or variety counts on the other side. And both similarity and dissimilarity exist.

On the other hand, if the whole range of types of religious experience have what Wittgenstein called "family resemblances," we might justifiably regard them as belonging to a single family. If religious experience constitutes an argument in support of a reality that might be regarded as the ultimate ground or source of the world and all things in it, perhaps we have no reason to assume that our experiences of that being, whoever or whatever it might be, must all be identical. Just as human individuals respond differently to the same aspects of nature, so might individuals, especially individuals in different cultures, apprehend and interpret experiences of the absolute, the ultimate, the ground-of-being, or whatever we might see fit to call it, differently.

But even if we are convinced that the nature of pure, uninterpreted religious experiences is sufficiently unanimous to support the unanimity thesis in some form, we never seem able to escape the lingering doubt that religious experience is grounded only in the human psyche and is not in touch with anything extramundane. The unanimity thesis might, after all, be explained by pointing out that all humans have a common physical and psychical apparatus. It should not be surprising that persons whose physical and psychological natures are identical in all cultures and eras should have similar experiences under similar conditions. Russell's analogy with the hallucinations of drunkenness lingers despite Broad's attempt to dispel it. And this casts a shadow of doubt on the argument from religious experience.

Still, there certainly are remarkable echoes of similarity from one religious tradition to another and from one historical period to another, despite the significant differences. The mystics themselves insist on the noetic quality of the experiences and report an overwhelming sense of the objective reference of their experiences — the sense that they are in touch with, and under the control of, something objective. If the reasons for rejecting such claims are not overwhelming, perhaps they should be given at least a tentative measure of credence. Although some mystical experiences such as *raptus* and *samadhi* have very strong overtones of psychological pathology that make the analogy with the delusions of drunkenness more plausible, this is not true of most religious experience. Many persons who have such experiences enjoy psychologically healthy lives and find their lives filled with meaning and their urge to live lives of holiness made firm as a result of their religious experiences. Such wholesome effects certainly do not flow from the experience of drunkenness.

Even if the dissimilarity issue can somehow be handled satisfactorily by means of typologies and the device of distinguishing between the experience itself and its interpretations, so that the unanimity thesis sustains its plausibility; even if doubts about the objective reference of the experiences can be assuaged, the question still remains concerning just *what* it is that religious experience proves. Christian mystics are convinced that it proves the existence of a theistic God, one who manifests as a Trinity, one who "spake by the prophets and was incarnate in Jesus Christ." Indeed, some Christian mystics say that their experiences are *of* such a God or *of* Jesus, the Blessed Virgin, or some Christian saint. Buddhist mystics, however, do not believe that their mystical experiences prove the existence of a theistic God. They often describe experiences of Lord Buddha or one of the previous incarnations of the Buddha, or else the experience of emptiness associated with the concept of not-self. Mystics in the Advaita Vedantic tradition believe that their experiences prove that reality is not a personal god but an impersonal Absolute. Even if we accept the claim that all mystical experiences, or at least those of the most profound and significant type, are in some sense the same and that only the interpretations differ, we still want to know which, if any, of these interpretations are warranted by the experience and by reason.

It certainly does not seem possible that all can be justified, in any literal sense, by an argument from religious experience. Perhaps the position called universalism, which we examined earlier in our discussion of revelation, might offer a metaphorical means of suggesting what the argument supports. Though it is surely too much to say that the argument proves in its entirety any one of the world views put forward by the various religious traditions, it might be suggested that we can understand how all, or at least several, of the religious belief systems might relate to mystical experience by the use of Vivekananda's image of the water and the many vessels. If reality or the ultimate, whether it be personal or impersonal, is accessible to human apprehension, even dimly, through mystical experience, perhaps each or at least several of our world religions are mythological elaborations of the fleeting glimpses vouchsafed to the most gifted of our prophets, saints, and avatars.

Undoubtedly some myth systems represent more adequately and with less distortion than others the true nature of reality. It might even be possible for reason to work out some vague principles for judging which distort less and which distort more, although we never could be very confident that we had got it right, or that our standards were not circular or based on unfounded presuppositions. But if we accept the unanimity thesis understood according to Katz's third formulation, then the more general, impersonal, and nonculture-specific the interpretations are, the more support they would receive from the argument; conversely, the more explicit, richly elaborated, and culture-specific the interpretations are, the less they can look to this argument for support. The detailed myth systems of most religious traditions are so filled with descriptions of personal gods, angels, saints, and avatars that they cannot hope, except in the vaguest and most indirect sense, to receive support from the argument from religious experience — and hardly any support at all for the details that believers often consider to be the most important aspects of the traditions.

Religious experience seems to suggest that there is something beyond the subjective human world of which many human individuals occasionally catch a glimpse; that this objective reality, whoever or whatever it may be, is not hostile to humans and their values; that indeed this ultimate reality supports at least in a very general way a world in which humans can pursue their projects and flourish. Whether this reality should be regarded as a being such as the God of several of the religions; as the natural world itself considered particularly with regard to its value dimensions, as some schools of nontheistic naturalism teach; or as an impersonal Absolute of the sort recognized in the Advaita Vedanta tradition or in some branches of Buddhism is a question not settled by the experiences themselves. This becomes a matter of interpretation, and interpretations tend to become elaborate, culture-bound, and richly worked-out mythologies, increasingly remote from the experience and the argument derived from it. In conjunction with well-formulated rational arguments, the argument from religious experience may contribute in some measure to a cumulative support of theism. But it seems more plausible to argue that religious experience offers better support for one of the alternatives to theism discussed in Chapter 5, such as some variety of religious naturalism or an impersonal absolutism like that taught by Advaita Vedanta.

In any case, religious experience does seem to offer support for the notion that there is an unseen reality with which humans can be in some kind of contact and whose nature is not unsupportive of the highest of human ideals and values. It seems to suggest the appropriateness of an attitude of reverence and gratitude toward whatever is regarded as ultimate, whether personal God or impersonal ground of being. It shows that there is joy and happiness to be experienced, despite the presence also of aversive experiences, and seems to intimate that the seeds of our greatest hopes and dreams can be sown in generally fertile ground. And it appears to encourage us to enjoy a sense of our own oneness with whatever is ultimate, as if we are sons and daughters and not just material objects; a sense of being at home in a universe of which we are inseparable parts; and a sense of confidence that human goals, motivated by solid rational ideals and good will, will turn out to be capable of realization.

These are the kinds of beliefs for which religious experience seems to provide us with a measure of evidence, rather than the detailed, culture-specific, sectarian mythologies that make up so much of the content of the great world religions. Perhaps the practice of religion would be impossible without these myth systems; perhaps the multifarious mythologies connected to the many different communities that make up human history are essential aspects of the cultural richness of our heritage. It may be appropriate, as such thinkers as Tagore and Vivekananda have argued, to cherish our different traditions, regarding them as ways of putting into practice in our community life what we take to be the implications of those glimpses of the ultimate that some of our sisters and brothers experience.

This last point will be a central issue in Chapter 8, when we turn specifically to the bewildering variety of beliefs and practices that have evolved in the great human religions. If religious experience is to count as a major source of evidence for the authenticity or validity of religious beliefs, however, we will have to remind ourselves carefully and frequently that it depends importantly on the unanimity thesis, which means that the evidence supports what is similar and not what is different from one religion to another. Religious experience supports the idea of being religious, in the sense of regarding the ultimate as the source of our being from which we come and to which in the end we return. Insofar as it supports the notion that humans are sisters and brothers, all children of one reality, it has also often been understood to imply moral obligations. Now it is time to turn to a consideration of the ground of our moral life and to ask if morality draws its authority from religion.

ANNOTATED GUIDE TO FURTHER READINGS

Hume, David. "Of Miracles." In *Philosophy of Religion: Selected Readings*, 2nd ed., edited by William L. Rowe and William J. Wainwright. New York: Harcourt Brace Jovanovich, 1989.

Hume offers a skeptical view of miracles and revelations. The text also contains a section that deals exclusively with mysticism and religious experience.

James, William. *The Varieties of Religious Experience.* New York: Macmillan, 1961.

This definitive classic covers the topics of religious experience and mysticism thoroughly; it is an excellent source for further examination of these subjects.

Katz, Steven T., ed. *Mysticism and Philosophical Analysis.* New York: Oxford University Press, 1978.

Provides a variety of viewpoints on religious experience and mysticism.

Stace, Walter T. *Mysticism and Philosophy.* Philadelphia and New York: J. B. Lippincott, 1960.

An outstanding source for the study of mysticism.

Stace, Walter T. *The Teachings of the Mystics.* New York: Mentor Books, 1960.

Distinguishes two types of mysticism, introversive and extroversive; examines the occurrence of mystical experiences within the religions of Hinduism, Buddhism, Taoism, Christianity, Islam, and Judaism.

Swinburne, Richard. *The Existence of God.* Oxford: Clarendon Press, 1979.

Applies the principle of credulity to religious experience: that is, that an experience is innocent until proven guilty. The religious perceptions of mystics, like other perceptions, should be taken seriously and should be accepted as long as no evidence proves otherwise.

Tagore, Rabindranath. *The Religion of Man.* Boston: Beacon Press, 1961.

Tagore's exposition of what he calls a "poet's religion," a theistic/humanistic interpretation of Vedanta that teaches the "humanity of God," and the divinity of "man the eternal."

Wainwright, William J. *Mysticism.* Madison, Wisconsin: University of Wisconsin Press, 1981.

Provides the reader with a thorough and diverse study of mysticism. Standard topics are covered along with sections on drug-induced mysticism and the relationship between mysticism and morality.

Zaehner, R. C. *Mysticism: Sacred and Profane.* Oxford: Oxford University Press, 1961.

Rejecting the unanimity thesis, Zaehner emphasized the rich variety of types of religious experiences, giving particular attention to monistic and theistic mystical experiences.

NOTES

1. Ronald W. Hepburn, "Religious Experience, Argument for the Existence of God," in Paul Edwards, ed., *The Encyclopedia of Philosophy* (New York: Macmillan, 1967), vol. 7, p. 165.

2. A Hebrew word related to the verb "to be" and transliterated "YHWH" or "Yahweh."

3. The Biblical account is to be found in Exodus, chapter 3.

4. E.g., the experiences of Noah, Genesis chapters 6ff; the call of Samuel, I Samuel chapter 3; the visions of Elijah, I Kings chapter 18; the vision of Isaiah, Isaiah chapter 6; and many others, particularly from the books of prophecy.

5. See *Bhagavad-Gita* (New York: Bantam Books, 1986).

6. Acts 9:1–9.

7. Rabindranath Tagore, "My Life," *Lectures and Addresses* (Calcutta: Macmillan, 1970), p. 13.

8. Ibid., p. 12.

9. Ralph Waldo Emerson: "Nature," *The Complete Works of Ralph Waldo Emerson*, Concord edition (Boston and New York: Houghton, Mifflin, and Company, 1904), vol. 1, p. 10.

10. William James, *The Varieties of Religious Experience* (New York: Macmillan, 1961), p. 37.

11. Ibid., chapter 3.

12. Walter Stace, *Mysticism and Philosophy* (New York: J. B. Lippincott, 1960).

13. William J. Wainwright offers a summary and a critique of Stace's two types in *Mysticism* (Madison: University of Wisconsin Press, 1981), pp. 8ff.

14. R. C. Zaehner, *Mysticism: Sacred and Profane* (Oxford: Clarendon Press, 1961). In later works Zaehner modified and refined his typology, expanding his classification to four.

15. There is a useful critical discussion of Zaehner's typology in Wainwright, *Mysticism*, pp. 11ff.

16. See, for example, Ninian Smart, "Interpretation and Mystical Experience," *Religious Studies*, vol. 1, pp. 75–87.

17. William James, *The Varieties of Religious Experience*, pp. 299f.

18. Ibid., p. 300.

19. Romain Rolland, *The Life of Ramakrishna* (Calcutta: Advaita Asrama, 1929, 1960), p. 76.

20. Ibid., p. 77.

21. R. M. Bucke: "Cosmic Conscious: A study in the Evolution of the Human Mind," quoted in William James, *The Varieties of Religious Experience*, pp. 313f. James has slightly paraphrased Bucke's wording. The original source is Richard Maurice Bucke, *Cosmic Consciousness* (Philadelphia: Innes & Sons, 1905), p. 8.

22. Quoted in William James, *The Varieties of Religious Experience*, p. 323.

23. See especially Rabindranath Tagore, *The Religion of Man* (London, George Allen & Unwin, 1931).

24. William James, *The Varieties of Religious Experience*, p. 324.

25. Ibid.

26. See, for example, John Hick, *Philosophy of Religion*, 3rd ed. (Englewood Cliffs, N.J.: Prentice-Hall, 1983), pp. 60ff.

27. John 1:14.

28. John 14:9.

29. John 10:30.

30. C. H. Dodd, *The Authority of the Bible* (Glasgow: William Collins Sons, 1978).

31. Genesis 12:1.

32. Exodus 3:4, 6.

33. David Hume, "On Miracles," *An Inquiry Concerning Human Understanding* (Indianapolis: Hackett, 1977), p. 81.

34. Acts 4:12.

35. E.g., John 1:14; 1:18; and 3:16.

36. John 3:18.

37. Qur'an, *Al-Mu'minun* (Surah 23).

38. Ibid., *Sad* (Surah 39).

39. Ibid., *Al-Taubah* (Surah 9).

40. Swami Vivekananda, *Jnana-Yoga* (Calcutta: Advaita Ashrama, 1915, 1976), pp. 379f.

41. Ibid., 352.

42. David Hume, *Dialogues Concerning Natural Religion* (Indianapolis: Hackett Publishing, 1980), p. 15.

43. Steven T. Katz, "Language, Epistemology, and Mysticism," in Steven T. Katz, ed., *Mysticism and Philosophical Analysis* (New York: Oxford University Press, 1978), pp. 23f.

44. See, for example, C. D. Broad, "Arguments for the Existence of God, II," *Journal of Theological Studies* 40 (1930), and *Religion, Philosophy and Psychical Research* (New York: Humanities Press, 1969).

45. William L. Rowe, *Philosophy of Religion* (Encino and Belmont, Calif.: Dickenson, 1978), p. 74.

46. Bertrand Russell, *Religion and Science* (London: Oxford University Press, 1935), pp. 187f.

47. Broad, "Arguments for the Existence of God, II."

7

Religion and Ethics

Morality concerns the distinctions we draw between right and wrong behavior, that is, between the kind of behavior that a society permits, encourages, or even commands, on the one hand, and the kind that it forbids on the other. Such distinctions seem to be as old as humankind itself. Every human culture evolves a system of morality, that is, a set of rules that designates what kinds of behavior are to be regarded as right, or morally permissible, and what kinds wrong, or immoral. **Ethics** is the branch of philosophy that examines such moral rules and attempts to develop them into a consistent and rationally justified system.

Most persons who have grown up in what we call the Western world have been influenced to one degree or another by the Judeo-Christian religious tradition. Jewish and Christian teachings have affected virtually every aspect of Western civilization, including art, architecture, music, law, family values, social institutions, political and economic structure, and morality. Western society has consequently always assumed a close interdependence between morality and religion. This assumption is expressed in the belief that morality is derived from religion. Both moral and legal principles are justified by appeals to the ten commandments or the teachings of Jesus. We look to religious leaders for moral guidance about social issues and moral justification of contemplated legislation. When hospitals began in the past few decades to form ethics committees to deliberate and advise on the moral implication of certain medical procedures, these committees nearly always included a minister, a priest, and a rabbi.

In Western society, then, we seem to take for granted that the ordained have special expertise about moral matters, with our conviction grounded in a vague assumption that morality comes ultimately from God. Some have gone so far as to suggest that without religion we would be without moral principles, or at any rate, without the sanctions that are thought to motivate us to obey moral rules. Such an attitude is enunciated explicitly in Dostoevsky's novel *The Brothers Karamazov* in the declaration that if God is dead, all things are permitted — in other words, that the absence of religion completely undermines morality.

THE DIVINE COMMAND THEORY OF ETHICS

This widespread assumption about the relationship between religion and ethics among both Christians and Jews has given rise to what is called the **divine command theory** of ethics. According to this teaching, morality is rooted in the will of God. Thus right means what God commands and wrong means what God forbids; and it is the fact that God commands or forbids it that makes an act right or wrong. The theory is based on the assumption of a Judeo-Christian deity who is omnipotent, omniscient, morally perfect, and the creator of the world. This God, who is the Lord of all creation and the source of everything in the world, has created all the laws of nature that determine how the world operates. God has created humans with the power of moral understanding and has promulgated laws to guide them in living a moral life. This is a view of ethics that makes immorality synonymous with sin and morality synonymous with righteousness. Although humans may understand some of the reasons that certain things are commanded or forbidden, they are to obey God's commandments whether they understand them or not. God, who determines all things, also determines what is right and wrong.

The Question of the Objectivity of Moral Rules

Moralists have argued at length about whether or not an objective ground for morality exists that determines universal standards of right or wrong for all persons. The divine command theory has a number of impressive advantages in this regard. For one thing, in response to claims of relativism it gives a definitive answer about the objectivity of moral principles. **Moral cultural relativism** teaches that morality is determined by the accepted practices of one's culture. Right and wrong are determined by the laws and traditions of one's culture. Thus it is wrong for persons living in England or the United States to have more than one spouse because this is what law and recognized moral custom dictate. It is not wrong, however, for a man living in Iran or Saudi Arabia to have more than one wife; the laws and moral customs of those societies authorize him to take up to four wives. An even more extreme form of relativism claims that morality depends on individual conscientious belief: If I sincerely believe that premarital sexual relations are morally wrong, then they are wrong *for me*; if you, on the other hand, conscientiously believe that premarital sex is not wrong, then it is not wrong *for you*.

The divine command theory solves all these problems. Right and wrong, it holds, do not depend on the customs of one's society or on an individual's conscientious beliefs; they are entirely objective. Right is what God commands or permits; wrong is what God forbids.

The Question of Arbitrariness

Although the divine command theory at first glance seems to set forth just what the religious person understands the correct relationship to be between religion and morality, closer examination reveals some serious problems with this position. One problem was already noticed in the ancient period by Socrates (c. 470–399 B.C.E.). Plato's dialogue *The Euthyphro* is a discussion between Socrates and the arrogant young man Euthyphro, who claims to be very knowledgeable about the meaning of "virtue." Virtue, he tells Socrates, is what is pleasing to the gods. But Socrates sees an important ambiguity in the claim and proceeds to bring it to light by asking this question: Is virtue pleasing to the gods because it is good, or is it good because it is pleasing to the gods?

At first glance the question might appear to be mere quibbling (as it did to Euthyphro, who seems never to have understood Socrates's point), but it actually marks a fundamental distinction. If virtue is good only because it is pleasing to the gods, then it would seem to be an arbitrary quality. For example, we believe that keeping our promises is morally obligatory. According to the divine command theory, however, it is so only because the gods command us to keep promises; they might instead have commanded us to make promises and then break them when we could make a profit by doing so.

Our immediate response to such a suggestion tends to be, "But God would never command such a thing!" This response, however, reveals something interesting about what (though we may not have noticed it) we actually believe about virtue — namely, that such things as promise keeping are objectively required by morality, whether God commands them or not. *Why* would God not command us to break our promises when we could make a profit? Because promise breaking is wrong and God would never command us to do what is wrong. According to the divine command theory, though, this reasoning is not correct. If God commanded promise breaking, then it would not be wrong. If virtue is good because the gods command it, then whatever they command—lying, cheating, stealing, or killing—would be good.

This logic implies that morality is actually nothing more than divine whim, that there is no other answer to the question, "Why did God forbid stealing?" than "Because he felt like it," or "Because that is what he chose to command." The gods of the ancient Greeks and the gods of the early Canaanites, beings whose own characters were often morally questionable, may have commanded humans to do senseless or hurtful things for no reason, but surely the rational and compassionate God of the Jews and the Christians would not determine anything as important as morality on the basis of mere whim. Our strong sense that morality cannot be based on arbitrary decree amounts to a tacit recognition that morality is objectively valid, binding whether or not it is commanded by God. And if morality does have objective grounds, then the divine command theory fails.

The Teleological Suspension of the Ethical

The notion that morality is exactly what God commands or forbids, as the divine command theory teaches, may certainly be found in some parts of the Hebrew Bible. Indeed, the seemingly arbitrary nature of morality is illustrated in one of the most celebrated events in the Hebrew religious tradition. The book of Genesis tells of Yahweh's covenant with Abraham to lead him to a land to be given to him and his heirs and to make him the father of a great and numerous people. But Sarah, Abraham's wife, was barren. How could Abraham be the father of a great people if he could not even be the father of one child? Finally, after many years of waiting and testing of Abraham's faith and after Sarah was far beyond childbearing age, the wondrous event happened. A son was born and given the name Isaac. But as the boy grew up, bringing great joy to his parents, God tested Abraham's faith once again. Yahweh appeared to Abraham and commanded him to take his son Isaac to the land of Moriah and offer him as a burnt offering on a mountain there. So Abraham took firewood and a knife, brought his son to the mountain, and built an altar for the sacrifice. Not until the child was bound and lying on the wood on the altar, the knife raised to kill him, did God send an angel to stay the hand of Abraham.

> He said, "Abraham, Abraham!" and he said, "Here am I." He said, "Do not lay your hand on the lad or do anything to him; for now I know that you fear God, seeing that you have not withheld your son, your only son, from me." And Abraham lifted up his eyes and looked,

and behold, behind him a ram, caught in a thicket by his horns; and Abraham went and took the ram, and offered it up as a burnt offering instead of his son.[1]

This is one of the most dramatic narratives in the Bible, cited frequently to show that Abraham was the paradigm of a good and faithful and righteous man. It is also, however, one of the most horrible, when we think of the unspeakable anguish it must have imposed on Abraham, not to mention his wife Sarah and the child Isaac.

The great Danish philosopher Søren Kierkegaard (1813–1855), meditating on the narrative, wrote four imaginative and poignant stories about what might have gone on in the minds of various parties to the affair as the drama unfolded.[2] He also discussed the implications of the story as a moral and religious teaching. Certainly what morality requires of a father is that he protect and care for his child. To kill one's child is a horrible, wicked, cruel, sinful, immoral, criminal thing to do, contrary to the most elementary requirements of morality. Such an act would properly entitle its perpetrator to be remembered by all future generations as a monster, not a righteous man, and yet it is held up as the standard of righteousness and obedience to God. Kierkegaard asks, then, whether any circumstance can transform a monstrous act of treachery and murder into an act of holy righteousness. The only one that possibly could would be what he calls a **teleological suspension of the ethical**. Are there circumstances, Kierkegaard inquires, under which, to achieve a higher purpose, we are obligated to set aside what ordinary morality requires and perform a dreadful act in obedience to God? The implications of the divine command theory for this question are clear enough: Because morality is a product of God's will, because moral rules have been decreed by God, God is certainly entitled to suspend them when, as in the case of Abraham and Isaac, that would serve one of his other purposes.

Such a concept, however, faces all the problems that accompany the divine command theory. The objection of arbitrariness seems particularly apt here. The idea that God would command such a cruel and barbarous act on the whim of seeing just how far Abraham would go in trusting him is keenly shocking to the moral sensibilities of any person with a developed sense of morality or a feeling for divine compassion.[3] We would indeed call any human being who made such a demand a fiend. Are we to think that God lives by lower moral standards than we do—indeed, that "vile and evil" means "good" if applied to something done or commanded by God?

Such an idea is absurd. We feel instinctively that a being as wise and loving as God would make provisions to achieve his purpose within the scope of rational morality and without recourse to any loophole as ad hoc as a teleological suspension of the ethical. Even if we are to believe that God might occasionally command a person to violate moral law for the sake of a higher cause, surely the cause must be something more worthy than God's alleged desire to have his own ego aggrandized by extreme feats of obedience to prove that his human servants are faithful. Arbitrary cruelty is unworthy of a God who deserves to be called good, and any theory that implies it fails to reflect the divine nature.[4]

Uncertainty about What God Commands

Another major problem posed by the divine command theory in general and the notion of the teleological suspension of the ethical in particular is how to know with confidence exactly what God commands. It did not seem to occur to Abraham that the voice he heard commanding him to commit a horrific act might not be the voice of God. We know that people do hear inner voices, voices that sometimes command them to commit crimes or to do cruel things, and we usually regard this as evidence of pathology. We do not normally nor properly take every experience that purports to be a hearing of the voice of God at face value; we must have some way of judging and deciding such phenomena.

Criteria to distinguish the divine voice from demonic voices would have to involve such characteristics as consistency with the character of God, and therefore consistency with morality, with lovingkindness and compassion, with pity and mercy and goodness. If rational criteria are required to ascertain a true command of God's, these criteria also determine whether or not an act is morally right, which amounts to abandoning the divine command theory. Indeed, the divine command theory makes no provisions for testing. It operates on the assumption that God's commands will always be recognized as such, leaving open the possibility that any deed whatsoever can be done in the name of divine command, no matter how irrational.

Inconsistency with God's Goodness

A final problem with the divine command theory is that it trivializes the claim that God is good. Goodness is usually regarded by theists as an absolutely essential attribute of God. Even the few theists who have been willing — in order better to deal with the problem of evil — to consider restrictive claims about God's power or knowledge have always held firmly to God's moral perfection. The divine command theory undermines or trivializes the claim that God's will or actions are good, for the theory tells us that goodness *means* what is willed by God. But if this is true, then to say that God's will is good means only that God's will is what is willed by God; equally, to claim that God always does what is good only means that God always does what God wills. The claim that God is good becomes empty if goodness means no more than willed by God.

To say that God always does what he wills is not what we mean when we say that God is good. This fact again suggests that we believe that goodness is independent of God's will. When we say that God is good, we mean that there is a real distinction between good and evil and that God always does what is good. Some thinkers claim that it is impossible for God to do evil; others say that although doing evil is within God's power, because he is supremely good we can be confident that God would never choose to do evil. If the divine command theory is true, these disputes become pointless, because good is defined by what God does and thus there could never be any question of God's doing anything that was not good. But at the same time, calling any deed good would be equally pointless since this would only be another way of saying that God did it. Unless goodness has some meaning independent of God's will, the attribution of goodness to God is so much empty talk. Christians and Jews (and persons of several other religions) praise God because they recognize a real standard of goodness, a standard independent of God's will, to which they believe God always conforms. And whether they believe that it is impossible for God to do evil, or that although possible God never chooses to do evil, they find God praiseworthy, not merely because God does whatever he chooses, but because he chooses what is truly good. The divine command theory, by undermining the possibility of such an objective standard of goodness, renders empty the attribution of goodness to God.

Morality Grounded in God's Character

So devastating have these criticisms been that for a time the divine command theory was virtually abandoned by philosophers of religion. Devout persons, unaware of the problems the theory raises, continued to assume it as part of their piety, but philosophers, believing it to have been refuted, mostly gave it up. Recently, however, a number of thinkers have attempted to rehabilitate the theory in modified form. The new version seeks to ground morality in God's character and not exclusively in God's will. Several contemporary philosophers have used the notion of the love of God to respond to the major weaknesses critics have pointed out.[5]

The two most serious criticisms the modified form of the theory attempts to answer are the claim that the divine command theory makes morality arbitrary and the claim that it trivializes the goodness of God. Adding the notion of love, however, first allegedly makes possible a response to the claim of arbitrariness. A position is not arbitrary if there is a reason for it. According to the modified command theory, the reason that God commands certain things and forbids others is that they are expressions of his loving nature. Most of the modified theorists admit that it is logically possible that God could command a horrific act like the slow torture of children; they all agree, though, that because of God's loving nature he never would. If God should command gratuitous cruelty, Robert Adams even asserts, it would not be wrong to disobey. But Adams goes on to explain that the reason is that if we became truly convinced that such a command had been given, it would mean that no loving God of the kind Christians believe in existed; thus all distinctions of right and wrong were destroyed and nothing would any longer be wrong. God commands loving acts, not cruel ones, because the divine nature is loving; thus God's commands are not arbitrary.

To deal with the other major objection — trivializing the goodness of God — the modified theorists draw a distinction that has not usually been a part of the divine command theory. They claim that although *moral* value is exclusively determined by God's will, so that only what God commands is morally right and only what God forbids is morally wrong, some things, such as happiness, love, kindness, beauty, have nonmoral value apart from the will of God. Although human behavior is morally praiseworthy only to the extent that it reflects respect and obedience to God, another factor that motivates humans to obey what God commands is that we place (nonmoral) value on many of the things, such as love, kindness, and happiness, that are the frequent consequences of moral behavior.

This new distinction between moral and nonmoral value provides an opening for answering the claim that the moral command theory makes trivial the attribution of goodness to God. To be sure, we do not praise God for doing what is morally right and refraining from what is morally wrong, and thus when we say that God is good we do not mean that God is *morally* good. But we do appropriately praise God for his qualities of character that have the kinds of nonmoral value that we recognize independently of God's will. To say that God is good is not to say that God is morally excellent; rather, it is to say that God has such good qualities as love, kindness, and concern for human well-being.

John Chandler has analyzed the modified divine command theory based on the principle of love[6] and concludes that it has "inherent and quite general defects"[7] that imply that it must be diagnosed as unsuccessful. Part of the problem is that "the appeal to God's love transforms the theory so that it is no longer a Divine Command Theory."[8] In the attribution of goodness to God, the distinction drawn between moral and nonmoral value fails for the following reasons. With regard to moral value, the modified theorists concede that it would be trivial to call God good — the main flaw that the critics have been pressing. But with regard to nonmoral value, what makes it possible to attribute goodness to God is the fact that the divine command interpretation has been given up. Happiness, beauty, love are not good because God commands them; they are good in themselves independent of God's commands. This is an explicit abandonment of divine command theory.

Responding to the criticism about arbitrariness, Chandler points out that the modified theory again in effect abandons divine command:

> If an action's being loving is a good (or compelling) reason for a loving God to command it, it must be an equally good reason for us to perform it insofar as we are loving in our limited way. That loving actions are commanded by God, may be an additional reason for believers to perform them; but there is already sufficient (justificatory) reason. It would also appear that God's will is so constrained by the requirements of love as to leave Him little if any discretion in what He commands, *qua* loving being. The content of the moral code can in principle be read off from the knowledge of which acts are loving, without reference to God.[9]

This amounts to a recognition that what makes an action morally right or wrong is not that God commands it but that it is or is not the loving thing to do. Thus the principle of love becomes the ultimate grounding of morality, binding even the will and commandments of God. And, like Socrates, we are driven to recognize that the gods command virtue because it is good (i.e., loving, according to this version of the theory) and not that virtue is good because the gods command it.

This is not the only problem with the modified divine command theory, however. Chandler concludes that it is unsatisfactory not only because it has ceased to be a divine command theory but also because the principle of love is too vague to serve by itself as a satisfactory foundation of morality. Moral principles must be loving, but if they are to provide a foundation for detailed ethical decisions about what is right and wrong the essential point is that they must be rational.

THE INDEPENDENCE OF ETHICS FROM RELIGION

Many religious people, particularly those who have come under the influence of Judaism and Christianity, seem to feel that for religious reasons the divine command theory is required of the devout or the faithful. After all, if God is the creator, a being worthy of love, and worship, he must also be the source of moral rules. Furthermore, since so many Westerners tend to assume that actual moral systems originated in and evolved out of religion, the divine command theory even appears — until the problems with the theory we have been examining here become apparent — too obvious to question. It is important, however, to pay attention to the extent to which these assumptions are unjustified.

Religion and Ethics in Primitive Societies

The close connection between religion and morality, so widely taken for granted among Christians and Jews, does not by any means characterize all religions. It is particularly absent from most pretechnological societies, both ancient and contemporary.[10] Western Christian thought about the evolution of moral systems, based on the assumption of a necessary dependence of morality on religion, surmised that primitives derived their beliefs about right and wrong from their priests and shamans, spokespersons for the deities. The inference was that humans initially developed religious beliefs intertwined with moral teachings, that these gradually became more sophisticated, and that only quite late, when a society reached a complex level of development, did morality begin to be explored apart from religious teachings and eventually formulated in a freestanding, secular fashion that obscured its former (presumed) dependence on religion.

So firm was the assumption of the dependence of morality on religion that early explorers and even some anthropologists tended not to notice that in fact religion has little to do with morality among contemporary primitives. Instead, religion functions primarily to placate the gods and the spirit forces through rites and sacrifices. The purpose of these religious practices is twofold: to ward off disasters thought to come from the wrath of the gods and to make provisions for the safety of the human spirit or shade after death. The favor of the gods is not thought to be won by living a life of moral goodness or righteousness. The gods are quite indifferent to the human practice of morality and, indeed, are not themselves beings of high moral character. What the gods want is worship, reverence, and sacrifices. Morality is a matter to be settled among humans.

This attitude about religion seems to have been as characteristic of the ancient Greeks and Romans as it was of both ancient and contemporary primitives. It is to be seen in the religions of the Vikings and early Scandinavians, in the Druid practices of Britain, among some Native American tribes, and in the contemporary primitive societies of the South Pacific. Religion pertains largely to what is not understood — natural disasters, sickness, infertility of cattle or wives — which is to be dealt with by rites performed by the priests. The gods are not concerned with human behavior except as it relates to the faithful performance of religious rituals.

Morality Developed Independently of Religion

The widespread belief that all religions included a preoccupation with morality turns out in fact to be mistaken. So also does the assumption that all great moral systems have evolved out of religions. Two of the greatest systems of moral philosophy in the West, Plato's and Aristotle's, were worked out philosophically by the use of reason, with virtually no concern for religion. Confucianism in ancient China is another example: Often called one of the great world religions — involving as it does the notion of piety toward the spirits of one's ancestors — Confucianism is actually almost entirely concerned with human morality and what might be called human etiquette. It is not theistic; there is no element of revelation or any sense of gods as moral lawgivers. Similarly, in the modern period, systems of ethics such as those of Immanuel Kant in the eighteenth, John Stuart Mill in the nineteenth, and the humanists in the twentieth centuries have been developed independently of religion. Of course, Kant, Mill, and the humanists were affected in some measure by the Judeo-Christian religious tradition because they were a part of a culture saturated with its influence. Their moral theories, however, were grounded in rational human principles and not derived from alleged revelation or religious teachings.

But even faced with these historical facts — the absence of moral concern in the religions of primitive peoples and the origin of sophisticated moral systems completely apart from religion — many people still feel that proper morality must ultimately be rooted in religion. They believe so not merely because most developed religious traditions include moral teachings as major ingredients of their theology, but also from a sense that a being whose power is so great, whose wisdom is supreme, and who exemplifies moral perfection uniquely has the right to command our obedience in matters of right and wrong. The clinching point in the minds of many, we may note, is the belief that the divine command theory belongs to orthodox Jewish and Christian theology.

Morality and Natural Law

It comes as a great surprise to some to learn that during much of the history of the West, even in the Christian tradition, the divine command theory has not been the standard or accepted position. Among the ancient Greeks, as we have said, morality was believed to be grounded in human rationality and had nothing to do with religion or the gods. The Romans developed a concept of law that recognized the objectivity of the principles of government as well as those of the detailed legislative regulations enacted and enforced by governments. The Romans also seem to be the originators of the concept of **natural law**, not only as a term to describe the regularities in the operation of the material world but also to name the principles recognized by human reason as valid for the regulation of human moral and political life. These principles have nothing to do with the gods or religion, but are written, as it were, into the very structure of reality itself and are discoverable by any humans who take the trouble to reason carefully. This, according to the Romans, is the reason that fundamental moral and social values are so similar from one culture to another despite their great differences in details.

This concept of natural law as the source both of political and moral law came to be incorporated into the thinking of the West and eventually found its way into Christian theology, where it was called the law of God. This view was refined and elaborated in detail by the great Catholic theologian of the late Middle Ages, Thomas Aquinas (1224–1274). And though Thomas taught that Christian revelation is a source of knowledge about what God commands, he explicitly rejected the divine command theory of morality, teaching instead that an **eternal law** provides the foundation both of God's commandments and of the insights about morality that come from human reason.

According to Thomas, natural law is universal, the same for all time and place. Local variations in human law and in moral prescriptions (apart from inattention to, or misunderstanding of, what natural law requires) arise from the differences of circumstances to which natural law comes to be applied. Civil law is thus the result of applying natural law to the specific circumstances of a society. Lawmaking in human parliaments is not actually a process of *making* laws; rather, it is a process of *discovering* what natural law, applied to these local conditions, requires. Thomas says that legislating is like the use of a syllogism, whose first premise is natural law (and thus identical for all times and places), whose second premise is a description of the conditions to which the law is to apply, and whose conclusion is the piece of civil legislation. An example may serve to make his point clearer: When we legislate such matters as speed limits, the stable, unchanging natural law (the first premise) is a dictate about concern for the safety of all persons, but the specific application of that concern differs because the hazards vary from place to place. If we legislate for a congested area or an area near a school (second premise), then the conclusion (civil law) is a slow speed limit. But if we legislate for open countryside, where persons are not likely to be walking in the road, this different second premise, along with the same first premise of natural law, permits a faster speed. In every case, however, what makes the specific law right (assuming that it is properly made) is its foundation in natural law.

Now natural law as a source for civil legislation and for moral rules is valid for all societies alike and is accessible to all rational persons in whatever time or place; it is not connected with any one religion. This means that morality is founded on principles independent of religion and of God. Its laws are rather like the laws of logic and mathematics, which are similarly universal and binding on all rational beings, human and divine.

In our discussion of the attributes of God in Chapter 2, we noted that some philosophers, such as Descartes, insisted that the omnipotence of God requires what we might call a divine command theory of logic and mathematics — that is, they claimed that the principles of reasoning are created by God and derive their truth from the fact that God prescribes them. This amounts to saying that *2 + 2 = 4* is true because God says it is, not that God says it is because it is true. It also implies that if God had said that *2 + 2 = 7*, this would have been true instead. But we argued that such a situation clearly renders all meaning and understanding impossible. Not even God himself could actually *think* such things, for they are simply impossible — they destroy the conditions under which thinking can occur or claims can have meaning. There seem to be overwhelming reasons to believe that even an omnipotent deity must conform to the principles of logic and mathematics if such a deity wishes to think or to create a world. What we have playfully called a divine command theory of logic and mathematics is, in the final reckoning, unintelligible and must be rejected. Logic and mathematics are in a sense antecedent to the will of God and govern that will so that even God cannot violate these principles.

The argument is much the same for the principles of morality. It amounts to saying that God forbids inflicting gratuitous suffering on the innocent because to do so is wrong, and not that it is wrong because God forbids it. This means that moral right and wrong are independent of God's will. Like the principles of mathematics, those of morality are objective, binding even on God, and thus not changeable by divine decree. If God declared that *3 + 3 = 7*, God would be wrong; if God declared that torturing the innocent is a moral duty, God would also be wrong. Of course, if God is omniscient in any proper sense of the word, he would never assert such a mathematical claim; similarly, if God is morally good, he would never make any such moral claim. There is an objective natural law from which morality can be inferred by any rational person, whether a religious believer or not. At least in principle, everyone who reasons carefully enough and succeeds in transcending the biases of his or her culture should arrive at the same set of fundamental moral principles binding for all.

Independence of Ethics from Religion

If there is indeed a natural law, valid for all time, written so to speak into the structure of reality and detectable by any carefully thinking rational being, why is it that moral beliefs seem to differ so drastically from one generation to another and from one culture to another? Should we not expect that reasonable persons would come to the same conclusions about what morality requires?

The belief that moral principles differ greatly from culture to culture and from age to age has been widespread, especially in the twentieth century, and has been buttressed by the campaign of anthropology against intolerant ethnocentrism. The efforts of anthropologists to engender a spirit of tolerance toward the beliefs and practices of other cultures was certainly justified by Westerners' arrogant, unthinking assumption of superiority and their attempts to impose their own beliefs and practices on the rest of the world. The result of these anthropologists' efforts was the spread of the concept of **cultural relativism** during the early years of this century. As anthropology matured, however, and as studies of non-Western cultures became more careful and detailed, the moral differences that had seemed so drastic at first came to be seen as differences in details; underlying moral principles were, in fact, remarkably similar across cultures.

A celebrated instance, often cited in anthropological literature on the controversy over relativism, is the custom among certain Eskimo groups of leaving the elderly to die once they become frail and unable to keep up with the migrations of the group. This practice was initially thought to imply a disrespect, even a moral disregard, for the elderly and was cited as a radical contrast to the veneration of the elderly in certain Asian societies and the respectful care for the aged in Western culture. Closer study revealed that the practice was grounded not in different beliefs about what is morally right, but in different beliefs about human afterlife. The Eskimos regard respect and care for the elderly to be an important moral value just as Asians and Westerners do. Leaving the aged to die is in fact an expression of their esteem because they believe that life in the next world begins at precisely the level of physical strength and health the individual possesses at the time of death. From this point of view, to keep old persons alive until they are bedridden and helpless would condemn them to an eternity of weakness and wretchedness.

Dramatic surface differences in moral beliefs, then, often prove to reflect differences in beliefs about situations to which moral principles are applied, not differences about the principles themselves. Another example closer to home may further serve to illustrate the point. In contemporary Western societies, there is a heated controversy about abortion.[11] One group maintains that abortion is morally unacceptable because it is an abominable act of murder; another holds that during the early weeks of pregnancy abortion is morally permissible under certain circumstances. There might seem to be sharp disagreement here about fundamental principles of morality, with one group holding human life to be sacrosanct and the other (as it is sometimes accused) disregarding this sanctity. The difference, however, has nothing to do with basic moral principles; both groups regard human life as sacred and murder as wrong. They differ only on the issue of whether or not the fertilized ovum is a human being during the early stages of its development. If it is, then to kill it (without strong justification, such as saving the mother's life) is clearly morally wrong. If it is not yet a human being, however, then removing it is not murder and is sometimes morally justifiable.

Many moral disputes seem to be of this sort. What appears to be a radical disagreement about a moral principle is actually a disagreement about the facts to which the principle is being applied. Rational, conscientious people seem nearly always to agree about the basic principles of morality: that murder, lying, stealing, cheating, torture, and such things are wrong. Most disagreement seems to involve the definition of these moral terms and whether a particular instance is or is not a case of murder, lying, and so on. Other differences relate to cases where the demands of morality conflict — a murder can be prevented only by lying; the killing of a large number of persons can be prevented only by killing a crazed fanatic, and so on — and value judgments have to be made about which principle is the more pressing. Differences of this sort, however, are also to be decided by the exercise of human reason, and although there will often be room for conscientious, rational disagreement, careful and open-minded reasoning should lead at least to mutual understanding and, in principle, to a narrowing of differences.

Probably the greatest hindrance of such a meeting of minds is prejudice and closed-mindedness. Humans are prone to hold to the beliefs they have been taught and refuse to listen to reason. We are apt to be so convinced that what we already believe is beyond doubt that we dismiss evidence and refuse to consider changing our minds. This regrettable tendency of ours is nurtured and aggravated by the propaganda efforts of groups similarly convinced of the unshakable truth of their views and eager to bring emotion to bear in preventing their members from listening to any evidence or argument that might not support the received belief. Patriotism is a lamentable case in point. Pride in one's nation and one's cultural traditions is an entirely appropriate attitude, but when it leads to the total denigration of all other nations and cultures it is vicious and despicable. Time and time again, inflamed patriotism has led to cruelty, ruthlessness, and war. Another case in point is religious fervor, which sometimes clouds human judgment and leads people to refuse to listen to evidence or reason that contradicts precious beliefs thought to be essential to the faith. This is what results in the clash between religions on points of morality and the clash of religious teachings with those of secular rational morality.

What we have discovered about the relationship of human rationality to moral understanding implies that ultimately there is no place for conflict about the basic requirements of morality. When differences appear, they must be understood as arising from different perspectives on the situations to which the principles apply (assuming that preconceived positions have been set aside and open rational discussion is joined). Morality is a matter of rational inquiry. It involves the exercise of a faculty — reason — that is the same in all normal human persons without regard to culture, religion, or time in history. Like the laws of logic and mathematics, the principles of morality bind every rational being, human and divine; they are not the product of divine command. This fact implies that religious believers do not have greater access to morality than anyone else and that religious leaders are in no better position to make pronouncements about morality than any other rational persons — just as they are in no better position to know what logic or mathematics implies or what scientific truth involves. Religion and ethics, like religion and science, are entirely separate and independent enterprises.

Thus the notion that morality would collapse if belief in God or practice of religion disappeared is totally misguided. The statements by Nietzsche and Dostoevsky that the death of God means that all things are permitted reflect a childish understanding of morality. Such a notion resembles the idea that the only reason why the child should keep out of the cookie jar is that his mother will slap his hand if she catches him; when Mother is not looking, everything is permitted. But there is a reason for what morality requires and forbids, and that reason remains valid and binding on rational persons whether Mother is watching or not, and whether there is a God to enforce it or not. We should stay out of the cookie jar because eating too many sweets is harmful to our health; we should refrain from lying because lying undermines the social intercourse on which a good life is dependent. In other words, we should refrain from what morality forbids because such things really are wrong and their being wrong has nothing to do with whether or not they are commanded by God.

The Relationship of Rational to Religious Ethics

Notwithstanding, many developed religions consider the teaching of morality — and the attempt to enforce on their members the practice of their sanctioned moral rules — to be one of their major functions. An appeal to divine command theory is sometimes made to reinforce the religion's claim to exercise authority over the moral behavior of its members — and sometimes to extend its moral power to matters of legislation binding even on persons who are not members. Thus many laypersons, who may not be knowledgeable about the relationship between religion and morality — that is, about the independence of morality from religion — feel obliged to obey the moral pronouncements of their religious leaders even when their own better judgment suggests that these pronouncements may not be right.[12] For example, many Catholics and Jews may feel obliged to refrain from the use of contraceptives, or a few Moslems may feel obliged to engage in acts of violence against non-Moslems, because some leaders of these religious groups say that such an obligation exists. Thus, even though philosophers discover that in principle there is no place for a conflict between what rational morality requires and what religions legitimately teach, because some religious leaders take it on themselves to make moral pronouncements they claim are authoritative, the philosopher must analyze the question of the proper relationship between rational (secular) morality and the moral sanctions of the various religions.

One of the problems with any moral scheme based in a specific religion or grounded on a divine command theory is that it is binding only on members of the religious tradition or persons who believe in the god alleged to have commanded it. Christian moral teachings are not obligatory for Buddhists, and morality commanded by God does not reach to atheists. But clearly morality applies to all human beings. Just as no one can claim to be above the laws of the society to which he or she belongs, so also no one can claim exemption from the principles of morality, because morality pertains to humans as humans. If murder is wrong — as it clearly is — it is just as wrong for Hindus as it is for Christians and just as wrong for atheists as for religious believers.

These insights imply that any teaching that contradicts the properly reasoned-out requirements of rational morality must be rejected. The person who claims the right to kill because he believes the voices of spirits told him to is not thereby justified. The person who claims the right to lie and cheat because she believes her government told her to is not thereby justified. The person who claims the right to kidnap or torture because he believes his religion tells him to is not thereby justified. The only thing that can justify acting contrary to a rational moral injunction is a rational argument showing that some other course of action takes moral precedence in the particular case. For example, the only justification I have for killing another human being is the clear realization that I have no other way to stop that person from killing others. Nothing takes precedence over rational moral commandments except other rational moral commandments supported by even stronger moral arguments, or arguments showing that the alternative course of action is even more urgent morally. In many cases, of course, what is required is difficult to ascertain. Sometimes there will be very good moral reasons supporting more than one incompatible course of action and no definitive way of deciding among these courses. These are the kinds of practical difficulties that accompany any kind of moral judgment, and in dealing with them one must proceed with considerable humility, recognizing one's fallibility and acting on one's most conscientious best judgment.

The principle, however, remains clear. When the requirement of rational morality can be ascertained, nothing else (except a more pressing moral requirement) can overrule it. This means that if a religion or a religious leader commands what rational morality forbids or forbids what rational morality commands, the requirement of rational morality must prevail. We have seen already that this should never happen provided those who speak on behalf of religion make open-minded and conscientious use of their reasoning faculty. But we know that sometimes the teachings of an earlier era, based on an undeveloped science or an incomplete understanding of the world, become enshrined even when the advancement of human knowledge has shown them to be inadequate. When pronouncements from religious authorities clash with the discoveries of science, a conflict may ensue. This was the case with the church's condemnation of Galileo's scientific findings (a matter of some embarrassment to the Church today) and continues today in some sects' positions concerning evolution. Similarly, when such outdated beliefs about the world are used in formulating moral injunctions there may be a clash between what the religion commands or forbids and what reason — rational morality — requires. In every such case, the dictates of reason must prevail.

This may sound like an attempt to drive religion out of the moral arena altogether. Actually, it is nothing of the sort — any more than the recognition of the independence of science from religion is an attempt to enjoin religions from having anything to say about the findings of science or the world to which those findings pertain. Science offers descriptions and explanations of how phenomena occur in the material world. These descriptions and explanations make no reference to gods and no pronouncements about the significance of the findings for the human spirit. But persons who believe in God are likely to believe that the world that science describes is a realm of divine creation and that the order scientists discover in the world is the result of God's orderly plan. Religious persons may also interpret the facts that science discovers as evidence of God's love and care for his human creatures and may find in them great significance for the worth of human existence. They may also sense the appropriateness of our taking an attitude of reverence for the world because they regard it as God's creation. None of these factors clashes with science nor suggests any area of conflict between the legitimate work of science and that of religion.

In a similar way, religion may interpret the requirements of rationality as commanded and supported by God. We have seen that the validity of these requirements does not derive from God's command, but it is entirely likely that a wise and loving God would command that we behave in accordance with the rules of morality. Religion can offer incentives for living moral lives that may supplement for believers the incentives that reasonable persons already recognize in the nature of moral situations.

Furthermore, religions can place additional obligations on believers beyond those required by secular morality, provided they do not contradict anything required by universal human morality. Morality forbids gratuitous cruelty and requires truth telling of all persons; these injunctions may very well be a part of religious morality as well. But Christianity may also require believers to attend mass or to say certain prayers. Rational morality does not require such things, but neither does it forbid them, so there is no inconsistency between the two moral codes. If a religious group, however, forbids the use of blood transfusions to save the life of a child, this may conflict with rational morality, which requires taking appropriate measures to save the life, in which case the religious injunction must yield.

We conclude, then, that religion and ethics are separate realms independent of each other. Morality is not derived from the teachings of religion nor from the will of God. Rather, it is discovered, like the laws of logic and mathematics, by the proper use of human reason. It applies to all human beings alike, whether they are devotees of one religion or another, or of none. Because religion in the past has often been active in teaching morality and promoting moral behavior, however, we hope and expect that it will continue to do so in the future.

Although we have taken into account in some measure the teaching of non-Western religions up to this point, we have not examined in any detail the philosophy of any of those other religions. This is not the place to undertake the comparative study of religion. But just as an understanding of the history, politics, economics, and culture of other societies contributes in invaluable ways to our understanding of our own, so also an understanding of the philosophical teachings of other religions can give us a valuable perspective on those religions most familiar to us. Just as it is undesirable to be provincial in cultural outlook, it is likewise undesirable — even dangerous — to be uninformed about other religions. It is time now to turn our attention away from our customary preoccupation with the religions of the West to consider briefly the philosophies of several of the other great world religions.

ANNOTATED GUIDE TO FURTHER READINGS

Kierkegaard, Søren. *Fear and Trembling*. Edited and translated by Howard V. Hong and Edna H. Hong. Princeton, N.J.: Princeton University Press, 1983.

Presents the notion of the teleological suspension of the ethical. Kierkegaard offers four alternate renditions of the biblical tale of Abraham and Isaac, examining what effect God's demand of sacrifice might have had on the characters.

Nielsen, Kai. *Ethics Without God*. London: Pemberton Books, 1973.

In this interesting and thought-provoking book, Nielsen contends that there can be meaning to our moral lives without God. He shows that ethics can be separated from religion, then develops and explains his own humanistic system of ethics.

Outka, Gene, and Reeder, John P., Jr., eds. *Religion and Morality*. Garden City, N.Y.: Anchor Books, 1973.

Essays dealing exclusively with the relationship between religion and morality.

Pojman, Louis P., ed. *Philosophy of Religion: An Anthology*. Belmont, Calif.: Wadsworth, 1987.

Part 8 offers a selection of readings focusing largely on the divine command theory. In the initial piece, Socrates poses the classic question: Is it God who defines what is good, or is goodness a standard independent of God's will? The opposing positions are defended and attacked by four thinkers.

Rachels, James. *The Elements of Moral Philosophy*. New York: Random House, 1986.

An excellent introduction to some of the basic concepts of moral philosophy. Rachels discusses the connection between religion and morality, the divine command theory, and natural law, with relevant modern examples such as abortion, homosexuality, and famine relief.

Stewart, David. *Exploring the Philosophy of Religion.* Englewood Cliffs, N.J.: Prentice-Hall, 1980.

Chapter 7 offers a wide range of viewpoints dealing with the relationship of ethics and religion, including selections by Nietzsche, Kai Nielsen and Paul Tillich, and Reinhold Niebuhr.

NOTES

1. Genesis 22:11–13.

2. Søren Kierkegaard, *Fear and Trembling*, ed. and trans. Howard V. Hong and Edna H. Hong (Princeton: Princeton University Press, 1983), pp. 10ff.

3. This seems to be the point made by Woody Allen in a satirical parody on the Genesis passage: "At the last minute the Lord stayed Abraham's hand and said, 'How could thou doest such a thing?' And Abraham said . . . 'Dost this not prove I love thee, that I was willing to donate mine only son on thy whim?' And the Lord said, 'It proves only that some men will follow any order no matter how asinine as long as it comes from a resonant, well-modulated voice." *Without Feathers* (New York: Random House, 1972), p. 23.

4. Another example from the Hebrew scriptures of what looks like God's arbitrary cruelty merely to test a human devotee is the great drama of the book of Job.

5. See, for example, Robert Merrihew Adams, "A Modified Divine Command Theory of Ethical Wrongness," in Gene Outka and John P. Reeder, Jr., eds., *Religion and Morality* (Garden City, N.Y.: Doubleday Anchor, 1973), pp. 318–347, and "Divine Command Metaethics Modified Again," *Journal of Religious Ethics* 7, 1 (Spring 1979): 66–80. See also Edward Wieregna, "A Defensible Divine Command Theory," *Nous* 17 (1983): 387–407; Philip L. Quinn, *Divine Commands and Moral Requirements* (Oxford: Oxford University Press, 1978); and Robert Burch, "Objective Values and the Divine Command Theory of Morality," *The New Scholasticism* 54 (1980): 279–304.

6. See, e.g., John Chandler, "Is the Divine Command Theory Defensible?" *Religious Studies* 20, 3 (September 1984): 443–452, and "Divine Command Theories and the Appeal to Love," *American Philosophical Quarterly* 22, 3 (July 1985): 231–239.

7. Chandler, "Divine Command Theories and the Appeal to Love," p. 235.

8. Ibid., p. 231.

9. Ibid., p. 236.

10. This claim is discussed and documented by Patrick H. Nowell-Smith in his article, "Religion and Morality," in *The Encyclopedia of Philosophy*, ed. Paul Edwards (New York: Macmillan, 1967), vol 7, pp. 150–158. This article concludes with a good bibliography on the topic.

11. James Rachels offers a helpful examination of the relationship of morality to religion and an illuminating discussion of the abortion issue. He points out that Thomas Aquinas taught that the human embryo does not have a soul until several weeks into the pregnancy and that Aquinas's view was officially sanctioned by the

Catholic Church at the Council of Vienne in 1312, an action that has not to this day been officially changed. See his book, *The Elements of Moral Philosophy* (New York: Random House, 1986), pp. 47–52.

12. Rachels points out that Thomas Aquinas teaches that it is a Christian's obligation to obey his conscience, which Thomas calls the "dictate of reason," in every case, even when it may run contrary to what the Church teaches. See ibid., p. 46.

8

Philosophy and World Religions

It is a fairly new thing for philosophers of religion to concern themselves with the issues that arise when various world religions confront one another. Philosophy of religion in the West has most often drawn its questions and issues largely from the Judeo-Christian religious tradition, and its answers are thereby custom made to suit a culture permeated by that tradition. But such a narrow approach is no longer justifiable. In recent times it has become increasingly obvious that the rest of the world and the other religions can no longer be ignored.

THE UBIQUITY OF RELIGION

So pervasive is the phenomenon we call religion that some have suggested that the proper name for human beings is *homo religiosus*. There seem to be no societies, ancient or modern, from which religion is absent. Our knowledge about preliterate cultures is necessarily limited, but the evidence we do find suggests that even our most ancient ancestors were, in some sense, religious. It has been noted that the Neanderthals who lived between 100,000 and 25,000 years ago buried their dead with the kind of care that suggests a belief in an afterlife. The Cro-Magnons, successors to the Neanderthals, also buried tools and food with the dead and made cave drawings that lend themselves to a religious interpretation. Similar evidence shows up in the archaeological findings from ancient peoples.

A number of contemporary cultures, however, and probably even more ancient cultures have no exact word for what we call religion. The people of India, for example, did not term Hinduism a religion until they came into close contact with the West and adopted that usage from Westerners. One reason for this is that the practices we call religious are not sharply distinguished from other cultural behaviors. Thus, when we study another culture and speak about its religion, we are unavoidably placing an interpretation on what we see that may not accurately reflect the significance of the practices to members of the culture itself. With an ancient culture our situation is even more precarious. Not only are we interpreting the beliefs and practices of strangers by means of our own concepts, which might differ significantly from theirs, we are often doing so on the basis of scant and ambiguous physical evidence: a few remains of bones, tools, jewelry, and occasionally a fragment of what we think might have been an altar or a place of religious practice. Obviously, then, we must proceed with caution if we are to understand other cultures and not simply read into them our own concepts and beliefs. Still, even when such precautions have been carefully taken, there seems to be very little doubt that something like what we call religion, with or without the name, is present wherever humans are found.

THE PHILOSOPHER OF RELIGION DRAWS COMPARISONS

The comparative study of religion has traced the history and mapped the beliefs and practices of many of humankind's religions — though undoubtedly many have flourished and disappeared without a trace during the long period before humans began leaving written records. It is not our purpose here to survey the work of those who have documented the many varieties of religious activities in which humans have engaged. We propose instead to look briefly at five of the great contemporary world religions, not as historians or phenomenologists of religion, but as philosophers of religion interested in learning how the issues that constitute the core of the philosophy of religion in Western philosophy are colored by the filters of these other major religious traditions.

The single issue looming largest in an age when the relative isolation of cultures has ended is the question of the appropriate attitude the practitioners of one religion must take toward those of the other religions. For the philosopher of religion, this becomes the question of how to judge the doctrinal claims of various religions when they are put forth as truth claims about the world and the human situation. We have seen in Chapter 4 that some thinkers such as Freud and Marx maintain that all religions are mistaken or misguided attempts to deal with aspects of human experience that actually need to be faced and handled scientifically. We found reasons to believe, however, that these skeptics have not established their case. Religion is not only a pervasive feature of human experience throughout our long history on earth; it seems also to be a needful, perhaps even an essential, aspect of our lives as humans. Neither in competition with science nor in danger of being undermined and eliminated by the progress of human knowledge, religion is a permanent part of the way human beings live and understand their lives.

What we must try to do, then, is attempt to understand this human phenomenon, and in particular to understand the significance of the variety of manifestations of religion in the many cultures of the world. If the teachings of religions are intended as truth claims about the natural and human world, then we must ask whether they are, as on the surface they appear to be, doctrinal systems that are mutually incompatible. If they are, the philosopher's problem is to test the various claims in order to decide which, if any, is correct or most nearly correct. On the other hand, some thinkers have argued that religions do not represent incompatible sets of claims but merely different interpretations of the same reality. If this is the case, then the philosopher's task is to attempt to collect the insights about reality each has to contribute, to explore the reasons that the teachings appear incompatible, and perhaps even to discover a way in which the apparently incompatible teachings can be reconciled.

On the practical level, devotees of the world's religions have engaged in dialogue off and on for quite some time. Recently such dialogue has begun among philosophers of religion as well, yielding three main perspectives. The first argues that the various religions are advocating mutually incompatible beliefs and thus that at most only one can be correct and the rest must be in error. Advocates of this point of view have usually reached the conclusion that their own tradition, whichever one it happens to be, presents the true view and that the others are, either totally or perhaps in varying degree, mistaken. The second approach, grounded in the philosophy of Ludwig Wittgenstein (1889–1951), maintains that religions are so many different "forms of life," essentially incommensurable and thus not really a proper subject matter for philosophical study or evaluation. Each group holds its beliefs and lives accordingly, and there is nothing more to say about it. Such a position appears at least temporarily as peacemaker among the traditions, but in reality it amounts to abandoning the philosopher's quest. The third approach claims that religions are different ways of expressing the common human experience of a single transmundane reality. The differing cultural beliefs and expectations that we bring to our religious encounters with the one reality result in differing interpretations of that reality. As we share the content of our experiences and reason about it, we can come to recognize the commonalities and thus to acknowledge that several of the great religions might be legitimate ways of understanding and dealing with religious reality.

Perhaps the most difficult thing about the philosopher of religion's task here is that it is almost impossible even to set out on such a study without at least tentatively, and sometimes unconsciously, having already adopted one of these three positions. And viewpoint, of course, plays an important if not a determining role in how the teachings of the religions are apprehended and the conclusions that will be reached. Perhaps the only honest thing to do is for the author to acknowledge at the outset his own proclivity for the third approach — and to resolve that he will attempt to be fair to the first. Because the Wittgensteinian stance rules out the project of this chapter altogether, we will simply leave it aside and assume that it is possible and profitable to attempt a rational comparative study of the great religions, hoping that the results of this study will justify the assumption. First, however, it is necessary to examine, by way of brief summary, some of their central teachings.

TWO GREAT RELIGIONS FROM INDIA

Although religions have originated in every corner of the world in every era of human history, those that have achieved status as world religions by sheer numbers of devotees have all originated in the East. The religions of Native Americans, Europeans, and Africans are just as important to their own followers as the so-called great religions are to theirs. But a very large book indeed would be required to examine all the major religions, and an even larger one if the smaller religious traditions were included. Our purpose in this chapter is to examine several great religions that represent large proportions of humankind in the contemporary world as well as considerable variety in belief and practice as test cases for our question: How should the apparently incompatible truth claims of these traditions about the world, and about the human condition and destiny, be understood? Thus we choose two major religions originating in India (omitting Jainism and Sikhism), and three from the Middle East (omitting Zoroastrianism). The religions of the Far East, such as Confucianism and Shinto, have been left aside. Good detailed studies of all the major and many of the minor religions are to be found in books on comparative religion, to which interested students are referred. [1]

Hinduism: Monotheism Amid Radical Pluralism

Although Hindus have a body of literature that they treat as sacred and that functions as scripture in the tradition, Hinduism was not founded by one person at a specific date by means of alleged divine revelation, as many world religions were. It has no official statement of orthodox beliefs; its scriptures have never been formulated into an authorized canon by a body of priests or theologians. It has no official governing body; no unified hierarchy of clergy; no recognized method of training, ordaining, or authorizing clergy; no standard set of rituals; and no single teaching about the gods, human nature, or the world. Some Hindus engage in religious practices closely resembling those of ancient and contemporary primitives that might properly be called animism — the worship of spirits in various objects in nature. At the other extreme, some Hindus teach highly sophisticated theistic doctrines and practice refined methods of worship and meditation. Between these extremes lies virtually every imaginable variation. Hinduism has been called the religion of 330 million gods and goddesses; in some of its more intellectual formulations it teaches what might be called a trinitarian doctrine of deity; and certain branches claim that it is actually monotheistic or monistic. Unfriendly critics from outside have condemned Hinduism as idolatry because of its extensive use of images in worship; others have called it pagan because of its continued use in a few temples of animal sacrifices and the pouring of blood onto the image of the goddess. But its techniques of religious self-discipline — yoga in particular — and its mystical meditation practices have been prized and studied throughout the world. It is such a rich, variegated, textured, multifaceted fabric of beliefs and practices that some have suggested that "Hindu" be regarded as an umbrella term for a very large number of different but related religions.

Some of the beliefs and practices that make up modern Hinduism go back to 2500 B.C.E. or earlier. In the valleys of the Indus River system (the name of the religion is derived from the name of the river) in today's Pakistan once flourished an ancient civilization that was virtually wiped out by repeated waves of invasions of Aryan peoples from Persia — what we now call Iran — occurring between about 1750 and 1200 B.C.E. Elements of the religion of the ancient conquered peoples and other indigenous peoples on the subcontinent blended over several millennia with those of the invaders into the complex system of Hinduism. Most of the multiple gods and goddesses from all the different groups were carried over in one way or another into the developed religion, together with rituals of worship; myths about the world and the human condition; and attitudes about race, social class, and color.

The Indo-European language spoken by the Aryans evolved into Sanskrit, the language in which the scriptures of Hinduism, known as the **Vedas**, came to be written. Thought to have been composed during the period between 1500 and 400 B.C.E., the Vedas consist of three types of sacred writings: hymns of praise to various deities, texts giving detailed instructions on how the religious rituals are to be performed, and philosophical writings about the nature of reality and ways of achieving knowledge of, or unity with, that reality. The third kind of scripture from the Vedas, called the **Upanishads**, together with the writings on law, especially the Code of Manu (written between 300 B.C.E. and 300 C.E.), and the Bhagavad-Gita (written slightly later during the same period) form the basis for most subsequent philosophizing and for the six major schools of Hindu thought that developed during the medieval period.

Many interpreters of Hinduism regard two concepts as fundamental: *dharma* and *moksha.*[2] **Dharma** (the word often used for what we call religion) means, roughly, duty, and it describes one's moral responsibilities, cosmic and social alike. A person's cosmic duty is to perform the rituals needed to help the gods uphold and perpetuate the process and order of the world. Social duty is determined by an individual's place in society within the caste system, of which we will have more to say shortly. **Moksha,** in contrast, involves not sustaining the system of the cosmos and earthly life, but achieving liberation from it. Hinduism teaches a doctrine of reincarnation, driven by **karma,** the fruits of one's actions, on a wheel of birth, growth, suffering, death, and rebirth to another life of suffering and death. The level of society, the **caste,** into which one is born is determined by the moral nature of one's deeds in the previous life. Because earthly life involves suffering, the ultimate objective of every Hindu is to escape the wheel of *karma* and achieve *moksha,* liberation. This is the **soteriology** of Hinduism, its salvation doctrine. And *moksha* is achieved through renunciation of earthly concerns and involvement in things of the spirit, particularly meditation and devotion to the gods. Thus these two key concepts, *dharma* and *moksha,* involve a tension, a pull in opposite directions, and much of the theology of Hinduism is concerned with resolving this tension.

Basically, resolution of the opposing forces is achieved by dividing the span of human life into four stages and devoting the early stages to *dharma* and the later stages to *moksha.* The Code of Manu describes the **four stages of life:** The first, *brahmacharya* (the word means "chastity"), is the student stage, when a youth studies especially the religious rituals it will be his duty to perform and prepares for adult life. The second, *grihastha,* is the stage of the householder, when a young adult pursues a career and raises a family. These first two stages are particularly dominated by *dharma.* But when a man (these teachings were traditionally intended only for males; the woman was bound by her *dharma* to serve her husband) has completed his duty to society, when his children are grown up and he has seen his grandchildren, he is entitled to turn his attention to his own individual interest in achieving *moksha.* The third stage, *vanaprastha,* was traditionally the time when a man left his home to dwell in the forest and meditate. Today it is the time when he retires from his work and devotes himself more fully to religious matters. The final stage, *sannyasa,* was the time in former days when the man became a wandering mendicant, having cut all family and earthly ties. *Sannyasa* involves austerities and ascetic practices designed to purify the soul and to ready it for **nirvana** (literally, "extinction"), the dissolution of all desire and absorption into **Brahman,** the absolute, formless ultimate reality — or, failing that, at least a more auspicious place in the next reincarnation.

A creation myth in the Hindu scriptures accounts for and justifies the caste system. According to the myth, a god created humans out of parts of himself, making the priestly and scholarly caste of Brahmins out of his head, the military and royal caste of Kshatriyas out of his arms, the Vaishya caste of merchants and farmers out of his torso, and the serving caste of Shudras out of his feet. The concept of *dharma* reflects the caste system in its teaching that certain duties pertain to each caste and that the virtuous person is one who performs just those duties and refrains from the functions that belong to other castes. There is no social mobility among the castes during a given lifetime of a soul; each person is born into the caste of his or her parents and remains there. Belief in reincarnation provides a way out, however: In the next life, one may be incarnated into a higher or lower caste as determined by one's *karma*, that is, by the extent to which one has followed the *dharma* of the caste in the previous life.

Given the variety of belief and practice within Hinduism, it should come as no surprise that many ways of seeking salvation are available. Among these, four major *margas* ("paths") are usually singled out for special study. Of these **four paths to salvation**, the one we have been discussing, seeking salvation by living a conventional life through the four *ashramas* (stages of life), is called *Karma Marg* because it relies on faithful performance of one's work and the duties of caste to effect one's eventual liberation. Three other ways are thought of as quicker and more direct paths. It was not possible for a man to attain *moksha* by means of the path of *Karma Marg* until he had worked his way up through successive lives to the Brahmin caste and perhaps lived many righteous lives as a Brahmin. But another way, called the *Bhakti Marg*, the way of devotion, taught that by diligent and enthusiastic devotion to one or more of the gods, anyone, even an untouchable or a woman, might possibly achieve *moksha* in one lifetime.

By the medieval period, three major gods had emerged from the huge pantheon of gods and goddesses. Some Hindu philosophers developed an interpretation vaguely similar to the Christian concept of the Trinity, suggesting that these three gods are all manifestations of a single deity. One widespread position, called the Vedanta school (discussed in connection with Sri Aurobindo's thought in Chapter 5), teaches that ultimate reality is one Absolute, formless, undifferentiated Being, called Brahman. To be able to think about this reality, humans give It form, and the various gods, such as these three and others, are those forms.

The so-called trinity of gods consists of the creator, **Brahma**, the destroyer, **Shiva**, and the preserver, **Vishnu**. It is a curious thing that no extensive cult of devotees has developed dedicated to Brahma, but very extensive *bhakti* cults have grown up around Shiva and Vishnu. Shiva, god of death, disease, destruction, and dance, is usually depicted dancing within a ring of fire on the body of a demon. Shiva is also associated with sexuality and procreation; the Shiva temple usually contains stone images called the *lingam* and the *yoni*, representations of the male and female sexual organs. Devotees of Shiva, called Shaivites, often insist that Shiva is not merely a representation of the ultimate Brahman, but is himself the ultimate deity performing all the functions of creation, sustaining, and destruction. Closely connected to Shiva worship is the *bhakti* cult to Shiva's wife, the terrible black goddess **Kali-Durga**, whose worship involves animal sacrifice because she loves to drink their blood.

Vishnu is a god of love and concern for human well-being. Vaishnavites teach that Vishnu has experienced a number of incarnations, and whenever a particularly serious crisis of human need occurs Vishnu takes form to bring aid. Some of the **avatars** or incarnations of Vishnu have been animals and some have been humans. **Krishna**, one of the two major characters in the Bhagavad-Gita, is one of the most popular and widely worshipped avatars of Vishnu. The *bhakti* cult of Lord Krishna has become well known in the West in the twentieth century by way of the activities of the so-called Hari Krishnas and their Society for Krishna Consciousness. During the period when Buddhism was being gradually overcome and reassimilated into Hinduism, Lord Buddha also came to be known as an avatar of Vishnu.

A third way of knowledge, *Jnana Marga*, is in some ways most important for the study of the philosophy of religion. This path to salvation has given rise to six major systems of knowledge or schools of philosophical thought and many minor ones, all claiming to be based on the Vedas, particularly the Upanishads. Some of these systems are dualistic or pluralistic, teaching that ultimate reality consists of two or more kinds of things; several are nontheistic, influenced by Buddhism's denial of deity; and several are monistic. The two best known and most influential systems are the yoga and Vedanta.

Yoga is a dualistic system, distinguishing the human spirit from God and having as its goal to link (*yoga* means "yoke") the spirit to God. In the West, we are most familiar with Hatha yoga, which involves discipline of the body through a variety of bodily postures, but this is only a technique designed to lead to the more important spiritual dimensions of yoga. The essence of yoga is meditation, and a number of specific techniques have been developed to aid in the grasp of knowledge or the encounter with reality through meditation. Meditation involves a number of stages, beginning with simple concentration on one's breathing, through the use of a *mantra* or special word repeated over and over to aid in focusing the mind, to the emptying of the mind, the stilling of thought, the quiet waiting, and the relaxed openness that may lead to *samadhi*. This ultimate stage resembles unconsciousness or even death, but is described as a state of brilliant superconsciousness in which the mind confronts reality and grasps truth directly.

Vedanta (*Vedanta* means "end of the Vedas" and thus is grounded particularly in the Upanishads) has become known in the West through the efforts of its most charismatic advocate, Vivekananda (1863–1902), who preached in America and Europe and organized Vedanta societies in many major cities that continue to operate today. Vedanta is a monistic system, teaching that the seeming duality or plurality of our ordinary experience is *maya*, illusion, and that ultimate reality is a single Absolute Being, **Brahman**. Salvation means ridding oneself of ignorance and illusion so that one knows directly and immediately the oneness of oneself with Brahman. **Atman**, the human spirit, is identical with Brahman, the Absolute spirit. Salvation means coming to know in all its fullness and directness that Atman *is* Brahman.

Hinduism, perhaps the oldest major religion, shows a youthful vitality even today. It has never been narrowly sectarian or exclusivistic. It does not prescribe creeds or rituals as conditions of membership. It does not expel anyone for heresy, nor does it attempt to convert persons from other religions. It is open to new ideas, even the idea of new avatars — Buddha was pronounced to be an avatar of Vishnu, and a few have even suggested that perhaps Jesus is also an avatar. In these ways, the radical pluralism of its beliefs, its religious practices, and its gods and goddesses has helped maintain its flexibility, its resiliency, and its persistent vitality.

Buddhism: The Middle Way

Like several of the other great world religions, Buddhism is an outgrowth of an already active religious tradition, beginning as another school of thought within the parent tradition. Unlike the Hinduism that fostered it, Buddhism does have a particular founder and a fairly definite date of commencement. The enlightenment experience of Gautama, who became the **Buddha** (*Buddha* means "Enlightened One"), and the preaching of his first sermon setting forth the most fundamental teachings of the faith occurred sometime around the year 525 B.C.E., which may be reckoned as the approximate date of the beginning of Buddhism.

The writings that became the scriptures of Buddhism, purportedly containing the teachings of the Buddha and his contemporary disciples, were carried in the memories of succeeding generations of the monks and were not written down until some three or four hundred years after Gautama's death. It should not be surprising, then, that disputes should have arisen among the followers concerning precisely what the teachings were and what kind of life they require of monk and layperson. A series of councils were called over the years in an effort to reach agreement, but despite these attempts the movement split into two major branches, **Theravada** ("tradition of the Elders," i.e., the monks who were contemporaries of the Buddha) **Buddhism** and **Mahayana** ("greater vehicle") **Buddhism**, along with numerous subbranches.

Gautama Siddhartha (c. 560–480 B.C.E.) was born into a prosperous Kshatriya family in Northern India about a hundred miles northeast of Varanasi (Benares) and grew up pampered and well cared for. The accounts of his childhood and youth, like the stories surrounding many other great religious personages, read like legends filled with omens and portents bordering on the miraculous. Scholars think it likely that many of these legends, like the birth narratives of Jesus, were added to the tradition by later followers who came to believe that one so great must have come into the world under unusually marvelous circumstances. According to one legend, it was prophesied in Gautama's childhood that if he ever saw either human wretchedness or the tranquil life of the monk, he would abandon the life of a Kshatriya and pursue a religious life. Thus his father allegedly went to quite extraordinary lengths to surround him with young, healthy attendants, and particularly to prevent him from seeing a dead body, a diseased person, a person bent and wrinkled from old age, or a monk.

Gautama was married at about nineteen years of age and fathered a son. In the course of time, however, he did see the ugly sights of death, disease, and old age and thus became aware of the fate that is the common destiny of all humans. And he also caught sight of a yellow-robed monk whose demeanor bespoke tranquility and peace. Troubled by the awful mystery of suffering, Gautama wanted to discover the path to tranquility. He left his home and his young family in the middle of the night, exchanged his fine clothing for those of a beggar, and entered a period of questing for understanding. He studied the various schools of philosophy taught by the Hindu saints and gurus, without finding satisfaction. Then he turned to the path of **asceticism**, widely accepted as the surest way to achieve enlightenment. For about six years Gautama practiced the most extreme self-denial, coming quite near to death from hunger, exposure, and neglect of the needs of the body.

Finally realizing that the path of asceticism, like that of philosophy, had failed, he ended his fasting and extreme austerities by taking an ample meal and then sat under a tree, resolving to remain there until he received enlightenment. It came in the form of a recognition that the endless cycle of birth, suffering, death, rebirth, suffering, death is fueled by craving. Our wretchedness results from desire and a dissatisfaction with what we have. It is not possible to escape from our misery by satisfying our desires, because desire is insatiable, perpetually outrunning and exceeding everything we can grasp to satisfy it. The only solution, then, is to curb desire. The person who desires nothing he does not have is not unhappy. Thus the answer is neither the extreme of sensuality in an effort to satisfy all desires nor the extreme of asceticism in an effort to deny all desires, but rather the **middle way** of desiring only what one has and refusing to desire what one cannot have.

At once Gautama sought out a group of monks with whom he had previously practiced asceticism and preached to them his new insights. They became his first disciples. This first sermon, preached in a deer park near Varanasi, at a place now called Sarnath, sets forth the central teachings of Buddhism in the form of the **four noble truths** and the **eightfold path**. The four noble truths are: (1) Life is suffering (*dukkha*); (2) the cause of suffering is craving (*tanha*); (3) the cure of suffering is to abandon or to renounce craving; and (4) the way that enables us to renounce craving is the eightfold path (rightness of views, intention, speech, action, livelihood, effort, mindfulness, and concentration). These truths are set forth in more detail in a passage from the first sermon:

> Now this, monks, is the noble truth of pain: birth is painful, old age is painful, sickness is painful, sorrow, lamentation, dejection, and despair are painful. Contact with unpleasant things is painful, not getting what one wishes is painful. In short the five groups of grasping are painful.
>
> Now this, monks, is the noble truth of the cause of pain: the craving, which tends to rebirth, combined with pleasure and lust, finding pleasure here and there, namely the craving for passion, the craving for existence, the craving for non-existence.
>
> Now this, monks, is the noble truth of the cessation of pain, the cessation without a remainder of craving, the abandonment, forsaking, release, non-attachment.
>
> Now this, monks, is the noble truth of the way that leads to the cessation of pain: this is the noble Eightfold Way, namely, right views, right intention, right speech, right action, right livelihood, right effort, right mindfulness, right concentration.[3]

To be born, to suffer, to die, to be reborn and to suffer and die again, over and over again, is the destiny of unenlightened humankind. It is to escape this wheel of suffering that one undertakes to follow the eightfold path. That path leads to *nirvana* ("extinction"), which is an end of craving and an extinction of unsatisfied desire. For the person who achieves *nirvana*, the wheel of rebirth ends.

Gautama, now known as the Buddha, founded a monkhood called the Sangha, a growing group of persons desiring to dedicate all of their energies to achieving *nirvana*. He laid down rules for how the *bikkhus*, as the monks were called, were to live, and also guidelines on how laypersons, in a less intensive way, might pursue the eightfold path. He taught no doctrines about gods and did not claim any supermundane status for himself. The Buddha insisted that his teachings were not to be accepted blindly as authoritative, but rather that each person should seek to understand the insights contained in them and that the teachings should be used as instruments through which each person would seek to attain enlightenment for him- or herself: The doctrines of the Buddha are a boat we use to cross over the water, but when we reach the other side we throw away the raft. The person who insists on clinging to every detail of the doctrine after enlightenment has been achieved is like the foolish man who allows himself to be burdened for his journey overland by attempting to carry the boat on his back.

Thus the Buddha's doctrines might more properly be characterized as a set of philosophical teachings than a religion. As teachings they were also demanding enough that only those persons willing to become monks could hope to follow them with enough effect to achieve *nirvana* after one lifetime. For laypersons, it was a matter of living in such a way that they would achieve a more favorable rebirth, with the hope that in some future life they would be in a position to become monks and achieve liberation.

Because the tradition deriving most directly from the Buddha and his immediate disciples, known to its advocates as Theravada, seemed to provide a vehicle for salvation for only the few, it came to be called by its opponents the Hinayana ("small vehicle") tradition. Hinayana was too demanding for ordinary people, requiring full-time devotion to study and meditation if salvation were to be achieved. Thus there developed the Mahayana ("great vehicle") tradition, which preached a much more liberal doctrine and offered greater hope to a much larger number of persons.

A basic Mahayana tenet is that some secret teachings of the Buddha were not a part of the elders' tradition. This claim opened the door to innumerable additional claims, and it was these that contributed most to making Mahayana a religion in the fullest sense of the word, with divine beings, worship, prayer, and the accumulation of merit. The Mahayanists taught that the Buddha was not merely human but a compassionate divine being in human form. They also taught that there were and are other Buddhas, some who lived before Gautama, some after, some yet to come. There are also **bodhisattvas** (enlightened beings) who delay passing into *nirvana* to offer help to humans. Thus human prayers and acts of worship may achieve two kinds of effects: help with concrete earthly problems, such as healing or better economic fortune, and aid in moving toward the objective of enlightenment. The Buddha himself explicitly rejected distinctions of caste, and taught that persons of any social level might achieve enlightenment. The Mahayanists embraced this teaching, thus providing a salvation path for persons from every walk of life.

The spread of Buddhism was greatly facilitated by the work of Ashoka, an emperor of India in the third century B.C.E., who enlisted and sent out missionaries to spread the new doctrine. It is said that his own son and daughter went to Sri Lanka, where the ruler was converted and the new religion spread rapidly. Missionaries also carried it to Burma and Southeast

Asia and eventually to China and Japan. The teaching that more than one Buddha exists made the spread of Buddhism easier, since the missionaries did not need to insist that the recipients renounce their old religious beliefs but could simply interpret their former gods as additional Buddhas. This openness of Mahayana Buddhism to blending with other religions contributed greatly to its increasing prosperity. At the same time, a similar openness in Hinduism led to the reabsorption of Buddhism into Hinduism in India through the teaching that the Buddha was another incarnation of Vishnu. Thus Buddhism virtually disappeared from the land of its birth just as it was becoming the major religion in much of the rest of Asia.

Although the Theravada tradition persisted, in Sri Lanka, Burma, and the countries of Southeast Asia, holding firmly to the old teachings of the elders and changing very little, Mahayana Buddhism developed and changed considerably over the centuries as it spread to other Asian peoples. Two of its more important new sects were Pure Land and Zen. **Pure Land Buddhism** is based on the belief that there are *bodhisattvas* who preside over other worlds, called pure lands, where humans who have made good progress toward liberation may be reincarnated for another lifetime, during which they may accumulate the remaining merit needed to achieve final salvation. The most popular of these *bodhisattvas* is **Amida**, a Buddha who governs "the pure land of the West." Salvation, or that step toward it that gets one to the pure land, is achieved by faith in Amida and through his grace. Worshippers pray to Amida and engage in ritual practices of chanting his name. This sect offers both a straightforward hope and a quick, direct path to salvation for anyone.

Zen (Ch'an) **Buddhism**, which has become quite popular in the West, is a more intuitive and nonrational approach to salvation through meditation than its Pure Land counterpart. Zen devotees claim that enlightenment comes suddenly in a flash as, allegedly, it did to the Buddha himself. The mind with its preoccupation with sense experience and rational thought presents a serious hindrance to the coming of enlightenment. Thus the Zen masters make use during meditation of puzzles and paradoxes (*koans*) to startle and puzzle the reason in an effort to free the mind to be open to sudden illumination.

By the twentieth century, Buddhism has evolved into a very complex cluster of interrelated sects all with certain elements in common but displaying such variety that it has been called not one but many related religions. But the same thing is true of Hinduism and, as we will see, of Christianity as well. The Theravada tradition remains basically nontheistic, offering immediate hope of salvation only to a few, and making use of relatively little by way of religious ritual. Some of the Mahayana traditions have become theistic, even polytheistic, with elaborate rituals of worship and prayer designed to provide concrete paths to salvation for anyone and everyone. Common to nearly all the various sects is the belief in *karma* and rebirth and the ultimate objective of *nirvana*. In the twentieth century Buddhism, like Hinduism, has shown a renewed vitality stimulated in part by a reaction to Christian missionary efforts and by a rising Asian nationalism that values the indigenous while rejecting the foreign.

THREE GREAT RELIGIONS FROM THE MIDDLE EAST

Four of the great world religions originated in India (Hinduism, Buddhism, Jainism, and Sikhism); another four (Zoroastrianism, Judaism, Christianity, and Islam) had their birth in that stretch of land between the east end of the Mediterranean Sea and the Persian Gulf that we call the Middle East and that many Asians call West Asia. There is evidence that all eight of these great religions have ancient connections with one another. In our discussion of Hinduism, we noted the repeated waves of invasion into the Indus River Valley of Aryan peoples from Persia and that Hinduism evolved as the culture and religion they brought with them blended with that of the Indian indigenous peoples. Subsequently, of course, Buddhism, Jainism, and Sikhism developed from within the Hindu milieu in India, each inheriting influences from all roots of the tradition.

Meanwhile, the religious beliefs and practices of the Aryans who remained in Persia, identical in the ancient period to those of the Aryans who invaded India, evolved in a different direction, eventually giving rise to Zoroastrianism. A study of ancient Persian and ancient Indian texts reveals very many of the same gods and rites of worship. The influence of the ancient Persian Aryans flowed not only onto the Indian subcontinent to the East, but as far as Greece and Rome to the West, where in the several centuries before and after the beginning of the Common Era mystery cults to some of the Persian gods flourished — particularly cults of Mithra, a god also important in ancient India. Although Zoroastrianism never became as widespread geographically or as successful in number of adherents as the other great world religions — and indeed has diminished in our time to a very small number, called the Parsis, located mostly in the vicinity of Bombay in India — it generated ideas and beliefs that found their way, either directly or indirectly, into all the other three Middle Eastern religions.

Judaism: The Chosen People of the Jealous God

The historical beginning of Judaism is usually traced to the career of **Moses** and the giving of the law after the exodus of his people from enslavement in Egypt, thought to have occurred around 1450 to 1400 B.C.E. (some place it as late as 1250 B.C.E.). But this people seems already to have had an oral tradition that remembered a history going back to an earlier great patriarch named Abraham. The Abraham stories may well reflect memories of waves of migrations around 1800–1500 B.C.E. of certain tribes who came from the region of Arabia near the place where the Euphrates River empties into the Persian Gulf and moved westward, ultimately reaching the land now known as Palestine.

The Hebrew Bible, however, sets these events into a context of universal history by means of myths about God's creation of the world and legends that reflect a series of disasters, from the murder of brother by brother in the very first family God created to the growth of so much wickedness that God decided to destroy all but a handful of humans in a great flood and begin the project over again. The descendents of Noah, the man saved from the flood, were no more obedient, so God seems to have decided to stop attempting to lead all humankind and select instead one man to become the father of a chosen people. Abraham was called to journey to a land that would be given to him and his descendents, and it was promised that he would become the father of a great people and a blessing to all the peoples of the earth. According to the legends, the descendents of Abraham were driven by famine into Egypt, where they were eventually enslaved. The account seems to become more historically reliable with Moses and the exodus.

It has been remarked that the religions of India and the Far East originate in the effort of humans to discover truth or to make contact with the gods, whereas the religions of the Middle East begin with a divine intervention into the affairs of humans. Judaism began when God spoke to Moses out of a burning bush in the desert of Sinai, revealed to him that the divine name is **Yahweh**,[4] assured Moses that he was the same God who had made promises to Abraham, and sent him to accomplish the liberation of the Hebrew tribes from Egyptian slavery. When the Pharaoh of Egypt was not eager to give up his slaves, the biblical account runs, a series of signs and wonders performed by Moses and plagues sent upon Egypt culminated in the death of the firstborn in every household. The Hebrews were protected from the death angel by religious rituals prescribed by Yahweh, including a blood mark on the doorpost of their houses. This episode is remembered and celebrated in the Jewish observance of Pesach, or **Passover**.

After a miraculous escape from pursuing Egyptian armies through a body of water said to have parted before them and to have surged back to drown the Egyptians, the Hebrews were led to Mount Sinai, where Moses had seen his original vision and received his call. There God gave Moses the ten commandments that became the foundation of Jewish law — and a cornerstone in the foundation of Western civilization. The commandments are both religious and moral in nature, reflecting a resistance to the polytheism and idol worship in the midst of which the Jews lived and establishing Judaism as an ethical monotheism. The commandments are found in the Bible in Exodus 10:1–17 and in Deuteronomy 5:6–21. The Exodus version may be summarized thus:

I am the Lord your God, who brought you out of the land of Egypt,
out of the land of bondage,
You shall have no other gods before me,
You shall not make for yourself a graven image, or any likeness of
anything that is in heaven above, or that is in the earth beneath, or
that is in the water under the earth; you shall not bow down to them
or serve them; for I the Lord your God am a jealous God, visiting the
iniquity of the fathers upon the children to the third and fourth generation of those who hate me, but showing mercy to thousands of
those who love me and keep my commandments,
You shall not take the name of the Lord your god in vain . . . Remember the Sabbath day to keep it holy. Six days you shall labor, and do
all your work; but the seventh is a Sabbath to the Lord your god; in it
you shall not do any work . . . for in six days the Lord made heaven
and earth, the sea and all that is in them, and rested on the seventh
day; therefore the Lord blessed the Sabbath day and hallowed it.
Honor your father and your mother . . .
You shall not kill
You shall not commit adultery.
You shall not steal.
You shall not bear false witness against your neighbor.
You shall not covet your neighbor's house; you shall not covet your
neighbor's wife . . . or anything that is your neighbor's.

On this skeleton grew up a detailed body of law that became the core of the
Hebrew Bible to be found in the books of Exodus, Leviticus, Numbers, and
Deuteronomy. Together with the book of Genesis these books of law make
up the Pentateuch, also called the **Torah**—although Jews sometimes use
the word *Torah* more broadly to refer to the entire Hebrew Bible, even
including the Talmud, the record of the interpretation of the law by
learned rabbis. These materials were probably written down long after the
events they reflect and codified later still, the Hebrew canon of scriptures
having been fixed by a council of rabbis about C.E. 90.

The Hebrews eventually reinvaded Palestine, gradually settling among
the other tribes living there. They carried with them the Ark of the Covenant, a casket said to contain the stone tablets on which the commandments were written, and the Tent of Meeting, which had served them as a
place of worship during their nomadic existence. A priesthood developed
along with a cult that involved the burning of sacrifices of animal flesh in
the open air before the tent. Eventually these people dominated most of
Palestine and established themselves as a nation in about 1030 B.C.E. King
Solomon built his royal palace in Jerusalem and constructed a great temple
for the worship of Yahweh. The greater ease and plenty which came with a
settled life also brought a loosening of the standards of morality, especially
in high places, and concessions to those interested in introducing aspects
of the religious practices of the indigenous tribes. This stimulated the rise

of a distinct religious movement, that of the prophet, who preached loyalty to Yahweh, moral righteousness, and purity of religious practice.

Palestine is located on the trade routes connecting several important parts of the world, a sort of thoroughfare of merchants and marching armies. Thus the Jewish kingdom was not able to stand independently very long. In 922 B.C.E. the kingdom split into two nations, the northern called Israel and the southern called Judah. Israel was destroyed by the Assyrians in 721 B.C.E., never to arise again. Judah survived until 586 B.C.E., when the Babylonian empire conquered Jerusalem, leveling the city, leaving the temple in ruins, and forcing most of the political and religious leaders into exile in Babylon.

The religion of Jews was forced to evolve during the period of Babylonian captivity. Conceived during the national period in somewhat narrow regional terms as a religion of people and place, Judaism began to be rethought in more universal terms; God began to be recognized as the deity who is present everywhere and who controls the affairs of the whole world. Deeds of enemies were seen as planned by God to punish and purify the people. When Cyrus, the Zoroastrian king of Persia, conquered Babylon in 538 B.C.E., freeing the Jews to return to Palestine, they understood this also as an act of Yahweh. Returning exiles rebuilt the city of Jerusalem and built the second temple, which served as the center of Jewish worship until it was destroyed by the Romans in C.E. 70. Only occasionally and sporadically did the Jews enjoy freedom during the period of the second temple in Jerusalem. Alexander the Great and then Rome soon extended empires to include Palestine and Judah became a vassal state.

The people chafed under foreign rule, but some of the greatest of their writings were generated in the periods of the exile and the return. The ethical monotheism of the Jews developed into a vision of a universal monotheism under the governance of a God who loved and ruled all the earth and whose chosen people were God's special instrument for dealing with humankind. The concept of Israel as the suffering servant of God on behalf of humanity was preached by the prophets, whose writings are preserved in the Books of Isaiah and Jeremiah, and the concept of the **messiah**, an anointed one, also sometimes referred to as the Son of Man, appeared. Some interpreted the messianic concept in terms of a great political and military leader who would overthrow the foreign rulers and restore the Kingdom of Israel; others understood it in more spiritual terms; and some believed it referred to an age to come, when there would be peace and suffering would end. Many men came forward declaring themselves, or being declared by their followers, to be the messiah. Among them was Jesus of Nazareth, whose followers founded Christianity after his execution.

After the destruction of the second temple in C.E. 70, the dispersion of Jews to many nations of the world, which had begun with the exile of 586 B.C.E., increased greatly. The **Diaspora**, as these Jews were called, settled into the nations of Europe and parts of Arabia, Asia, and Africa, developing in varied ways as they were influenced by the surrounding culture, but preserving a core of Jewishness that involved faithfulness to the law as taught by the Torah and the Talmud. With the temple destroyed, the center of Jewish life for the Diaspora became the **synagogue**, an assembly primarily for study of the laws and celebration of the holy days that bring to remembrance the great events in the history of the people. With no temple there remained no priesthood. The religious leader became the rabbi, a person learned in the law and prepared to teach it to the community.

The fortunes of the Jews of the Diaspora have shifted greatly from one period to another and from one country to another, but more frequently than not discrimination and often open persecution has been practiced against them. This was partly the result of the tendency of Christians to blame all Jews for the death of Jesus; in some parts of the world it was related to the practices of Islam, which sometimes attempted forced conversions. In Europe Jews were frequently persecuted and confined to ghettos, segregated quarters of the city, the only parts where Jews were permitted to live. The most devastating example of persecution was the Holocaust in Germany during World War II, when some 6 million Jews were methodically rounded up and killed.

After World War II ended, the demand for a homeland somewhere in the world for the Jews weighed heavily on the consciences of the nations of the West. Various locations were explored, but the Zionist movement of Jews insisted that Palestine, their historical homeland, promised to them by God, was the only suitable place. In 1947, the United Nations divided Palestine into two countries, declaring the western part as a homeland for the Jews, thus reestablishing after some 1800 years a nation of Israel. As is well known, the Palestinians already living in the land given to Israel were relocated into settlement camps, where many continue to live under very difficult conditions. The fact that both the Palestinians and the Israelis claim the land of Palestine creates one of the unresolved political and religious crises of our times.

Although Judaism developed a theology that understood Yahweh as the God of all humankind, it did not develop a missionary movement designed to convert others, as Christianity and Islam did. And although Judaism evolved a clearly articulated conception of the personal and loving nature of God as well as a detailed and sensitive set of teachings about personal and social morality, its eschatology remained ambiguous and its soteriology vague. Just what the concept of the messiah means in Judaism is still not agreed on; what the nature of the future destiny of Judaism is to be is left unspecified; and the position on what happens to a person after death is not enunciated clearly, although for the most part Judaism contains no teaching of personal immortality.

In the modern world three major branches of Judaism have developed: orthodox, conservative, and reformed. Orthodox Jews make the greatest attempt to practice biblical and Talmudic Judaism. Even in societies where Saturday is a regular workday, they are careful to keep the Sabbath observances as required by law. They conduct worship in the Hebrew language on Friday evenings, separating men and women in their synagogues, and requiring both to cover their heads; they are also very careful to observe kosher food laws, a set of dietary practices derived from scripture and intended to guarantee the ritual purity of food. Conservative Jews are somewhat less strict about the details of biblical rules and much more concerned with the scientific study of the Bible. They worship in synagogues on Saturday morning, using a combination of vernacular language and Hebrew. Many conservatives are also careful to observe Sabbath and kosher food laws.

Reform Judaism, widespread in the United States and Europe, is an attempt to adapt Jewish religious and cultural practice to modern Western life. Reformed Jews worship on Friday evenings in synagogues, which they call temples; men and women sit together and are not required to cover their heads; the services are mostly in the vernacular. They are much less strict than orthodox or conservative Jews about Sabbath and kosher food laws. Recently the reform movement has even taken the step of ordaining women rabbis.

Christianity: Salvation Through Believing in Christ

Christianity began as a sect of Judaism. **Jesus** of Nazareth, on whose life and teachings it was founded, was a Jew, and so were all his earliest followers. There was no suggestion during Jesus' lifetime of any thought of establishing a religion separate from Judaism. The leaders of the movement after the death and alleged resurrection of Jesus preached primarily to Jews and seem to have presumed no separation. But the earliest controversy to arise within the Christian movement concerned the question whether Gentile (that is, non-Jewish) converts to Christianity must also become Jews — that is, whether they had to undergo the rite of circumcision and observe the sabbath and kosher dietary laws. It was at this time, when the movement began to spread to Gentiles, largely through the efforts of the missionary Paul, that the issue was forced, and it was decided that Christians did not have to be Jews, in effect separating the movement from Judaism.

After Jesus' death, alleged resurrection, and ascension, his followers seem to have believed that he would return within a very short time to bring about the Kingdom of God — whatever they may have understood that to mean. Thus they did not bother to write accounts of his life and teachings until at least forty years had passed. Most of the Epistles, especially those of Paul, were written sooner, but they contained very little detail about Jesus' life. The occasion to begin writing about the life and teachings of Jesus was the aftermath of the abortive Jewish rebellion against

Rome, which began in C.E. 66. By C.E. 70, Jerusalem had been destroyed, the temple lay in ruins, and many of the persons who had known Jesus were dead or were scattered to other parts of the Roman Empire. Those remaining were forced to realize that Jesus had not returned to precipitate a new era of history, and it became necessary to reinterpret their eschatological expectations. Only then did his followers begin to write down what they remembered of his life and teachings.

The earliest Gospel, perhaps that of Mark,[5] seems to have been written during or shortly after the rebellion in around C.E. 68 to 70. Luke and Matthew followed perhaps during the next decade, and John, reflecting a much more settled church community, probably dates from some time between C.E. 90 and 120. Written long after the events they purport to describe, by followers interested in promoting the new religion and supporting their claim (rejected by so many Jews) that Jesus was indeed the expected messiah, these documents were not concerned first and foremost with accuracy of historical detail. The four **Gospels**, and especially the first three so-called synoptic Gospels,[6] agree to a certain extent about events in Jesus' life, but there are also very serious differences, aggravating the problem of ascertaining the historical facts. And yet they are virtually our only sources about Jesus' career. He is mentioned in very few secular sources and these provide little useful detail. Some critics suggested that there never was such a person; that the life was fabricated by the founders of the faith to give it the greater appearance of authenticity. Such speculations cannot be positively disproved, but most scholars consider them quite implausible and highly unlikely.[7]

The historical circumstances, however, provide us with only very scant information. There is very little about Jesus' life before he began his public ministry. The birth narratives in Matthew and Luke have the air of pious tales added by devout believers not so much out of their memories as their imaginations. The allegation that Jesus was born miraculously of a virgin mother (similar claims were made about other religious figures of the period) seems grounded in a mistranslation in the Septuagent[8] of a verse from the Prophet Isaiah, "Behold, a young woman (*almah*, "young woman" in Hebrew, but translated *parthenos*, meaning "virgin" in the Greek) shall conceive and bear a son, and shall call his name Immanuel" (Isaiah 7:14). The Gospel writer apparently interpreted this verse as a prophetic foretelling of the coming of the messiah, and since he believed that Jesus was the messiah he applied it to Jesus in composing the birth narratives. Besides these birth stories, the Gospels contain only one story from the childhood of Jesus.

Christianity is possibly the religion that places the greatest importance on faith and on holding the right beliefs. Such an emphasis might lead us to expect a set of teachings clearly enunciating the correct principles to be believed. When we search the Gospels for truths of this sort, however, we find no coherent set of affirmations. Indeed, they contain teachings on each of opposite sides of several issues. For example, Jesus seems to have opposed the legalistic attitudes of the Jewish religious party of Pharisees, who insisted on scrupulous observance of every detail of the ancient Jewish laws on diet and the Sabbath. Jesus appears to have regarded such attitudes as niggling, placing the letter of the law above the well-being of persons. He performed healings on the Sabbath, he and his disciples plucked grain in the fields on the Sabbath, and he is reported to have said, "The Sabbath was made for man, not man for the Sabbath."[9] Yet at other times Jesus teaches great regard for the law:

> Think not that I have come to abolish the law and the prophets. . . . till heaven and earth pass away, not an iota, not a dot, will pass from the law until all is accomplished. Whoever then relaxes one of the least of these commandments and teaches men so, shall be called least in the kingdom of heaven.[10]

A number of other passages might be cited that likewise seem to advocate contradictory positions.

Jesus' famous sermon on the mount, often taken as the summary of his teachings, begins with the celebrated **beatitudes**, which pronounce persons blessed who possess such qualities as meekness, mercy, hunger and thirst for righteousness, and purity of heart. Citing a number of traditional Jewish moral teachings, Jesus asserts in each case that his teachings impose an even higher standard.

> You have heard that it was said, "An eye for an eye and a tooth for a tooth." But I say to you, Do not resist one who is evil. But if any one strikes you on the right cheek, turn to him the other also; and if any one would sue you and take your coat, let him have your cloak as well. . . . You, therefore, must be perfect, as your heavenly Father is perfect.[11]

Another major source of Jesus' teachings is a series of parables he spoke that make use of commonplace situations to illustrate a moral or religious principle. Several of these parables teach a sense of rejoicing over the recovery of something lost. A woman with ten coins loses one; a shepherd has a hundred sheep, one of which strays from the flock; and, perhaps most famous of all, the man with two sons, one of whom—the prodigal son—leaves home. Each parable ends with great rejoicing when what was lost is recovered, bringing home the moral that there is equally great rejoicing in heaven when one sinner repents and comes back to God.

It is not easy to distill the teachings of Jesus into a set of principles that Christians are supposed to believe. Much is already familiar from the ancient Jewish writings. When a Pharisee asks what the most important commandment is, Jesus quotes from the Hebrew scripture:

> You shall love the Lord your God with all your heart, and with all
> your soul, and with all your mind. This is the great and first com-
> mandment. And a second is like it, You shall love your neighbor as
> yourself. On these two commandments depend all the law and the
> prophets.[12]

Perhaps this is the core of Jesus' teachings. Many parables and sayings also
reflect the commandment to love one's neighbors and even one's enemies,
and to give expression to this love in deeds of kindness. And yet nothing in
the recorded teachings of Jesus comes even close to being a creed. The
creedalism of Christianity — its tendency to formulate sets of beliefs and to
insist that all Christians affirm them — is a later development growing out
of controversies about what it means to be a Christian, controversies that
continue to our day.

Some have plausibly suggested that the act of faith that accomplishes
salvation in the Christian movement is not just giving intellectual assent to
a set of teachings, but giving loyalty — that is, giving one's life commitment —
to Jesus himself. An often-quoted verse from the Gospel of John says:

> God so loved the world that he gave his only Son, that whoever
> believes in him should not perish but have eternal life. . . . He who
> believes in him is not condemned; he who does not believe is con-
> demned already, because he has not believed in the name of the only
> Son of God.[13]

And a verse in the book of Acts suggests that salvation can be obtained in
no other way than through believing in Jesus: "There is salvation in no one
else, for there is no other name under heaven given among men by which
we must be saved."[14] Such a teaching is easier to understand if we understand that the disciples of Jesus claimed that Jesus was the messiah while
most of their contemporaries, particularly the Jewish authorities, rejected
the claim. Perhaps, among the very early advocates of Christianity, the
condition thought necessary to achieving salvation was to believe in
Jesus — that is, to believe that Jesus was the messiah, and to commit oneself
to follow him. Some modern interpreters of Christianity have made a similar suggestion: No body of beliefs taught by Jesus makes up the revelation
he mediated; rather, Jesus himself is the revelation. This claim implies a
substantial body of theology about the divine nature of Jesus and about the
meaning of his death and resurrection, doctrines that were not explicitly
worked out until much later.

Jesus lived and preached in a Palestine that was ruled by the Roman
Empire, a Palestine charged equally with resentment against Rome and
with keen messianic expectations that have been interpreted in a wide
variety of ways. Jesus' own life seems to have lasted from around the year
4 B.C.E.[15] until he was executed on charges of insurrection and claiming to
be a king sometime around C.E. 28–30. The Gospels offer details about

only a few years of his adult life. By far the largest portion of the Gospels concerns the last weeks of Jesus' life, leading up to the crucifixion and resurrection, events regarded as the key to the whole Christian phenomenon. But the Gospels also describe a public ministry of perhaps two or three years, beginning with Jesus' baptism by John the Baptist in the Jordan River. After a period of fasting and reflecting on the nature of his mission, Jesus travels the country preaching, teaching, and performing wondrous signs such as healing the sick, casting out demons, and changing water into wine.

During this period many disciples followed Jesus, but twelve were called to be his closest associates. Jesus seems to have struggled to deflect militaristic messianic expectations that certain persons wanted to fasten on him, teaching his disciples that his ministry was one of sacrifice and suffering and claiming at his trial before Pontius Pilate that his own kingdom was not of this world. Responsibility for his arrest and execution has often been placed on the Jewish leaders as the historical excuse for Christian persecution of Jews. In fact, Roman soldiers arrested him, led him before both the Jewish high court, the Sanhedrin, and the Roman authorities, and carried out his crucifixion. Jesus died and was buried on a Friday. By Sunday, according to the Gospel accounts, the tomb was found empty and his disciples were proclaiming that he was resurrected from the dead. The Gospels describe several postresurrection appearances by Jesus, culminating in his command to his disciples to go into the world and make disciples of all persons and then his ascent into heaven.

The disciples were so stunned by the turn of events resulting in Jesus' death that at first they contemplated returning to their old vocations, abandoning the movement. But on Pentecost, the fiftieth day after Jesus' crucifixion, they gathered in Jerusalem and began boldly preaching that Jesus, who had been crucified, was alive and the messiah of a spiritual kingdom. The resurrection proved that Jesus was Lord over death; those who believed in him would similarly be resurrected to everlasting life and bliss.

The conversion of Paul, a Pharisee who had previously opposed the Christian movement, marked the beginning of a rapid spread of the religion beyond Palestine and to non-Jews. Paul was not only an extraordinarily effective evangelist, able to persuade and convert great numbers of persons, he was also an enthusiastic theologian. Paul took the simple and unsystemized sayings of Jesus, blended them with ideas from Greek philosophy, and developed them into a complex, sophisticated, tightly argued theology — one that Jesus probably would not have recognized as his own. The beliefs that eventually became prescriptive creeds of Christianity are thus at least as much the fruit of Paul's as they are of Jesus' thinking.

Interpreting the death of Jesus as part of Yahweh's divine plan to save his lost people, Paul expounded the doctrine of **original sin** — the claim, namely, that through the sin of Adam, our first parent, all humankind lost the image of God in which we had been created. Through Adam's disobedience, all children of Adam became lost sinners, estranged from God. Paul called Jesus the second Adam, the person who made right what Adam had made wrong. He said that just as Adam's sin made us all sinners, Jesus' righteousness, and especially his redemptive sacrifice, on our behalf made us all children of God. Jesus took on himself, perfect and without sin as he was, the punishment that each human deserved because of Adam's and our own individual sins, and paid the price to free humankind from the condemnation that was our heritage from Adam.[16]

The Greek and Roman world of Jesus' day was a sort of religious vacuum in which many yearned for something to replace the pagan religions that they no longer found credible. The promise of resurrection and everlasting life was a powerful appeal not to the Jews, but to the Gentiles. The Jews had a religion they found satisfactory and thus they rejected Christianity. The Gentiles were ripe for a new religion, and so Christianity spread rapidly among them. There were periods of official persecution by Rome, but within 300 years the new faith had seeped upward through the levels of society until it reached the imperial palace. The emperor Constantine was baptized on his deathbed, and in the fourth century the emperor Theodosius made Christianity the official religion of the empire.

The destiny of the Christian church was determined by many political, economic, and social circumstances having nothing to do with the intrinsic nature of the religion itself. The decline and fall of Rome left a power vacuum that the church moved shrewdly to fill. As it consolidated its power, the church was also busy solidifying its theology, stamping out a number of teachings it labeled heresies. An early statement of the essentials of the faith, called the **Apostles' Creed** though it almost certainly dates from no earlier than the third century, affirmed the trinitarian nature of God; the virgin birth; the resurrection, ascension into heaven, and expected second coming of Jesus; and the forgiveness, resurrection, and eternal life of Christians. To settle early controversies focused on the exact status of Jesus, the Church finally declared him to be "of the same substance" as God, an inseparable part of the trinitarian nature of God along with the Father and the Holy Ghost. The **doctrine of the Trinity** is a mystery beyond rational understanding: There is only one God, supreme and eternal, who nevertheless exists in three persons, Father, Son, and Holy Ghost. And Jesus, the Christ, is to be considered fully and completely human, yet at the same time fully and completely divine.

The vague statements about the forgiveness of human sin and the attainment of salvation through faith in the name of Jesus came to be elaborated into detailed doctrines. A system of seven **sacraments**, or sacred rituals, was developed to cover every aspect of human life: (1) *Baptism*, usually administered in infancy, removes original sin and initiates the individual into the church; (2) *Eucharist*, the holy meal in which it was said that the bread actually changed into the body of Christ and the wine into his blood, confers on the individual the saving power of Christ by reenacting the sacrifice by which Christ paid for human sin; (3) *confirmation* marks the attainment of adulthood and entitles the teenager to begin to participate in the eucharist; (4) *penance* is the confession of actual sins; the priest offers absolution, often prescribing penitent acts such as saying prayers, lighting candles, or making an offering; (5) *marriage* gives the blessing of the Church to the formation of a new family; (6) *unction*, or anointing of the sick, is a sacrament of healing usually reserved for the gravely ill to prepare them for death; and (7) *holy orders* is the sacrament whereby individuals are set aside and ordained as priests.

The long history of Christianity has witnessed the splintering of the church into many separate bodies that differ on issues of doctrine, the nature of the sacraments, the status of the clergy, and the authority of church administrators. The earliest major division took place between the Western church, administered by the bishop of Rome, and the Eastern church, which developed no centralized focus of power. The occasion of this split was the moving of the administrative headquarters of the Roman empire under Constantine from Rome to Byzantium (renamed Constantinople) as the empire began to fall apart. The single most significant split in Christianity, however, came in the sixteenth century, when a monk named Martin Luther enunciated a long list of charges of corruption against the Church and precipitated what came to be called the **Protestant Reformation**. Luther objected to the use of the sacraments for raising money in the Church and many other corrupt practices. He asserted that a direct relation existed between Christian individuals and God without the need of the Church to mediate. Salvation is achieved by faith in Christ, he insisted, not by the good works of penance that the Church had increasingly imposed.

The outcome of this challenge to the sole authority of what now came to be called the **Roman Catholic Church** was the formation of many churches independent of Rome and of one another. By the twentieth century there were several hundred such independent Christian churches, each offering its own theology and method for attaining salvation. Some consist of only one or a handful of local congregations with only a few hundred members; others are worldwide organizations with thousands of local congregations and millions of members. Of all these, the Roman Catholic Church remains by far the largest. The number of active participants (in contrast to nominal members) in the various churches is impossible to ascertain, however; even the claim that Christianity is by far the largest religion in the world may not be justified for reasons of inaccuracy of counting.

Because Christianity has practiced vigorous missionary activities with concentrated efforts to persuade persons to convert, it has become a worldwide religion represented on every continent and in virtually every country of the world. Its splintering into branches introduced so much variety, however, that, as with Buddhism and Hinduism, there is some justification for saying that Christianity has become a cluster of similar religions rather than a single religion. Because the notion of right beliefs has been held to be of such importance in this religion, many branches insist that they alone are the true Church, often claiming that salvation is to be attained not just by believing in Christ, but by following their own specific prescriptions. Some effort has been made through the ecumenical movement to reverse the effects of splintering, and there have been a few mergers of Protestant denominations, but attempts to unite the larger branches continue to be frustrated by inflexibility on the points of difference in theology, church polity, ecclesiastical authority, sacramental practice, and numerous other matters.

The rapid expansion experienced by the various branches of the Christian church in the nineteenth century, when so many were engaged in active missionary programs, has slowed and stopped during the late twentieth century, and many denominations are experiencing a decline. This is true in the Western nations, where Christianity has long been the dominant religion; it is also true in the developing nations, where nationalistic feeling brings with it a resurgence of the ancient indigenous religions, although Christianity continues to grow in Africa. Heady aspirations enunciated by certain Christian denominations during the nineteenth century to convert the whole world to Christ in the next hundred years are rarely heard today. Even those groups still engaged in concerted missionary efforts seem to concede that for many years to come Christianity will be one among many other religions and will not soon be able to "save the world."

Islam: No God But Allah; Muhammad the Final Prophet

The great prophet of Allah rose from beginnings nearly as obscure as those of Jesus and during a short ministry of about twenty years laid the foundation for the very rapid spread of a new faith. **Muhammad** was born around the year C.E. 570, the son of Abdallah, a minor official in charge of the pilgrimage shrine at Mecca. An admirer of the monotheism of the Jews and the literary foundation of their religion in a great book of scripture, Muhammad dictated the material that became the holy book of Islam as a result of a series of revelation experiences he had beginning in C.E. 609, making the oneness of God the key concept.

Whereas Christianity is a direct offspring of Judaism, the relationship of **Islam** to its predecessor religions, Judaism and Christianity, is more indirect. Unlike Jesus, Muhammad was not himself a Jew, and neither were his early disciples. And yet Jews of the Diaspora, some displaced as early as the exile of 586 B.C.E., others fleeing the Roman repressions of C.E. 70 and C.E. 135, lived in many parts of the Arabian peninsula. There were several Jewish desert tribes, and there were communities of Jews living in such oasis towns as Mecca and Yathrib (later known as Medina). Muhammad and his early followers admired the strict monotheism of the Jews, which contrasted sharply with the polytheism and idolatry of the indigenous desert peoples. They were also impressed by the fact that the Jews had a great book that contained the record of divine dealings with humankind.

The Christianity to which Muhammad and his associates were most directly exposed in the seventh century was engaged in fierce theological controversy over the status of Jesus. The Christian doctrine of the Trinity was still being worked out; claims about Jesus ranged from the notion that he was a human teacher or prophet, to the position that he was God incarnate, to the Gnostic claim that he was a spiritual being whose body was only an apparition. Jesus' followers declared that he was the Christ, but there was considerable disagreement about what that meant. To outsiders the religious doctrines of Christianity must have seemed very confused. Its teachings about the threefold nature of God made the religion appear polytheistic rather than monotheistic; and misunderstanding of the sacrament of Eucharist occasionally led to accusations that Christians practiced cannibalism, eating human flesh and drinking human blood.

Muhammad, however, regarded Christians as nonpagans because they believed in the God of Adam, Abraham, Moses, and Elijah — the God of the Jews — the same God more perfectly revealed to Muhammad. They were respected because they, too, were a "people of the book." According to Islam, though, both the Christians and the Jews were unfaithful to the message revealed to them from God. Muhammad proclaimed that **Allah** or God is one, the sovereign ruler of the entire universe, and that although Allah has revealed himself to other peoples, such as the Jews through their patriarchs and prophets and the Christians through John the Baptist, Mary the Mother of Jesus, and Jesus, only through the Koran or **Qur'an**, the holy scriptures mediated by the last prophet Muhammad, is Allah made perfectly known to humankind. Because Jews and Christians had already received a portion of God's message, Muhammad expected that they would readily respond to his teachings. The fact that they did not was explained as proof of the extent to which they had misunderstood the message revealed to them. The Jews, already far adrift from the monotheism taught them by Abraham, failed to recognize and accept the new revelation mediated through Jesus. And the Christians distorted Jesus' message by claiming that he was divine, thus turning Christianity into a religion of three gods.

The Muslim calendar dates not from the birth or death of Muhammad, but from September 24, C.E. 622, the date when he moved from Mecca to Medina to assume the position of judge of that city. His journey is called *Hijrah* ("migration"); thus the years in the Muslim calendar are designated

"A.H." (*Anno Hegirae*). Islam uses a lunar calendar with twelve months, some with twenty-nine and some with thirty days. Days are added to the last month of the year at designated intervals to bring the lunar calendar more nearly into alignment with the solar calendar, but there is still a discrepancy of about three years in each century.

Mecca was already an important religious center and place of pilgrimage for the Arabs before the birth of Muhammad. A large black meteorite, fallen there at some time in the remote past, had become the object of religious veneration. The pre-Islamic Arabs were polytheistic and animistic in their religious life, worshipping images, trees, stones, wells, and animals. At some point long before the lifetime of Muhammad a square enclosure called the **Ka'bah** had been built around the meteorite, and over the years images and paintings representing the whole pantheon of Arab divinities accumulated in the shrine. Pilgrims came from all over Arabia to worship at the Ka'bah.

Muhammad was born into the clan at the time in control of the Ka'bah. His father died before he was born and his mother died when he was six years old. Reared by an uncle, Muhammad had no opportunity for formal education; he is said not even to have known how to read or write. He worked as a camel driver with caravans that traveled the trade routes all over Arabia and into neighboring regions. On these journeys Muhammad must have met Jews, Christians, and Zoroastrians and learned something of the teachings of these religions. At the age of twenty-five he married a wealthy widow named Khadija, owner of a camel caravan. She bore him six children, but only one daughter survived her father. Although the marriage brought wealth and opportunity for leisure to Muhammad, it was not just a marriage of convenience. Khadija was a strong supporter of Muhammad when he began to preach the new religion, and although they lived in a society where polygamy was more the rule than the exception, he did not take another wife as long as she lived.

Muhammad used his increased leisure to meditate on religious matters and became convinced that there is only one God supreme over all creation. He also became increasingly troubled about the religious behavior of his countrypersons, whose idolatry he believed must offend the one true God. During a period of reflection in a cave on a mountain near Mecca, he had a religious experience that he understood to be a visitation from an angel named Gabriel, bringing him a revelation from Allah.[17] From time to time during the remaining ten years of his life, he was visited by the angel and given more of the divine revelation. Muhammad memorized the message that, apparently, he was unable himself to write down and dictated it to a scribe, who wrote it for him. The resulting document is the Qur'an.

Muhammad recognized Allah as the God who had revealed himself through a series of prophets. He believed that the revelation comes from a book in heaven and was dictated to him so that it could also be written in a book available to humans. Earlier revelations to other peoples may have been incomplete, but they were just as much the word of God as that which Muhammad received. The Jews and Christians, however, were not careful to preserve what they received, and it had become corrupted. Muhammad became convinced that he was the last and greatest of the prophets bringing God's complete revelation in unspoiled form. Neither Muhammad nor his followers claimed that he, as Prophet, was divine; he was human like any other person. The revelation did not come from Muhammad; it only came *through* him. Once it was written and preserved correctly, there would be no need for any other prophet. Now all that was needed is to study, understand, believe, and live by the word of Allah as recorded in the Qur'an.

When Muhammad began to preach his message, he was very disappointed with the response. Contrary to his expectations, Jews and Christians did not accept the new teaching; the worshippers of the many gods did not take kindly to his declaration that they were idolators; and his condemnation of idol worship threatened to hurt the business of those who depended on pilgrims who came to Mecca to worship the idols. Thus there arose strong hostility against Muhammad and his followers. He attempted to move from Mecca to a nearby town but was not permitted to live there. News of his practical sagacity had reached leaders of several warring tribes in Yathrib, some 250 miles away, however, and they invited Muhammad to come to that city as an impartial judge. Active attempts on his life in Mecca made it necessary for his followers to leave a few at a time, and in secret. But on September 24, 622, Muhammad himself escaped from Mecca and migrated to the city that became known as **Medina**. Although his political work there was well received, his religious teachings at first were not. But slowly the Muslim numbers grew, and by 630 a force of about 10,000 attacked Mecca and took the city. Muhammad purified the Ka'bah, destroyed the idols, and made it the central shrine of his religion. He only lived two years after this cleansing of the Ka'bah.

According to the majority tradition in Islam, Muhammad died without designating a successor or making any arrangements for the leadership of the movement. According to the minority tradition, he did name a successor, but other followers took over, crowding out the person named by the Prophet. This dispute became the occasion for a major split of the religion into two branches, the Sunnis and the Shi'ites. The **Sunnis** believe the proper successor to Muhammad was his close friend **abu-Bakr**, whom the Prophet had appointed to lead the community in prayer. The **Shi'ites**, in contrast, insist that as he was returning from his farewell pilgrimage to Mecca shortly before his death, Muhammad stopped at a place called Ghadir al-Khumm because a revelation had come to him that he should designate **Ali**, his cousin who was also his son-in-law, as his successor. They cite a passage from the Qur'an allegedly spoken to Ali before all the people on that occasion by Muhammad, although Ali's name does not explicitly appear:

> O Messenger, deliver that which has been sent down to Thee from thy Lord; for if thou does not, thou wilt not have delivered the message. God will protect thee from the people of the unbelievers. [18]

In any case, abu-Bakr became the first *caliph* (literally, "deputy" or "representative") and two others followed him before Ali finally assumed the position, only to have it taken forcefully from him by those who made the caliphate into a kingly position by forming the dynasty of the Umayyads.

The split between Sunnis and Shi'ites grew into a significant theological difference within Islam. The Sunnis, who make up about 85 percent of all Muslims, consider themselves the orthodox of Islam. As Islam grew and spread, the Sunnis became divided into four schools of thought concerning the proper interpretation of the Qur'an.

The Shi'ites, who make up only about 14 percent of Muslims, take their name from the Arabic expression *Shi'at 'Ali* (literally, "faction or party in support of Ali"). They distrust the text of the Qur'an as it has been handed down, suspecting that it was altered from the original words delivered by Muhammad, particularly since it does not contain the name of Ali. They also believe that revelation did not end with Muhammad and the Qur'an but that other, later revelations took place. They believe also that a *madhi*, a figure like the Jewish messiah, will come some day to usher in an era of peace and justice. The Shi'ites look with distrust at the present world order and thus are stronger advocates of theocratic political arrangements in Moslem countries, with the Qur'an as the supreme document of law. They are more willing to accept suffering and even martyrdom for their faith because of a belief that the religious martyr goes directly to paradise, and to trust the leadership of an **Imam**, the head of a mosque, or an **ayatollah**, a high-ranking imam, not only on religious but also on political matters.

In the decades following Muhammad's death, Islam gathered momentum and spread with astonishing speed. Within a hundred years the religion had conquered Arabia, Palestine, Persia, Egypt and all of North Africa, and even Spain. Within the next few centuries it found its way into India, the islands of the Pacific, and China.

During a long period of time in the Middle Ages when Christian culture in Europe reached a very low ebb, Islamic culture flourished, producing great works of literature, philosophy, and art. For most of the twelfth century, the Christian crusaders did battle with the Muslims and took possession of the sacred sites in Jerusalem, and clashes continued for several hundred years. Then, as Europeans began shaking off the lethargy of their feudal economies, Muslim culture started to go into decline. While the West modernized and industrialized, the Muslim nations became less open to change and their economies remained largely preindustrial. In the twentieth century, the discovery of huge petroleum reserves in the Middle East brought great wealth to several nations and rapid industrialization to some, but the growth in power of the more conservative elements of Islam slowed the process of modernization.

As Islam has been brought dramatically into contact with the values, religious and cultural, of the Western world, it has issued several contradictory responses. On one hand, small reform movements have emerged promoting a scientific critical study of the Qur'an and the modernization of laws pertaining to such things as marriage and divorce and penalties for crimes. On the other hand, large conservative movements have urged a return to a strict, literal understanding of the Qur'an and its religious and moral requirements. An even more extreme fundamentalist movement has demanded that the Muslim nations be made into theocracies where the religious leaders make and enforce the laws in strict conformity with the literal teachings of the Qur'an. Because Islam has come to feel itself on the defensive, it has become generally more conservative, entrenched, inflexible — and, at the same time, more aggressive. A conspicuous example of the resurgence of Islam is its forceful missionary activity in Africa.

The word *Muslim* literally means "submitter," that is to say, one who submits to the will of Allah. The central doctrines, the so-called **five pillars of Islam**, summarize the most important ways in which Muslims express their submission to Allah. The first is the creed or *shahadah*[19] recited frequently every day by every believer: "There is no God but Allah; Muhammad is the Prophet of Allah." The recitation of this affirmation is an act of merit for a Muslim.

The second pillar is *salah*, the daily prayers. At five designated times each day Muslim men (women are excluded from this rite) are expected to perform rites of purification — washing face, hands, and feet — and to prostrate themselves facing toward Mecca, touching the forehead to the ground as they pray. In Muslim towns and villages a man called a *muezzin* climbs to the minaret of the mosque or to some other high place, such as the roof of a house, and cries out loudly to all within hearing that it is time for prayer. The proper times are at dawn, noon, mid-afternoon, sunset, and dusk. Prayers can be said anywhere, wherever the Muslim happens to be when the time of prayer comes, except that on Friday, the holy day of Islam, the noon prayers should be said in concert with the community of Muslims in a mosque (the word *mosque* means literally "place of prostration"). Noon prayers in the mosque on Friday are usually accompanied by a sermon delivered by the imam, the person who also coordinates the prayer ritual.

The third pillar of Islam is the *sawm*, or fast, that takes place during **Ramadan**, the ninth month of the Muslim calendar, the month when Muhammad received his first revelation. For the entire month, Muslims whose health permits it are expected to refrain from all food, drink, and sexual activity during the daylight hours, from the first light of morning until darkness falls in the evening. Because the lunar Muslim calendar does not match the solar calendar, Ramadan occurs at various times of the year. When it occurs during the time when the daylight hours are the very longest, it becomes an occasion of substantial sacrifice and self-discipline, particularly in parts of the world that are very hot and dry. Ramadan is supposed to be a time when the power of the spirit over the demands of the flesh is cultivated, and the degree of one's devotion to Allah is tested. The believer is permitted to take food and drink before dawn in the morning and after dark in the evening, but none during the hours of light. When the month has ended, there is a period of feasting and thanksgiving.

The fourth pillar is *zakah*, or almsgiving. All Muslims are expected to give of their material wealth or possessions for causes of charity and to support the growth of the faith. The Qur'an mentions gifts of charity to parents, kinsmen, orphans, the needy, and travelers. From the very beginning the Islamic states have regarded almsgiving as a duty that is more than voluntary and have expected a designated proportion of all personal wealth to be collected and then distributed for the stipulated purposes.

The fifth pillar is the *hajj*, or pilgrimage to Mecca. We have already noted that Mecca was a place of religious pilgrimage from very early times. Muhammad reinterpreted the meaning of pilgrimage, setting it in the context of an account of the significance of the great black stone and the Ka'bah. The stone was said to have fallen to earth during the time of Adam,[20] the first human and first Prophet of Judaism, according to Muhammad. Islam teaches that the Arabs are descendents of Abraham through his son Ishmael, as the Jews are descendents of Abraham through his son Isaac. The Hebrew Bible tells how Sarah, when she finally succeeded in bearing a child, persuaded Abraham to send the concubine, Hagar, and her son Ishmael away. Muslims believe that Hagar and Ishmael went to Mecca and that in later years Abraham visited them there. On this visit, according to the account, Abraham built the Ka'bah around the sacred stone.

The pilgrimage involves specific ritual acts performed at the mosque where the Ka'bah is located and at several other holy sites. Pilgrims are required to wear garments consisting of plain white or black cloth, allegedly so that differences in wealth or station that ordinary clothing might reveal can be left behind in a ritual of equality and unity. Every Muslim who has the means is expected to make the *hajj* at least once in a lifetime; so important is this religious duty that every pilgrim who has accomplished the pilgrimage adds the word *hajj* to his or her name.

In addition to the five pillars, there are other duties expected of Muslims. Like Jews, they are forbidden to eat pork; unlike Jews, they are forbidden to drink intoxicants. Gambling is also forbidden. One of the most troublesome and controversial duties is the **jihad**, the holy war. It is an obligation connected with the protection of Islam, and sometimes with the propagation of the religion and the wiping out of the infidels. It is worth remembering, however, that Muslims are by no means the only group who have gone to war for the sake of their religion, nor the only ones who find in their scriptures justifications for acts of violence against persons of other faiths.

Because Islam has always taught that faith is more than merely an inward feeling and must be expressed in outward acts such as prayer and almsgiving, Muslims show less of a tendency to pursue a life of asceticism or contemplation. Nevertheless, a mystical movement did develop in Islam. The **Sufis** claim that the concerns of Muslims with political matters lead to a neglect of the simple life of the spirit. To reclaim the spiritual life and to realize union with Allah, the Sufis adopted many practices like those of mystics of other religions: self-discipline, poverty, and sometimes celibacy (*Sufi* means "woolen" and refers to a coarse robe, symbolizing poverty and renunciation of the world). The most conspicuous manifestation of Sufi mysticism is the *dervish* who spin round and round for hours in an effort to attain union with God.

EXCLUSIVIST CONQUEST OR INCLUSIVIST TRANSFORMATION?

John Hick uses an analogy to depict the confrontation of the many religions in the world during modern times. We have been, he says, like a "company of people marching down a long valley, singing our own songs, developing over the centuries our own stories and slogans"[21] without realizing that in other valleys beyond our surrounding hills other groups are doing the same thing. "But then one day they all come out into the same plain, the plain created by modern global communications, and see each other and wonder what to make of one another."[22]

In the previous sections of this chapter we have briefly listened to a few of the songs, stories, and slogans rising up from five of Hick's valleys. Now we stand on the plain where the five troops, and others, have converged. They continue singing their songs and shouting their slogans, and we confront a cacophony. Must it continue until one group has shouted the others down? Must we attempt to retreat into our separated valleys, where we don't hear or disturb one another? — but that is no longer really possible. Or is there some way that we can live together on the plain, talking to and not shouting at one another, singing in harmony rather than in discord?

For the devotees of these five religions the problem is an urgent, practical one. Indeed, it has an important impact on the lives of everyone, even those who attempt to remain aloof from religion, since religion drives the political, economic, and military relations of nation with nation everywhere in the world. In some nations, religion is an inseparable part of the political order; thus toleration of other religious points of view is in theory contrary to policy — when toleration occurs, it is inadvertent or by default.

Even in nations where separation of religion and politics is constitutionally
established, and thus toleration of all religions is official policy, religious
considerations nevertheless exert pressure on both internal and international practices. Many groups continue to sing their songs and shout their
slogans, some of them explicitly attempting to shout the others down.
Religious dialogue has sometimes been motivated by those practical considerations that have to do with the possibility of peace and freedom of
religion — that indeed may determine whether or not the human race
comes to a juncture of confrontation on which its very survival on earth
might hinge. The Catholic theologian Hans Küng has stated the message
very graphically: "There will be no peace among the peoples of this world
without peace among the world religions."[23]

These practical considerations concern philosophers of religion as
well, although, in our capacity as philosophers, we work primarily with
theoretical issues. Thus our central question here must be: How can we
understand and evaluate the cognitive content of the claims made by the
various religions? Are there criteria by which we may measure the contending claims and decide which religions are in some sense better, truer, more
adequate than others? And although as philosophers we must reason in as
disinterested a manner as possible and not with an eye on the practical
implications, nevertheless how we answer these theoretical questions, particularly if our answer is compelling and becomes widely known and accepted, may quite possibly influence the course of practical affairs.

Basil Mitchell (1917–   ) suggests that one way to approach the question is to regard their cognitive portions as world views or metaphysical
systems, comprehensive theories that attempt to integrate and explain human knowledge and experience in its entirety.[24] Certainly most of the
great religions do offer accounts, more or less well worked out, of reality as a
whole, of the mundane world of human affairs, and of the supermundane
dimension of reality in which this world and this life are presumed to be
grounded. Such world views are not alternatives to science nor competitors
with science, because science takes for its universe of discourse more limited regions of reality and restricts its attention to circumscribed areas of
the mundane only. An adequate world view would have to integrate into
itself the warranted findings of science and place these in the larger context
of a theory that treats reality comprehensively. It is plausible to regard the
cognitive aspects of the more fully developed religions as attempts to present at least the outlines of such an overarching world view.

Now the attempt to compare and evaluate such mammoth and un-
wieldy theories is notoriously difficult. This is the reason, in part, that the
great comprehensive philosophical theories continue to contend with one
another, none having succeeded in establishing itself as the most adequate
and crowding out the others. But the problem is not different in kind, only
in scope, from that posed by comprehensive scientific theories. In the field
of cosmology, for example, where theories attempt to account for the ori-

gin (if any) and comprehensive development of the whole physical universe throughout the entire stretch of time, several theories continue to contend with one another, none having been decisively established. The philosopher of science Thomas Kuhn (1922–   ) has argued that comprehensive scientific theories, or what he calls scientific paradigms, are not refuted but rather gradually come to be recognized as less and less satisfactory as more knowledge accumulates; eventually they are abandoned in favor of other paradigms that comprehend and explain the same phenomena in more satisfactory ways.[25] The standards of what counts as explaining in more satisfactory ways are vague, and there are no mechanical rules for applying these standards or deciding just when a scientific paradigm has outlived its usefulness. Yet gradually Ptolemaic gives way to Copernican and Einsteinian astronomy, the old biological viewpoint is replaced by Darwinian biology, and plate tectonics crowds out older explanatory schemes in geology.

If the cognitive portions of the great religions are to be regarded as world views, or what Stephen Pepper (1891–1972) called "world hypotheses,"[26] we can no more expect to show one of them to be decisively best and the others definitely mistaken or clearly inadequate than we can expect to do the same for metaphysical theories or even comprehensive scientific theories. But this fact does not need to drive us to the Wittgensteinian position, which holds that religious doctrines must be regarded as incommensurable, incapable of being compared or judged. What it means instead is that the criteria by which they can be compared and evaluated are more general and less decisive and that the conclusions they support are more a matter of considered and thoughtful judgment about which honest and justified disagreement is likely to continue. But even the conclusion that several religions satisfy most of the criteria about equally well, if that should be the outcome of our inquiry, should have the practical effect of enlarging our understanding and perhaps diminishing the mutual intolerance among religions.

Several thinkers have attempted to offer criteria and guidelines for comparing and evaluating comprehensive world views. Stephen Pepper suggests that one world hypothesis is relatively more adequate than another if it exceeds the other in scope and precision. By scope he means that it takes in, integrates, and explains a larger range and quantity of data; by precision he means that the explanation is less vague and more detailed.[27] William Wainwright offers a list of twelve criteria that metaphysical systems should meet if they are to be judged adequate:

> (1) The facts that the system explains must actually exist . . . (2) A good metaphysical system should be compatible with well-established facts and theories . . . (3) It must be logically consistent . . . (4) It shouldn't be "self-stultifying" . . . (5) Adequate metaphysical systems should be coherent . . . (6) Simpler systems are preferable to complex ones . . . (7) Good metaphysical systems should avoid ad hoc

hypotheses . . . (8) Metaphysical explanations should be precise . . .
(9) A system's scope is also important . . . (10) One should consider a
system's fruitfulness . . . (11) Good metaphysical systems provide illuminating explanations of the phenomena within their explanatory
range . . . (12) Philosophical theories should be judged by their effi-
cacy in the life-process of mankind.[28]

Everyone who discusses these issues agrees that there is no mechanical way
in which our criteria can be applied to the great religious systems so as to
arrive at the conclusion that a certain one is most adequate and the others
definitely less adequate. W. H. Walsh suggests that our evaluation of overarching world views might more fruitfully be conceived not as similar to
testing a simple logical syllogism for validity or testing some simple chemical substance in the laboratory, but rather as comparable with the way that
historians evaluate disparate accounts of a period of history or art critics
evaluate works of art.[29] We often find that a given historical period lends
itself to more than one interpretation. Of course, not just any interpretation will do; criteria do exist. Any satisfactory historical perspective on an
era must get its facts straight, present a coherent account, attempt to avoid
deliberate distortion or bias, and so on. But several accounts may satisfy the
criteria, and it may not be possible to say definitely that one is right and the
others wrong, or even that one is the most adequate. Similarly, there is
likely always to be room for reasonable disagreement about which painting
or poem is greater, or which critic's interpretation of an art movement is
most adequate. But again criteria exist, and room for justified disagreement
lies within limited parameters. Whether Monet is greater than Renoir or
the other way around is certainly a question about which reasonable and
well-informed persons may disagree; yet nearly everyone who is knowledgeable about art agrees that the French Impressionists are better than the
American Impressionists, and nearly every accomplished critic of poetry
agrees that William Blake is better than Edgar Guest.

If we apply Walsh's insight to the contending great world religions, we
may find room for reasonable disagreement, for example, about whether a
theistic religion such as Christianity or Islam provides a more satisfactory
account of ultimate reality than a nontheistic religion such as Theravada
Buddhism, or the other way around. There is likely to be much more widespread agreement, however, that polytheistic and animistic religions do
not provide satisfactory integrated accounts. And it seems likely that one
religion may be more adequate by one criterion and a different religion may
better satisfy another criterion. For example, Christianity may be subject
to the charge of inconsistency when it claims both that God, the compassionate creator and father of humankind, desires that all should be saved
and claims at the same time that salvation is to be attained only through
Jesus Christ — thus apparently cutting off a large proportion of the human
race who have never heard of Jesus Christ from salvation. Hinduism, on
the other hand, must be judged morally less adequate to the extent that it

persists in upholding a caste system, because rational morality discovers no human differences sufficient to justify caste or class discrimination. Both Christianity and Islam seem blameworthy to the extent that they make use of their scriptures to justify war and other acts of violence. It may well be that all but the fundamentalists of these various traditions would insist that such unsatisfactory features are not essential to their religion; that as the religious traditions grow and adapt to the demands of the global village, exclusivist salvific claims and religious justification of caste and gender discrimination, violence, and war can and must be left behind along with the outmoded prescientific statements about nature that also found their way into scriptures in an earlier era.

Both the **exclusivist** and the **inclusivist views** recognize that there are important differences in the teachings of the various world religions, although one approach tends to emphasize their differences and the other their affinities. William Abraham points out some of the differences:

> The world religions differ on matters of fundamental significance. They differ on whether God's will is made known in the Koran or the Bhagavad Gita or the Bible; they differ on whether God became incarnate in Jesus Christ; they differ on whether the divine reality is personal or non-personal; they differ on whether human beings become reincarnate on earth, and so on.[30]

Abraham's "and so on" could be continued at length. They differ in soteriology—how salvation or enlightenment or liberation is to be attained. They differ in eschatology—that the future holds or what the end of human history and the destiny of human individuals will be. They differ about questions of social justice—caste ranking or equality; equality or subjugation of women—and on and on. These are not small differences, and this fact gives plausibility to the claim that the traditions advocating them cannot all be right and that they cannot be reconciled. Because these differences are important, people hold very strong convictions about them that they do not surrender or compromise lightly. Such intellectual convictions, strengthened and bolstered by practical considerations, find expression in adamant affirmation of exclusive claims and often in harsh condemnations of opposing views. And the exclusivists have a point. Some claims do appear more reasonable than others, implying that the religious system with the most such reasonable claims has the strongest title to being considered "right."

Yet exclusivism at its worst becomes nearly as petulant as a pack of children each shouting, "My father is smarter than your father." Inclusivists emphasize the social and cultural context in which beliefs and practices arise to explain why they seemed proper within the tradition, and they insist that in changed circumstances some religions have shown themselves able to adapt and change. Besides, the inclusivists insist, religions show important similarities as well as differences, particularly if we are willing to probe beneath the surface to the fundamental issues. William James has suggested that all major religions agree about the reality of the unseen and that the unseen is the source of the significance of the seen. They all recognize that the mundane is not all there is: even naturalism, while denying anything supernatural, still recognizes, in the order of nature, a source of ideals and values worthy of an attitude of reverence. William Wainwright points to another area of agreement:

> There is a broad ethical consensus among the higher religions. All prize justice, loyalty, compassion, and so on. Furthermore, the faithful in these traditions embody these values. Devout Hindus, for example, are neither more nor less just, loyal, and compassionate than are devout Muslims or Christians.[31]

And even if the major religions teach differing paths to salvation, Hick argues that they are about equally successful in enabling their devotees to achieve it:

> If by salvation we mean a radical turning from self to the ultimate Reality that we Christians know as God, and thus a transformation of human existence from self-centeredness to Reality-centeredness, then so far as we can tell this takes place to about an equal extent within each of the great world faiths.[32]

Some thinkers go even further, offering interpretations that they claim show that concepts in one religion correspond to others in another religion, even when that correspondence does not at first appear obvious. As early as about C.E. 153, Justin Martyr taught such an idea through what has come to be known as *Logos theology*, based on the opening verses of the Gospel of John.

> In the beginning was the word [*Logos*] and the Word was with God, and the Word was God. He [i.e., the *Logos*] was in the beginning with God; all things were made through him. . . . In him was life and the life was the light of men. . . . And the Word became flesh and dwelt among us, full of grace and truth.[33]

Justin believed that the Word, or **Logos**, was an eternally existing divine being, or an aspect of God, that became incarnate in Jesus but that was also present in the work of the Hebrew prophets and the Greek philosophers. Contemporary theologians such as John Cobb give a wider interpretation of the doctrine, suggesting that the divine Logos is responsible for the revelations that occur in all the great world religions. The Logos is the Word of God; thus the same Logos speaks through the Bhagavad-Gita, the Bible, the Qur'an, etc.[34]

Cobb proposes an even more radical idea. He discusses the notion of the *bodhisattvas*, who, according to the Pure Land branch of Mahayana Buddhism, preside over other realms where humans may go for help on their path to *nirvana*. According to this Buddhist doctrine, it is by faith in

Amida, the best known of such *bodhisattvas*, and through his grace that persons achieve salvation or help on the path to enlightenment. Christianity teaches that humans achieve salvation by faith in Christ and through his grace. Drawing out the affinities of Amida and Christ, Cobb concludes that Amida *is* Christ: "The features of the totality of reality to which Pure Land Buddhists refer when they speak of Amida is the same as that to which Christians refer when we speak of Christ."[35]

The inclusivists take different positions about the implications of their view for the future of the great religions. Some, such as John Cobb, argue that the time for dialogue is past and the time has come for mutual transformation. Cobb believes that each of the religions has much to contribute to the others and to gain from them. In the process, a Christianity will evolve that is changed and made truer and better by incorporating insights offered by Buddhism and the other religions; similarly, these other religions will also be transformed and made better. The implicit suggestion, not fully elaborated, seems to be that eventually there might be just one religion, bringing together in a coherent whole the multiple revelations mediated by all the great traditions.

Vivekananda (1863–1902), the great nineteenth-century Hindu preacher of Advaita Vedanta and founder of missions in the West, was a strong advocate of religious dialogue and was eager to have the religions learn from one another. He was convinced that all the major religions are in touch with the same Ultimate Reality and simply express their experiences in differing ways because of the different cultural assumptions with which they begin. In Chapter 6 we cited his analogy of the lake and the different vessels: There is only one lake from which all the religions draw their water. The water is the same; it takes different shapes only because we carry it in different vessels. Vivekananda did not advocate the merging of all religions into one, however. He believed that each religion has a unique value, special insights, and spiritual and aesthetic contributions to make through its myths, art, and literature. Thus, though he advocated sharing and learning from one another so that we can all escape the naive assumption that ours is the only right way, he also urged that Christians remain Christians, but become better Christians through what they learn from Hindus, and vice versa.

One of the most thoughtful and persuasive inclusivists on the contemporary scene is John Hick. Hick illustrates his conviction that all religions are in touch with the one Reality through a retelling of the familiar story of the blind men and the elephant: Certainly the blind man who only felt the leg and thought an elephant was like a tree was in contact, however incompletely, with the same elephant as the one who only felt the trunk and thought that an elephant was like a snake. Hick also cites the distinction drawn by the German philosopher Immanuel Kant (1724–1804) between reality as it exists in itself apart from human thought (what Kant calls the "thing-in-itself") and the picture of reality we create in our minds as we attempt to express our experience of that reality (what Kant calls the "phe-nomenon").[36] Reality in all of its infinite fullness is beyond our complete comprehension; yet we confront it and it enters into our experience. This is particularly true in our religious experiences. My vision of this Reality does not fully match yours, because I see it with different eyes, with different expectations, with different preconceived ideas. But you and I could im-prove our understanding of that Reality if, instead of insisting that what we saw is all there is, we pool and share our visions, as the blind men might have done about the elephant.

Despite the discouraging persistence of religiously motivated conflict in the world, many inclusivist scholars are optimistic that religious dia-logue is beginning to bear fruit and will ultimately lead both to the transfor-mation of the religions themselves and to more cooperation and less strife. Hick notes that progress within the Christian tradition has been excruciat-ingly slow, but he believes that some softening of rigid attitudes and some increased openness among the various Christian groups have taken place. The philosophers and theologians of the world religions who are engaged in dialogue have made remarkable progress toward understanding, mutual re-spect, and even mutual transformation of religious beliefs. These changes are very slow in trickling down to the ordinary layperson in the church, mosque, temple, or synagogue. Practical considerations, indeed, are far more urgent than the theoretical; often real-life crises have been the instrument forcing reluctant, self-satisfied believers to rethink the theoretical foundations of their practices. But many times real-life crises serve only to harden atti-tudes so that minds are even more closed to any consideration of other views. The religions are out on the plain and there is no turning back to the isolation of our separate valleys. There is much cacophony; there is also a little harmony. What the future holds is perhaps known only to the gods.

It is time now to turn to the impact religious belief and disbelief have on human happiness and the quest for a meaningful life. Questions of this sort, after all, give more than just a theoretical importance to the work of philosophers of religion. In every age some have found a good life apart from religion, but certainly religion has been the source of meaning and hope for great numbers of persons in every era of human history. These are the issues that we must examine in the closing chapter.

ANNOTATED GUIDE TO FURTHER READINGS

The Religions

Ellwood, Robert S., and Wiggins, James B. *Christianity: A Cultural Perspective.* Englewood Cliffs, N.J.: Prentice-Hall, 1988.

Reads easily, almost like a story at times, and offers a good exposure to the basic principles of Christianity, Christian society and culture.

Hopfe, Lewis M. *Religions of the World*, 3rd ed. New York: Macmillan, 1983.

> *An excellent introductory text, with a chapter on each of the major religions. Of special interest to some may be specific chapters devoted entirely to Native American religions and African religions. Includes excerpts from the scriptures of each religion.*

Jacobson, Nolan Pliny. *Understanding Buddhism.* Carbondale, Ill.: Southern Illinois University Press, 1986.

> *Relates Buddhism to Western philosophical thought, combining a scholarly presentation of the basic facts of Buddhism with a lucid writing style that transcends these facts.*

Martin, Richard C. *Islam: A Cultural Perspective.* Englewood Cliffs, N.J.: Prentice-Hall, 1982.

> *A useful introductory text that deals with more than just the basic principles of Islam; examines life within the Muslim culture, art, and the Islamic community.*

Morgan, Kenneth W., ed. *The Religion of the Hindus.* New York: The Ronald Press, 1953.

> *Six chapters, each written by a different Indian scholar, provide the reader with a good introduction to the Hindu religion. Also contains selections from the Hindu scriptures.*

Neusner, Jacob. *From Testament to Torah: An Introduction to Judaism in Its Formative Age.* Englewood Cliffs, N.J.: Prentice-Hall, 1988.

> *The focus is basically historical, namely, three pivotal stages in the history of Judaism: the fall of the temple of Jerusalem, the fall of the second temple of Jerusalem, and Constantine's Christianization of Rome.*

Noss, David S., and Noss, John B. *Man's Religions*, 7th ed. New York: Macmillan, 1984.

> *A basic resource in the study of religion, this text is notable for its extensive use of primary sources. Focuses on Buddhism, Christianity, Confucianism, Hinduism, Islam, Jainism, Judaism, Shinto, Sikhism, Taoism, and Zoroastrianism.*

Comparative

Cobb, John B., Jr. *Beyond Dialogue.* Philadelphia: Fortress Press, 1982.

> *Through dialogue the differing world religions can transform one another. Cobb focuses on the interaction between Christianity and Buddhism.*

Dharmasiri, Gunapala. *A Buddhist Critique of the Christian Concept of God.* Antioch, Calif.: Golden Leaves, 1988.

> *A valuable resource for the Western reader because of its Eastern point of view. The author considers the Christian religion to be primitive, perhaps even dangerous. Dharmasiri feels strongly that we must not blindly surrender our individual freedom to the self-proclaimed authority of religion.*

Hick, John, and Meltzer, Edmund S., eds. *Three Faiths: One God.* Albany: State University of New York Press, 1989.

An interpretation of the common heritage of Judaism, Christianity, and Islam including chapters on God, the world, and humankind by major thinkers from the three religions.

Oxtoby, Willard G. *The Meaning of Other Faiths.* Philadelphia: Westminster Press, 1983.

Provides a useful basic discussion of the relationship of the world religions. Oxtoby, coming from a Christian background, examines his faith's view of other religions from both historical and contemporary perspectives.

Peters, F. E. *Children of Abraham.* Princeton, N.J.: Princeton University Press, 1982.

Islam, Judaism, and Christianity have a special relationship with one another because they share a common ancestry. Peters examines the link between these three great world religions by comparing their scriptures, traditions, and theologies.

Smart, Ninian. *A Dialogue of Religions.* London: SCM Press, 1960.

An original and interesting work. Smart adopts the format of a dialogue in which characters from the world religions address one another and discuss such topics as revelation, rebirth, and theism.

Smith, Wilfred Cantwell. *Towards a World Theology.* Philadelphia: Westminster Press, 1981.

Focuses on the historical aspect of the religions of Christianity, Judaism, Islam, Hinduism, and Buddhism, emphasizing the unity rather than the separateness of humankind's religious life.

NOTES

1. See, for example, John B. Noss and David S. Noss, *Man's Religions,* 7th ed. (New York: Macmillan, 1949, 1980); Lewis M. Hopfe, *Religions of the World,* 3rd ed. (New York: Macmillan, 1983), and Niels C. Nielsen, Jr., et al., *Religions of the World* (New York: St. Martin's Press, 1988).

2. See, for example, David Kingsley, *Hinduism* (Englewood Cliffs, N.J.: Prentice-Hall, 1982), pp. 82–104.

3. *Early Buddhist Scriptures,* translated by E. J. Thomas (London: Kegan, Paul, Trench, Trubner & Co., 1935), pp. 29f.

4. The Hebrew text contains only the consonants, which are transliterated into English as YHWH. The vowels were omitted probably because the divine name was considered to be too holy to pronounce. In many translations, the word "LORD" is used when YHWH occurs in the text.

5. Much effort has been devoted to the task of ascertaining the earliest Gospel and the dates of their writing. The matter is far from settled; some scholars argue that Mark is the latest rather than the earliest Gospel.

6. Matthew, Mark, and Luke are referred to as the *synoptic Gospels* (synoptic means "to see together") because their account of Jesus' life and teachings are fairly similar, whereas the picture presented in the Gospel of John is rather different.

7. See Albert Schweitzer, *The Quest of the Historical Jesus* (London: Adam and Clark Black, 1910).

8. The Septuagent is a translation of the Hebrew Bible into Greek undertaken in Alexandria in the third century B.C.E. for the benefit of Jews of the Diaspora who no longer understood Hebrew.

9. Mark 2:27.

10. Matthew 5:17–19.

11. Matthew 5:38–40, 48.

12. Matthew 22:37–40. Jesus is quoting the first great commandment from Deuteronomy 6:5 and the second from Leviticus 19:18.

13. John 3:16, 18.

14. Acts 4:12.

15. If he was born, as Gospel passages suggest, during the reign of Herod, his birthdate could be no later than 4 B.C.E., the year that Herod died.

16. These doctrines are set forth particularly in the Epistles of Romans and Galatians.

17. The Arabic word *Allah* is not like the Hebrew YHWH, or Yahweh, which is the name of God; rather, it seems to be linked linguistically to the Hebrew word *El*. Both words mean "God."

18. Qur'an 5:71.

19. The word *creed*, used by Christians, comes from the Latin *Credo*, meaning "I believe," the expression with which most Christian affirmations of faiths or declarations of belief, such as the Apostles' Creed or the Nicene Creed, begin. *Shahadah* means "to witness." Many verses in the Qur'an begin, "I witness": for example, "I witness that there is no Allah but Allah; Muhammad is the Prophet of Allah."

20. A different legend says that the stone was given to Abraham by the angel Gabriel and that it was originally white but has been blackened by the sins of humanity.

21. John Hick, *God Has Many Names* (Philadelphia: Westminster Press, 1982), p. 41.

22. Ibid.

23. Hans Küng et al., *Christianity and the World Religions* (Garden City, N.Y.: Doubleday, 1986), p. 443.

24. Basil Mitchell, *The Justification of Religious Belief* (London: Macmillan, 1973).

25. Thomas Kuhn, *The Structure of Scientific Revolutions*, 2nd ed. (Chicago: University of Chicago Press, 1970).

26. Stephen C. Pepper, *World Hypotheses* (Berkeley: University of California Press, 1961).

27. Ibid.

28. William J. Wainwright, *Philosophy of Religion* (Belmont, Calif.: Wadsworth, 1988), pp. 171ff. Wainwright attributes the twelfth criterion to Paul Tillich, *Systematic Theology* (Chicago: University of Chicago Press, 1951). The eighth and ninth criteria obviously come from Pepper, although Wainwright does not acknowledge that source.

29. W. H. Walsh, *Metaphysics* (London: Hutchinson University Library, 1963).

30. William J. Abraham, *An Introduction to the Philosophy of Religion* (Englewood Cliffs, N.J.: Prentice-Hall, 1985), p. 215.

31. Wainwright, *Philosophy of Religion*, p. 178.

32. John Hick, "Rethinking Christian Doctrine in the Light of Religious Pluralism," *IRF: A Newsletter of the International Religious Foundation* 3, 4 (Fall 1988): 2.

33. John 1:1, 3, 4, 14. Each time that "Word" appears capitalized in these verses, the Greek expression is *Logos*.

34. See, for example, John B. Cobb, Jr., *Beyond Dialogue: Toward a Mutual Transformation of Christianity and Buddhism* (Philadelphia: Fortress Press, 1982).

35. Ibid., p. 128.

36. John Hick, *God and the Universe of Faith* (London: Macmillan, 1977).

9

Religion and the Meaning of Life

Many might say that the meaning, significance, purpose, or value (if any) of human life is the big question, the one that takes precedence over all the others and gives them any point they may have. To be sure, from a cosmic perspective that question might seem small, even trivial. After all, humans are one species of animal life among millions of living organisms. We occupy one planet orbiting a relatively small star, one of billions in a galaxy that is itself one of countless numbers of galaxies scattered in a stretch of space and time so immense that no scale we can imagine would enable us to measure it in a way intelligible to us. So far as we know, life has appeared only on this microscopic speck called Earth, and only after long and tortuous paths of evolution has it reached a level of complexity that manifests consciousness and a propensity to ask questions about the origin of the universe, and the meaning, if any, of its own existence. The universe, we believe, has existed for some 18 billion years, but life itself has existed for only about 4 billion years, and humans for perhaps forty or fifty thousand. How can any phenomenon, so new, so rare, so very small on any scale of cosmic measurement, presume to claim that the most important question in the universe is why it is here and what its destiny will be?

Someone has remarked that even though from the point of view of astronomy, a human is a creature of no importance at all, from the point of view of astronomy, we humans are the astronomers. However trivial humans might seem to be in the total scheme of things, it appears that nothing else in existence — except God, if such a being exists — has even any notion that such a total scheme of things exists. Some argue, particularly those philosophers who call themselves personalists, that apart from God human persons are the only value-conscious and thus value-creating beings in the universe. Such thinkers insist that if the materialists are correct in their claim that everything which happens is the result of unplanned reshuffling of material substance, then there can be no source of worth or value anywhere except in the conscious experience of human persons. Where there is no consciousness, nothing has any meaning. If, of all the objects that exist, only humans have consciousness, then they are the source of all meaning and all worth — if, indeed, there is any. If there *is* another source of meaning, such as a deity, then whatever else that God may be, he must be at least a conscious being who is aware of values.

In this chapter we will examine a cluster of questions that relate to the concept of human existence and human destiny. Religion has been the source of meaning and hope for countless humans in every society and every era of human history. One of the most widespread traditional theories about the meaning of human life is the belief that each person is a part of a divine plan, a plan that holds not just for this life but for an unending life after death. Others have argued that the question of life after death is entirely irrelevant to the question of the meaning of life, and some have insisted that if meaning is to be found it need not, or perhaps even cannot, be through religion. In the twentieth century the claim that human existence is accidental, fortuitous, and therefore absurd and without meaning has been vigorously argued, particularly by the existentialists. Some have concluded, from this position, that life is therefore not worth living; others have insisted that even in the absence of an objective meaning, life can be meaningful and good.

We will look first at the phenomenon of death and the religious debate surrounding it. Then we will examine briefly the thought of two major existentialists on the meaning and value of human existence. We conclude with a brief look at some of the central teachings of the theologian Paul Tillich on what religion can contribute to understanding these issues and whether life even apart from religion can have meaning.

DEATH AND HUMAN DESTINY

Death has always been the ultimate human puzzle. Some have said that death is the father of the gods because it clamors for a supermundane explanation. Religion provides rituals to bless all the major transitions of life and theories to explain them, but the true stimulus for the creation of religion may have been the need to manage this final transition in particular. Archaeological evidence suggests that our most ancient ancestors buried their dead with ceremony, reverence, and the expectation that death was not the end. Until fairly recent times the belief seems to have been widespread that death is not a natural phenomenon but always the result of either accident or the evil designs of an enemy. It was a step forward when humans gradually came to realize that nearly every living thing dies naturally. Certain simple one-celled organisms may not have a natural life span and may die only through accident, but nearly all living things seem to have a built-in natural life span and for the most part die, as we say, of old age.

Yet to humans death does not seem just. Why should we die? Especially, why should *I* die? Every culture seems to have produced attempts to explain death and discover what we can do to escape it. In certain ancient cultures the mystery of death seems to have been answered in a tribal way; the person dies but the tribe lives on, and thus in some sense the dead person lives on in the tribe. In ancient Egypt life after death seems to have been the special privilege of the wealthy and powerful, who could afford to have their bodies made into mummies and buried with food and implements needed for the next life. But the rise of individualism — briefly in ancient Greece and Rome during the first several centuries before the Common Era, and not significantly again until around the sixteenth century in Europe and Britain — brought a new attitude toward death and the hereafter. Individualism suggests that the indignity of death as a final end for anyone of any rank is unacceptable. For individualism, grounded in egalitarian political notions and Protestant Reformation teachings about the direct access of each believer to God, teaches the ultimate importance or value of each individual. How, then, could a rational universe, especially how could a just and loving God, permit even one person to perish?

Modes of Survival

Among contemporary pretechnological societies we sometimes find vague beliefs about the survival of the dead in the form of ghosts that wander the earth, sometimes causing problems for those still alive. The ancient Greeks believed the dead survived only as shadows in a most undesirable place called Hades. Their dread of death was made worse because the dead were thought to be beings drained of all powers — not actively tortured as in medieval visions of the Christian Hell but formless, emptied of all good, wretched, and poor. The Hebrew Bible contains few references to survival after death, but there are occasional references to the ghost of a person going to a place called Sheol, a vision of human destiny resembling very much that of the Greeks. When the question of **immortality**, or surviving bodily death, came to be examined carefully by philosophers and theologians, the resulting doctrines have taken one of three major forms:

reincarnation of the soul in another earthly body; immortality of the disembodied soul; and resurrection of the body to rejoin a surviving soul.

Reincarnation.   The belief in the **reincarnation** of the human soul in a
newly born body has been fairly widespread, especially in the East. It is an
integral part of the Hindu tradition, and a somewhat similar belief is found
among Buddhists as well. In Hinduism belief in reincarnation is connected
with the doctrine of karma, which relates to a person's actions and the
fruits of those actions. According to this teaching, the station of the reincarnated person is determined by his or her behavior in the previous life. In
the context of the caste system, a person who has fulfilled faithfully his
caste duties in the previous life will be reincarnated in a higher caste in
the next.

Such a belief gains a measure of plausibility because it provides an
explanation of why some are born to a lowly station and others to a much
more privileged place. But are there strong reasons to accept it as true? The
most direct evidence offered in support of reincarnation consists of alleged
memories of previous lives. Certainly most persons do not remember having lived before this life — and the lack of continuity in memory from a
previous life is a serious argument against the theory. But a few do claim
such memories. Perhaps the most interesting examples are children who
spontaneously begin to talk of the events they seem to remember from a
previous life. In India and other Asian countries it has been reported that
certain children claim to remember having experienced events independently verified to have happened a few years before the children were born.
Carefully controlled studies, however, would be necessary to authenticate
such cases and rule out the possibility that the children had heard the
details they relate during this life. More impressive are cases where children are alleged to recite lengthy and complex passages of scripture in an
ancient language such as Sanskrit or Pali, material they are very unlikely to
have been capable of learning during their childhood. But the reports remain to be fully studied and documented; anecdotal accounts do not provide very strong proofs.

A different kind of argument for reincarnation has been offered by
such Western philosophers as Plato. It is based on the distinction between
two different kinds of knowledge and the way in which individuals learn
them. Much of our knowledge is acquired through our senses by observing,
measuring, counting, keeping records, and finally drawing conclusions.
All such knowledge is fallible; we never can be sure that further observation will not force us to modify the conclusion we reached. For example, we
might conclude after extensive observation that birds are flying animals
until we encounter an ostrich, which is surely a bird but not a flying one.

Consider, however, a different kind of knowledge and how we acquire
it. The teacher shows the young school child two pencils and then two

more and points out that together they make four. Then she points to two chairs and two more and observes that together they make four. Very quickly the child's mind will make what seems to be an infinite leap and recognize that two of anything added to two more will always make four. There is no need for tedious observation of hundreds of examples. Furthermore, once we understand the principle of arithmetic, we believe it with total conviction. We see that there is no possibility of coming across an exception that will require revising the belief, as happened with the ostrich. How is such a thing possible? Plato suggests that before we were incarnate in this body we have all lived in another realm where such truths as $2 + 2 = 4$ were apprehended directly by the soul. When we are reincarnated, we may not immediately recall these principles; as soon as something happens to bring them to mind, however, we know them with absolute conviction, because we have experienced them before.

The reincarnation theory, though, might not be the only possible explanation for this phenomenon. Humans may possess a faculty of intuition or reason that enables them to grasp such things quickly and discern that knowledge acquired in this way is not empirical — that is, it is not dependent on accumulating many sense observations, but rather on seeing the necessary relations between numbers or other concepts.

Reincarnation also raises the problem of personal identity (discussed as a separate topic later in this chapter), a problem involved with each of these modes of alleged survival after death. How can we be sure that someone now alive is the same person as one who lived and died before? If everyone or nearly everyone had distinct memories of a previous life, that might constitute sufficient reason to believe in reincarnation. But most people do not, and even those few who claim to have such memories might be mistaken, their claims having not been carefully documented. Without demonstrated continuity of some sort, reincarnation remains an interesting hypothesis that may perhaps be true but that falls very short of established.

Immortality of the Disembodied Soul. Reincarnation theories sometimes involve the claim that the ultimate objective of human life is to escape the ongoing process of reincarnation. Hindus seek to escape reincarnation and achieve *nirvana*, which means extinction. Some interpretations teach that when this much-to-be-desired state is reached, the person ceases to exist as a separate entity, like a drop of water that returns to the ocean. What was separate ceases to be separate and dissolves again into the great unity of Being itself. We might call this a form of immortality — the drop of water, and the soul, do not cease to exist altogether — but it is certainly not individual immortality. The person ceases to exist as a differentiated unity of consciousness and experience, and this is not what is usually meant by the immortality of the disembodied soul.

Dualistic theories in Western philosophy have asserted that a human individual consists of two kinds of things, a material body and a spiritual soul. Both Plato and Descartes taught such a dualism. Plato, however, believed that the human soul existed before its incarnation in its present body — indeed, that it might go through many reincarnations before it achieved its final immortality apart from the body — whereas Descartes believed that the soul began to exist when its present body came into being but would continue to exist disembodied after the body died. (It is not clear the extent to which Descartes had in mind the Christian doctrine of resurrection; he may have believed, as Christian theology suggests, that the soul lives on in a resurrected and transformed spiritual body.) Plato regarded the body as the prison house of the soul, weighing it down and limiting its rational and intellectual powers. Thus the desired consummation of human existence seems to be to shed the body permanently, thereby freeing the intellect from its material burden and enabling it to function to its fullest.

The principal argument Plato offered to support the belief that the soul continues to exist after the death of the body is a response to an argument put forward by the Greek materialists against survival. The atomists of ancient Greece regarded the soul as a material substance that occupied the body during life but streamed out and dispersed like a vapor after the body died. Plato argued that the only way in which something can be destroyed is for it to be broken up into its parts. This is what happens to the body: When the body dies, the chemicals it consists of disperse and find their way into other things. But this dissolution cannot happen to the soul, Plato maintained, because the soul does not consist of parts. The soul is simple, unitary, self-identical, and therefore incapable of being dissolved. Thus the very essence of the disembodied soul is immortality. This theory raises very difficult problems about personal identity, but we will wait until the next section to address them.

It is easy to see, with Plato and Descartes, that the soul (if it exists) is something very different from the body. The body occupies space; it is located in a specific place at a specific time and can move from place to place; it has a certain size and shape and weight. None of these things can sensibly be said of soul. We may say that the body weighs 62 kilograms, but how much does the soul weigh? The question makes no sense at all. The concept of the soul involves something that does not occupy space, that has no size or shape or weight. And although we can speak of losing parts of one's body, such as a leg or an arm, it makes no sense to speak of losing part of one's soul. The soul seems to be an all or nothing affair, and this is just Plato's point. Although the soul contains many thoughts, feelings, beliefs, desires, and the like, it does not *consist* of these things. The soul may acquire new beliefs and lose old ones, but it remains the same soul. Since the destruction of anything consists of dissolving it into its component parts, and the soul has no parts, it follows that the soul cannot be dissolved. Thus it must be immortal.

Many have found the assumptions of this argument to be implausible. The dualism on which it depends has resulted in some of the most intractable problems in modern philosophy since Descartes put that theory forward so forcefully in the seventeenth century. Dualism may allow us to formulate a theory about immortality, since it explains how body and soul can be separated, but how can we explain how these two radically different kinds of substance, material body and spiritual soul, can be connected or related in the same human being?

David Hume argues, on empirical grounds and contrary to Plato, that when we look into ourselves we do not observe a soul or anything else over and above our perceptions, thoughts, feelings, desires, and so on. Many people agree with Hume that we do not seem to have any convincing reason to believe that there is any such thing as the soul. Certainly psychology, that science which studies human individuals, has long since abandoned any notion of a soul as a substance existing over and above the body and the mental phenomena that accompany it and are now usually thought to be dependent on it. Most of the widely accepted theories in the philosophy of mind today deny that soul or mind is an entity. For example, behaviorism regards mental terms — such as belief, attitude, thought, decision, changing one's mind, and so on — as a function of behavior, activity of the body, or predispositions to behave in certain ways. Central state materialism regards mind or soul as a function or an epiphenomenon of the brain, supervenient on certain brain processes. These theories clearly imply that there is no such thing as a soul that could in any sense survive the disintegration of the body (see the discussion of materialism in Chapter 5).

Finally, it can be argued that dissolving things into their component parts does not seem to be the only way in which they can cease to exist. Pain disappears apparently without being broken up into constituent parts; hopes disappear when their object fails. Even if there is a soul and even if it is unitary and does not consist of parts, there does not seem to be any necessary reason why it might not disappear or be annihilated. Immanuel Kant (1724–1804) argued that even if the soul is an immaterial substance with no extensive quantity and thus incapable of being destroyed by dissolution into parts, it still might have what he called intensive quality, which could be diminished in degree until it reached zero. For example, the soul is conscious, but its consciousness admits of degrees and might be reduced to zero. If this happened to all its qualities, the soul would have been destroyed. It may be admitted, then, that the notion of an individual soul, with memory, character traits, and personality intact, surviving the death of that body through which it acquired all its sensations and expressed all its desires and choices in this life may be intelligible — although some have argued that it is not. Moreover, such survival has not been shown to be impossible. The evidence, however, in its favor is at best inconclusive.

Resurrection.   The Christian teaching about what happens to the individual after death is the doctrine of the **resurrection** of the body. Platonic and Cartesian dualism has been so widespread that many Christians believe that their church teaches the immortality of the disembodied soul. That position, however, is significantly at variance with perhaps the central teaching of Christianity. The most important event in the history of the Christian religion, marked by Easter, the most important holiday, is the alleged resurrection of Jesus from the dead. It was the claim that Jesus had been resurrected that became the foundation of the teaching that death had been conquered. The insurmountable evidence that God can raise believers from the dead to everlasting life, so the early Christians taught, is the fact that God has raised Jesus.

The doctrine of the resurrection is based on a certain understanding of what it means to be human. In the context of the Jewish tradition of shades living on in Sheol and the popular Greek ideas of shadows of the deceased lingering in Hades, belief in a joyful future life as a disembodied soul seemed too incongruous to consider. The surviving ghosts were not complete persons precisely because they were disembodied. Meaningful life after death must involve the survival of the whole person, and that was thought to include survival of the body. But such a belief presented very serious problems. Death means the loss of the body; dead bodies decay and turn to dust. This was one reason that Egyptians believed it was vital to preserve the body as a mummy so that the next life could be a full one and not just a shadowy half existence. Not only does the body decay when it dies; it becomes weak, feeble, sick, dysfunctional when it ages. Surely everlasting life in a feeble and sickly body is not anything to rejoice about.

It fell to Paul, the convert to Christianity who had been reared as a Jewish Pharisee and who had been schooled in Greek philosophy, to work out the theology of resurrection. As a Pharisee, he already believed in resurrection even before he became a Christian. A resurrected life involving the complete person requires a body. To avoid the problem of a mortal, sickly, frail body, however, this has to be a transformed body. Paul construed Jesus as the new Adam who restored the condition that the first Adam had destroyed, and he introduced the paradoxical notion of a spiritual **resurrection body:**

> In fact Christ has been raised from the dead, the first fruits of those who have fallen asleep. For as by a man came death, by a man has come also the resurrection of the dead. For as in Adam all die, so also in Christ shall all be made alive. . . . What you sow does not come to life unless it dies. And what you sow is not the body which is to be, but a bare kernel, perhaps of wheat or of some other grain. But God

gives it a body as he has chosen. . . . So it is with the resurrection of the dead. What is sown is perishable, what is raised is imperish- able. . . . It is sown a physical body, it is raised a spiritual body. . . . When the perishable puts on the imperishable, and the mortal puts on immortality, then shall come to pass the saying that is written: "Death is swallowed up in victory." "Oh death, where is thy victory? O death where is thy sting?" . . . Thanks be to God, who gives us the victory through our Lord Jesus Christ.[1]

It is necessary, argues Paul, for the corruptible physical body to die and decay just as the seed corn dies and decays, so that from it may spring the new and transformed body that God gives. Clearly such a doctrine depends on its hearers' prior belief in God and their acceptance of the framework of the Judeo-Christian world perspective. Divorced from such an antecedent set of beliefs, claims of resurrection of the body have little rational appeal. If the theistic arguments have been found convincing and the divine per- fections plausible, then one would expect God to make provisions for the survival of living creatures beyond this life. A God who can create the universe and all that is in it, as Christian philosophy teaches, could surely sustain an individual human spirit and create a new body for it.

Personal Identity and Arguments for Survival

We have examined some of the arguments for and against surviving death. The central question about any kind of claim of survival involves **personal identity:** What does it mean to remain the same person through the great transition of death? A valid claim that a person has survived or may survive death requires that the surviving person be the same one as the person that died. We must look at the kinds of criteria available for establishing per- sonal identity.

Ordinarily, we use the criterion of bodily appearance to establish iden- tity. If I know a person well, I know what that person's body looks like. When I see a body that looks relevantly similar, I assume that it is the same body and thus the same person. There are times when this rule of thumb fails — as in the case of identical twins or persons we have not seen for many years. When bodily appearance fails, there are other tests we can call on. If an accident victim arrives at the hospital in a coma and unable to tell the doctors who she is, we may use dental records to establish that this is the body of Susan, and as soon as we have done so we say with complete confi- dence that this person is Susan. In other cases, we do not know quite what to say. Suppose an individual suffering from amnesia establishes a new identity over many years. When someone who knew the person before the loss of memory — a close relative, let us say — recognizes the person, is this truly the same person her cousin remembers from twenty years ago?

Our dilemma about the true identity of the amnesiac brings out another criterion we frequently use to establish personal identity, namely, *continuity* — of memory, character, and personality. I may soon realize that the person I am talking with is not my friend Robert, however much he may look like him, because he does not remember the trip Robert and I took together last month, and because the attitude he expresses toward big business or labor unions is entirely out of character for Robert. But if this other person, who does not look very familiar, remembers the details of the pranks Tom and I used to pull in college, and tells just the kind of jokes Tom used to tell, I am likely to conclude that the extra thirty pounds and the grey hair are not sufficient reason to doubt that this is really Tom.

Bodily appearances change, memories fade, personalities evolve, character can undergo radical transformation, but these criteria work fairly well within the confines of this life if we are in a position to apply them rigorously and to use both kinds. If we can establish not only that this body looks like that of my old friend Joe but that in fact it is spatially and temporally continuous with the friend I knew years ago; *and* if we can ascertain that this individual has memories, personality, and character traits that are similarly continuous with those of my old friend, then we can be confident that this is indeed old Joe.

If continuity of memory, personality, and character is essential to personal identity, reincarnation doctrines fail, but disembodied immortality might meet the test. If continuity of body is the essential factor, both disembodied immortality and reincarnation fail the test. At best, only a survival doctrine involving resurrection of the body could satisfy these two theories. Indeed, it would not be easy to justify the claim that this resurrected body was indeed the same body, even if it looked very much the same. Still, let us suppose that a person with a body that appears relevantly similar, a rich store of memories, and a personality and character just like that of someone who had died appears somewhere beyond this earthly realm. If we knew about it, we would be inclined to say that this was the same person as before and that he or she had survived death. If a disembodied spirit with all the relevant memories and personality and character traits appeared, we might feel a little more uncertain, but even if it lacked a body we might be inclined to concede that this is probably an instance of the survival of a person's soul. Let us concede, then, that survival in one or both of these modes is conceivable. Is it probable? Are there good reasons to believe that it happens? Several arguments support such a belief; several also oppose it.

Two types of argument based on individual experiences have raised considerable controversy. The first involves claims of communications from the dead through mediums. The study of these claims has been one of the projects of the British and the American Societies for Psychic Research for nearly a hundred years. The most interesting cases are those in which the medium reveals substantial amounts of information about the earthly life of the deceased person that he (the medium) could not independently have known. H. H. Price (1899–1984), a professor of philosophy at Oxford, was convinced that there are cases where plenty of verifiable information is communicated and suggests two possible ways to explain the phenomenon: (1) the medium is indeed in touch with the surviving spirit of the departed individual, and (2) the medium is acquiring the information by a process of extrasensory perception. Price regarded the second suggestion as the more unlikely one and thus argued that "some mediumistic communications do provide us with *evidence* for continued existence of human personality after death."[2] Price stated, however, that he was very far from regarding the evidence as conclusive.

Many critics would seriously question Price's assumption of authenticated cases where verifiable information is communicated that require explanation either as extrasensory perception or as actual communication from the dead. Alleged communications have been associated with a range of phenomena that have aroused deep suspicion. Some cases of alleged paranormal phenomena have been frankly fraudulent; others have not stood up under the bright light of scientific control. After nearly a hundred years of study, there does not seem to be sufficient agreement among the investigators to inspire widespread confidence. Indeed, quite the contrary: It is remarkable that the claims persist and have been taken seriously by a number of highly reputable scholars. So far, these alleged phenomena do not constitute a convincing argument for personal survival of death.

Another phenomenon that some consider suggests possible survival of death is the experiences reported by persons who have been clinically dead, that is, persons whose respiration and heartbeat have stopped for some period of time but who have been resuscitated. Advances in medical practice have made such resuscitation of clinically dead persons fairly commonplace. Raymond Moody recounts many such case histories and is impressed by the similarities in accounts of this experience. On the basis of his study he offers a summary or composite embodying the common elements. None of the patients experienced all of the factors included in this summary, but most experienced a large proportion of them. We will quote it in its entirety.

> A man is dying, and as he reaches the point of greatest physical distress, he hears himself pronounced dead by his doctor. He begins to hear an uncomfortable noise, a loud ringing or buzzing, and at the same time feels himself moving very rapidly through a long dark tunnel. After this, he suddenly finds himself outside of his own physical body, but still in the immediate physical environment, and he sees his own body from a distance, as though he is a spectator. He watches the resuscitation attempt from this unusual vantage point and is in a state of emotional upheaval.
>
> After a while, he collects himself and becomes more accustomed to his odd condition. He notices that he still has a "body," but one of

a very different nature and with very different powers from the physical body he has left behind. Soon other things begin to happen. Others come to meet and to help him. He glimpses the spirits of relatives and friends who have already died, and a loving, warm spirit of a kind he has never encountered before — a being of light — appears before him. This being asks him a question, nonverbally, to make him evaluate his life and helps him along by showing him a panoramic, instantaneous playback of the major events of his life. At some point he finds himself approaching some sort of barrier or border, apparently representing the limits between earthly life and the next life. Yet, he finds that he must go back to earth, that the time for his death has not yet come. At this point he resists, for by now he is taken up with his experiences in the after life and does not want to return. He is overwhelmed by intense feelings of joy, love, and peace. Despite his attitude, though, he somehow reunites with his physical body and lives.[3]

Moody makes no sweeping claims about how these experiences should be interpreted. He acknowledges that there may be mundane explanations grounded in the patients' medical condition, bodily chemistry related to therapeutic pharmacological substances administered, or cultural expectations. Most of the accounts came from patients in American hospitals, and many describe their experiences in terms that involve Christian or Judeo-Christian concepts. It will be interesting to know, when such studies are completed in other cultures, whether, as one would expect, patients conceptualize their experiences in terms of the religions prevailing in their culture. Certainly one explanation is that such persons have actually glimpsed a future life that awaits us all. At this point, however, there seems no way to decide whether that explanation is correct. So these experiences, though suggestive, do not constitute very strong evidence of an afterlife.

An argument of a different kind for the soul's immortality was offered by Immanuel Kant (1724–1804) in connection with his moral argument for the existence of God, discussed in Chapter 3. Kant points out that humans experience a sense of moral obligation, an imperative to conform to moral law. Such an urgent moral sense would be inappropriate if it were impossible for us to conform to it. Kant's way of putting this is to say that "I ought" implies "I can," which entails that we cannot have a moral obligation to do anything it is not possible for us to do. Because we experience such a strong sense of obligation, whose ultimate implication is the duty to achieve moral perfection, it must be possible to do so. Clearly this is not possible in this life; indeed, it appears to require an eternity to fulfill. Thus moral reason requires us to postulate an eternal continuation of our moral life so that we can progress onward toward perfection. This is an ingredient in Kant's moral argument for the existence of God. As we have seen in Chapter 3, Kant claims that God is a necessary postulate both of pure and of practical reason, that is, both as the creator of the postulated world of things in themselves and as the guarantor of our immortality and thus the foundation of morality.

Although Kant's argument has some strength, it is not compelling. Perhaps what our sense of moral obligation obliges us to do is not to achieve moral perfection but simply to strive for it, something we can certainly do in this life. Furthermore, the fact that we experience a sense of obligation may not justify inferring that the realization of what that sense requires is supported by the world or by God. We experience desires whose satisfaction the world does not always make possible. Those who find Kant's argument for the existence of God unconvincing or who simply believe that there is no God are not likely to be convinced by the moral argument for immortality.

Perhaps the most threatening argument against human survival of death is the one that points up the seemingly inseparable connection between mind and body. Bertrand Russell (1872–1970) offers a statement of this argument.

> All that constitutes a person is a series of experiences connected by memory and by certain similarities of the sort we call habit. If, therefore, we are to believe that a person survives death, we must believe that the memories and habits which constitute the person will continue to be exhibited in a new set of occurrences. No one can prove that this will not happen. But it is easy to see that it is very unlikely. Our memories and habits are bound up with the structure of the brain. . . . But the brain . . . is dissolved at death, and memory therefore must be expected to be also dissolved.[4]

The very close dependence of thought on the body, and especially on the brain, is easy to illustrate. We know that injury to the brain causes profound changes in mental functioning and can severely handicap the thinking process or render it impossible. Many chemical substances can also be taken or introduced into the body to produce changes in mental functioning, such as altered feelings, intoxication, irrationality, hallucination, delusion, unconsciousness. Surgery on the central nervous system provides additional evidence of the connection of brain with mind or the dependence of mental activity on brain activity. We seem to depend entirely on our body for the sense experiences from which most if not all of our knowledge comes. If we add to this the argument that we have no evidence to show that a mind or a person can ever exist apart from a functioning nervous system, the presumption against survival of bodily death seems to be very strong.

Such a presumption, however, may not be compelling. J. M. E. McTaggart (1866–1925) has pointed out that our dependence on our brains to function in this life might actually be, as Plato had suggested, a handicapping condition.

> *While a self has a body*, that body is essentially connected with the
> self's mental life. . . . It might be that the present inability of the self
> to think except in connection with the body was a limitation which
> was imposed by the presence of the body, and vanished with it. . . . If
> a man is shut up in a house, the transparency of the windows is an
> essential condition of his seeing the sky. But it would not be prudent
> to infer that, if he walked out of the house, he could not see the sky
> because there was no longer any glass through which he might see it.[5]

McTaggart also offers an argument designed to take some of the sting out of
the claim that the mind must be dependent on the brain because brain
injury or chemical substances affect mental functioning.

> Many things are capable of disturbing thought, which are not essen-
> tial to its existence. For example, a sufficiently severe attack of tooth-
> ache may render all consecutive abstract thought impossible. But if
> the tooth was extracted, I should be able to think. And, in the same
> way, the fact that an abnormal state of the brain may affect our
> thoughts does not prove that the normal states of the brain are neces-
> sary for thought.[6]

The suggestion seems to be that a disembodied self might perceive without
bodily sense organs just as the person who has walked out of the house
might see without looking out through a window. Equally, a person in a
transformed resurrection body might think as clearly, perhaps more clearly,
than a person in an earthly, fleshly body.

McTaggart's argument, however, is by no means a decisive answer to
Russell. At the very best, it can only enlarge our vision of the possibilities
for survival of bodily death. Interpreted more strongly, it becomes an appeal to ignorance, an explicitly invalid way of reasoning. It is certainly
true, as McTaggart points out, that the fact that mental functioning depends on a nervous system *in this life* does not *prove* that there could not be
mental functioning without a body. It is certainly *conceivable* that disembodied spirits continue to exist after the death of their bodies or find their
way into new resurrection bodies. But the fact that something is conceivable does not provide any evidence at all for the claim that it is true.

The most we can concede is that McTaggart has suggested other possibilities without offering any substantial evidence that they are anything
more than possibilities. The survival of bodily death by humans is a very
plausible belief, *if* theism is true. And it *may* be true. We found strength in
the theistic arguments when we examined them in an earlier chapter; we
also found strength in the objections to theism. Apart from a fairly firmly
established theism, prospects for a convincing doctrine of individual survival appear rather bleak. Although we concluded that it is rational to
believe theism, we found that it is also rational to reject it, from which we
can only conclude that as a theory theism does not appear to be firmly
established.

Death, Immortality, and the Question of Meaning

The outlook on human life and the possibility of happiness and meaningfulness is said by many to depend on our survival of bodily death. In any case, the human prospects are supposed to be radically different if theism is true than if no loving deity exists to watch over us. The Christian religion has taught that God created each human person for a specific purpose and that it is our duty to discover that purpose and realize it in our lives; in some other theistic religions we also find similar beliefs. It is in living the life that God has planned for us that we find meaning and value in what we do. Those who accept and live according to God's plan may not be privileged in this life, they may face hardships and suffering, but they can be sure that their strivings and their adversity are not in vain, for their lives serve a higher purpose in fulfilling God's cosmic plan for all creation. And they live in the confidence of a consummation of the meaning and value of their lives when death brings a transition from the earthly world of labor and pain to the joys of everlasting life that God has in store for his own. If theism is true, far from robbing life of its meaning, then, death becomes the door through which we pass to a realization of that meaning in all its fullness.

On the other hand, if theism is not true and death is the end of our existence, if all our effort and pain lead only down to the dust of the grave, then some people would say that life itself becomes meaningless and not worth living. Unless the values we strive here to realize, unless the hopes and dreams that this short life provides the opportunity to envision can be preserved and fulfilled in an everlasting life in the future, even the relatively carefree, happy earthly life becomes a cruel hoax. The life filled with sorrow and disappointment, if it cannot hope for something better in the world to come, is a bitter cup, a mouthful of ashes.

The gist of these beliefs, both affirmative and negative, is that earthly life can be meaningful only if it is a prelude or a preparation for a fuller life that is eternal. But some argue that whether or not life continues beyond the grave is irrelevant to the issue of the meaning of human existence; some even suggest that an everlasting life would be monotonous and devoid of all meaning and that the brevity of earthly life is what makes it so precious. Quite apart from theism, the advocates of humanism (which we discussed in Chapter 5) find the prospect of an earthly life in which by human effort we strive to create a truly humane world, exemplifying the highest of human dreams and ideals, an exciting, zestful, and altogether meaningful challenge.

We turn now to look briefly at a modern philosophical movement whose primary focus was on the question of what (if anything) does or might make human life meaningful. When we have completed our examination of existentialism, we will ask again, in a larger context, the question of whether everlasting life is a necessary condition for life's having a meaning.

EXISTENTIALISM AND THE CREATION OF MEANING

The rise of **existentialism** in the West in the twentieth century was part of a complex process of social change. It grew up partly as a result of an erosion of the beliefs, especially the religious beliefs, that had given stability to Western civilization for hundreds of years. The progress of science was the most conspicuous single contributing factor to this decline, but it was by no means the only one. By the middle of the nineteenth century a few persons of unusual foresight, such as Søren Kierkegaard (1813–1855) and Friedrich Nietzsche (1844–1900), had already begun to realize that the core of Western ideals and values were threatened; it remained for a group of twentieth-century philosophers, theologians, and literary figures to explore the implications. Existentialism is not a philosophical position with an agreed-on set of teachings; rather, it involves a wide range of beliefs, including atheism, agnosticism, and theism; a variety of attitudes, ranging from nihilism to optimism; and a diversity of modes of expression, varying from tightly argued, jargon-filled philosophical treatises to essays, novels, and plays. The thread of unity seems to be a response to the malaise of Western civilization in the face of attacks on its core religious, political, economic, and social values.

Core Beliefs of Western Civilization

For at least a thousand and perhaps for nearly two thousand years, Western civilization has been unified by a cluster of beliefs or assumptions, sometimes not well articulated but always taken for granted. The implications of these beliefs have been elaborated in a variety of ways; during certain periods some of the beliefs have faded into the background; individuals and groups have questioned or rejected these beliefs. For the most part, however, they have been stable fixtures in the Western mind for a very long time. Three of the most important are: (1) an objective reality that can be known by the human mind; (2) a stable human nature the same in every human person; (3) a set of objective moral and social laws that the human mind can discern and that constitute the foundation of political order and individual morality.

The belief in an objective reality that the human mind can know has usually involved the further belief that God is the most important aspect of that reality and that revelation and religious experience are the most important modes by which reality comes to be known. This is not quite true for Plato, who thought that ultimate reality consists of a realm of Forms or Essences, what we might think of as perfect patterns that the imperfect material objects in this world copy or imitate. For Plato, the concept of God was not of central importance, but when Christian thought began to dominate the West, the Essences of which Plato's ultimate reality consists became the rational plans according to which God creates, or the order of nature that God imposes. The West came to believe in a universe with earth at the center and the sun, all the planets, and the stars revolving around it. This universe was created by God specifically as the home for humans, God's finest creation. The vision was rounded out with images of heaven and hell, the eternal places of reward for the godly and punishment for the wicked, located a convenient distance above and below the material universe, the whole scheme directed and presided over by God.

Plato and Aristotle had slightly different conceptions of human nature, but it never occurred to either to doubt the existence of a fixed human nature, the same in all persons. Christian thought presupposed a human nature created in God's image and fallen through Adam's sin, but still the same in all persons. It added a plan of salvation through which Jesus, the second Adam, makes possible the restoration of God's image in those humans who respond to the divine invitation.

Plato's realm of Essences contained the essences of justice, beauty, goodness, and the like that make up the foundation of objective morality. The ancient Roman notion of natural law taught that principles of political and moral right are written, as it were, into the structure of the world, similar to the natural laws of the material world discovered by science. These ideas were elaborated particularly in the work of Thomas Aquinas into a doctrine of natural law derived from God's eternal law. John Locke made the notion of natural law the foundation of his work on political democracy, and Thomas Jefferson gave these ideas life in the American republic under the name of natural rights.

It was a cozy world, understood, if not by everyone, at least by God's designated representatives. It might involve hardship, but there was a reason for everything that happened, a purpose for every detail, a scheme of unfailing divine justice, and an ultimate outcome which offered hope and meaning.

The "Humiliations of Man"

Cracks in the foundation of this impressive intellectual structure started to appear significantly as a result of progress in the study of astronomy which began to cast doubt on the notion that the earth is the center of the universe. The work of such astronomers as Copernicus (1473–1543), Galileo (1564–1642), and Kepler (1571–1630) revealed an earth that was one of several planets circling the sun, and in succeeding centuries the emerging vision of the universe cast the solar system itself as a minor player in a gigantic cosmic frame. From a secure position at the very center of creation, humans found themselves and their earth cast off into perhaps endless, expanding space, lost amid systems of stars and galaxies too vast to conceive. The blow to the human ego was devastating, and religious leaders attempted to stem the tide by denouncing the new astronomy and punishing the scientists. But the truth could not be contained, and the mind of the West was forced to adjust and accept a somewhat more modest place for itself in the scheme of things.

This reconciliation had hardly been made when another blow came, this time from the science of biology. In 1859, Charles Darwin (1809–1882) published his famous theory of evolution, which taught that living species develop through a long process of change as a result of natural selection of those best adapted to survive in the particular environment. The clear implication was that the world has existed for eons longer than the creation date (4004 B.C.E.) put forward by certain Christian thinkers and that humans are one species among many that have evolved from simpler life forms during that very long period of biological development. A being in the image of God, created "a little lower than the angels" according to the Psalmist, is suddenly lowered to a position only a very little above that of the beasts. From their status as a special creation of God, humans suddenly saw themselves depicted as offspring of monkeys or apes. We have not yet recovered from this blow to human pride. This discovery sparked the creation of fundamentalism among Christian church leaders, who tried, as others before them had done with the threat of astronomy, to prevent its spread. Fundamentalists are still denouncing evolution and trying to prevent their children from learning about it, but the truth will not go away, and the effect on how humans feel about themselves and the meaningfulness of their lives is reflected in much of the thought of the twentieth century.

A third process that added to the growing crisis was the development of techniques of literary and source criticism and the application of these techniques to the Bible. The discovery that the so-called books of Moses could not possibly all have been written by Moses and that they are probably a blending or collage of materials from at least four sources; the analysis of the Gospels that indicated that they were written too late to be reliable eyewitness accounts of the activities of Jesus; the recognition that the texts of the scriptures have gone through processes of redaction that may well have altered what they originally said — all these developments contributed to undermining the belief that the Bible is the very word of God, trustworthy in every detail and for every purpose. Fundamentalism tried to turn back the implications of these findings, too, but mostly by dogmatically asserting that the scriptures are infallibly true.

These are the so-called "humiliations of man" that strike at the roots of the traditional beliefs of Western civilization. They are among the chief intellectual factors contributing to the malaise of our age, which has manifested itself in existentialist thought and in the so-called "death of God" theology. Yet at the same time these movements arose during an era of almost unprecedented optimism in the West, especially in the United States. The progress of science may have had disquieting implications, but these were obvious only to specialists and academicians. Science was providing a practical cornucopia of ingredients for the good life, including not only energy-saving devices and conveniences but also medical products that cured diseases and promised longer and much healthier lives. Technology made tasks previously considered impossible easy. If a handful of intellectuals interpreted evolutionary theory as implying that human life is merely the life of beasts, many ordinary people understood it to mean that things naturally get better and better. Liberal religious groups, undisturbed by modern astronomy, biology, and biblical criticism, which they cheerfully embraced, captured a prevailing late nineteenth- and early twentieth-century mood in forthrightly predicting "the inevitable progress of mankind, onward and upward forever."

It required a series of social catastrophes to bring home to the ordinary Westerner what some specialists had already foreseen. And these events came with a vengeance in the twentieth century. World War I delivered a severe shock, but it was rationalized as the war to end all wars, the war to make the world safe for democracy. Then came the most devastating economic depression Westerners had ever known, threatening the prosperity and even the livelihood of virtually everyone. The drastic reform measures introduced in the United States by President F. D. Roosevelt, moving the republic toward socialism and the welfare state, as some saw it, were barely going into effect when an even more horrific war overcame much of the world. Besides the barbarities of warfare itself, World War II brought with it the inconceivable horror of the Holocaust with the brutal, calculated extermination of many millions of innocent persons, mostly Jews. This war was brought to its conclusion by the introduction of a new weapon of unthinkable destructiveness, a weapon that ushered in the era in which humans had in their hands for the first time the power to destroy all life on earth. Even the new United Nations, with its fabled vision of a world of peace, co-operation, and progress for the whole family of nations, proved unable to prevent or control the persistent warring passions of persons and nations. And between the superpowers the open hostility of war was replaced with what seemed an intractable, lasting stance of belligerence called the Cold War. With the fading of superpower competition and its specter of nuclear war, the end of the century finds the world faced with widespread ethnic conflict and environmental problems of unimaginable proportions.

The themes of the existentialists began to be heard amid the somber circumstances of World War II. We will discuss here only selected ideas of two of the most popular, Jean-Paul Sartre and Albert Camus, as they relate to the philosophy of religion and particularly to the question of the meaning of life.

Sartre: Existence Before Essence

Jean-Paul Sartre (1905–1980) enunciated, in a three-word phrase, a slogan that encapsulates a major theme of existentialism and at the same time contradicts all three main core beliefs of Western civilization we have just examined: "Existence precedes essence."[7] In the West we have always believed that essence precedes existence. This is the explicit teaching of Plato's philosophy: the Forms or Essences subsist eternally and the particulars, the material things in the mundane world, come into existence patterned after those Forms. One of these eternally subsisting Forms is the essence of the human being; when individual women and men appear in the world they imitate that Form, so that each particular human being is a more or less perfect copy of the essence "human." Furthermore, the laws that nations enact, properly made, reflect the Forms of justice or, as the Romans would say, of natural law.

Christian teachings also clearly affirm the priority of essence over existence. The most fundamental being is God, whose existence is said to be identical with His essence. And God creates all things according to the essences that are the patterns of His own eternal reason. The physical universe is governed by God's eternal natural laws, and the principles of morality for both individuals and nations derive from God's divine and natural law. All these things are thought to be eternal. First are essences; then particular things come into existence and exemplify in one degree or another those eternal essences.

Sartre's pronouncement denies the whole tradition. First, we particular human persons exist, he says, and then we *create* our essences, each of us individually, by our free actions. Sartre is convinced that in the twentieth century the speculative teachings of Plato have lost whatever credibility they ever had. He also insists that no reasonable person can any longer seriously believe in any such being as God. Indeed, Sartre asserts that the very conception of God is self-contradictory. There are two kinds of beings: *être-en-soi*, or being-in-itself, and *être-pour-soi*, or being-for-itself. Being-in-itself is being with a fixed essence. A table, for example, is just what it is; it has no power to do anything about it. It cannot choose to change its essence and become something else. But there is another kind of being, Sartre says, that is not what it is but rather is what it is not. That is to say, *être-pour-soi* is a being with a free will. It has no antecedent essence; it has only the essence it has given to itself by its choices and actions. The human being is an example of this kind of being.

The definition of God, however, implies that the deity is *être-en-et-pour-soi*. Yet this clearly means that a God so defined is a being with a fixed essence that has no fixed essence—an obvious contradiction. So much of the theological talk about God concerns itself with just what kind of being God is: omnipotent, omniscient, immutable, impassive. A being with such a set of essences, however, cannot be free. To be free means to be able to change, and to change is to lose one essence and take on another. This is the very reason why many theologians insist that God cannot change. If God were to change, he would no longer be omnipotent or omniscient or immutable — that is to say, he would no longer be God. Yet God could not be God if he is not free to do as he wills, free to act, free to change. God must have always and unchangingly those essences by virtue of which he is God; yet God must be able to act and thus to change. Thus God is a being with an (immutable, unchangeable) essence that has no essence (i.e., that is free to change). Such a concept is contradictory; that, according to Sartre, is why there cannot be a God. (Sartre is also said to have remarked that if there were a God, he, Sartre, could not stand not to be He.)

Whatever exists, then, is either *être-en-soi* or *être-pour-soi*. Most objects in the world are simply things, beings with unchanging essences and no freedom. This is not true of humans, however; Sartre says that "man is a hole in being." There is no such thing as human nature; there are only free, individual human persons, each what she or he has freely made of her- or himself by the actions resulting from personal choice. We are what we do. Because we are nothing at all initially, a hole in being, we fill in our essence by choosing and acting. This means that our essence is not fixed but is constantly subject to change. By an act of the will, we can shed the essence of our lifetime up to now and become a different being. Indeed, if we do not approve of who we are, then we ought to decide to become someone else and act to create that new character of which we do approve.

It is because our existence precedes our essence that we are, each of us, completely free and totally responsible for what we are. But we have a great tendency to try to duck that responsibility by blaming our actions, and therefore our character, on others or on circumstances. Sartre insists that there is no such thing as extenuating circumstances. The greatest human evil is what Sartre calls bad faith, which simply means refusing to acknowledge our responsibility. We make excuses. We blame others. We claim that we could not help what we did. We insist that anyone in similar circumstances would have done at least as badly. When we finish our excuses, Sartre reminds us that no one but we ourselves can decide what we do; no one else can determine our attitudes, our habits, our loves and hates or, in a word, our character. We are today just who we have chosen to be. And who we will be tomorrow we determine by the choices we make today.

Because there is no God and there is no human nature, there is also no objective standard of morality or of politics. Human institutions, like human character, are human creations. The person who claims to be king by the grace of God is a pretender; the government that claims to be established on eternal natural law is no less so. There are no eternal guidelines of human behavior, and so we must work out our own salvation by thinking responsibly about the kind of human character we can conscientiously approve and the kind of human institutions we can sincerely support; then we must act freely to bring them into existence. Above all, we must be true to our own vision of what is right and what is good. The belief in anteced-ent essences allows us to shirk the responsibility to think for ourselves, to claim that there are roles prescribed by God or nature which we are des-tined to play, and thus that we are not to blame if things do not go well. In fact, we are always to blame — or to credit — for how things go, since it is up to us to choose how they will go and then to make them go. If the great sin, according to Sartre, is bad faith — refusing to acknowledge responsibility for our deeds — then the great virtue is authenticity. Authenticity is the opposite of bad faith. It means recognizing and embracing our freedom and thus taking on the responsibility for creating our own essence.

The absence of antecedent essences, the death of God, the awesome responsibility of human freedom — none of these factors implies that life has no meaning or worth. They do, of course, imply that there is no objec-tive or antecedent meaning. But the life of the person who embraces com-pletely his or her freedom and lives authentically, who creates a character of which he or she can approve, is a meaningful life. The characters Sartre depicts in his novels and plays very rarely succeed in doing so; most exhibit, in painfully duplicitous ways, the many forms of the life of bad faith. The three characters in his best-known play, *No Exit*,[8] are paradigms of bad faith, and even the famous oft-quoted (and very often misunderstood) cli-max line "Hell is other people!" is an ironic exemplification of blaming others and refusing to acknowledge one's own responsibility. (Sartre's point is that hell is *not* other people; it is ourselves; so also is heaven.) Sartre is keenly aware that the world does not make it easy to live authentically. Some critics suggest that Sartre never convinced himself that it was even possible. Certainly his is not a philosophy of cheap optimism, but at least one of Sartre's characters — Orestes in the play *The Flies*[9] — does seem to succeed to a substantial extent. Perhaps that is Sartre's conclusion: that 95 percent of humankind lives in bad faith; only the rare, heroic one may manage to achieve a measure of authenticity.

Camus: The Most Important Question

Albert Camus (1913–1960) addresses the question of this chapter much more directly and offers his answer in a much less roundabout way than Sartre.

> There is but one truly serious philosophical question, and that is sui-cide. Judging whether life is or is not worth living amounts to answer-ing the fundamental question of philosophy. All the rest . . . are games.[10]

The implication seems clear. If life has no meaning and thus is not worth living, suicide is the reasonable response. Thus the question becomes: Has life a meaning? or: What is necessary for life to have a meaning?

Camus suggests that the loss of what has previously given us a reason to live results in the sense of **the absurd**. We normally suppose that we understand the world, that there is a reason for everything that happens. The reason that is operative for an individual, however, is usually not one that she has thought out for herself, for we ordinarily adopt unconsciously the explanations our society offers. This is the reason such an overwhelming crisis occurs when the fundamental beliefs of a civilization, the ways in which the peoples of a culture have made sense of their world, crumble. This is the reason the "humiliations of man" and the social crises of the twentieth century created for so many people the feeling of absurdity. The atrocities of war, the devastation of economic depression, the horror of witnessing unbridled brutality perpetrated on great numbers of persons for the most spurious reasons—more correctly, for no reason at all—these horrific events occurring in the midst of a loss of traditional beliefs and values, as happened in the West in the twentieth century, leave us with the anguished, empty, nihilistic feeling that nothing matters any more, that no one thing is any more important than any other thing, that we are living in a wonderland where reason does not function and events are random, not caused. Life in the twentieth century, as Camus saw it, might be described by borrowing a line from Shakespeare's vision in an earlier century: "a tale told by an idiot, full of sound and fury, signifying nothing."[11]

Camus depicts this desolate sense of absurdity in many of his works of fiction. For example his novel *The Stranger* (1942) depicts a character living his life largely by default, not deciding what to do but drifting with the tide. When he attends his mother's funeral, everyone is scandalized because he sheds no tears, as if her death did not matter to him. His lover asks him if they could get married, and he says he doesn't mind—they could if she wants to—it really makes no difference. He is walking along a beach and kills a person he meets for no reason except that it is hot and the sun is in his eyes. Sentenced to death for the murder, he muses that it does not really matter how or when a person dies since everyone does, at one time or another:

> What difference could it make if, after being charged with murder, he were executed because he didn't weep at his mother's funeral, since it all came to the same thing in the end. . . . What difference could they make to me, the death of others, or a mother's love . . . or the way a man decides to live, the fate he thinks he chooses. . . . Nothing, nothing had the least importance.[12]

This, Camus seems to be saying, is what life has become in our times: meaningless, irrational, absurd.

Camus's most graphic presentation of this vision of the absurdity of life is in his short retelling of the famous myth of Sisyphus. Sisyphus was condemned by the gods to a task of ceaseless toil: rolling a rock to the top of a mountain, where it would roll back down, to roll the rock up again, over and over without end—an eternity of backbreaking toil that accomplished exactly nothing. What meaning could there be in such a life? Sisyphus is the absurd hero, and, all the more tragically, he is a god and cannot die. Not even suicide can free Sisyphus from his wretched condition.

Sisyphus' condition, Camus suggests, is not really very different from ours — except that we are not gods and can die. A parent toils for hours to prepare a delicious and attractive meal for a family; in a matter of a few minutes they swarm to the table and reduce the work to scraps, and the whole process must begin again the next day. The professor labors all semester to impart a modicum of knowledge to her class; then she returns the next term to find that her classroom has been invaded by another horde of barbarians, and she must once again shoulder her rock. The lives of all of us are an endless round of doing the same thing over and over again, and where does it all lead? What Camus says sounds altogether like the slang expression, "Life is a bitch, and then you die." If life is absurd and has no meaning, the next step seems to be that it is not worth living; thus the only truly serious philosophical conclusion would seem to be that suicide is the only sensible response.

But first we must finish examining the myth of Sisyphus. Camus pays particular attention to the time when the stone reaches the top and Sisyphus begins his long walk down to the bottom again. During this period of respite that unfailingly punctuates his never-ending suffering, Sisyphus has the opportunity to look up and marvel at the stars, to reflect on his own life, a life that is the consequence of his own choices. Sisyphus received the gods' judgment because of his own deeds. There are times when the burden seems too heavy and he is tempted to blame the gods, but then he recognizes that whatever one is obliged to do, there is freedom in *how* one will do it. The gods may chain one's body, but they cannot chain the unyielding will.

> All Sisyphus' silent joy is contained therein. His fate belongs to him. His rock is his thing. Likewise, the absurd man, when he contemplates his torment, silences all the idols. . . . There is no sun without shadow, and it is essential to know the night. The absurd man says yes and his effort will henceforth be unceasing. . . . He knows himself to be the master of his days. . . . The universe henceforth without a master seems to him neither sterile nor futile. . . . The struggle itself toward the heights is enough to fill a man's heart. One must imagine Sisyphus happy.[13]

Happy? But if Sisyphus in his situation can create meaning, if he can transcend his fate through the strength of his own will, how can we then bemoan a meaningless life? To be sure, like Sartre, Camus discovers no reason to find an objective meaning in God or any cosmic purpose. This is the sense in which life is absurd: Life *has* no meaning prescribed from before eternity.

> Hitherto . . . people have . . . pretended to believe that refusing to grant a meaning to life necessarily leads to declaring that it is not

worth living. In truth, there is no necessary common measure between these two judgments.[14]

For a life that has no objective meaning prescribed for it by God can be
supremely worth living. Camus, who is convinced that belief in God is
entirely unjustified, suggests that a life programmed and supervised by a
deity would be the insufferably meaningless one. "If God exists, all depends
on him and we can do nothing against his will. If he does not exist, everything depends on us."[15] If we found at best a glimmer of hope in the work of
Sartre, we find a sizeable beam of encouragement in Camus's thought.
Even the overbearing fate of Sisyphus can be transcended; surely the much
smaller difficulties most of us must face can be transformed into opportunities to create meaning, to demonstrate worth, and to live life to its
fullest. If Sisyphus is happy, surely we can be, too.

We have looked in only the sketchiest way at a few of the central ideas
of just two existentialists. There are many other important thinkers in the
movement, some representing points of view significantly different from
those of Sartre and Camus. Both of our examples are atheists, but there are
theistic existentialists as well. Our concern here, however, is to examine
the single issue of life's meaning and to ask whether only the life of a religious believer can be worth living. We have already clearly seen in the
thought of Camus that an atheist can create meaning in his life and can
find life worth living—can even see ways of living it that make it joyful
and happy. It is time now to reflect on the question of meaning in a more
general way.

RELIGION AND THE MEANING OF LIFE

The traditional assumption that meaning can be found in our lives only
through religious belief has been seriously challenged by the arguments we
have examined. The power of religious belief and practice to convey meaning, however, continues to be put forward by reasonable persons through
persuasive arguments. Paul Tillich argues that no one is truly without religion and that whatever gives meaning to a person, her or his object of faith,
constitutes the religious dimension of that person's life. Tillich, a religious
existentialist, offers a new and constructive approach to the question of
meaning. Before we look at his thought it will be useful to examine more
closely what we mean when we ask whether or not life has a meaning.

The Meaning of "Meaning"

The word "meaning" has mainly to do with language. A word or a phrase
has a meaning in this primary sense, but an object, a class of things, or a
state of affairs does not. "Life" has meaning in this linguistic sense; life does

not. Some have attempted to dispose of questions about the meaning of life by insisting that the expression involves a mistake about what can and cannot have meaning. It does not make sense to ask such questions as, "What is the meaning of trees?" or "What is the meaning of time?" or "What is the meaning of people?" Neither does it make sense, others have suggested, to ask, "What is the meaning of life?"

This move, however, is a dodge and not a successful one. The primary sense of "meaning" is not the only one. If I come home to find my wife walking out of the door with suitcases in her hands, I may quite properly ask, "What is the meaning of this?" It is a perfectly intelligible question that admits of several very different answers. "I've had enough of your taking me for granted. I'm leaving you," she might say, and this tells me in no uncertain terms what her actions mean. Or she might explain that her sister has been hospitalized and that she is going to help out for a few days—another entirely intelligible explanation of what the packed suit- cases mean.

We need not explore all the different kinds of meaning in order to recognize that not just words, phrases, sentences, and paragraphs, but also such things as actions (leaving home, pounding the table, ripping up a letter), objects (packed suitcases, a puddle of water on the floor), and events (an ambulance approaching one's house, the lights suddenly going out) can have meaning. When I say that the puddle on the floor means that my attempt to patch the roof was unsuccessful, I am saying that an object or an event suggests, points to, or justifies our inference of some other factor. We also recognize that the meaning of something can change, or even that something can lose the meaning it had for us. "I used to see you at the theater quite often," my friend might say, "but I haven't seen you there in a long time now." And I might explain that drama used to mean a lot to me but that I no longer have any time for it; that it bores me and I would rather spend my time doing something else. What "meaning" means in this con- text is importance or value. Something important or worthwhile has lost its meaning; that is to say, it has ceased to be important or worthwhile for me. All these are quite proper senses of "meaning"—and so is the sense we intend when we speak of the meaning of life.

The Meaning of Life

What, then, does "meaning" mean when we speak of the meaning of life? It means several things. Perhaps the primary one—at least in Western thought, where religion has been closely bound up with these issues—is purpose. When we ask whether life has a meaning, we may be asking whether it has a purpose. "Why are we here?" or "Why was I born?" may amount to "What is the purpose of human life?" or "For what purpose was I put on this earth?" This is certainly the way in which the question is usually expressed in the Christian tradition, with the implication that where a purpose exists, there is also a Purposer, someone who had a purpose in mind that explains why the world is as it is. Christians have been taught that the world was created by a rational God with a plan in mind who is working out a grand scheme through creation. They are also taught that God has a purpose for each of them individually that is a part of the overall scheme. A person's life has meaning because it has a purpose; it is up to the person to discover what part his life is supposed to play in God's scheme so that he can act accordingly.

Persons who take this point of view are likely to hold that human life would be meaningless if God did not exist. Theists sometimes like to contrast the happy circumstance of believers with the tragic outlook of unbelievers: The unbeliever is a person whose life is without meaning or hope, and death brings home in its most urgent and poignant way the futility of existence without God. The apostle Paul argues this point most insistently, asserting that it is Christ's resurrection from the dead which guarantees that we too will be resurrected, and that a good life here on earth is not nearly enough to justify the claim that life is worthwhile.

> If Christ has not been raised, then our preaching is in vain and your faith is in vain. We are even found to be misrepresenting God. . . . For if the dead are not raised, then Christ has not been raised. If Christ has not been raised, your faith is futile and you are still in your sins. Then those also who have fallen asleep in Christ have perished. If for this life only we have hoped in Christ, we are of all men most to be pitied.[16]

According to this viewpoint, survival of death is a necessary condition for life to be called meaningful, not only in having a purpose but also in being worthwhile. God is necessary to guarantee that death is not the final end for us.

Some go even further and argue that an unbeliever may mistakenly think that her life is meaningful or happy when it is not grounded in what is permanent, objective, divine. David F. Swenson makes such a point:

> Just as life is not life unless it is happy, so happiness is not happiness unless it can be justified. In order really to be happiness it requires to be interpenetrated with a sense of meaning, reason, and worth. . . . It is possible to believe oneself happy, to seem happy to oneself and others, and yet in reality to be plunged in the deepest misery.[17]

Without immortality guaranteed by an all-powerful God, there can be no such meaning, reason, and worth. Thus, as Paul would say, even those who believe themselves to be supremely happy in this life, if there is no God to give them hope of immortality, "are of all men most to be pitied." The happiness of a Sisyphus, and that of humans who like Sisyphus affirm and joyfully live their lives as atheists, is not real happiness, according to this way of thinking.

Even such atheistic thinkers as Sartre and Camus seem to make some of the same assumptions about God, death, and meaning. Because there is no God, they say, there is no one whose plan for the world gives it objective meaning and purpose. It follows that life is meaningless. Camus suggests that when we can understand the reason for something, it has a meaning, but when something exists for no reason at all — as he believes is true of the world and of humans — then it is absurd. We appear out of the darkness of nonbeing for no reason at all; for a brief season we flourish like the lush grass of spring; but pain, toil, disease, despair, and death come upon us, and we plunge again into the dark abyss of nonbeing, to disappear without a trace as though we had never existed. Even if pain comes sparingly and pleasant occupations and diversions keep us from despair, life is still absurd.

Although these atheistic existentialists, perhaps without realizing it, make the same assumptions as the theists about the necessity of objective purpose to give life meaning, the similarity between their positions ends there. The theists affirm that there is a God, a purpose, and therefore a meaning; thus they infer that because life has a meaning, it is worth living. As Swenson would say, the life of the believer is *really*, not just seemingly, happy. Indeed, the life of the believer, even when it involves much adversity and suffering and does not appear to be at all happy, is actually happy because of its eternal outcome. On the other hand, the atheistic existentialists assert that there is no God, no purpose, and therefore no meaning. But they do not take what the theists believe is the next logical step: that life is therefore not worth living, or that the seemingly happy life is really miserable. Instead, as we have seen, they suggest that even a meaningless life can be happy, can have great value, and thus can be worth living. Or sometimes they put it differently; they tell us that life *has* no meaning, that is, no objective meaning antecedent to the living of it, but a particular life can come to have a meaning depending on how the individual lives. In other words, it is possible to create meaning where there was none by living authentically, by embracing one's life and its possibilities, living them honestly and to the full.

As we have seen, for many people it is the prospect of death as the annihilation of the individual that threatens to render life meaningless and not worth living. Some even argue that a life that leads to no other end than the grave is so worthless that it is better to die than to live. Such a position is usually the corollary of the teaching that any measure of suffering and wretchedness in this life is to be counted as trivial since this life is after all only the brief prelude to an eternity in which those who bear their earthly adversities in the right spirit can expect a never-ending life of bliss. But if the suffering of this life is nothing, so also is its happiness. Even a comfortable and prosperous life in this world is dust and ashes unless there is an eternity of joyful life in the world to come.

Many nontheists suggest that the complete otherworldly orientation of such theists yields a distorted and even morbid view of the good and wholesome happiness of this world. Why should we denigrate the happiness a person achieves in this life just because we may believe that that happiness will not last forever? Why, indeed, should humans demand eternal life, as if it were something to which they are entitled? Is it, in fact, really something greatly to be desired? Perhaps the shortness of life is what makes it precious; maybe the fact that we have only limited time and finite opportunities gives such great value to what we do have. To live forever in the gardens of bliss described in the Christian or the Moslem traditions has been thought by some sensitive persons to be insufferable, boring, stagnant, stultifying. It was the fact that he could not die that made Sisyphus' predicament so tragic. But would it be any less so if the existence to which he was condemned were an eternity of lying on a couch sipping wine and watching dancing girls? To live robustly, to design grand projects and use up all one's strength and life itself to complete them, to think new thoughts, to create with original and powerful imagination, to dream dreams and to see visions of what one human life in a brief precious span can be; and to bring it to pass, to risk one's all and often fail, but occasionally to triumph — this is the vigorous and adroit happiness of a well-lived earthly life. Is it to be scorned as not *real* happiness?

For the most part, the insistence that eternal life is a necessary condition for meaning and happiness has been characteristic just of cultures strongly influenced by the Christian and the Moslem religions. The cultures of Asia have quite a different attitude about what is to be hoped for after earthly death. In societies where belief in reincarnation is widespread, continued existence in another earthly life is generally regarded as undesirable and the objective is liberation from the unending cycle of rebirth and redeath. The contrast has sometimes been drawn by saying that Christians seek eternal life whereas Hindus and Buddhists seek eternal death. *Nirvana*, after all, means extinction. Interpreters of Hinduism and Buddhism sometimes argue that this means extinction of suffering or of unsatisfied desire, not extinction of the person, but one suspects that this interpretation reflects the influence of Christian beliefs about the afterlife and also perhaps a growing individualism in Asian cultures. The conditions of modern life may have blurred the understanding of *nirvana* just as they have certainly blurred the Christian teachings about the afterlife. The orthodox Hindu and Buddhist view of *nirvana* seems to be extinction of the individual. This is interpreted, at least by such sects as the Advaita Vedantists, to be the reabsorption of what was separate into the great One. The outcome in any case is the complete disappearance of the individual.

Plato, in *The Apology*, offers an account of Socrates's deliberations concerning death which led him to the conclusion that whatever death may be, it is nothing to be dreaded or feared. *The Apology* presents the

speech Socrates is supposed to have made to the people of Athens in his
own defense when he had been charged with teaching what is contrary to
the religion of Athens. After Socrates was found guilty and sentenced to
death, he made his closing speech a reflection on death. He mentions some
of the theories put forward by the poets about the afterlife, but he finds only
two possibilities that reason recommends as plausible. Neither suggests
that there is anything dreadful about death.

> Either death is a state of nothingness and utter unconsciousness, or,
> as men say, there is a change and migration of the soul from this world
> to another. Now if you suppose that there is no consciousness, but a
> sleep like the sleep of him who is undisturbed even by dreams, death
> will be an unspeakable gain.[18]

This alternative seems really to amount to annihilation; it is perhaps an
equivalent of *nirvana*. To be at rest after the adventures and toils of a busy
human life seems to Socrates, and to many persons after him, not at all
horrific but rather appealing.

The other possibility is a continued conscious existence in some other
realm where those who have died before us also dwell.

> But if death is the journey to another place, and there . . . all the dead
> abide, what good . . . can be greater than this? . . . What would not a
> man give if he might converse with Orpheus and Musaeus and Hesiod
> and Homer?[19]

To be sure, Socrates's arguments do not suffice to prove that these two
possibilities are the only rational ones and that the many others put forward
are not possibilities. Instead, he rests his case on a solid confidence in the
ultimate justice of the world, even apart from any belief in a supreme God.
He concludes his discussion of death thus: "Be of good cheer about death,
and know of a certainty, that no evil can happen to a good man, either in
life or after death."[20] One might conclude, then, that on the central point
the theists, the atheists, the Platonists, and the existentialists agree: What
is important is the moral quality of a person's life. For the theist, living such
a moral life will guarantee entry into the blissful life of the world to come.
For the atheist, living such a moral life will itself make one's days, be they
many or few, meaningful, happy, and worthwhile.

Religion and Meaning

Over and above the arguments philosophers have offered to support the
truth claims of religion or of certain religious teachings, many thinkers
have championed religion for pragmatic reasons. William James argued
that religious belief is a source of solace because it gives to our lives a sense
of importance, an intensity, a purpose, and a hope that the values we

cherish will be preserved permanently. He insisted that we must proportion our beliefs about any subject to the evidence when the evidence is decisive, but maintained that when the evidence is indecisive and the issue is of great importance to our lives we are entitled to decide on practical grounds and accept the belief that will contribute most constructively to our happiness and well-being. Because the evidence and the arguments do not succeed in establishing that the claims of religion are either definitely true or false, and because believing can energize and enrich our lives whereas refusing to believe can bring hopelessness and despair, we ought to will to believe. Indeed, on the question of whether life has a meaning, James says that what we believe will determine the answer to the question. If we believe that life does not have a meaning, we will be right, because we will live in the dark shadow of that belief, bereft of any motivation to put our heart and our will into making our lives worth living. If, on the contrary, we believe that life is meaningful and good, it will be because we will live it in such a way as to make it so. To suspend judgment in such a situation, where the evidence is indecisive but the outcome is of such importance, is foolish. Here our believing becomes a major factor in determining that the belief is true.

But this presumes that religious belief is a necessary condition for life to be meaningful and happy. We have seen reason to suggest that this is not true. In every age some people have rejected religion, in any ordinary sense of the word, and have nevertheless lived happy, energetic, zestful, constructive lives that they themselves have found meaningful; and there seems no justification for denying that they really were so.

Yet unquestionably it has been through religion that great numbers — perhaps the major portion — of humankind have found meaning in their lives. Some would even claim that what we really mean by religion is that path, of whatever nature, through which meaning is to be found. This implies that anyone who has found life meaningful has a religion, even without any connection to recognized or organized religion. This claim, though plausible, does not appeal to everyone. Yet it is approximately the position taken by the influential German-American theologian Paul Tillich (1886–1956), whose thought we will examine briefly here.

Faith, Tillich argued, is the integrating factor in human life, without which a personality disintegrates and the individual loses the ability to function as a sane, whole person. The faith of some persons is very immature and idolatrous, according to Tillich, and that of others is mature and authentic; but every functioning individual is a person of faith. Tillich defines faith not as endorsing certain beliefs, but as **ultimate concern** about whatever the individual takes to be of greatest importance. Persons orient their lives around one or another of a great variety of concerns — wealth, social status, nation, class, a political movement, the betterment of humankind, God, the Bible, pleasure, and the like. The focus of concern gives unity and integrity to the individual personality.

Almost any conceivable object of faith, even a very superficial one, may serve to bring wholeness to a personality, at least so long as the individual does not recognize that the object is not ultimate. Unfortunately many of the things, causes, movements that we make the objects of our faith, that we treat as our gods, are finite and unable to bring the ultimate fulfillment that is the promise of an ultimate concern. Tillich cites nation worship as a conspicuous example. He himself fled from Germany during the rise of the Nazi regime. He watched the German people give their hearts and souls and consciences totally to Hitler and his ideals, and he watched the disintegration of their lives as their ideals were revealed to be empty and evil. Faith as ultimate concern about an object that is not ultimate Tillich calls idolatry. Genuine faith takes Being-itself, that which is truly ultimate, as its object of ultimate concern.

Tillich has been called a Christian existentialist in part because he was keenly sensitive to the threat of meaninglessness and despair that the existentialists addressed in their writings. Tillich spoke of three kinds of **existential anxiety** as a permanent part of the human condition in every age: the anxiety of fate and death, the anxiety of guilt and condemnation, and the anxiety of emptiness and meaninglessness. These anxieties afflict every person, in varying degrees; they also affect every era of human history, with a different anxiety dominating different eras. Our own era, Tillich says, is particularly afflicted with the anxiety of emptiness and meaninglessness. These anxieties cannot be cured the way pathological anxieties can; they can only be faced and dealt with through what Tillich calls the **courage to be**, which he defines as "the ethical act in which man affirms his own being in spite of those elements of his existence which conflict with his essential self-affirmation."[21]

Tillich discusses three major kinds of the courage to be that help humans deal with the three major kinds of anxiety: the courage of participation; the courage of individualism; and the courage of transcendence. The courage of participation means affirming oneself as a part of a larger group, a nation, a religious organization or a social movement. Participation enables persons to cope with the anxiety of death, because even though individuals die, the group lives on, preserving the contributions made by the members. The group also assuages the individual's guilt and provides a purpose or a sense of value that gives the person's life a meaning. But all the groups of which we may be a part are themselves finite; even the church as the representative of God loses its ultimate status when overwhelming doubt destroys our ability to believe in God. Thus, although the courage of participation continues to bring integrity into the lives of many who are not aware of the doubts or who can keep them in the background, it does not succeed in the final analysis in overcoming existential anxiety for an increasing number for whom doubts have overwhelmed belief.

The courage of individualism has come to the fore in the twentieth century and is the stance recommended by existentialism, as exemplified by Sisyphus. It is the courage to stand alone without dependence on a group and without reference to external or objective standards. It is the affirmation of one's own life and the standards and values that only come from within. It accepts death as final; it deals with guilt by the attempt to live up to one's own moral vision while rejecting objective standards imposed by society; and it deals with meaninglessness by the project of creating meaning. Yet it is such a lonely and demanding way of life that only the few great heroes such as Sisyphus and Orestes can achieve it. Furthermore, it affirms only the individual, finite self. Though the courage of individualism appears satisfactory to the few who can live up to it, it is actually an ultimate concern addressed to what is not ultimate.

The type of courage Tillich believes to be finally authentic is what he calls the courage of transcendence. This is courageous affirmation of oneself as related to Being-itself, which Tillich designates the **God beyond God**, the God that appears when the God of theism has dissolved in the doubt of skepticism. The God beyond God is not a person nor even a being—on the basis of this point some have called Tillich an atheist—but is Being-itself. Because it is ultimate, we cannot know its nature, nor can we describe or define it. We can only recognize that it is ultimate and that it is the ground of all being; it is that on which everything depends, that of which everything is a part and an expression, that from which we come, in which we are rooted, and to which we return.

Because we cannot comprehend the ultimate, we can only express our faith through myths and symbols.[22] A **symbol** is a concrete object or action whose importance is that it points beyond itself and puts us in touch with that greater reality which it symbolizes. The flag, for example, is a symbol of the nation, awakening in us all those sentiments of patriotism and loyalty that citizenship involves. **Myths** are the windows through which we see beyond the mundane to the ultimate. Our lives have meaning, value, authenticity, worth as we achieve the courage to be, the courage of transcendence, the courage to affirm ourselves as rooted in the ground of being that is eternal, accepting, and the source of all meaning. This is the life of faith, the life of ultimate concern about what really is ultimate, expressed through an adequate system of myths and symbols and ideally through a community of faith. Each of the great religions presents such a community of faith and a system of myths and symbols. Tillich is persuaded that the Christian church, to the extent that it avoids idolatry and keeps its symbols transparent to ultimacy, is the most adequate community of faith.

Tillich's theology implies that all persons (except those whose personality or sanity is either temporarily or permanently disintegrated) live by faith—either idolatrous or authentic. This amounts to much the same thing as the claim that only through religion can persons achieve meaning in their lives, and thus that everyone living a meaningful life must be religious. Within the specialized context of theological discussion, when what is meant by faith or by being religious has been carefully delineated, such a claim might be justified. Out of context, it sounds at best paradoxical. Many persons whose lives are perfectly well integrated, who live vigorous, healthy, happy, and meaningful lives, would not call themselves persons of faith or religious persons. To insist on fastening those titles on them is perhaps too much. It certainly remains true that religion has been and is the source of meaning and worth in the lives of very great numbers, perhaps even the majority, of people. It seems also true that being religious in the prevailing sense of that term is not a necessary condition for a meaningful life.

CONCLUSION

Our examination of the arguments dealing with the whole range of religious beliefs has shown that the arguments and the evidence supporting many of the truth claims of religion are substantial. It has also shown that the contrary evidence is weighty as well. We find ourselves in a situation that, on the account of rationality given in Chapter 1, justifies our believing, and also justifies our declining to believe. The major, rationally elaborated religious doctrines are not supported by such overwhelming evidence that reason requires us to believe, nor are they undermined so decisively by counterevidence that reason forbids us to believe. Neither do pragmatic considerations, such as those of William James, either require or forbid belief. Each reasonable person will have to make up her or his mind, based on both cognitive and pragmatic considerations, whether or not religious belief and practice will have a place of importance in her or his life. But the study of human religious beliefs and practices raises what are probably the most important and interesting questions the human mind has learned how to ask. To be a religious believer or an unbeliever without thinking through these questions carefully and honestly is to lack understanding and justification for the stance one takes; it is to miss the intellectual gratification that characterizes the quest for understanding. Thus the philosophy of religion remains a central endeavor of philosophy and of the whole human intellectual enterprise.

Often the purpose of taking a journey lies in the traveling itself, not in reaching some destination. Certainly the purpose of study is not to arrive at the point where we can declare ourselves learned or be certified by some authority no longer to need to learn anything more. The purpose of study is to grow, to increase in understanding, to grasp and grapple with the issues that have intrigued the minds of the greatest of human thinkers. The more we study; the more we become captivated by the charms of the intellectual enterprise itself and the rewards of thinking, questioning, and discovering, the more we come to realize that the questions always open out before us. The conclusions we reach are always tentative, temporary resting places from which we are eager to embark again to explore yet unmapped intellectual territory.

Thus the importance of what we have done here cannot be summed up in a few lines at the end, marking conclusions we have reached. What matters is the exercise of the mind, and the lifting of the spirit, that can come as the issues presented here come alive and lure the inquiring mind. We have looked at a fair sampling of the questions asked about religion and the answers offered by philosophers. We have briefly glimpsed the teachings of five major world religions. These teachings constitute the concrete belief claims out of which our philosophizing arises and to which in some sense it must remain responsible, if it is to claim to be the philosophy *of religion.* Human thought about these questions is far from finished, however: Indeed, we might say that it is only now in a position to make a great new beginning. The author, like the teacher, can point out the prominent landmarks in the terrain over which the human mind has thus far come. More than that he cannot do — except to point ahead, and to promise that the journey yet to be made will surely be at least as new, as fascinating, and as gratifying as any part of what has gone before!

ANNOTATED GUIDE TO FURTHER READINGS

Camus, Albert. *The Myth of Sisyphus and Other Essays.* New York: Alfred A. Knopf, 1955.

When we abandon the screens which we hide behind and embrace the absurdity of our existence, we find meaning in our lives, according to Camus, who uses the myth of Sisyphus, the story of a man eternally condemned to rolling a rock up a mountain, to illustrate this point and to explain why suicide is an unacceptable action even if human existence is absurd.

Flew, Antony. *The Logic of Mortality.* New York: Basil Blackwell, 1987.

A thorough and critical examination of the concept of immortality of the soul. Emphasizes the theories of Plato; the contributions of Descartes, Aristotle, and Aquinas are examined as well, along with a chapter devoted to parapsychology.

Frankl, Viktor E. *Man's Search for Meaning.* New York: Pocket Books, 1963.

The fascinating and powerful story of Frankl's experiences in a Nazi concentration camp and how this led him to the creation of a philosophy he calls logotherapy: Each individual must decide on and affirm the thing that provides his or her life with meaning; in this action the meaning of life resides.

Hick, John. *Death and Eternal Life.* New York: Harper & Row, 1976.

The issue of what happens after death is approached from a number of perspectives: Eastern and Western religious thought; sociological, psychological, and humanist perspectives; the views of specific authors. Hick suggests the possibility of an all-inclusive eschatological reality that transcends worldly boundaries.

Klemke, E. D., ed. *The Meaning of Life*. New York: Oxford University Press, 1981.

An excellent collection of essays, divided into three sections: the theistic perspective, the nontheistic perspective, and the claim that the question "What is the meaning of life" does not make any sense.

Kramer, Kenneth. *The Sacred Art of Dying: How World Religions Understand Death*. New York: Paulist Press, 1988.

A useful and easily understandable introductory text covering Hinduism, Buddhism, Taoism, Judaism, Christianity, and Islam as well as Native American, Egyptian, and ancient Greek thought.

Moody, Raymond A., Jr. *Life After Life*. New York: Bantam Books, 1975.

Examines case studies in which the subjects were clinically dead for a period of time and then resuscitated. Moody finds these near-death experiences suggestive evidence of an afterlife but stresses that they do not provide a definitive proof.

Pojman, Louis P., ed. *Philosophy of Religion: An Anthology*. Belmont, Calif.: Wadsworth, 1987.

Contains a good selection of essays on death and immortality presenting both sides of the argument concerning immortality of the soul or resurrection of the body.

Price, H. H. "The Problem of Life After Death." In *Philosophy of Religion: Selected Readings*, 2nd ed., edited by William L. Rowe and William J. Wainwright. New York: Harcourt Brace Jovanovich, 1989.

Price concentrates on such matters as ESP and mediums who claim to communicate with the dead. Other pieces on death and immortality in this anthology are by Anthony Quinton, Bertrand Russell, and J. M. E. McTaggart.

Sartre, Jean-Paul. *Existentialism*. New York: Philosophical Library, 1947.

Absolute freedom is at the center of Sartre's existentialist philosophy. He insists that there is nothing external to humankind, no God or human nature, that provides humans with purpose. The individual human being is left with the freedom, and the responsibility, to define him or herself and create meaning.

Tillich, Paul. *The Courage to Be*. New Haven: Yale University Press, 1952.

Tillich states that the anxieties aroused by the threat of our nonexistence are best met with courage. Ideally, we need to accept our anxieties as a part of ourselves. This is the courage to be, and it is realized when the theistic God is transcended and the God that lies beyond is affirmed.

NOTES

1. I Corinthians 15:20–22; 36–38; 42; 44; 54–55; 57.

2. H. H. Price, "The Problem of Life After Death," *Religious Studies* 3 (April 1968): 459.

3. Raymond A. Moody, Jr., M.D., *Life After Life* (New York: Bantam Books, 1975), pp. 21f.

4. Bertrand Russell, *Why I Am Not a Christian* (London: Allen & Unwin, 1957), p. 89.

5. J. M. E. McTaggart, "The Dependency Argument," *Some Dogmas of Religion* (London: Edward Arnald, 1906), pp. 105f [italics in the original].

6. Ibid.

7. Jean-Paul Sartre, *Existentialism*, translation by Bernard Frechtman of *L'Existentialism est un humanisme* (New York: Philosophical Library, 1947), p. 18.

8. Jean-Paul Sartre, "No Exit," *No Exit and Three Other Plays* (New York: Alfred A. Knopf, 1948).

9. "The Flies," ibid.

10. Albert Camus, "An Absurd Reasoning," in *The Myth of Sisyphus and Other Essays* (New York: Alfred A. Knopf, 1955), p. 3.

11. William Shakespeare: *Macbeth* V: 5.

12. Albert Camus, *The Stranger*, trans. Gilbert Stuart (New York: Alfred Knopf, 1946), p. 152.

13. Camus, "The Myth of Sisyphus," *Myth of Sisyphus and Other Essays*, pp. 90f.

14. Ibid., p. 7.

15. Ibid., p. 80.

16. I Corinthians 15:14–19.

17. David F. Swenson, "The Dignity of Human Life," in *Kierkegaardian Philosophy in the Faith of a Scholar*, ed. David F. Swenson (Philadelphia: Westminster Press, 1949), p. 16.

18. Plato, *The Apology*, in *The Works of Plato*, trans. Benjamin Jowett; selected and edited by Irwin Erdman (New York: Modern Library, 1928), 40 c–e, p. 87.

19. Ibid., 40 e–41 a, p. 87.

20. Ibid., 41 c–d, p. 88.

21. Paul Tillich, *The Courage to Be* (New Haven: Yale University Press, 1952), p. 3.

22. For a detailed discussion of faith and of myths and symbols see Paul Tillich, *The Dynamics of Faith* (New York: Harper & Row, 1957).

Glossary

absolute idealism: a philosophical system that teaches that only mind is real; ultimately there is only one Mind, of which all the particular things that make up the world are manifestations or parts.

Absolute, the: the one mind that is the only ultimate reality.

absurd, the: a concept said by certain existentialist philosophers, particularly Albert Camus, to be aptly descriptive of the human situation; meaningless; without rhyme or reason.

abu-Bakr: one of the first converts to Islam and the person appointed as the first caliph or successor to Muhammad. He is recognized by Sunni Muslims as the legitimate successor, but Shi'ites insist that Ali was the legitimate heir.

Advaita Vedanta: a monistic (nondualistic) Hindu school of philosophy based mostly on the Upanishads.

agnosticism: the refusal to affirm any belief, or the claim not to know.

Ali: the cousin and son-in-law of Muhammad. The Shi'ites claimed that he was the rightful heir of the Prophet.

Allah: the Moslem name of God, from the Arabic. Some scholars believe it is related to *El*, a Hebrew word for God.

Amida: a Buddha who presides over the "pure land of the West" and is able to aid humans in their quest for enlightenment, according to Pure Land Buddhism.

animism: an early form of religious belief and practice that holds that nature is animated or alive with spirits; that trees, rivers, stones, and other natural objects have such spirits; and that these spirits need to be placated by human ritual.

anthropomorphism: conceiving the deity as having human forms or characteristics.

Apostles' Creed: an early Christian affirmation concerned especially with the nature of Christ and the doctrine of the Trinity; attributed to the Apostles but probably much later, perhaps no earlier than the third century of the Common Era. It is still used in worship in some Christian churches.

a priori: not derived from or dependent upon experience. An *a priori* proposition is one whose truth depends on the meaning of the constituent terms; for example, "A bachelor is an unmarried man."

argument: a series of statements related to one another in such a way that some, called premises, provide evidence or reasons for accepting another statement, called the conclusion.

argument, cosmological: a form of argument for the existence of God that observes that the world and the things in it are contingent and require an explanation. The sequence of causes and effects we observe in the world cannot extend infinitely into the past because such a supposition would imply no first cause; without a first cause there would be no subsequent causal chain; thus, there must be a first cause and this is said to be God.

argument, deductive: a form of logical argument that establishes the truth of its conclusion with certainty, provided the premises are true, because the propositions in the argument are related to one another in such a way that it is impossible for all the premises to be true and the argument to be valid without the conclusion also being true.

argument, inductive: a logical argument usually based on empirical evidence which amasses a measure of evidence short of conclusive evidence for its conclusion.

argument, moral: an argument for the existence of God put forward by Immanuel Kant that claims that because we experience such an uncompromising sense of moral obligation, it must be possible for us to achieve moral perfection, and that the existence of God is a necessary condition for the realization of human moral perfection.

argument, ontological: an argument for the existence of God that claims to make use of no empirical premises and to prove God's existence from the meaning of the idea "God." The classic formulation of the argument comes from Anselm (1033–1109): God is that than which nothing greater can be conceived. God must exist because otherwise another with all his attributes plus that of existence could be conceived, which would be greater, and that would be a contradiction.

argument, pragmatic: an argument for the existence of God that attempts to show that, even in the absence of direct proof, when the evidence is evenly balanced we are justified in believing in God because of the practical benefit such belief brings to our lives.

argument, teleological: an argument for the existence of God that takes for its premise the order or design alleged to be observed in the world and argues that such design requires a God as its designer or cause.

asceticism: the practice of strict self-discipline, renunciation of the sensual, usually involving physical austerities such as fasting, wearing coarse clothing, and the like.

atheism: the belief that there is no God.

atman: the human soul or self, according to several Hindu schools.

avatar: an incarnation of a deity. In Hinduism, for example, Krishna is said to be an avatar of Vishnu.

ayatollah: a high-ranking imam, or leader, in the Moslem religion.

beatitude: literally, "blessedness." In Matthew 5:3–11, a portion of the sermon on the mount, Jesus makes a series of statements about the type of persons who are especially blessed ("Blessed are the pure in heart . . . blessed are the merciful . . . " etc.); these statements are known as the beatitudes.

Bhagavad-Gita: one of the books of holy scripture in Hinduism, a part of a longer epic work called the *Mahabharata*.

bodhisattva: a future buddha. A bodhisattva has achieved enlightenment and is entitled to enter *nirvana*, but delays the final entry in order to help humans along the path to enlightenment.

Brahma: one of the three gods of the Hindu "trinity" said to be incarnations of Brahman; the other two are Shiva and Vishnu.

Brahman: in Hinduism, the absolute, formless ultimate reality. The lesser gods are said to be incarnations of Brahman.

Buddha: literally, the "enlightened one"; the title assumed by Gautama Siddhartha after he achieved enlightenment.

Buddhism, Mahayana: *mahayana* means "greater vessel." A form of Buddhism less strict than Theravada, it attracted greater numbers of followers with its teaching that a person does not need to become a monk to reach *nirvana*. Mahayana is the major form of Buddhism in China, Japan, and other East Asian nations.

Buddhism, Pure Land: a sect of Mahayana Buddhism that teaches that there are other Buddhas who are divine beings presiding over realms to which the human may go after death and receive help in the final effort to achieve *nirvana*. The most popular such divine being is Amida, who is said to preside over the "pure land of the west."

Buddhism, Theravada: *theravada* refers to the elders, the monks immediately associated with the Buddha. Theravada Buddhism (sometimes called Hinayana, "the lesser vessel," by the Mahayanists) is more conservative than Mahayana and claims to be the orthodox form of Buddhism that preserves the true teachings of the Buddha himself. It is found primarily in Sri Lanka, Burma, Thailand, and Cambodia.

Buddhism, Zen: a meditative sect of Mahayana Buddhism, widespread in Japan (known as Ch'an in China), that teaches that the rational mind is a hindrance to enlightenment. Zen makes use of paradoxical or nonsense sayings (e.g., "Think of the sound made by one hand clapping") to weary the mind and persuade reason to give up so that enlightenment may come as a sudden intuition.

Carvakist school: a materialist and atheistic philosophical tradition in India that rejected the Vedas and belief in any spiritual reality.

caste system: the hierarchical division of Hindu society into several castes or classes with limited and strictly regulated intercourse among members of different castes and with certain vocations and levels of social status assigned to the different castes.

compatibalist: a philosopher of religion who believes that the complete omnipotence of God, and thus divine predestination of all human actions, is compatible with human free will and responsibility.

compossible: able to exist together. An omnipotent being is sometimes said to be one who is able to create *any* possible state of affairs and *every* *com*possible state of affairs, that is, every state of affairs that does not involve mutually incompatible features.

conversion: a form of religious experience, particularly in Christianity, that marks a shift in orientation, often sudden and radical, from indifference or resistance to religion to intense involvement and commitment; occasionally, a shift away from religious involvement; or a similar shift in orientation from one secular concern to another; or a shift from one religion to another.

courage to be: a concept introduced by Paul Tillich to name what he takes to be the appropriate human response to the existential anxieties that he believes are an inescapable part of the human condition.

deism: the belief that the world was created by a deity that no longer concerns itself in the ongoing affairs of its creation.

determinism: the belief that every event is caused or determined by antecedent circumstances.

determinism, economic: a doctrine of Marxism that the social, religious, and cultural beliefs and practices of a society are determined by the dominant mode of production and distribution of goods in any given era.

dharma: duty; social and moral obligation. One of the four goals of life according to Hinduism. Also, the word usually used to name what in the West is called religion.

Diaspora: Jews scattered away from Palestine to many parts of the world, beginning as early as the conquest of Judea by Babylon in 586 B.C.E.

disproof, ontological: an argument designed to be the reverse image of the ontological proof or argument. As the ontological proof is supposed to prove that God exists, the ontological disproof is designed to prove that God does not exist.

divine command theory: the theory that what makes an action right is that it is commanded by God and what makes an action wrong is that it is forbidden by God.

dogma: a system of religious or political teachings; doctrines enunciated as orthodox on the basis of authority.

dukka: a Sanskrit or Pali term meaning craving or unsatisfied desire. The second noble truth of Buddhism is: The cause of suffering is *dukka.*

eightfold path: the Buddhist teaching concerning how to achieve cessation of suffering or craving. The eightfold path consists of right views, right aspirations, right speech, right conduct, right livelihood, right effort, right mindfulness, and right contemplation.

élan vital: the vital impetus that, according to such naturalists as Henri Bergson, drives the process of nature whereby evolution, striving ever upward, creates higher and more complex levels of order each with its new qualities.

empiricism: the view that all knowledge derives from sense impressions.

epistemology: theory of knowledge; the branch of philosophy that concerns itself with questions of knowledge and truth.

eschatological: having to do with the end of the world, with final judgment, or with what happens at the end or in the next world.

ethics: the study of the principles of right and wrong behavior.

ethnocentrism: the assumption that the beliefs and practices of one's own society or culture are the right ones and that those of other societies or cultures that differ from one's own are either wrong or inferior.

être-en-et-pour-soi: literally, "being-in-and-for-itself"; Jean-Paul Sartre's term for God. Since Sartre is convinced that the concept is self-contradictory, he says that there cannot be a God.

être-en-soi: literally, "being-in-itself"; Jean-Paul Sartre's term for material objects that lack freedom and thus have a fixed, unchanging essence.

être-pour-soi: literally, "being-for-itself"; Jean-Paul Sartre's term for humans, beings with free will, who therefore have no fixed essence because they can always change.

evil, moral: evil, such as suffering of humans or animals, caused by human actions; examples are murder and torture.

evil, natural: evil, such as suffering of humans or animals, not attributable to human actions; examples are natural disasters and disease.

evil, the problem of: the problem raised for philosophers of religion by the existence of evil in a world believed to have been created by a God who is omnipotent (and thus able to prevent evil), omniscient (and thus aware of evil), and benevolent (and thus desirous of preventing evil).

existential anxiety: the condition of a human who recognizes her or his finiteness. Paul Tillich names three kinds of existential anxiety: th anxiety of fate and death; the anxiety of guilt and condemnation; and the anxiety of emptiness and meaninglessness.

existentialism: a twentieth-century philosophical movement, particularly in Europe, that responded to the "humiliations of man" and the horrors of war. A central teaching of existentialism is that existence precedes essence, not the other way around.

experience, mystical: a form of religious experience said to involve a direct, immediate encounter between a human and a deity.

experience, religious: a term covering experiences ranging from very mild feelings of awe or divine presence through conversion, which involves transformation of life orientation, through various levels of mysticism, which involve a sense of unity or oneness with God.

faith: belief in or devotion to a being or concept such as God, nation, or the like, or acceptance of a system of doctrines. Sometimes contrasted with reason, suggesting acceptance on authority without rational justification ("blind faith"). According to Paul Tillich, faith means not just believing and especially not believing without warrant; it means, rather, concern about whatever is understood to be ultimate.

five pillars of Islam: the obligations individuals must fulfill in order to be good Muslims. They are: frequent repetition of the creed ("There is no God but Allah; Muhammad is the messenger of Allah"), prayer five times a day facing toward Mecca, almsgiving, fasting during the month of Ramadan, and the pilgrimage to Mecca.

five ways: the five Christian arguments for the existence of God given by St. Thomas Aquinas in his *Summa Theologica*; the first four are varieties of the cosmological argument; the fifth is the deductive form of the teleological argument.

four noble truths: a fundamental teaching of Buddhism: (1) Human life is suffering; (2) the cause of suffering is craving (*dukka*); (3) the solution of the problem of suffering is the cessation of craving; (4) the way to achieve the cessation of craving is the eightfold path.

four paths to salvation: the major paths or *margas* of Hinduism are *karma*, the way of action, doing the work proper to one's caste; *bhakti*, the way of devotion, worshipping and serving one of the gods or goddesses; *jnana*, the way of knowledge, studying the sacred writings and the various systems of philosophy; and *Raja yoga*, the royal way of meditation.

four stages of life: in Hinduism the stages are: *bramacharya* (literally, "celibacy"), the stage of the student; *grihastha*, the stage of the householder; *vanaprastha*, the stage of the forest dweller, retired from household and family life, cultivating spiritual concerns; and *sannyasa*, the stage of the wandering mendicant, all ties to the world severed, seeking *moksha* or salvation.

free will defense: a proposed solution to the problem of evil that argues that if humans are to have free will, without which they cannot be fully human, it is not possible for God to prevent all evil, since free beings might commit evil acts.

functionalism: the doctrine that mind is a function of the body or of parts of it, such as the central nervous system, or that all psychological terms can be analyzed in functional terms; a position held by certain materialist philosophers in the philosophy of mind.

fundamentalism: inflexible insistence on the acceptance of certain beliefs and practices alleged to be fundamental to a specific religion. Fundamentalism originated as a conservative Christian response to Darwinian evolutionary theory in the early twentieth century, when several preachers published a list of five fundamental beliefs acceptance of which they insisted was indispensable to being a Christian. The term has been extended to apply to any dogmatic imposition of rigid beliefs and practices, religious, political, or ideological.

God beyond God: the God that appears after the God of traditional theism disappears in the skepticism of doubt, according to Paul Tillich.

Gospel: the teaching, or "good news," of Christianity. The first four books of the Christian Scriptures—Matthew, Mark, Luke, and John—are called the four Gospels because they teach the Gospel of Jesus Christ.

Great Chain of Being: a vision of the world as a hierarchy with everything in its proper place and no gaps, accepted especially in the late Middle Ages in Europe. God is at the top; matter is at the bottom; in between are plants, animals, humans, and various ranks of angels.

hajj: the pilgrimage that every Muslim is supposed to make at least once in a lifetime to Mecca and surrounding shrines; the fifth pillar of Islam.

henotheism: the worship of a god thought to belong exclusively to one's own people while believing that other gods exist that belong exclusively to other peoples.

humanism: a variety of naturalistic philosophy that denies supernaturalism and finds the supreme value in human ideals and possibilities.

humiliations of man: the term used to name three events said to have dealt severe blows to the human self-concept: Copernican astronomy, which destroyed the conception of earth as the center of the universe; Darwinian biology, which questioned the status of humans as specially created and suggested that they are animals evolved from lower life forms; and biblical criticism, which indicated that the Bible cannot be regarded as the literal words of God.

imam: the leader of Moslem prayers in the mosque; the leader of a local congregation of Muslims.

immortality: survival of bodily death, especially survival of a disembodied soul; taught by Plato and others.

immutability: unchangeability; the same eternally. One of the metaphysical attributes of the God of Western theism.

impassibility: not dependent on anything other than itself. One of the metaphysical attributes of the God of Western theism.

impeccability: flawlessness; without fault; perfect, especially morally perfect. One of the metaphysical attributes of the God of Western theism.

Jesus: the founder of Christianity, called Jesus of Nazareth and Jesus Christ (*Christ*, the Greek translation of the Hebrew word *messiah*, means "anointed one"). Born in Bethlehem around 4 B.C.E. and crucified and allegedly resurrected about thirty years later.

jihad: holy war or striving; a controversial doctrine in Islam. Used from time to time to justify war against infidels (non-Muslims) in connection with the promise that the warrior killed in *jihad* will go directly to paradise.

Ka'bah: the building in Mecca surrounding and enclosing the black stone that is the focal point of prayers and of the *hajj* or pilgrimage for Muslims.

Kali-Durga: the ferocious Hindu goddess consort of Shiva, usually depicted as black, wearing a necklace of human skulls, and drinking blood. The object of *bhakti* devotion, especially in the vicinity of Calcutta, she was worshipped as the mother goddess, the destroyer of demons, by Ramakrishna.

karma: action and the fruits of action in Hinduism. Accumulated *karma* determines one's fate, good or ill, in the next life. *Karma marga* or *karma yoga* is a path to salvation through faithful performance of one's caste duty.

Krishna: one of the most popular of the Hindu gods; an avatar of Vishnu. The object of bhakti (devotion) in many Hindu temples; often depicted as playful, dancing and playing the flute.

law, eternal: as taught by Thomas Aquinas, the rational order of God's reason according to which God creates and governs the world. Derived from eternal law are natural law, which can be discovered by human reason, and divine law, which comes to be known to humans only through revelation.

law, natural: the order of nature and the principles of morality and political order believed by the ancient Romans, Thomas Aquinas, John Locke, and others to be the objective foundation of social order. Aquinas taught that the natural law derives from God's eternal law; it is that part of God's law that can be discerned by human reason.

logical positivists: a group of early twentieth-century philosophers who attempted to redefine philosophy as a discipline legitimately concerned only with claims that can be verified either through analysis of the meaning of the terms they contained or empirically. Their verifiability criterion proved self-refuting, and the movement declined.

logic, modal: the logic of necessity, possibility, and impossibility. Recent philosophers of religion have made extensive use of modal logic in constructing arguments for the existence of God, especially the modal ontological argument.

Logos: a Greek word meaning "reason," "teaching," or "word" (it forms the last part of many English words such as biology, sociology, theology, etc.). The author of the Gospel of John interpreted Jesus of Nazareth as the divine Word of God made flesh.

materialism: the belief that there exists only one kind of substance, matter, and that all things that exist and all events that happen can be explained as various configurations of the single material substance.

materialism, central state: a philosophical position that undertakes to explain mental events and activities as manifestations of material events in the central nervous system.

maya: literally, "illusion." Certain Hindu and Buddhist thinkers claim that the empirical or material world is *maya* and that the only ultimate reality is mind, God, or Brahman.

Mecca: the holy city on the Arabian peninsula where the Ka'bah containing the meteorite venerated by Muslims is located, toward which prayer is said five times daily and to which Muslims make pilgrimage or *hajj*.

Medina: the city on the Arabian peninsula where Muhammad spent much of his lifetime and to which, along with Mecca, Muslims make *hajj*.

messiah: a Hebrew word meaning "anointed one." After the fall of the Hebrew nation in 586 B.C.E., there developed a "messianic expectation," the hope that a great messiah would come to restore the kingdom. Christians believe (and Jews do not believe) that Jesus of Nazareth is the messiah, the leader not of an earthly, but of a spiritual, Kingdom of God.

metaphysics: the branch of philosophy that attempts to understand the nature of that ultimate reality believed to lie behind the fluctuating appearances of the senses.

middle way: according to the Buddha, the path between the extremes of sensuality and asceticism.

miracle: an event thought to have occurred in violation of the laws of nature through the power of God or a god.

moksha: literally, "liberation." The word for salvation in Hinduism, meaning escape or liberation from the wheel of *karma*, the round of birth, suffering, death, and rebirth.

monism: the belief that all reality, the impersonal deity as well as the material world, are one being.

monotheism: the belief that there is only one God.

monotheism, ethical: the belief that the one God is just and righteous and demands justice and righteousness of his followers.

Moses: the founder of Judaism. Born to a Jewish slave couple in Egypt, possibly in the sixteenth but more likely in the thirteenth centur

B.C.E., reared in the palace of the Pharaoh, called by Yahweh to liber-
ate Israel from slavery, Moses led his people through the desert of
Sinai, delivered to them the ten commandments, and set the stage for
their invasion of Palestine.

Muhammad: the founder of Islam, the prophet said to be the heir to Jewish
and Christian revelation, bringing the final revelation of the one true
God, Allah, through the Qur'an. Muhammad was born around C.E.
570, began receiving the message that became the Qur'an in 609, and
died in 632.

mysticism: a form of religious experience which is said to involve a direct,
immediate encounter between a human individual and the deity.

myth: a story that may or may not be literally true but whose importance is
for its symbolic rather than literal teachings.

naturalism: a philosophical theory that teaches that all reality is contained
within the realm of nature and that there is nothing supernatural.

naturalism, emergent: a philosophy that denies the supernatural but
teaches that there are creative forces in nature that generate increasingly complex beings whose new qualities are not reducible to, or pre-
dictable from, those of the next lower level from which they emerged.

nirvana: literally, "extinction"; the state of emancipation and bliss
achieved once the cycle of rebirth and redeath has been escaped according to Buddhism.

nisis: a term introduced by Samuel Alexander to name the force that
drives and guides the process of evolution as it generates ever higher
and higher life forms.

noetic: purporting to convey knowledge; for example, mystical experience
is often said to be noetic in this sense.

omnibenevolence: all loving. One of the three central traditional attributes of God, according to Western theism.

omnipotence: all powerful. One of the three central traditional attributes
of God, according to Western theism.

omniscience: all knowing. One of the three central traditional attributes
of God, according to Western theism.

orison: prayer and the state of consciousness that accompanies prayer, especially the prayer of a mystic who feels powerfully the presence of God.

pantheism: the belief that everything is god or that there is no distinction
between God and nature and humankind.

Passover: a Jewish holy day that celebrates the occasion when the death
angel killed the firstborn of every household of Egypt but passed over
the homes of Jews who had marked their doors with blood.

personal identity: doctrines that allege survival of bodily death confront
the problem of personal identity, that is, the problem of establishing
that the surviving (reincarnate, resurrected, or disembodied) individual is the same as the one who died.

phenomenology: the study of what is observed that excludes interpretation; for example, the phenomenology of mysticism is the examination of what actually happens or what is actually experienced when persons have mystical experiences. Phenomenology does not ask what the experiences mean, but only how they are to be described.

philosophy of mind: a branch of philosophy concerned with the nature of mind, consciousness, thought, awareness, and the like. It also deals with artificial intelligence, the aspects of mind that may be duplicated by machines such as computers.

polytheism: the belief in several or many gods.

possible worlds: worlds that do not actually exist but whose constituents are not contradictory or incompatible and that therefore might have existed. The concept of possible worlds is used by philosophers of religion particularly in connection with modal arguments for the existence of God and in responding to the problem of evil.

predestination: the doctrine taught by certain Christians groups that God predetermines the course of history and in particular predetermines those persons who are to be saved.

principle of sufficient reason: the principle that claims that for the existence of anything or the occurrence of any event there must be a cause great enough to bring it about or a reason adequate to make it intelligible. A premise of most versions of the cosmological argument, it amounts to a denial that things happen for no reason at all.

process philosophy: a view of reality that regards process as more fundamental than substance. Taught by Heraclitus in ancient Greece and by such thinkers as Alfred North Whitehead and Charles Hartshorne in the twentieth century.

proof: an argument that is valid and whose premises are known to be true. The theistic arguments are often called proofs although, strictly speaking, few if any of them are.

prophecy: an utterance alleged to be divinely inspired and often involving a warning, a rebuke, or a call back to godliness. Prophecy was an important dimension in the development of Judaism; the work of Muhammad is also regarded as prophecy.

Protestant Reformation: a movement led by Martin Luther (1483–1546) to protest perceived abuses and corruptions in the Roman Catholic Church, resulting in a split in the Church that persists until today; the Protestant movement has subsequently splintered into more than 200 sects.

Qur'an: the holy scripture of Islam. Dictated to a scribe by Muhammad, who received the revelation through a series of experiences beginning in C.E. 609.

rabbi: a Hebrew word meaning "my teacher." A reform movement in Judaism begun in 650 B.C.E. consolidated priestly sacrifice at the Temple c

Jerusalem and established the synagogue, led by the rabbi, as the center of Jewish activity elsewhere. After the destruction of the first temple in Jerusalem in 586 B.C.E., and especially after the destruction of the second temple in C.E. 70, the office of priest disappeared in Judaism, to be replaced by that of rabbi, the teacher of Bible and tradition and the leader of the synagogue.

Ramadan: the month of fasting in Islam during which no food or drink is taken from dawn until dusk.

raptus: an intense religious experience reported by some Christian mystics involving joy, bliss, and a sense of oneness with God.

reductio ad absurdum: an argument designed to refute a position or claim by showing that, if taken to its logical conclusion, such a position implies an absurdity.

reductivism: the process of explaining higher or more complex phenomena in terms of lower or simpler ones, advocated by certain philosophers as a part of the "unity of science" movement. Critics of materialism say that reductivism distorts or oversimplifies when it attempts to explain life in terms of complex arrangements of inorganic substance or mind in terms of complex material processes in the brain. Naturalism claims superiority over materialism because it allegedly avoids reductivism; contemporary materialists claim also not to be reductivists.

regression, infinite: going on into the past endlessly. The cosmological argument for the existence of God denies the infinite regression of causes and claims that there must be a first cause, God.

reincarnation: reborn in a new body; several religions and philosophies, (e.g., Hinduism and Platonism) claim that individual human souls are reborn in new bodies after the death of their old bodies.

relativism, cultural: see **relativism, moral cultural.**

relativism, moral: the belief that there are no moral absolutes or objective moral rules binding on everyone.

relativism, moral cultural: the belief that what is morally right and wrong is determined by the moral teachings and practices of a given culture; what is morally right or wrong in one culture might not be right or wrong in another.

religion, exclusivist view: the belief that one of the world religions is true and that all others are mistaken or at least further from the truth.

religion, inclusivist view: the belief that all or several of the great world religions are in touch with the same ultimate reality and that the differences between them result from differing cultural expectations. Inclusivists usually advocate interreligion dialogue, learning from one another, sometimes mutual transformation of the religions through such interaction, and occasionally merging of the religions into one.

resurrection: a human's return to life in the body that died; a central teaching of Christianity is that Jesus Christ was restored to life three days after his crucifixion and that individual Christians will also be resurrected.

resurrection body: the "spiritual body" that, according to certain biblical passages attributed to the apostle Paul, resurrected Christians will have.

revelation: messages alleged to come from God to humans through religious experiences and preserved in the scriptures of the great religions. One view of revelation claims that God himself is revealed rather than information or commandments.

Roman Catholic Church: the Christian church whose headquarters are the Vatican in Rome and whose supreme earthly pontiff is the Bishop of Rome, also known as the Pope.

sacrament: a sacred act or ritual performed by priests or other authorized persons to accomplish specific religious objectives. In the Roman Catholic Church, seven sacraments are practiced: baptism, confirmation, Eucharist (also called mass or holy communion), penance, marriage, holy orders, and extreme unction. Most Protestant churches recognize only two: baptism and Eucharist (also called holy communion or the Lord's supper). Although non-Christian religions tend not to use the term, they do have sacramentlike rituals, such as circumcision and the *bar mitzvah* in Judaism; *upanayana* (adolescent sacred thread ceremony) in Hinduism; and the taking of *prashad* (somewhat like communion) in Sikhism.

samadhi: a word in several Asian languages referring to death or to a cemetery or crematorium; also frequently designating a mystical state in which the mystic becomes unresponsive to stimulation, greatly slows breathing and heartbeat, becomes stiff like a corpse, and appears to be dead. Persons achieving such a state claim that they are superconscious, not unconscious.

satchitananda: from Sanskrit-based languages. *Sat* = being; *chit* = consciousness; *ananda* = bliss. *Nirvana* is sometimes said to be *satchitananda*, that is, a state of being and consciousness of joy or bliss.

Shi'ites: one of the two major branches of Islam, comprising about 14 percent of all Muslims. The term literally means "the party of," referring to the party of Ali, those Muslims who believed that Ali, Muhammad's cousin and son-in-law, was his legitimate successor. They also believe that revelation did not end with Muhammad; they especially prize martyrdom; and they distrust the traditional reading of the Qur'an, which they think may have been modified by the Sunnis to suit their own purposes.

Shiva: one of the gods of the so-called trinity of Hinduism (the others are Brahma and Vishnu). Shiva is often depicted performing the dance of cosmic creation surrounded by a circle of fire.

sin, original: a Christian doctrine that the disobedience of Adam, the first man, tainted the human race and lost for all humans the image of God in which humans had originally been created. All humans are said to be guilty of Adam's original sin and in need of forgiveness in order to be saved. The death of Jesus is the sacrifice that is supposed to have redeemed humans from sin; baptism is the sacrament through which each person receives the benefit of Jesus' sacrifice and is cleansed of original sin.

skepticism: an attitude of doubting everything and refusing to affirm anything or to claim that one has any knowledge. Extreme skepticism becomes self-refuting since it amounts to the claim that nothing (presumably including this claim itself) can be known.

soteriology: salvation doctrine. The teachings of a religion on how individuals are to attain salvation, enlightenment, liberation from the human condition, and so on. For example, Buddhist soteriology concerns *nirvana* and Hindu soteriology pertains to *moksha.*

Sufis: the word refers to a coarse woolen robe worn by Muslim mystics, and by extension to the mystics themselves.

Sunnis: one of the two major branches of Islam, comprising about 85 percent of all Muslims. Sunnis accept the traditional lineage of the caliphs and regard the Prophet as the only mediator of revelation.

supernaturalism: the belief that the natural world is not the totality of reality; there is something greater than nature, usually a deity or God.

symbol: an object or act that stands for and points to something else; for example, the flag is a symbol of the nation and the cross is a symbol of the Christian religion. Religious language is often said to be composed of symbols and myths, designed to point beyond themselves to beings and truths that cannot be conveyed through the literal meaning of language.

synagogue: place of assembly for Jews, especially Jews of the Diaspora; when a reform movement in Judaism in about 650 B.C.E. consolidated priestly worship at the great temple in Jerusalem and abolished temple worship elsewhere, the synagogue emerged as a center of Jewish community life and a place particularly of teaching, presided over by a rabbi (teacher). A synagogue can be any place where ten adult Jewish males assemble and there is a copy of the Torah, or scripture.

teleological suspension of the ethical: the claim, pointed out particularly by Søren Kierkegaard, that the requirements of morality may legitimately be set aside or suspended when God specifically commands something contrary to established moral rules. The example usually cited is God's command that Abraham violate the moral rule that requires a father to protect his son and instead kill and offer his son as a burnt sacrifice to God.

theism: the belief in the existence of God.

theodicy: an account of the divine nature which exonerates God of evil.

theology: the study and usually also the defense of the doctrines of a specific religious tradition.

Torah: a Hebrew term referring to law or divine revelation. It is sometimes used to refer to the first five books of the Hebrew Bible, or more generally to designate all the sacred writings of Judaism.

Trinity, doctrine of the: in Christianity, the teaching that God is three beings inseparably joined and identified in one: God the Father or creator, God the Son or redeemer (identified with Jesus Christ), and God the Holy Spirit. Some schools of Hinduism also affirm something like a doctrine of the Trinity, namely, that the Ultimate formless Deity, Brahman, has three manifestations, Brahma, Shiva, and Vishnu.

ultimate concern: the meaning of faith, according to Paul Tillich.

unity of science: a project undertaken by the logical positivists in the 1930s to unify all the sciences by showing that the principles of the more complex sciences such as psychology and biology can be reduced to the principles of physics. See **reductivism**.

universalism: similar to religious inclusivism, the view that God reveals himself to persons in all eras and in every part of the world; that the various religions all represent, in culturally modified ways, human understandings or interpretations of the one revelation; advocated particularly by Vivekananda (1863–1902). Also the belief that all humans will ultimately achieve salvation.

Upanishads: a portion of the Hindu scriptures. Each of the Vedas is divided into four parts; the fourth part of each, the most philosophical material that became the basis for Hindu philosophy, is called Upanishads (literally, "sitting near," i.e., a teaching obtained by a disciple from a guru). The earliest of the Upanishads are thought to have been composed during the ninth century B.C.E. and the latest during the sixth century C.E.

value, instrumental: the value something has, not in itself or for its own sake, but for acquiring or achieving some other value. For example, money has instrumental value for purchasing something needed or desired.

value, intrinsic: the value something has in itself or for its own sake. We cherish art, music, aesthetic experience, and religious experience not for their instrumental value, but for their own sake.

Vedanta: literally, "the end of the Vedas." See **Advaita Vedanta**.

Vedas: the basic sacred scriptures of Hinduism, generally thought to have been composed between 1500 and 400 B.C.E.

verifiability criterion: a standard offered by the logical positivists to discern meaningful and nonsense statements. According to this standard, to be meaningful a sentence must be either analytic (true or false by virtue of the definitions of its terms) or empirically verifiable. The criterion itself was soon discovered to be neither analytic nor empirically verifiable, and thus by its own standard literally nonsense.

Vishnu: one of the gods of the so-called trinity of Hinduism (the others are Brahma and Shiva). The creator and sustainer of the world, Vishnu takes earthly form to provide help whenever his earthly creation is in great need. Krishna is an avatar, and some interpret Buddha as an avatar of Vishnu.

Yahweh: The name of the God of the Jews. In the Hebrew scriptures we find only the letters, which are transliterated YHWH. The vowels are thought to be missing because the divine name was too holy to be pronounced.

yoga: from a Sanskrit word meaning "yoke." Yoga involves bodily exercises (Hatha yoga), control of breathing, and particularly meditation in an effort to achieve union ("yoking") with the Absolute.

Index